A MONETARY AND FISCAL HISTORY
OF THE UNITED STATES, 1961–2021

A Monetary and Fiscal History of the United States, 1961–2021

Alan S. Blinder

PRINCETON UNIVERSITY PRESS

PRINCETON AND OXFORD

Published by Princeton University Press
41 William Street, Princeton, New Jersey 08540
99 Banbury Road, Oxford OX2 6JX

press.princeton.edu

Library of Congress Control Number: 2022936806

ISBN 9780691238388
ISBN (e-book) 9780691238395

British Library Cataloging-in-Publication Data is available

Editorial: Joe Jackson, Josh Drake
Jacket Design: Karl Spurzem
Production: Erin Suydam
Publicity: James Schneider, Kate Farquhar-Thomson

This book has been composed in Adobe Text Pro and Gotham.

Printed on acid-free paper. ∞

Printed in the United States of America

10 9 8 7 6 5 4 3 2 1

CONTENTS

Introduction

Those who cannot remember the past are condemned to repeat it.
—GEORGE SANTAYANA

These famous words have been repeated so many times since George Santayana wrote them in 1905 that they have become a cliché. But remember, clichés often capture important grains of truth. Mark Twain was probably more accurate when he (allegedly) asserted that "history doesn't repeat itself, but it often rhymes."[1] Sad to say, many economists and policy makers are not very skilled at picking up rhyming schemes. This book is intended to help.

During fifty-plus years as an academic economist, one thing I have learned is that my fellow economists have a remarkable propensity for forgetting or ignoring the past. Such lapses of memory may not be terribly problematic in the world of pure theory. After all, scientific progress is rarely made by looking backward, the most reliable route to academic success is jumping onto the latest bandwagon, economic theory runs in fads, and many fads don't last long. But forgetfulness in the world of policy can lead to errors, maybe even

1. It is not clear that Twain ever wrote those exact words, but he penned similar thoughts.

1

to grievous errors with serious consequences, which, I suppose, is what Santayana had in mind when he chose the verb *condemned*.

Policy makers and their economic advisers must resist fads. But they must also avoid getting trapped in the past. Walking that fine line is one of the key ways in which the *science* of economics merges into the *art* of economics. Sometimes the merger works well, but often it doesn't. And that's part of the story I tell in these pages.

This book is light on economic theory, and equations are rarer than dodo birds. However, a number of the theoretical and empirical controversies that have surrounded—and sometimes enveloped—monetary and fiscal policy find natural homes here. Furthermore, part of the evolution of thought on macroeconomic policy involves or was even spurred by developments in theory. So, several aspects of macroeconomic theory necessarily play roles in the historical narrative.

That said, this book is a work of *history*, not of *theory*, so I studiously avoid sojourns into theory for its own sake. Rather, I limit myself to theoretical developments that had serious bearings on policy making. So, for example, you will find much in these pages about monetarism, rational expectations, and even supply-side economics but little about such popular (among academic economists!) topics as Ricardian equivalence, time inconsistency, and the fiscal theory of the price level. As far as I can tell, those (and other) topics had little or no bearing on actual policy making.

The worlds of ideas and policy have always interacted strongly, and the sixty-year period covered in this volume is no exception. Developments in the world of ideas (usually coming from academia) *sometimes* have major impacts on the world of policy. Developments in the world of events (including policy events) *sometimes* have major impacts on thinking in the academy. This two-way interaction is a natural and necessary subtheme of this book, and so is its opposite: cases in which policy makers resisted sensible ideas and academics ignored reality.

A second, more important, subtheme is the interaction between policy and *politics*. In the realm of monetary policy, where the Federal Reserve normally sets short-term interest rates and its other policy instruments independently, politics has mostly been a sidebar issue—though with some notable exceptions (e.g., Richard Nixon and Arthur Burns). Technocrats, mostly economists, make the policy decisions.

But in the realm of fiscal policy, where publicly debated budget issues are at the forefront, politics rules the roost. Fiscal policy decisions are made by elected politicians, though hopefully informed by facts and by sound economic thinking. These politicians are guided by forms of logic that are alien to economists—I've called them *political logic* to distinguish them from Aristotelian logic (Blinder 2018). Nonetheless, no history of fiscal policy can avoid delving, sometimes deeply, into the politics of the day. Writing a history of fiscal policy in America that ignored the politics would be leaving out of the play not just the Prince of Denmark but also Ophelia, Laertes, and Polonius.

So, you will find substantial political discussion of fiscal policy in these pages, though I emphasize the economics far more than the politics. In that regard, I should level with the reader by stating right up front that I have long been a center-left Democrat. However, in writing this book (unlike in writing my op-ed columns) I have tried hard to relegate my personal political views to second or third fiddle. Where there were controversies in policy making, I don't shy away from the issues. Instead, I try to give the reader a sense of the arguments on both sides—though without hiding my own views.

The book is designed to serve two audiences. One is my fellow economists or at least those of them who wish to learn some of the lessons of history, lessons that their graduate educations probably did not teach them and that they, in turn, probably don't teach to their students. Such readers may browse selected portions of the book and then place the volume on their bookshelves for future reference.

The other audience is the general reader who is interested in economic policy, or at least in *macroeconomic* policy. How does the past shape today's attitudes, options, and debates over monetary and fiscal policy? What worked and what didn't—*and why*? For those readers especially, the book is arranged chronologically, not thematically, starting in 1961 and continuing to the end of 2021. It is meant to be read as one continuous story, a *nonfiction* story to be sure.

The title is not accidental but rather an intentional homage to Milton Friedman's and Anna Schwartz's monumental *A Monetary History of the United States, 1867–1960* (Princeton University Press, 1963), from which the doctrine of monetarism and our current view of the Great Depression, among other things, derives. Two changes from their title are obvious. First, I pick up the story exactly where they left off—in 1961. Although I am far from a monetarist, I have no desire to engage in debate with the ghosts of Friedman and Schwartz. This work is in no sense a sequel to theirs.

Second and much more important, inserting the words "and Fiscal" into the title reflects a major change in focus. This volume tells the sixty-year story of monetary *and* fiscal policy as those two types of stabilization policy struggled—sometimes cooperatively, sometimes combatively—to fight recessions, unemployment, and inflation in the United States. One can argue that there was no such thing as "fiscal policy" in the United States prior to 1961 anyway, but I'm not going to engage in that argument. There certainly has been lots of fiscal policy since then. And it has mattered.

Old age offers precious few advantages—except in writing history. I began studying economics as a Princeton University freshman in the fall of 1963, which means I have lived through virtually all the events recounted here—not just lived through them but also *observed* them and sometimes even *participated* in them. I have also been writing about economic policy ever since I penned my first op-ed over forty years ago (Blinder 1981a). I have served as an informal adviser to many U.S. policy makers, including several presidential candidates, for decades and intensely so as a member of President Bill Clinton's original Council of Economic Advisers in 1993–1994. Following that stint of about a year and a half, I briefly became an actual policy maker as vice chair of the Federal Reserve Board in 1994–1996. And I have kept in pretty close touch with many Federal Reserve policy makers and with economists in Democratic (and even some Republican!) administrations ever since. So, some portions of the history recounted in this book are based on firsthand experience, and a great deal is based on close secondhand knowledge.

Finally, while it's an overused and sometimes abused adjective, my macroeconomic framework is decidedly *Keynesian*. How could it be otherwise if you want to make sense of history? Rival doctrines to Keynesianism have come and gone over the decades covered in this volume: monetarism, new classical economics, supply-side economics, and others. But only one survived. The competitors to Keynesian economics all either fell of their own weight (e.g., monetarism) or saw their most useful aspects incorporated into the Keynesian tradition (e.g., rational expectations). Keynesian economics circa 2021 differs in many ways from the theory originated by John Maynard Keynes in 1936, but the family resemblance remains. As Mark Twain might have said, it rhymes.

Acknowledgments

This book represents a life's journey through macroeconomics, and as such my first debts of gratitude go to the dozens of teachers, scores of colleagues, thousands of students, and even some journalists who have helped sharpen my thinking on these matters. Teaching helps you learn. As this manuscript was taking shape, I benefited enormously from helpful comments and suggestions on earlier drafts from my friends Ben Bernanke, Michael Bordo, William Dudley, Barry Eichengreen, Philip Friedman, and Robert Solow, plus three fine anonymous reviewers arranged by Princeton University Press. I know that some of these readers disagree in part with what I have written, which is probably inevitable and certainly healthy. They should not be implicated in my opinions.

I also owe a large debt of gratitude to Stephanie Hu for skillful and thorough research assistance including an uncanny ability to find the unfindable, and to Will McClure and Shirley Ren for helping a man who needed help to produce the many graphs in this volume—often under time pressure. Overseeing all this, my wonderful longtime assistant, Kathleen Hurley, watched every detail carefully, saved me from numerous errors, produced the references and captions for the figures, and generally kept the proverbial trains running on time—as she always does.

Writing this book took longer than it should have because of the COVID-19 pandemic. Through it all, I benefited from release time from Princeton University, financial support from Princeton's School of Public and International Affairs, and research support from the Griswold Center for Economic Policy Studies. I thank them all.

Once the manuscript was near completion, it went into the capable hands of the folks at Princeton University Press, led by Joe Jackson (Senior Editor) and Josh Drake (Editorial Associate) and including Karl Spurzem (cover design), Carmina Alvarez (design), and James Schneider (publicity). PUP staff were accommodating and efficient at every stage, making my job easier, not harder. The people at Westchester Publishing Services, who processed the manuscript, impressed me with their skill, speed, and responsiveness. I thank, especially, Christine Marra, Yvette Ramsey, JodieAnne Sclafani, and Theresa Carcaldi. I am a fussy author who is often at war with his copyeditors. Not so with Christine and Yvette, who were a pleasure to work with.

But most deeply of all, I thank my wife and life companion, Madeline Blinder. We have been married for almost as long as the six decades covered in this book. Not only has Madeline been a loving partner, she was instrumental in several crucial decisions that account for the firsthand nature of parts of this book. Much of my personal involvement in the *Monetary and Fiscal History of the United States, 1961–2021* is due to her. "Thank you" is far too weak a phrase.

1

Fiscal Policy on the New Frontier

Now, let us turn to the problem of our fiscal policy. Here the myths are legion and the truth hard to find.

—JOHN F. KENNEDY, COMMENCEMENT ADDRESS,
YALE UNIVERSITY, JUNE 11, 1962

The beginning of the "New Economics," a term coined by the media for the already old idea of using fiscal policy to influence economic activity, can be dated precisely to June 7, 1962. At a press conference that day, President John F. Kennedy promised to ask Congress for "an across-the-board reduction in personal and corporate tax rates which will not be offset by other reforms—in other words, a net tax reduction" (Stein 1969, 407). His tax proposal took a long time to be put into concrete form within the administration and then to wend its way through a recalcitrant Congress. It eventually became law in February 1964, after his death and at least in part as a tribute to the assassinated president. The Kennedy-Johnson tax cut, as it has been called ever since, was quickly hailed as a great success.

Fiscal stimulus had been deployed before, of course, by the Swedes in the 1930s (Türegün 2017) and by Franklin Roosevelt's New Deal, although the magnitudes then were puny relative to the immense need,[1] and on a massive scale during World War II, though the last of these was certainly not motivated by any Keynesian reasoning. So, the New Economics was not as new as the media made it out to be. Still, it was a sharp departure from the fiscal legacy of Dwight Eisenhower's administration.

Background: Eisenhower and the Three Recessions

As Herbert Stein (1969) argued in his definitive history of how the "fiscal revolution" came to America, Eisenhower and his team understood basic Keynesian ideas but were reluctant to employ them because the president did not want to stray far from a balanced budget. Eisenhower was also almost obsessed by fears of inflation, which he associated with budget deficits (Stein 1969, chap. 11), even though the inflation rate (as measured by the Consumer Price Index [CPI]) averaged a mere 1.4 percent during his presidency.[2] Although the average real growth rate over Eisenhower's eight years was a respectable 2.9 percent, one reason why inflation remained so low was that his two terms were marred by three recessions.

The first of these, in 1953–1954, was basically caused by a sharp fiscal contraction. In part, this recession was a normal adjustment from wartime to peacetime: federal defense spending fell sharply as the Korean War ended. But it was not necessary to couple that drop in *defense* spending with declines in *nondefense* spending too—unless you were firmly tied to the mast of the balanced budget ideology. Eisenhower was.

Unlike 1953–1954, the recessions of 1957–1958 and 1960–1961 cannot be laid directly at the doorstep of the Eisenhower administration. The former was part of a worldwide slowdown, though a

1. E. Cary Brown's (1956) once-classic paper concluded that "fiscal policy . . . seems to have been an unsuccessful recovery device in the 'thirties—not because it did not work, but because it was not tried."

2. Here and throughout the book, I use modern data, not the real-time data policy makers would have seen at the time, with some rare exceptions. The differences rarely matter much, and where they do I take note of them.

tightening of monetary policy played some role too. (Inflation was still the main worry then.) Fighting inflation with monetary policy probably played a larger role in causing the 1960–1961 recession. More to the point of this chapter, the administration and Congress did little to mitigate either slump.[3] The fiscal inaction as the 1960–1961 recession developed was particularly noteworthy because it greatly chagrined the vice president, Richard M. Nixon, who fought a losing battle for fiscal stimulus within the administration and then lost the 1960 election to Kennedy by a razor-thin margin (Nixon 1962, 309–10). Nixon believed that the recession cost him the 1960 election, and he may well have been right. As we will see in chapter 4, it was a lesson he would not forget.

The New Frontier and Tax Cuts

Attitudes began to change quickly when Kennedy replaced Eisenhower as president in January 1961, but you couldn't have anticipated that from Kennedy's 1960 campaign. The young senator from Massachusetts campaigned on a pledge to "get America moving again," as if the country had stood still under Eisenhower. Yet Kennedy also ran as a fiscal conservative, seeing no contradiction there (Stein 1969, 376). That fiscal conservatism perhaps reflected the views of his wealthy and domineering father, who had been a titan of Wall Street and held views that were characteristic of that circle at that time (Tobin 1974, 19). If anything, Nixon sounded a bit more Keynesian than Kennedy during the 1960 campaign.

But Kennedy, who was born in 1917, had grown up in the Keynesian era, was intellectually curious, and wanted to hear from the experts he had brought to Washington. That group of advisers, led by Walter Heller of the University of Minnesota, chair of Kennedy's original Council of Economic Advisers (CEA), was composed mostly of enthusiastic Keynesians, which was probably no coincidence.

---

3. On this episode, see Stein (1969, chaps. 12–13).

One member of that stellar group was the estimable James Tobin of Yale, a subsequent Nobel Prize winner whom Kennedy hired as a CEA member. Tobin famously demurred when the president-elect called to ask him to join the new administration. "I'm afraid you've got the wrong guy, Mr. President," Tobin replied. "I'm an ivory tower economist." Kennedy responded, "That's the best kind. I'm an ivory tower president" (Noble 2002). (It is easy to imagine Kennedy smiling his famous smile as he said this over the phone.) Tobin later recalled that, true to that vignette, "Innocent of economics on inauguration day, he was an interested and apt pupil of the professors in the Executive Office Building" (Tobin 1974, 24).

So what was new about the New Economics? Certainly not the basic theoretical framework. The underlying ideas dated from Keynes's *General Theory*, which had been published in 1936. By 1961 its message was standard fare, at least in left-of-center circles and probably beyond, even though many conservatives of the day condemned Keynesian ideas as "socialist." (They weren't strong on definitions.) Heller later noted that "the rationale of the 1964 tax-cut proposal came straight out of the country's postwar economics textbooks" (1966, 72). Indeed, the premier such textbook of the day was written by MIT's Paul Samuelson (1948), who was the acknowledged intellectual leader of Kennedy's team of economists even though he never took a position in Washington.

Perhaps the most important and obvious feature of the New Economics was that the Kennedy-Johnson tax cut was the first deliberate and avowedly Keynesian fiscal policy action ever undertaken by the U.S. government. While the ideas were not new, acting on them was. It is in this sense that the Kennedy-Johnson tax cut is rightly seen as a watershed event.

It was also considered revolutionary at the time to cut taxes when the federal budget was already in deficit and the economy was recovering rather than mired in recession. Indeed, Robert Solow, who was on the CEA staff then, recalled to me (in personal correspondence) that the Kennedy economic team went through mental gymnastics to argue that the deficit would not exceed Eisenhower's largest deficit. That was deemed important.

Prior to the Kennedy tax proposals,[4] countercyclical fiscal policies were considered emergency measures to be reserved for deep recessions, such as the situation faced by Roosevelt. Looking back a few years later, Heller wrote, with perhaps a tinge of hyperbole, that: "John F. Kennedy and Lyndon B. Johnson stand out, then, as the first modern economists in the American Presidency. Their Administrations were largely free of the old mythology and wrong-headed economics which had viewed government deficits as synonymous with inflation; government spending increases as a likely source of depressions that would 'curl your hair'; and government debts as an immoral burden on our grandchildren" (Heller 1966, 36–37). Were Heller alive today, he probably would be shocked to see that all three of these pre-Keynesian ideas live on, if only at the lip service level.

While Heller doubtless exaggerated, there does seem to have been a sharp intellectual break between the Eisenhower and Kennedy administrations. In a 1972 lecture at Princeton, Tobin looked back at what he saw as "new" in the New Economics, listing three main items:

1. The notion "that government could and should keep the economy close to a path of steady real growth at a constant target rate of unemployment" (which the New Frontiersmen set at 4 percent) (Tobin 1974, 7);
2. getting rid of "the taboo on deficit spending" (10); and
3. seeking "to liberate monetary policy and to focus it squarely on the same macro-economic objectives that should guide fiscal policy" (11).

The first item represents clear advocacy of what would first be praised and later derided as "fine-tuning." An even clearer clarion call for fine-tuning came from Heller in his (1966) book in which he asserted that fiscal policy appropriately "became more activist and bolder" in the early 1960s (68). In fact, he claimed, "we now take for granted that the government must step in to provide the essential

4. I use the plural here because the Investment Tax Credit, originated by Kennedy's CEA, was enacted in 1962.

stability at high levels of employment and growth that the market mechanism, left alone, cannot deliver" (9). This necessary activism, he added, means that "not only monetary policy but fiscal policy has to be put on constant, rather than intermittent, alert" (69). Precious few economists would go that far today.

The third item on Tobin's list is notable in light of the monetarist-Keynesian debate that would follow (see chapter 2), one in which Tobin would play a leading role. But it is even more notable—indeed jarring from a modern perspective—for its lack of fealty to the now-sacred doctrine of central bank independence. It may seem amazing from a modern perspective, but belief in central bank independence was *not* holy writ then, not even among economists. Indeed, the January 1964 *Economic Report of the President* had warned the Federal Reserve—in print—that "it would be self-defeating to cancel the stimulus of tax reduction by tightening money" (CEA 1964, 11). Gardner Ackley of the University of Michigan, who replaced Heller as CEA Chair in November 1964, was even more blunt: "I would do everything I could to reduce or even eliminate the independence of the Federal Reserve" (Meltzer 2009a, 457). Modern-day Ackleys would never say such a thing. The belief in central bank independence now runs deep.

Allan Meltzer, the renowned monetarist and historian of the Federal Reserve, has criticized Fed Chair William McChesney Martin for being too pliant at the time. "Policy coordination ensnared Martin in administration policy," Meltzer claimed. "He willingly sacrificed part of the Federal Reserve's independence for the opportunity to be part of the economic 'team,' make his views known to the president, and coordinate policy actions" (Meltzer 2009a, 445). This judgment seems harsh in view of Martin's subsequent clash with Johnson (see below). Besides, is policy coordination really such a bad thing, especially if it does not imply Federal Reserve subservience to the White House? If the Fed saw that a big tax cut was coming, might it not want to adjust monetary policy accordingly? Yale's Arthur Okun, who succeeded Ackley as chair of the CEA, rendered a much kinder judgment: "The Federal Reserve . . . Board put on an outstanding performance in 1966, making wise judgments and, most of all, having the courage to act promptly and decisively on them" (Okun 1970, 81).

My own view—and I think it is the historical consensus—is far closer to Okun's. And don't forget that the dominant attitude in the early to mid-1960s was that the Fed would and should "accommodate" expansive fiscal policy,[5] an early version of what modern economics now calls "fiscal dominance."[6] When it came to stabilization policy, monetary policy occupied the back seat, not the driver's seat, at the time. Indeed, Kennedy confessed that he helped himself remember the difference between fiscal and monetary policy by the fact that "monetary" and "Martin" both began with the letter M (Stein 1969, 4),

But it was the second item on Tobin's list that was the real political stickler. The balanced budget ideology was not only alive and well at the time, it was dominant. And it made Kennedy hesitant to propose anything as radical as a tax cut with the budget already in deficit. Heller, Samuelson, and Tobin worked hard to persuade the new president intellectually. But support from Congress was underwhelming, and his own treasury secretary, C. Douglas Dillon, a Wall Street Republican, opposed the idea. (Dillon favored tax reform, not a tax cut.) Hard as it is for a modern reader to imagine, selling a tax cut to Congress in those days was hard work! Political gravity pulled strongly toward a balanced budget.

President Kennedy nonetheless decided to make a large tax cut the centerpiece of his New Economics. His stated intention when he announced the tax cut on June 7, 1962, was to get it through Congress quickly. But that was not to be—not even close. The idea of enacting a fiscal stimulus in a nonrecessionary environment was considered revolutionary, even heretical, at the time. Congress and the White House also had to decide on how much tax reform should be packaged with the tax cut (in the end, there was little) and how

5. CEA (1965, 66) As one small indicator of lack of independence, what is now known as the Troika for macroeconomic policy (the Treasury, the Office of Management and Budget, and the CEA) was then organized to include the Fed and became known as the Quadriad.

6. Many scholarly papers discuss and model fiscal dominance. Among the earliest is Leeper (1991).

much expenditure cutting should accompany the tax bill (in the end, there was some), for both of those decisions would influence the impact of the tax package on the budget deficit and therefore the legislation's prospects in Congress. Last, but not least politically, Congress and the administration had to decide on the distributional aspects of the tax cut—who would gain how much? There were also a few other "minor" distractions that year, such as the Cuban Missile Crisis of October 1962 and the November 1962 midterm elections!

Kennedy's CEA thought that a tax cut of about $10 billion—then about 13 percent of federal income tax receipts and about 1.4 percent of gross domestic product (GDP)—was about right. It would approximately close both what we now call the GDP gap and what they then called the full-employment surplus.[7] It is unlikely, however, that such macroeconomic subtleties swayed many members of Congress, who loved the idea of cutting taxes but were still strongly attached to the balanced budget ideology. Nonetheless, the Revenue Act of 1964, when fully phased in, reduced federal tax receipts by about $11.5 billion per year—close to the CEA's original target.

The bill that finally passed Congress in 1964 was a tax *cut*, not tax *reform*. It reduced the top marginal tax rate for individuals from a confiscatory 91 percent to "only" 70 percent (times have certainly changed!), and it reduced the lowest bracket rate (other than zero) from 20 percent to 14 percent. It also shaved the top corporate rate from 52 percent to 48 percent.[8]

With a peak multiplier of, say, 1.5, a tax cut of that size would have been expected to boost real GDP by about 2.5 percent. But the Heller CEA expected far more. According to Stein (1969, 431–32), the CEA based its analysis on a multiplier closer to 3 than to 1.5, perhaps assuming monetary accommodation.[9] Consequently, real GDP growth (using today's data) rose from a healthy 4.1 percent

7. Stein (1969, 431–33). It is worth remembering that measuring potential GDP, which Okun did as a CEA staffer, was a new idea in those days. Current CBO estimates show very small GDP gaps then.

8. These and other historical tax rates come from the Tax Foundation (n.d.).

9. In the mainstream theory of the day, just as in the mainstream theory of today, fiscal multipliers are larger when monetary policy prevents (or limits) interest rate increases.

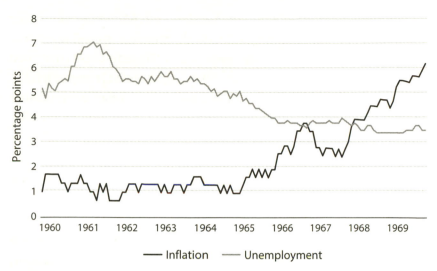

FIGURE 1.1. Unemployment and inflation, 1960–1969.
Source: Bureau of Labor Statistics.

pace over the four quarters of 1963 to an even healthier 5.2 percent over the four quarters of 1964 (remember, the tax cut did not pass until late February) and then to a perhaps unhealthy 8.5 percent pace during the four quarters of 1965. The economy was skyrocketing. Consistent with this, the unemployment rate dropped from 5.5 percent in December 1963 to 5 percent in December 1964 and then to 4 percent in December 1965 (figure 1.1). The Kennedy team's interim unemployment target was achieved.

Yet inflation remained quiescent. Using the December-to-December CPI measure, the inflation rate dropped from 1.6 percent during 1963 to 1.2 percent during 1964 and then rose only to 1.9 percent during 1965 (see figure 1.1).[10] What would soon become the "Vietnam inflation" was barely getting started by late 1965.

On balance, the U.S. economy in 1965 really did look and feel like Camelot. Commensurately, the New Frontier's economists looked like geniuses. As Okun, a member of the CEA at the time, remembered it, "The high-water mark of the economist's prestige

10. In those days, there was no need to distinguish between "core" inflation, which excludes food and energy prices, and "headline" inflation, which includes them. The food and energy shocks that drove this distinction would come later.

in Washington was probably reached late in 1965. At that point, for a brief moment, even congressmen were using the appellation 'professor' as a term of respect and approval" (Okun 1970, 59). I served in Washington in the mid to late 1990s, first on Bill Clinton's CEA and then on the Federal Reserve Board, during what was probably the next high-water mark for economists. I can assure you that the "water" then never rose that high.

Was Kennedy's economic team really a bunch of geniuses? Well, with Tobin as a member of the CEA, the likes of Robert Solow and Kenneth Arrow on the CEA staff (imagine that!), and Paul Samuelson kibitzing from the sidelines, one could certainly answer yes. That's four future Nobel Prize winners. But the New Frontiersmen were simply acting like good textbook Keynesians. And their leader, Walter Heller, was blessed with the kind of political and media savvy that you don't often find in academia. He understood Washington.

As noted earlier, Kennedy's CEA pegged what would later become known as the natural rate of unemployment at 4 percent. It was an educated guess based on paltry data. Looking back today, the Congressional Budget Office (CBO) estimates that number to have been far higher at the time: 5.7 percent in the fourth quarter of 1965. If the CBO's modern estimate is even close to correct, the United States already had a sizable inflationary gap in 1965, meaning that economists should have been expecting rising inflation, which by then was just barely visible. But they weren't.

In fairness, the Kennedy-Johnson economists could not have predicted the sharp military buildup that followed, though they did have a better inkling than most (including the Federal Reserve) because the administration's budget planning preceded the actual surge in Vietnam-related spending. Real defense spending jumped by 15 percent from 1965:4 to 1966:4 and then by another 7 percent from 1966:4 to 1967:4.[11] Largely for that reason, the economy overshot full employment, and the inflation rate (December-to-December CPI) rose to 3.3 percent in both 1966 and 1967 and then to 4.7 percent in

11. Here and throughout, dates like 1965:4 are shorthand for the fourth quarter of 1965.

Walter Heller (1915–1987)

Leader of the New Frontiersmen

Walter Heller of the University of Minnesota was the acknowledged leader of the band of economists who came to Washington with President Kennedy in 1961, acknowledged not so much for his intellectual prowess—in that regard, he was no match for future Nobel Prize winners such as James Tobin and Robert Solow—but rather for his teaching ability (in the broad sense), his political sensibility, and his knack for turning a phrase. Heller may well have been the most influential chair of the CEA in history. Indeed, he called himself an "educator of Presidents" (Kilborn 1987b), a claim not made by many CEA chairs since.

Heller was born in Buffalo, New York, to German immigrant parents. He attended Oberlin College and received his PhD in economics from the University of Wisconsin in 1941. After teaching there for a few years he joined the University of Minnesota faculty in 1946, where his early academic work focused on taxation. That specialty led him to an interlude as tax adviser to the U.S. military government in West Germany before and during the early years of the Marshall Plan. In that post, he was involved in both the currency and tax reforms that helped West Germany recover.

Heller met Kennedy mostly by chance: Minnesota senator Hubert Humphrey introduced them at a campaign event in 1960. After the two chatted, Heller went home and wrote Kennedy a single memo. It must have been an exceptional one, because President-elect Kennedy shocked Professor Heller by offering him the chairmanship of the CEA (*TIME* 1961). It was a surprising choice made, according to Kennedy biographer Richard Reeves (1993, 26), "mostly because he was not from Harvard or Yale. There were too many Ivy Leaguers around [Kennedy] already."

As an enthusiastic Keynesian who had Kennedy's ear, Heller helped persuade the young president to advocate a sharp cut in *marginal* tax rates, even though the economy was recovering and there was a budget deficit. The media dubbed this idea the New Economics. Later Heller helped Kennedy develop "voluntary" wage-price guidelines, which they hoped would keep inflation in check as the economy boomed. (Less luck there.)

Heller stayed on at the White House after Kennedy's assassination and suggested what became the War on Poverty to President Lyndon Johnson. But when Johnson insisted on huge new spending on the Vietnam War without raising taxes, Heller resigned in November 1964 on the grounds that such a policy would be inflationary. He was clearly a two-sided Keynesian. Sometimes Keynesian thinking called for expansionary fiscal policy, but sometimes it called for contractionary policy. Politicians tend not to like the latter.

After his White House years, Heller returned to the University of Minnesota, where he spent the rest of his professional life, although he traveled to Washington often. He subsequently chaired the university's economics department, helping to build it into one of the world's best. In recognition of his valuable service and sterling career, a building on the Minnesota campus bears his name.

1968 (see figure 1.1). Americans viewed that inflation rate as excessively high at the time, just as they would today.

So, price stability went by the board due to what economists—
both then and now—would brand a policy error: piling a mountain
of defense spending on top of an economy that was already at (if you
believed in 4 percent) or well beyond (if you believed in 5.7 percent)
full employment. Astute readers will notice the similarity to the fiscal
policy choices of the early Trump administration in 2017–2018, when
Congress cut taxes and raised spending even though the unemployment rate was then near 4 percent (more on that episode in chapter 17). As Hegel (1899, 6) had sagely observed, "What experience and
history teaches us is that people and governments have never learned
anything from history, or acted on principles deduced from it."

Meanwhile, Back at the Fed

The unsustainable boom started losing steam at about the same time
that inflation began to climb. Over the five quarters from 1966:2
through 1967:2, real GDP growth slowed to a 2.4 percent annual
rate—including one quarter of roughly zero growth (1967:2). In
some business cycle chronologies this episode is called a "growth
recession," a term that was once in common use but seems to have
disappeared from the lexicon once real recessions started reappear-
ing. What slowed the economy down then? Not fiscal policy. (More
on that shortly.) It was mostly monetary policy.

The federal funds rate—which was not the Fed's primary policy tool then—had been creeping up slowly, almost unnoticed, for
years, starting at around 2 percent in the summer of 1961 and topping 4 percent by November 1965. From a modern perspective, it
seems inconceivable that Presidents Kennedy and Johnson, not to
mention their economic advisers, could have failed to notice this
development. However, in those days more attention was paid to
the money supply, and M2 growth (as we measure it today)[12] was

---

12. M2 today includes cash held by the public, checkable deposits in banks,
small-denomination time deposits, and balances in retail money market funds
(MMFs). MMFs did not exist in the 1960s.

not doing anything exciting.[13] Besides, you would certainly expect a strengthening economy to push up interest rates. So, you might argue that the Fed was just being passive, perhaps too passive, in letting the market raise rates.

In those early days, however, the task of actively managing aggregate demand growth was thought to fall more in the province of fiscal policy. The Federal Open Market Committee, at the time, saw itself as a bulwark against inflation, not as an agency responsible for steering, not to mention fine-tuning, the economy (FOMC 1975, 70). The Fed's famous dual mandate for low inflation and low unemployment was not added to the Federal Reserve Act until 1977.

While most Fed officials could not be called practitioners of Keynesianism at the time—indeed, Martin was not trained in economics at all—they understood that part of their duty was described by Chair Martin's famous aphorism: "The Federal Reserve . . . is in the position of the chaperone who has ordered the punch bowl removed just when the party was really warming up."[14] And by 1965, Martin and his colleagues felt that the "party" was getting too hot. He began speaking publicly about his concerns that the economy was in danger of overheating due to growing expenditures on the Vietnam War.[15]

In June 1965, Martin laid down the gauntlet in a speech at Columbia University in which he worried out loud about the "disquieting similarities" between the current economic and stock market situations and those of the 1920s. Oh my, 1929 *redux*? That thought sent a shiver down traders' spines, and the market fell. More to the current point, Martin's speech angered President Johnson so much that he asked his attorney general if he could legally remove the Fed chair from office. (He couldn't without cause.)

Late in November 1965, Martin warned Henry Fowler, then Johnson's treasury secretary, that the Fed might vote to raise the

13. The measured Ms have, however, changed numerous times since then.

14. The exact words are often quoted differently. My source is the Fed's history website (Martin 1955, 12).

15. The history of this episode, including all the quotes that follow, comes largely from Granville (2017).

discount rate at its next meeting on December 3. Fowler relayed that Thanksgiving cheer to Johnson along with some advice that the president didn't need: "We ought to really try to hold him back now." As noted earlier, central bank independence was far from the accepted norm then.

Johnson replied ominously that he was "prepared to be Jackson if he [Martin] wants to be Biddle." The president apparently knew his monetary history. The reference was to the so-called Bank War between President Andrew Jackson and Nicholas Biddle, the president of the Second Bank of the United States, in 1833–1836. That "war" ended badly for Biddle, leaving the United States without a central bank for seventy-eight years.

But Martin, though warning his Fed colleagues of the potential threat to their independence, did not hold back. The December discount rate hike passed by a 4–3 vote, which meant that Martin had cast the deciding vote. A livid President Johnson, who was recuperating from surgery at his Texas ranch at the time, summoned the Fed chair down to banks of the Pedernales River for one of his famous barbecues.

Though I imagine Texas beef was served, the real purpose was to barbecue Martin. "Martin," complained the president, "my boys are dying in Vietnam, and you won't print the money I need." The Fed chair was apparently unmoved, telling Johnson that the president and the central bank had different jobs to do and that the Federal Reserve Act gave the Fed authority over interest rates. No fiscal dominance there. The president must have accepted Martin's assertion, if reluctantly, since he nominated him for yet another term a year later. It no doubt helped that the long boom of the 1960s kept on going. The 106-month expansion (by National Bureau of Economic Research dating) lasted until December 1969 and in so doing smashed all previous records.

Bill Martin, who by then had been the Fed's chair for over fourteen years, wasn't the only observer who worried about an overheating economy and inflation in 1965 and 1966. So did the thoroughly Keynesian members of Johnson's CEA, which was then chaired by Gardner Ackley and included as a member Arthur Okun, who would later succeed Ackley.

William McChesney Martin (1906–1998)

The Fed's Longest-Serving Chair

William McChesney "Bill" Martin, unlike most subsequent chairs of the Fed, had no degree in economics. From the Fed's founding in 1913 through Martin's era, U.S. presidents did not deem formal training in economics important to the job. Rather, they sought to appoint hard-money men (until Janet Yellen became chair in 2014 they were all men) with integrity and judgment. Martin was all these and more. You might even say he was born to the office: his father had served as president of the Federal Reserve Bank of St. Louis.

Martin's sterling career on Wall Street began with the St. Louis brokerage firm A. G. Edwards, where he became a full partner after just two years. By 1931 he had a seat on the New York Stock Exchange (NYSE). His work on stock market regulation in the wake of the 1929 crash landed him first on the NYSE's board of governors and then, at age thirty-one, in its presidency. That meteoric rise earned him the nickname "the boy wonder of Wall Street."

After World War II Martin entered government service, landing in the Treasury Department at a time (1949) when the Federal Reserve was trying to reclaim its independence from the Treasury. (The Fed had lost that independence while pegging interest rates during the war.) He wound up part of the Treasury–Federal Reserve team that negotiated the famous Accord between the two in 1951. Almost immediately thereafter, President Harry Truman appointed Martin chair of the Fed, perhaps mistakenly thinking that Martin would help him bring the Fed to heel again.

But Martin proved to be an effective defender of the Fed's independence, clashing with several presidents—most notably with President Johnson in 1966. Nonetheless, as noted in the text, Johnson reappointed Martin—just as Truman, Eisenhower, and Kennedy had done before him. Martin was truly an institution, the longest-serving Fed chair in the central bank's history. One of the Fed's two main office buildings in Washington bears his name.[16]

While Bill Martin is famous for his punch bowl quip, inflation nonetheless—and ironically—rose from about 1.5 percent to over 5 percent late in his tenure as Chair. Martin was not happy about that part of his legacy.

Johnson's economists argued that the coming surge in aggregate demand from defense spending could and should be countered, or at least mitigated, either by cutbacks in civilian spending or by tax increases. In the modern argot, the federal government should "pay for" the upsurge in military spending. But Johnson rejected spending cuts because they would have crimped his Great Society plans. For him, it would be guns *and* butter. In his words, "I was determined to be a leader of war and a leader of peace. I refused to let my critics push me into choosing one or the other. I wanted both" (Goodwin 1976, 283). The president also rejected tax increases

16. The other is named for Marriner Eccles.

because they would have made the costs of the Vietnam War much more visible to the voters and thereby undermined support for the war. So, in Okun's words, "the economists in the administration watched with pain and frustration as fiscal policy veered off course" (Okun 1970, 71). It would not be the last time economists watched fiscal policy decisions "with pain and frustration."

This failure to turn from fiscal stimulus to fiscal restraint, or at least toward less stimulus, was notable for three reasons. Most obviously, it opened the door to what became the Vietnam inflation; by 1969, the inflation rate was up to 6 percent (see figure 1.1). Less obviously but at least as important for the themes of this book, it gave Keynesian economics a bad name—unfairly. Critics would soon start claiming that Keynesian policies had an inflationary bias. Keynesians, it was alleged, advocated stimulus when the problem was fighting unemployment but did not advocate restraint when the problem was fighting inflation. The charge wasn't true then, and it isn't true now. But the criticism gave a big boost to the rise of monetarism (see chapter 2) and is occasionally leveled even today. For example, two economists criticized the "Keynesian" nature of the Coronavirus Aid, Relief, and Economic Security (CARES) Act, the first big fiscal package enacted to combat the recession of 2020, writing that "the last thing we need at this moment is a Keynesian stimulus. Since the lockdowns constrain supply, stimulating demand would lead only to a rise in prices" (Seru and Zingales 2020). They were as wrong in 2020 as wrong can be. But they were not alone.

Finally, a die (of sorts) was cast. In theory, fiscal policy is symmetric. You raise taxes or cut spending to rein in aggregate demand, just as you cut taxes or boost spending to spur aggregate demand. In practice, however, fiscal policy in the future would be used (with rare exceptions) only to expand demand. When contracting demand was the order of the day, policy makers would turn to monetary policy instead, thereby taking the onus off politicians and lodging it squarely at the Fed's Constitution Avenue headquarters.[17]

17. Symmetrically, a folk adage of the day held that monetary policy only worked in the contractionary direction. Monetary expansion was like "pushing on a string."

This is good politics, I suppose. But introductory textbooks explain why it is bad economics. Looser budgets and tighter money will generally produce higher real interest rates, hence a lower investment share in GDP and eventually a slower growth rate of potential GDP. This is precisely what happened in the 1965–1968 period. For example, the share of business investment in GDP fell from about 18 percent in 1966:1 to about 16 percent in 1967:2, and the CBO now estimates a sharp drop in potential GDP growth after 1968.[18]

The fiscal spigot was not turned off until a tax increase finally passed in June 1968, and then its power was undermined by making it explicitly temporary.[19] Monetary policy was left to shoulder the burden of fighting inflation alone. As mentioned earlier, the Fed raised its discount rate in December 1965, and the federal funds rate drifted up to 4.1 percent by November 1966.

The financial events of 1966 were quickly dubbed a "credit crunch." In those days, monetary policy derived much of its power from what was called "disintermediation" due to the Federal Reserve's Regulation Q, which placed ceilings on the interest rates that banks were permitted to pay to their depositors. Regulation Q, a leftover from the reactions to the Great Depression, was based on the quaint theory that ruinous competition for deposits had been a major factor behind bank failures in the 1930s. The regulation was defanged in stages by the Depository Institutions Deregulation and Monetary Control Act of 1980, leaving monetary policy less powerful (but also less distortionary), and finally eliminated entirely by the Dodd-Frank Act of 2010. But in Regulation Q's heyday, which included the 1966 credit crunch, banks and thrifts would see deposits flee to higher-yielding alternatives whenever market interest rates rose above the regulation's ceilings—a process dubbed disintermediation.

Such reallocations of households' liquid assets might seem inconsequential; after all, the funds didn't disappear. But the sloshing around of money had profound effects on the housing sector because

18. I don't want to exaggerate the point. The CBO's estimated drop in potential GDP growth is too large to be explained by a two-point drop in the investment share in GDP. See, for example, CBO (2021).

19. See, among others, Eisner (1969) and Blinder (1981b). For more on this issue, see chapter 2 in this volume.

FIGURE 1.2. Federal funds rate, 1964–1970.
Source: Board of Governors of the Federal Reserve System.

financing for home mortgages came from banks and thrifts, not from Treasury bills and money market instruments, and there was no such thing as mortgage-backed securities then. So, any serious bout of disintermediation threw housing into a slump. Residential investment fell by 22 percent between 1966:1 and 1967:1.

The growth recession and perhaps even Johnson's attacks on the Fed, induced the central bank to ease up a bit in 1967. But much more tightening was to come. By November 1967 the federal funds rate was up to 4.1 percent, and it eventually peaked at 9.2 percent in August 1969 (figure 1.2). Three months later, with the unemployment rate sitting at 3.5 percent, the U.S. economy slipped into the 1969–1970 recession, which would raise the unemployment rate to 6 percent—its highest level since late 1961.

A second, now-archaic, factor also pushed the Fed toward tighter money at intervals during the late 1960s and early 1970s: gold outflows. The U.S. dollar, in particular its peg to gold at $35 per ounce, was the linchpin of the Bretton Woods system of fixed exchange rates. The other leading industrial countries pegged their currencies to the dollar so that, for example, with the value of the French franc pegged at 20 cents, France was effectively on an ersatz "gold standard" at 175 francs per ounce of gold. There was a catch, however. The international exchange value of the dollar could not fall when

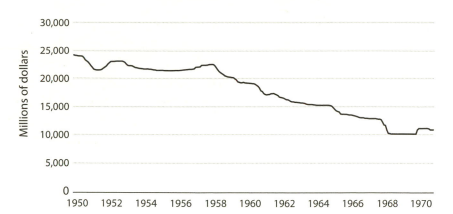

FIGURE 1.3. U.S. monetary gold stock, 1950–1970.
Source: Federal Reserve Bank of St. Louis.

it needed to—say, when U.S. inflation ran repeatedly above German inflation. Instead, the U.S. balance of payments deficit would widen, and gold would in principle flow out.

Back in the 1960s, "losing gold" would alarm Federal Reserve officials—and others too. Losing gold created a presumption that interest rates should rise, thereby mimicking what would have happened automatically under the classical gold standard. Importantly, the loss of gold reserves turned out to be a secular problem: the U.S. monetary gold stock declined steadily from the late 1950s to the late 1960s (figure 1.3), until President Nixon finally broke the link to gold in August 1971 (more on that in chapter 4). But gold was at least a putative influence on monetary policy during the Kennedy-Johnson years.

Chapter Summary

Keynesian economics came to U.S. fiscal policy in the New Frontier. Monetary policy was seen as subsidiary then, its main job being to "accommodate" the 1964–1965 tax cuts. And Federal Reserve independence was far from being a sacred cow. In fact, it was barely a sacred calf. What we might call a "soft landing" in 1965—at 4 percent unemployment and sub-2 percent inflation—was upset by the

Vietnam buildup shortly thereafter. It was a classic case of excess demand, making the remedy clear: tighter monetary and fiscal policies. But both monetary and fiscal policy fell "behind the curve" in the fight against inflation, although the Fed did jack up interest rates substantially, thereby drawing the ire of President Johnson. As the 1960s drew to a close, the United States was entering a mild recession, but inflation was still the problem of the day. And Keynesian economics had been tagged, unjustly, with a reputation it would struggle to shake off for decades: it was allegedly inflationary.

2

Inflation and the Rise of Monetarism

Inflation is always and everywhere a monetary phenomenon.
—MILTON FRIEDMAN (1956)

The Kennedy-Johnson tax cut of 1964 was, as noted in chapter 1, the first deliberate use of fiscal policy to speed up the growth of aggregate demand in the United States. (Such policies had, however, been used in several European countries much earlier.) Its success gave the idea a good name. But that was all about boosting demand and pushing the economy forward.

The first deliberate use of fiscal policy to slow down the growth of aggregate demand came in 1968 in the form of a temporary surcharge on income tax payments. The surcharge was not successful, and it is hard to find many (any?) subsequent examples of fiscal tightening for stabilization purposes in U.S. history.[1] There are, of course, obvious political reasons why politicians eschew tax hikes. Nonetheless,

---

1. As will be clear in this book, there have been fiscal tightenings for other reasons, such as to reduce the budget deficit.

the failure of the 1968 surcharge may have had momentous consequences. Why did it fail?

The Long Delay in Fighting Inflation, 1965–1968

Recall that President Lyndon Johnson's economic advisers began
urging him, pretty much unanimously, to pursue a contractionary fiscal policy in late 1965, and they never relented. But Johnson
was unmoved for more than a year. Only by January 1967, with the
unemployment rate down to 3.8 percent and the inflation rate up to
3.4 percent, was he persuaded by his Troika (Treasury, the Office
of Management and Budget, and the Council of Economic Advisers
[CEA]) that a tax increase was in order (Okun 1970, 84–85). Johnson
initially spoke of a 6 percent surcharge on both personal and corporate
income tax payments, exempting taxpayers in the lowest brackets. But
by the time Congress acted, the overheating of the economy had worsened, and the surtax rate was eventually set at 10 percent.

Johnson's request may have been long overdue, but it nonetheless
received a frosty reception on Capitol Hill. To cite just one prominent example, Congressman Wilbur Mills (D-AR), who chaired the
powerful House Ways and Means Committee, observed at a hearing
in November 1967 that "I have not seen as yet any evidence that we
are currently in any demand-pull inflationary situation that requires
immediate action" (Okun 1970, 87). If you paid attention to neither
theory nor economic forecasts—which was (and is) no doubt the
position of most members of Congress—Mills had a point: inflation
at the time was stable to falling.

Much more important, elected legislators knew that taxpayers
never like higher taxes and that the unpopularity of the Vietnam War
made any patriotic appeal for revenue to finance the war a political
nonstarter. The war did not grow more popular as time passed, but
public and congressional opinion against inflation began to stiffen
as the inflation rate crept up from its low point of 2.3 percent in
May 1967 to 3.3 percent by December 1967 and 4.2 percent by
June 1968 (figure 2.1).[2] Where would it stop?

2. Here, as usual, I use the twelve-month Consumer Price Index inflation rate
as recorded in today's data.

FIGURE 2.1. Consumer Price Index inflation rate, January 1965–December 1969. *Source*: Bureau of Labor Statistics.

Interestingly, in view of the cavalier attitudes toward central bank independence at the time, the Federal Reserve explicitly joined the administration's call for fiscal restraint in early 1968. The February 1968 *Economic Report of the President* observed that "it has been and remains the conviction of both the Administration and the Federal Reserve System that the Nation should depend on fiscal policy, not monetary policy, to carry the main burden of the additional restraint on the growth of demand that now appears necessary for 1968" (CEA 1968, 84–85).

From a modern perspective, two remarkable—and long-rejected—ideas are packed into that sentence. First, the Fed was ceding to the administration the "main burden" of fighting inflation. Really? When's the last time the Fed thought *that* would work? Or when did you last hear an economist voice that view? Second, not only did the CEA speak for the Fed (in its *Economic Report*), but the Fed explicitly endorsed the administration's fiscal policy. Did it not occur to Fed Chair Bill Martin that the Johnson administration or future administrations might not return the favor by endorsing the Fed's monetary policies? Had he forgotten that politicians don't like to see punch bowls being taken away from parties?

The Revenue and Expenditure Control Act of 1968 was finally signed into law by President Johnson in late June 1968, retroactive to April 1 for individuals and to January 1 for corporations. It was estimated to raise about $10.5 billion per year once fully phased in,

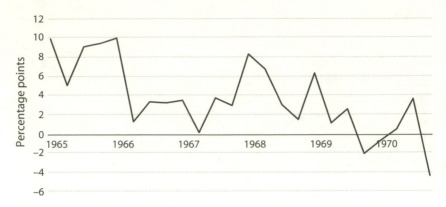

FIGURE 2.2. Annualized growth rate of real GDP, quarterly, 1965–1970.
Source: Bureau of Economic Analysis.

which was roughly 1.2 percent of GDP at the time. Notice that the magnitude almost undid the Kennedy-Johnson tax cut of 1964. The act also reduced federal spending by $6 billion. Together, both parts of the acts represented a sizable fiscal contraction, nearly 2 percent of GDP. It was late for sure, but not trivial in size.

Because the historical verdict on the 1968 surcharge—a verdict that came quickly—is so negative, it is worth pointing out that real GDP growth (in today's data) slowed from 5.5 percent in the four quarters before the 1968 act to 3.1 percent in the four quarters after. Negative growth did not show up until the final quarter of 1969, when a short and shallow recession began (figure 2.2).

Did people at the time expect a faster or sharper slowdown than that? I suppose some did, but the CEA's January 1969 forecast predicted only "less than 3%" real growth over the four quarters of 1969 (CEA 1969, 56). Modern data show the actual figure to have been 2.1 percent, so the CEA forecast was basically on the mark. Robert Solow and I (Blinder and Solow 1974, 103–15) subsequently noted that the surtax was battling a list of contemporaneous forces that were expanding aggregate demand, such as a surge in spending on automobiles and the lagged effects of the highly expansionary monetary policy that had followed the credit crunch. So, perhaps the surtax was more effective than widely believed. All that said, however, inflation rose after the tax hike from 4.2 percent in June 1968 to

5.5 percent in June 1969 and 6 percent in June 1970 (see figure 2.1). This outcome was not expected, and it seemed perverse. The surtax was branded a failure.

The comparatively weak effect of higher taxes on real demand is not hard to explain, however. The law imposed the surtax for just one year (it was later extended to a second year). As Robert Eisner (1969) observed at the time and as subsequent research confirmed, albeit not without controversy,[3] explicitly temporary income tax increases (or decreases for that matter) should pack less punch than permanent ones. Okun (1971) subsequently used four macroeconometric models to estimate that the surcharge on personal income taxes, which averaged $9 billion (at annual rates) over the four quarters of 1969, should have reduced consumer spending by about $4 billion, or less than 0.5 percent of GDP.

Thus, the puzzle, to the extent there is one, is not why consumption did not fall more but rather why inflation continued to rise. The answer is obvious to a modern economist, though it wasn't to many economists of the day: unemployment remained substantially below its natural rate throughout the period, not reaching even 5 percent until July 1970. But the Keynesian economists of the day, perhaps wed to President John F. Kennedy's 4 percent "full employment" target, were loath to accept that proposition. Indeed, the natural rate hypothesis itself, though already introduced by Friedman (1968) and Phelps (1967, 1968), was not yet widely accepted (more on this in the next chapter). People looked instead to ephemeral phenomena such as "wage push," "administered pricing," "bottlenecks," and the like.

Milton Friedman and the Birth of Monetarism

As the New Frontiersmen were bringing Keynesian policy into mainstream American practice, Milton Friedman and Anna Schwartz were rewriting American economic history in a decidedly non-Keynesian way. The bold opening sentence of their epic 1963 work (from which this book draws its title) is at once accurate and a gross

3. See, for example, Okun (1971) and Blinder (1981b).

understatement of the book's intent and achievements: "This is a book about the stock of money in the United States" (Friedman and Schwartz 1963, 3). Yes, it was about the money stock—and a lot more.

Friedman and Schwartz's *A Monetary History of the United States, 1867–1960* rewrote macroeconomic history with a heavy emphasis on fluctuations in the money supply. (Money looked much better as a predictor of nominal GDP and inflation in the 1950s and 1960s than it would later.) Among other things, the pair famously laid responsibility for the length and depth of the Great Depression squarely on the "inept" (their word) policies of the Federal Reserve. They insisted that "though the Reserve System proclaimed that it was following an easy-money policy, in fact it followed an exceedingly tight policy" (Friedman and Schwartz 1963, 699), allowing the money supply to contract. To Friedman and Schwartz, monetary stringency, not credit conditions, had squeezed aggregate demand and turned what might have been a recession into a severe depression.

Nearly four decades later, Ben Bernanke, a Fed governor at the time and later the Fed's chair, offered a famous apology to Friedman and Schwartz at Friedman's ninetieth birthday celebration in 2002. "I would like to say to Milton and Anna: Regarding the Great Depression. You're right, we did it. We're very sorry. But thanks to you, we won't do it again" (Bernanke 2002). When Great Depression 2.0 threatened to engulf the U.S. economy in September 2008, Bernanke and the Fed most emphatically didn't "do it again." Nor did Chair Jerome Powell in 2020.

In the Friedman and Schwartz view, the Fed's grievous errors in 1929–1933 not only made the Depression worse—which was bad enough—but also left a damaging intellectual legacy. "The contraction shattered the long-held belief . . . that monetary forces were important elements in the cyclical process and that monetary policy was a potent instrument for promoting economic stability. Opinion shifted almost to the opposite extreme, that 'money does not matter'; that it is a passive factor which chiefly reflects the effects of other forces; and that monetary policy is of extremely limited value in promoting stability" (Friedman and Schwartz 1963, 300).

Friedman and Schwartz, of course, rejected every aspect of that "shattering"; they favored returning to the "long-held belief." Notice in particular the quotation marks around the phrase "money does not matter," suggesting, without citation, that it was a widely voiced notion at the time. But was it? Or was it a straw man?

More the latter, it appears. I am unable to find any American economist at the time who denied that monetary policy mattered. That Heller, Tobin, Ackley, and Okun were not in that camp is on the record. They all said so clearly. Ditto for such other Keynesian luminaries as Samuelson, Solow, and Franco Modigliani. What is true is that a number of U.S. economists, looking back at the Great Depression, had observed that a liquidity trap could conceivably rob monetary policy of its efficacy—something Keynes had pointed out in 1936. None, however, saw the liquidity trap as relevant to the 1960s.[4]

Looking for extreme "fiscalists" was perhaps a bit more promising in the United Kingdom, where Nicholas Kaldor and Joan Robinson are sometimes offered as examples. But their central complaint against monetarism was not that monetary policy was powerless but rather that the money supply was endogenous, so M should not be looked upon as a control variable (Iša 2006). It is true that the denigration of M as an exogenous policy instrument, which many of the aforementioned American economists shared, is a rather different gestalt than what is found in Freidman and Schwartz. But it is a long way from claiming that "money does not matter."

Regardless of whether many (or even any) economists ever said that money didn't matter, there is little doubt that Friedman and Schwartz's monumental work—bolstered significantly by Friedman's personal persuasiveness and skill in debate—changed intellectual history. Even though the term *monetarism* never appears in their volume, there is little doubt that their *Monetary History* is one of the wellsprings of that doctrine.

A second wellspring that became famous at the time but is mostly forgotten today is Friedman and David Meiselman's (1963) lengthy paper "The Relative Stability of Monetary Velocity and the

---

4. In late 2008, however, the liquidity trap idea made a surprising comeback.

Investment Multiplier in the United States, 1897–1958," written for the Commission on Money and Credit. The commission was established in November 1957 by the Committee for Economic Development to make the first extensive investigation of the U.S. monetary system since the Aldrich Commission of 1908–1911, which turned out to be a step toward founding the Federal Reserve. Although the commission's report was published in June 1961, a multivolume series of supporting studies, which included Friedman and Meiselman's soon-to-be-famous paper, appeared only in 1963.

Friedman and Meiselman asked, in an exceedingly simple way, whether velocity was more or less stable (and hence reliable) than the Keynesian multiplier. Specifically, they asked which was the better predictor of consumer spending (C): what we now call M2 or what they classified as "autonomous expenditure" (A), conveniently eliding the facts that M had clearly *not* been the Fed's policy instrument over most of this period and that the United States didn't even have a central bank in 1897–1913.[5] Their basic methodology was to run statistical horse races between M and A via univariate regressions—that is, to regress C on either M or A—and see which gave the better statistical fit. In Friedman and Meiselman's work, M won this horse race with plenty to spare. But evidence as simplistic as that was not very convincing—unless you were already convinced.

Their salvo, however, was just the beginning of what would become a decades-long empirical battle. Very quickly (given publication lags), Albert Ando and Franco Modigliani (1965) disputed both Friedman and Meiselman's methodology and their conclusions in the pages of the *American Economic Review*. Friedman and Meiselman (1965) replied at length in that same issue. They started their reply with these modest words: "Because our article ventured into almost virgin territory, it was necessarily tentative, probing, and imperfect. Because it questioned the new orthodoxy, we expected it to provoke controversy" (753). It certainly did!

---

5. In fairness to them, money creation could influence output and spending even without a central bank.

Under the influence of its hawkish president, Darryl Francis, and its research director, Homer Jones, the Federal Reserve Bank of St. Louis became the hotbed of monetarism within the Federal Reserve System. In 1968, two of the bank's research economists, Leonall Andersen and Jerry Jordan (1968), published a paper in the *Federal Reserve Bank of St. Louis Review* that caused a sensation and became a defining event in the monetarist-Keynesian debate.[6] That paper evoked, although it did not cite, Friedman and Meiselman's analysis; indeed, looking back years later, Jordan wrote that "we considered the AJ article to be a sequel to the FM article" (Jordan 1986, 6).

But the Andersen-Jordan approach was considerably more sophisticated than Friedman-Meiselman's, especially about such matters as allowing for lags in the effects of policy and including both monetary and fiscal variables in the same regression. Using either the money stock or the monetary base as the measure of monetary policy and either the high-employment surplus or its revenue and expenditure components separately as the fiscal policy measure(s), Andersen and Jordan presented a series of multivariate regressions covering the years 1952–1968. These purported to show that monetary policy did a vastly better job than fiscal policy in explaining quarterly movements in nominal GDP.

Keynesians were aghast, and research critical of Andersen and Jordan started to appear everywhere.[7] I still remember a visit by Andersen to MIT to present a seminar on their results when I was a graduate student there in 1969–1970. When Andersen made some nonincendiary remark about how *both* monetary and fiscal policy might matter, Paul Samuelson popped out of his seat to declare, "If you believe that, you're not a monetarist. You're a member of the human race!" The fact that the great Professor Samuelson chose to attend the seminar at all indicated how important the Andersen-Jordan

6. Jordan would later become president of the Federal Reserve Bank of Cleveland.

7. A fledgling Princeton economist named Alan Blinder participated in this effort a few years later. See Goldfeld and Blinder (1972). We showed that, for example, perfect fiscal stabilization policy would destroy any statistical correlation between GDP and the fiscal policy variable.

results looked in academia, even though they were not published in a peer-reviewed scholarly journal. His not-very-polite remark was indicative of the heat that surrounded the debate.

The term *monetarism* appears to have been coined by Karl Brunner. Brunner and his frequent coauthor, Allan Meltzer, were perhaps the most prominent monetarists of the day after Friedman himself. Brunner described the core of the doctrine as comprising three propositions. "First, monetary impulses are a major factor accounting for variations in output, employment and prices. Second, movements in the money stock are the most reliable measure of the thrust of monetary impulses. Third, the behavior of the monetary authorities dominates movements in the money stock over business cycles" (Brunner 1968, 9).

Most Keynesians of the day accepted the first of these propositions and perhaps the third as well.[8] But they choked on the second. At the time, the Federal Reserve was using "free reserves" as its instrument,[9] mostly as a way to control short-term interest rates. It was certainly not targeting the money supply by anybody's definition. But that just describes how the Fed was actually behaving at the time. It leaves open the question of whether it could have done a better job of conducting monetary policy by targeting the money supply instead. Monetarists insisted that it could—and should.

Notice that Brunner's list does not include the notion that fiscal policy does not matter, even though the Friedman-Meiselman and Andersen-Jordan results both pointed in that direction. In his then-famous 1968 debate with Friedman, Walter Heller stated that "the issue is *not* whether money matters—we all grant that—but whether *only* money matters, as some Friedmanites, or perhaps I should say Friedmaniacs, would put it" (Friedman and Heller 1969, 16). Friedman replied that this is a "straw man. . . . I do not think that it is a meaningful statement" (46). But a few pages later he stated that "in

8. Years later, there was a sizable academic literature on endogenous money. It did not, however, grow out of Kaldor's and Robinson's objections but instead came from "inside" the monetarist camp. See, for example, King and Plosser (1984).

9. Free reserves were defined as excess reserves minus borrowings from the Fed.

my opinion, the state of the budget by itself has no significant effect on the course of nominal income, on inflation, on deflation, or on cyclical fluctuations" (51). Isn't that saying that fiscal policy doesn't matter?[10] Friedman's explanation then was what we would now call complete crowding out of deficit spending if it is financed by issuing bonds. This became the issue: Does a larger fiscal deficit, not accompanied by increasing the money supply, expand aggregate demand?

Simple versions of the monetarist model—which answered *no* to that question—required that the demand for money, and hence velocity, be insensitive to interest rates. In the economists' jargon, the LM curve summarizing the dependence of the demand for money on interest rates and GDP is vertical. But the zero elasticity idea was easily debunked empirically. A famous, or perhaps infamous, paper by Friedman (1959) had claimed to have found a zero interest elasticity, but no one else could. Okun's (1970, 146–47) book listed twenty-five "articles [that] report empirical results showing a negative relationship between the demand for money and the rate of interest" and only one—Friedman's 1959 article—showing no relationship.[11]

However, establishing that the demand for money does in fact depend negatively on the nominal interest rate by no means ended the Keynesian-monetarist debate. One prominent monetarist recalled that "as the decade of the 1960s ended, the lines had been drawn for a prolonged intellectual battle. The Keynesian revolution was still dominant, but the challenge of the monetarist counterrevolution had been initiated" (Jordan 1986, 6). The battle was indeed long, raging on through the 1970s, the 1980s, and even into the early 1990s, which is when Federal Reserve Chair Alan Greenspan officially announced that the Federal Open Market Committee (FOMC) would no longer pay attention to the growth rates of the monetary aggregates.[12] By the time he made that statement, attention to the

10. In fairness, however, the budget deficit is at least an endogenous as the money supply.

11. Okun's list included papers by prominent monetarists such as Karl Brunner, Allan Meltzer, and David Laidler.

12. See, for example, his testimony before the Senate Banking Committee (Greenspan 1993).

Ms at the Fed, which had been a legal requirement since 1975, had already been reduced to lip service. Greenspan just put an end to the lip service.

Were Keynesians Inflationists?

But I am getting ahead of the story. The 1968 tax surcharge failed to curb inflation. In retrospect, no one should have expected it to. But the plain—and painful—fact that inflation rose to levels not seen in almost two decades was counted as a failure of Keynesian economics and therefore gave monetarism a strong boost in both intellectual and policy circles.

Perhaps by coincidence, most Keynesian economists tended to be both liberal and a bit dovish on inflation,[13] while monetarists tended to be conservative and decidedly more hawkish on inflation. Samuelson and Friedman were quintessential examples of each camp. So, there was an underlying grain of truth to the monetarist charge that Keynesians were soft on inflation—but only a grain. Remember, it was President Johnson's Keynesian economists who had lobbied for a contractionary, anti-inflation policy as early as 1965. The political aspects of the Keynesian-monetarist divide probably stemmed more from Friedman's advocacy of fixed policy rules than from anything having to do with money per se. After all, liberals typically look toward government for solutions, while conservatives look away.

In any case, rising inflation certainly gave the rise of monetarism a big assist. In 1969, the Consumer Price Index inflation rate topped 6 percent for the first time since 1951. The proverbial horses were out of the barn. As noted earlier, both fiscal and monetary policy had already turned restrictive by then to fight inflation, and to no one's surprise, a mild recession began in December 1969. Partly in consequence, the inflation rate tracked down to about 5.5 percent a year later and to about 4.5 percent when President Richard Nixon

13. But not all, either then or now. Herbert Stein was a prominent conservative Keynesian back then; Ben Bernanke is today.

invoked wage-price controls in August 1971 (more on price controls in chapter 4). Arguably, monetary and fiscal policies were working, albeit slowly, when Nixon, anxious about his 1972 reelection prospects, ran out of patience. But the entire episode was read, especially by monetarists and other conservatives, as discrediting Keynesianism.

To Milton Friedman, the remedy for the disease of inflation was simple: just slow down the growth rate of the money supply. Hence, the genesis of his famous k-percent rule for money growth, which predated the term *monetarism* by many years.[14] The constant *k* was supposed to be the estimated growth rate of potential GDP plus the target rate of inflation—nowadays 2 percent, though Friedman might have preferred zero or even negative (Friedman 1969). Regarding inflation fighting, he wrote that "I don't think monetary policy has to be backed up by fiscal policy at all. I think monetary policy can curb inflation" (Nelson 2007, 1). Friedman's reasoning was simple and familiar: "A budget deficit is inflationary if, and only if, it is financed in considerable part by printing money."[15] Notice that Friedman was once again skating perilously close to the extreme "fiscal policy doesn't matter" position that he had attacked as a straw man.

Remember also that his policy prescription, the k-percent rule, predated the birth of monetarism by years and was not part of Karl Brunner's definitional list in 1968. In fact, the Brunner quotation above, taken in isolation, could easily be read as a brief for activist monetary stabilization policy—something that a younger Milton Friedman had once advocated (Friedman 1948).[16] Nonetheless, the k-percent rule soon became an essential part of the monetarist policy prescription, if not of monetarist theory. Friedman, a libertarian distrustful of government, naturally believed in elevating rules over human discretion. Many monetarists sympathized with that view. Arthur Burns, though a conservative, did not (more on Burns in chapter 4.)

14. Friedman had advocated it in his 1960 book (Friedman 1960).

15. From a newspaper interview, as quoted in Nelson (2020, 437n162).

16. His idea there was that with fixed fiscal policies, the business cycle would naturally produce deficits and surpluses that should be financed by creating and destroying high-powered money.

Milton Friedman (1912–2006) Monetarist Extraordinaire

Few economists who never held a high position in government ever had as extraordinary an influence on public policy as Milton Friedman. He did it all by the force of his intellect, a deft pen, and an amazing talent for debating.[17] His book *A Monetary History of the United States, 1867–1960* (with Anna Schwartz), published in 1963, is, of course, the inspiration for this book's title.

Friedman was born in Brooklyn, New York, but raised in New Jersey by parents who were immigrants from what we now call Ukraine. A brilliant high school student, young Milton won a scholarship to Rutgers, which was then private but is now the state university of New Jersey. There, studying economics and mathematics, he encountered a teacher named Arthur Burns, thus starting an association that would prove to be both long-lasting and influential. But Friedman's original goal was to become an actuary!

Upon graduation from Rutgers, Friedman turned down a scholarship to study mathematics at Brown in favor of one to study economics at the University of Chicago. It was a fateful decision, for "the Chicago school" and "Friedman" subsequently became nearly synonymous. As a graduate student at Chicago, Friedman was influenced by the likes of Jacob Viner, Frank Knight, and Henry Simons. Perhaps more important, Friedman met and fell in love with his wife, Rose Director.

Ironically, given what was to come, Friedman's first job after obtaining his PhD in 1935 was in Washington, DC, as a bit player in Franklin Roosevelt's New Deal working for—hold your breath—the National Resources Planning Board. A few years later, he was back in the government as an adviser to the Treasury Department during World War II.

Obviously, this attachment to federal service didn't stick. Virtually all of Friedman's fabled career was spent in academia, mostly at the University of Chicago (from 1946 to 1977), and much of it attacking government actions as foolhardy or worse. At the University of Chicago, Friedman published such notable works as *A Theory of the Consumption Function* (1957), the aforementioned *Monetary History*, his celebrated 1967 American Economic Association presidential address "The Role of Monetary Policy" (1968), a collection of essays entitled *The Optimum Quantity of Money and Other Essays* (1969), and much more. He was awarded the Nobel Prize in 1976.

Friedman's keen intellect and talent for persuasion were evident in a number of popular books (*Capitalism and Freedom* [1962] and *Free to Choose* [1979]), in widely read *Newsweek* columns for about eighteen years, and in advocacy of a number of "crazy" ideas that subsequently became realities such as floating exchange rates, the negative income tax, an all-volunteer army, and school vouchers.

In the realm of monetary and fiscal policy, however, Friedman is clearly most notable for practically inventing the doctrine that Karl Brunner later labeled "monetarism." That meant both positive monetarism, which argued that the growth rate of the money supply was far and away the most important determinant of inflation, and normative monetarism, which held that the central bank should stabilize the growth rate of the money supply. There aren't many monetarists left today. But in its heyday monetarism was enormously influential, as was Milton Friedman.

---

17. Personal note: I debated him once. It was an event for which I prepared more assiduously than I ever prepared for anything else. Debating Milton was frightening.

While monetarists insisted on the central importance of monetary policy, often denigrating fiscal policy, they were just as insistent that the Federal Reserve was committing grievous errors by targeting a short-term interest rate rather than the growth rate of (some measure of) the money supply. M, the monetarists argued, was a better control instrument than r. As Allan Meltzer put it years later, "To a monetarist economist, [the simple] view of the transmission process is overly restrictive and mechanical. A monetary impulse that alters the nominal and real stocks of money does more than change a single short-term interest rate or borrowing cost" (Meltzer 1995, 52). Whoever argued with that? Wealth effects, for example, would boost consumer spending. It was another straw man. But it left open the question of whether M or r was a better target for the Fed.

This important practical question was addressed theoretically in a landmark paper by William Poole (1970), a onetime Friedman student who was then a staff economist at the Federal Reserve Board. Poole would later become an academic and, subsequently, president of the Federal Reserve Bank of St. Louis. Like many good ideas, Poole's original framework was strikingly simple, though it was later complexified by other economists in several dimensions.[18] Here is his basic idea.

If the central bank fixes the money supply (M), thus giving rise to the textbook IS-LM system, both output (y) and interest rates (r) will fluctuate in response to stochastic shocks to either the demand for money ("LM shocks" or "velocity shocks") or real spending ("IS shocks"). If, on the other hand, the central bank fixes r, letting M adjust period by period to achieve the desired interest rate, LM shocks become irrelevant to y, whose variance depends only on IS shocks. But those demand shocks now have larger effects on y than when an upward-sloping LM curve cushions them. So, there is a trade-off. Targeting M rather than r mutes the effects of IS shocks but adds LM shocks to the mix. Depending on which type of shock is more troublesome, the monetary authority might prefer one type of policy or the other.

Poole, who went on to become a prominent monetarist, was relatively agnostic about the choice in that 1970 paper. It was a work of

---

18. One such extension, by Sargent and Wallace (1975), turned out to be a landmark in the rational expectations revolution. See chapter 6.

scholarship, not advocacy. He did, however, observe that "it could be argued that much more is known about the monetary sector than about the expenditure sector" (Poole 1970, 206), which if true would push a central bank toward targeting M rather than r. Subsequent events, especially waves of financial innovation in the 1970s and 1980s, spurred both by inflation and Regulation Q restrictions, would demonstrate the power of Poole's simple (and intuitive) analysis. But they would also prove his hunch wrong. We did not know more about the monetary sector. Rather, huge and recurring velocity shocks gradually led one central bank after another to give up on monetarism. As Bank of Canada governor Gerald Bouey famously quipped, "we didn't abandon monetary aggregates, they abandoned us" (Bouey 1982).

The Fed's brief flirtation with monetarism in 1979–1982 will be described in chapter 7. But monetarism's rise in the late 1960s and early 1970s had enough influence in the real world that financial markets began to dance to the tune of the Fed's weekly announcements of the money supply (by several different definitions!), even though those high-frequency numbers were mostly statistical noise. The FOMC itself began to specify "ranges of tolerance" for M1 and M2 in 1974. Then in 1975, the Fed received instructions from Congress to include annual growth targets for M1, M2, M3, and bank credit in its semiannual reports. Monetarists rejoiced at this "major change in monetary policy—perhaps the most important change since the banking acts of the 1930s," in Milton Friedman's overly exuberant words (Friedman 1975a, 62).

Finally, a 1977 amendment to the Federal Reserve Act directed the Fed to "maintain long run growth of the monetary and credit aggregates commensurate with the economy's long run potential to increase production, so as to promote effectively the goals of maximum employment, stable prices, and moderate long-term interest rates." Modern attention focuses on the last part of that instruction, the Fed's so-called dual mandate. But reread the first ten words. Congress had enshrined a role for the Ms into law.[19] Monetarism had (sort of) been endorsed by Congress.

---

19. On the matters in this and the next paragraph, see Bernanke (2006).

After the Volcker experiment in 1979–1982, the Fed rapidly backed away from its allegedly monetarist operating procedures. In Ben Bernanke's words in 2006, "It would be fair to say that monetary and credit aggregates have not played a central role in the formulation of U.S. monetary policy since that time" (Bernanke 2006). That was an understatement. When the statutory reporting requirements lapsed in 2000, the Fed ceased setting target ranges for the monetary aggregates. By then, monetarism was pretty much a dead intellectual doctrine anyway. Empirical realities had trumped theoretical reasoning—not for the first time and not for the last.

But monetarism had left its mark. As early as 2009, inflation hawks were worrying out loud about the potential inflationary consequences of the mountain of reserves the Fed had created to fight the world financial crisis, despite the evident facts that (a) nervous banks wanted to hold enormous volumes of idle reserves and (b) those reserves now paid interest. For example, at a House hearing in July 2009, Congressman Ron Paul (R-TX) criticized the Fed after its massive first round of quantitative easing. "The true definition of 'inflation' is when you increase the money supply. . . . You have doubled the money supply. . . . So it seems to me that you are in the midst of massive inflation" (U.S. House Committee on Financial Services 2010, 19). Paul's "true definition" seemed to reverse the roles of horse and cart. But then again, logic is never required in a congressional hearing.

Now, you might write off Paul as an anti-Fed crank—and you would be right to do so. And rising inflation never came. In January 2010, however, with the economy still in the doldrums, Thomas Hoenig, then president of the Kansas City Fed, was dissenting against the Fed's hyperexpansionary policies partly on the grounds that "the combination of near-zero interest rates with the size of our balance sheet will cause long-term inflation expectations to systematically, over time, become less well anchored" (FOMC 2010a, 188). Not quite monetarism but perhaps a first cousin.

Monetarist-like thinking reemerged even more strongly during the pandemic of 2020–2021. As M2 growth soared by 35 percent during the year and a half from February 2020 to August 2021, more and more voices started pointing to money growth as a harbinger of inflation. And inflation did indeed rise in 2021, although most contemporary observers attributed it more to sectoral supply bottle-necks than to the money supply.

Chapter Summary

Monetarism rose to prominence on a combination of some hotly dis-puted scholarly work, Milton Friedman's singular brilliance and skill in debate, and perhaps most important the rise of inflation in the late 1960s (due to excess demand) and the early 1970s (due mostly to the supply shocks discussed in chapter 5). Keynesianism was unjustly tagged as inherently "inflationary," and monetarism stepped forward as the replacement.

Monetarist doctrine died in both the academic and policy realms for the same reason, though with different timing in different coun-tries: the behavior of velocity became erratic and unpredictable. That happened, however, only after monetarism had registered substantial influence on policy formulation in the United States, the United Kingdom, Germany, and elsewhere. The policy debate was not, as Friedman and others sometimes claimed, over whether monetary policy mattered. It was about whether fiscal policy *not accommodated by monetary policy* mattered. As it turns out, it did.

3

The Phillips Curve
Becomes Vertical

There is need for much more detailed research into the relations between unemployment, wage rates, prices and productivity.

—A. W. PHILLIPS (1958)

The epigraph is the final sentence of one of the most famous papers in the history of macroeconomics, published in 1958 by A. W. Phillips (1958, 299), who was then a professor at the London School of Economics (LSE).[1] The sentence reads very modestly, as does the whole paper. Despite his astounding life story, Phillips was apparently a modest man. But his 1958 paper caused a sensation and has had profound and lasting effects on fiscal and especially monetary policy around the world.

Before Phillips

To appreciate why Phillips's 1958 paper made such a splash, a quick review of the intellectual framework of the 1950s is useful. The Keynesian revolution had swept through much of academia by then—skipping,

---

1. This chapter contains a few simple equations. Readers who are allergic to equations can skip over them and read the accompanying prose.

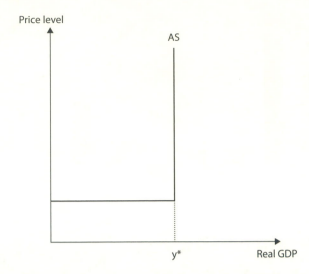

FIGURE 3.1. The backward L-shaped aggregate supply curve.

of course, the University of Chicago. But early Keynesian models, as exemplified by the ubiquitous IS-LM model, had no theory of inflation. Taken literally, IS-LM itself was a fixed-price model; the price level never changed. No one believed that described reality, of course. Common renderings of what might be called "crude Keynesianism" sometimes conceptualized the aggregate supply curve as approximated by a backward L: flat until the economy approached full employment (at y* in the graph), then rising almost vertically (figure 3.1).

Notice the stark empirical implication of this crude Keynesian model: expanding aggregate demand by monetary or fiscal policy does not cause inflation until you pass the kink in the aggregate supply curve at "full employment." After that, any further increases in aggregate demand cause only inflation, with no further increments to output. If you really believed in such a naive view of the world, then either monetary or fiscal policy could be employed to boost employment, but not to reduce inflation, when the economy was operating below full employment; the opposite would be true beyond full employment. Pretty simple.

Far too simple, in fact. I doubt that anyone ever believed that the real world was that binary. All you had to do to refute the stark

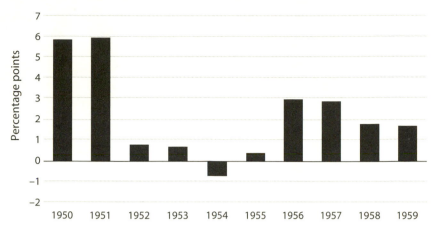

FIGURE 3.2. The U.S. inflation rate, 1950–1959 (December-to-December Consumer Price Index).
Source: Bureau of Labor Statistics.

dichotomy depicted in figure 3.1 was open your eyes. The data on inflation, displayed in figure 3.2 for the decade of the 1950s, certainly did not support the inflation-on or inflation-off view. Inflation moved up and down. Attempts to reconcile this extremely naive theory with the facts gave rise to debates over cost-push versus demand-pull inflation, the possible importance of sectoral bottlenecks, and so on. The profession was looking, desperately you might say, for a way to integrate variable inflation into Keynesian theory.

What Phillips Found

While he eschewed making sweeping claims, Phillips filled this intellectual gap by offering a smooth empirical curve to replace the reverse-L in figure 3.1—a curve he "fit" to British wage inflation data by what can only be called unusual methods. What would soon be named the Phillips curve showed a strong negative relationship between the rate of change of money wages and the unemployment rate in the United Kingdom over the years 1861–1913. Finding such a negative relationship was hardly a surprise. The first sentence of Phillips's famous paper (1958, 283) was a straightforward statement: "When the demand for a commodity or service is high relative to

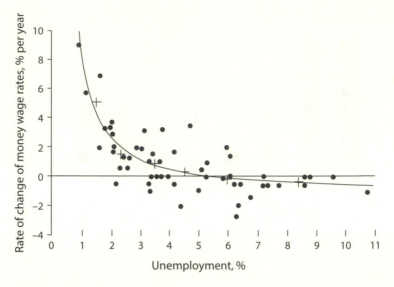

FIGURE 3.3. Phillips's original curve: UK data, 1861–1913.
Source: Phillips (1958).

the supply of it we expect the price to rise." I presume that students at the LSE knew that at the time.

What was surprising in Phillips's paper was the seeming durability and consistency of the relationship. His original curve, reproduced here as figure 3.3, was based on data from 1861 to 1913. That's a long time span. Even more amazingly, however, the data points for the years 1948–1957 (the most recent ten years at the time) fell almost exactly on the curve Phillips had fit to the older data. Thought of as a test of postsample stability of an estimated equation, the econometrician had skipped thirty-five years of data and then estimated almost exactly the same equation. Remarkable. No wonder Phillips's paper attracted so much attention.

It did not take long to notice that it was a quick hop, step, and jump from an equation for nominal wage increases to an equation for price increases. The Phillips curve thus "closed" the Keynesian model by providing the missing equation for inflation. Notably, however, Phillips's original wage equation included no inflation term whatsoever. Think about that. He was seeking a statistical explanation for the rate of change of nominal wages, and yet he omitted inflation as a determinant. From a modern perspective, that seems incredible. And Phillips did not just forget about inflation; he mentioned it and dismissed its importance: "It will be argued here . . . that cost of living adjustments will have little or no effect on the rate of change of money wage rates" (Phillips 1958, 283). Really?

Two years later, Phillips's LSE colleague, Richard Lipsey (1960),[2] remedied this omission by estimating a coefficient of 0.37 on inflation in a Phillips curve of the form

$$w_t = \alpha \pi_t + f(U_t) + \varepsilon_t, \tag{1}$$

where w_t is the rate of change of nominal wages, $f(U)$ is a nonlinear function of the unemployment rate, π_t is the inflation rate, and ε_t is a stochastic error term. When Lipsey estimated that same equation over more modern (at the time) data rather than 1861–1913, his estimate of α rose to 0.76 (with standard error 0.08). Lipsey probably never imagined how important that estimated parameter would subsequently become.

That same year, Paul Samuelson and Robert Solow (1960) brought the Phillips curve to America in a paper presented at the December 1959 meetings of the American Economic Association. Their august professional status alone guaranteed that their paper would garner a great deal of attention. And it did.

Using inflation on the vertical axis rather than the rate of change of nominal wages, Samuelson and Solow (1960) sketched what they called a "modified Phillips curve for the US." Perhaps most noteworthy and consistent with the discussion in their paper, they captioned that figure as follows: "This shows the menu of choice between different degrees of unemployment and price stability, as roughly estimated from the last twenty-five years of American data" (192). Roughly estimated, indeed. The Samuelson-Solow Phillips curve was a freehand sketch, not an econometric estimate. While I was writing this book, Solow recalled to me in private correspondence that neither he nor Samuelson had a computer at the time! Yes, and that was at MIT.

---

2. Lipsey (1960), unlike Phillips, estimated the Phillips curve by conventional econometric methods. He also found a less striking fit than Phillips did.

A. W. "Bill" Phillips (1914–1975)

Engineer Turned Economist

Bill Phillips is, of course, most famous for discovering what came to be called the Phillips curve. (He did not give it that name himself!) But his life before economics is little short of remarkable.[3]

Phillips was born on a farm in New Zealand, left high school at the age of fifteen to become an electrical engineering apprentice, and six years later moved to Australia, where he bounced around for about two years holding jobs as diverse as electrician at a gold mine and crocodile hunter. In 1937, he set off on the long journey to England, part of which was via the Trans-Siberian Railway. Once in London, he qualified as an electrical engineer. But when World War II war came, he joined the Royal Air Force. While traveling to Java by sea in 1942, Phillips's ship was attacked by enemy aircraft, and his bravery handling a machine gun later earned him his Member of the Order of the British Empire award. Not many economists ever did that!

Unfortunately, Phillips was captured by the Japanese in Java. During his three and a half years in prisoner-of-war camps, he built and operated a clandestine radio, learned Chinese from fellow prisoners, and developed the bad nicotine habit that probably contributed to his early death.

Returning to England in 1946, Phillips enrolled at the LSE for a sociology degree but quickly developed an interest in economics and in Keynesian theory in particular. Seeing the analogy between economic flows and hydraulic ones, he built a machine in which water literally flowed through clear plastic tubes to depict the Keynesian circular flow of income and expenditure. The machine was a sensation at the LSE, graced the school's basement for years, and was later put on display in London's Science Museum. It now resides at the Reserve Bank of New Zealand.

Phillips joined the LSE faculty in 1950, and his rise was meteoric by the standards of the day: to professor by 1958. That was also the year in which he published his famous paper, "The Relation between Unemployment and the Rate of Change of Money Wage Rates in the United Kingdom, 1861–1957." The rest, as they say, is history.

In 1967, Phillips moved back to Australia to assume a chair at the Australian National University in Canberra. But in 1969, he suffered a stroke and retired to Auckland, where he died in his native land in 1975.

Interpreting the Phillips curve as a "menu of choice" became the central intellectual frame after the Samuelson-Solow article, at least among Keynesians. Policy makers could choose, say, a combination of high inflation and low unemployment or a combination of low inflation and high unemployment. Pretty soon, the conventional wisdom held that liberal Democrats preferred to ride up the Phillips curve toward lower unemployment and higher inflation,

3. Much of this profile is based on Barr (2004).

while conservative Republicans preferred to ride down the Phillips curve toward lower inflation and higher unemployment. Indeed, that became a hallmark distinguishing liberal from conservative macroeconomists.

If you read Samuelson and Solow carefully, however, they hedged their bet: "All of our discussion has been phrased in short-run terms, dealing with what might happen in the next few years. It would be wrong, though, to think that our . . . menu that relates obtainable price and unemployment behavior will maintain its same shape in the longer run" (1960, 193). But lest you think they correctly anticipated what would happen over the next ten to fifteen years, the esteemed pair did not pin these possible shifts of the Phillips curve mainly on changes in expected inflation. Others subsequently did so, however.

Milton Friedman's presidential address to the American Economic Association in December 1967 received the most attention—immediately. He argued that the menu of choices allegedly offered by a negatively sloped Phillips curve was a mirage because it ignored the evolution of expected inflation. Once you took the adjustment of inflationary expectations into account, he argued, the only level of unemployment sustainable in the long run was its "natural rate," which was "the level that would be ground out by the Walrasian system of general equilibrium equations" (Friedman 1968, 8). Most important, the natural rate of unemployment was impervious to monetary policy. (Friedman didn't think or write much about fiscal policy.)

The mechanism was straightforward. If monetary policy pushed the unemployment rate (U) below its natural rate (U*), both inflation (π) and the rate of increase of money wages would start rising. If firms caught on to what was happening before workers did (his general presumption), then prices would rise faster than wages, so real wages would fall. Lower real wage costs would, in turn, motivate firms to boost employment, thereby pushing U below U* in the short run. Over time, however, workers would catch on, real wages would rise back to their equilibrium levels, firms would have no extra incentives to hire, and U would return to U*. The true menu of long-run choices, Friedman argued, consisted of the unique unemployment rate, U*, coupled with any rate of inflation policy makers chose. To wit, the long-run Phillips curve was vertical.

Edmund Phelps (1967, 1968) developed a similar though more formal model in which both firms and workers were fooled by inflation at first, leading to transitorily higher employment. But both eventually caught on, leading to a conclusion identical to Friedman's: there is no trade-off in the long run. Given what was to come later, it is worth pointing out that neither Friedman's verbal analysis nor Phelps's equation-laden model embodied what would soon be called *rational* expectations. Rather, each of them viewed expectations as lagging behind reality but eventually catching up—something approximating adaptive expectations. During the transition period when U was below U*, π^e would systematically lag behind π, which was rising. Robert Lucas and others would subsequently argue that such lagging, and therefore biased, expectations were not "rational." But in 1968, hardly anyone was thinking that way.[4]

As Robert Gordon pointed out decades later, the timing of Friedman's presidential address and Phelps's two papers "was impeccable and even uncanny" (2011, 16). The Kennedy-Johnson tax cuts followed by the Vietnam War buildup had pushed unemployment well below any reasonable estimate of the natural rate, and inflation rose throughout the 1960s—just as the Friedman-Phelps model had predicted (figure 3.4). Thus, the new natural rate theory both enhanced the charge that Keynesian demand-management policies were inflationary and buttressed the claim that monetarism provided a better, or at least less inflationary, policy frame.

Keynesian "theory" was wounded though, as it turned out, not mortally. As Solow reflected decades later, "Maybe a patchwork of ideas like eclectic American Keynesianism, held together partly by duct tape, is always at a disadvantage compared with a monolithic doctrine that has an answer for everything, and the same answer for everything" (2018, 424). But back to the Phillips curve—and the duct tape.

To incorporate the Friedman-Phelps analysis into the Phillips curve (1) above, add a (presumably negative) constant (because price inflation

---

4. Lucas was just beginning to. See Lucas and Rapping (1969).

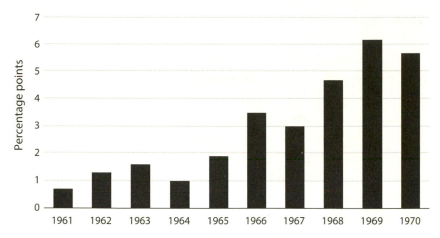

FIGURE 3.4. The U.S. inflation rate, 1961–1970 (December-to-December Consumer Price Index).
Source: Bureau of Labor Statistics.

runs below wage inflation) and, much more important, replace *actual* inflation on the right-hand side by *expected* inflation to get

$$\pi_t = \theta + \alpha \pi_t^e + f(U_t) + \varepsilon_t. \tag{2}$$

In equilibrium $\pi_t = \pi_t^e$, so equation (2) reduces to

$$(1 - \alpha)\, \pi_t = \theta + f(U_t),$$

which defines a negative relationship between π and U, to wit, a long-run sloping Phillips curve of the sort that Samuelson and Solow (1960) had depicted. If $\alpha = 1$, however, you get $0 = \theta + f(U_t)$ instead, which defines a unique equilibrium level of unemployment, Friedman's natural rate, and a vertical long-run Phillips curve. Hence, empirical attention started to focus on estimating the parameter α. Was it equal to or less than 1?

Remember, Lipsey (1960) had estimated α to be less than 1; so did a number of papers that came after his. For example, the first in what was destined to become a long series of Phillips curve estimates by Robert Gordon (1970) estimated α to be only 0.45.[5] Lipsey and

5. In those days it was common to estimate a price equation with the rate of change of money wages on the right-hand side and a separate wage equation with

Gordon were not alone in estimating $\alpha < 1$. I entered graduate school in the fall of 1967, first at the LSE (the former home of Phillips) and then at MIT (the home of Samuelson and Solow). The view in such places at the time, I well remember, was that while Friedman and Phelps had made convincing theoretical cases that α should be equal to 1, the empirical evidence virtually screamed out that $\alpha < 1$. It was one of those stark cases in which theory and empirics clashed sharply. As Groucho Marx memorably asked, "Who are ya gonna believe, me or your own eyes?" The view at MIT, as I recall, was go with your own eyes.

Meanwhile, a young economist at the University of Pennsylvania named Thomas Sargent (1971), a subsequent Nobel Prize winner, was demonstrating—in a beautiful five-page paper that was under-appreciated at the time—that the debate over the estimated parameter α was beside the point. His argument, based on an early use of rational expectations, was this. It had become common econometric practice to proxy the unobservable expected inflation rate in (2) by a distributed lag of past actual inflation rates. Thus, people were actually estimating Phillips curve equations of the form

$$\pi_t = \Sigma \alpha_j \pi_{t-j} + \theta + f(U_t) + \varepsilon_t, \tag{3}$$

and the standard test of verticality-in-the-long-run was whether the sum $\Sigma \alpha_j$ was 1.0 or less than 1.0. Every empirical estimate said less.

Sargent explained why this test is irrelevant under rational expectations. To illustrate his argument, suppose the true model is

$$\pi_t = \pi_t^e + \theta + f(U_t) + \varepsilon_t. \tag{4}$$

Since a coefficient of 1.0 sits in front of expected inflation, the implied long-run Phillips curve is vertical, just as Friedman and Phelps insisted. But suppose the stochastic process generating inflation is, say,

$$\pi_t = \rho \pi_{t-1} + u_t, \tag{5}$$

---

expected inflation on the right-hand side. The reduced form of that two-equation system resembled (2). In his paper, Gordon (1970) used long-term interest rates to develop a statistical proxy for expected inflation.

with $\rho < 1$. (This simple version has just one lag; Sargent's argument was more general.) Under rational expectations, (5) implies that $\pi_t^e = \rho \pi_{t-1}$. Substituting this into (4) yields

$$\pi_t = \rho \pi_{t-1} + \theta + f(U_t) + \varepsilon_t, \tag{6}$$

with $\rho < 1$, which is what an econometrician using the distributed lag methodology would estimate. Equation (6) looks like a long-run sloping Phillips curve because $\rho < 1$. But it's a mirage. The ρ in (6) is not the coefficient on π_t^e in (4), which is 1.0. Rather, it's the autoregressive parameter describing how inflation evolves in (5). If that parameter changes, the estimated coefficient in a Phillips curve such as (6) will change as well.[6]

As mentioned, Sargent's important point was not absorbed right away. People kept on estimating equations that looked like (3) and testing whether $\Sigma \alpha_j = 1$ or $\Sigma \alpha_j < 1$. As time went by, however, and inflation rose, the theory and the empirical evidence came into better alignment. Already in his 1972 Brookings paper, which made no mention of Sargent's then-recent paper, Gordon (1972) estimated a nonlinear α coefficient, finding that α rose as expected inflation rose, reaching about 1.0 when expected inflation was 7 percent. (CPI inflation was 3.4 percent in 1972 and 8.9 percent in 1973.) So, by about 1972 or 1973, the empirical debate over the verticality of the long-run Phillips curve was all but over. It was vertical both in theory and in the data. Keynesians and monetarists (and economists who would soon be called "new classicals") agreed on that. It was a clear triumph of theory over (flawed) empirics.

As academic economists rushed to embrace rational expectations, it was soon noticed that even the short-run Phillips curve should be vertical under rational expectations (Sargent and Wallace 1975). Look back at equation (4). Under rational expectations, π_t will differ from π_t^e only by a random expectational error, which must have zero mean and be independent of π_t^e. Putting that idea into (4) brings us right back to $0 = \theta + f(U_t)$, that is, to a vertical Phillips

---

6. This was an early application of what would later become known as the Lucas critique. See chapter 6.

curve at U*. But this time verticality obtains even in the short run. That stunning implication of rational expectations was revolutionary at the time. It was also wildly at variance with observed reality. So, while academic economists doted on it, real-world policy makers never paid it much attention (more on this in chapter 6).

Another problem with the rational expectations revolution went virtually unnoticed. Lucas's (1976) famous econometric policy critique held, correctly, that observed empirical relationships—such as $\pi_t^e = \Sigma\alpha_j\pi_{t-j}$ could change if policy reactions changed. As just mentioned, Sargent's (1971) important point, which predated the critique by five years, was an apposite example. But *could* is not *will*, and change does not necessarily connote change by a large amount. In the rush to revolutionize macroeconomics and, in the process, destroy Keynesianism, no one, it seemed, paused to ask whether the Lucas critique was empirically important in the context of the Phillips curve.

Well, almost no one. In a 1988 paper that garnered virtually no attention,[7] I estimated a series of Sargent-style autoregressions of the form

$$\pi_t = \Sigma\alpha_j\pi_{t-j} + u_t$$

for U.S. inflation over the period 1955:2 to 1987:4 (Blinder 1988). I then tested for the presence of a statistically significant break in this inflation-forecasting equation at the ends of 1970, 1971, 1972, and 1973—just when inflation was rising. The estimated F statistics ranged from 0.2 to 0.9, none of them coming remotely close to statistical significance. What that means is that, Lucas notwithstanding, the best-fitting autoregression for U.S. inflation remained reasonably stable through the early 1970s even though inflation itself did not. Sargent (1971) was right in principle, of course. So was Lucas (1976). But at least in this application, the Lucas critique appeared not to be quantitatively important.

Yet the old-fashioned Phillips curve did indeed fall apart later in the 1970s. Why? It was not for Lucas-Sargent reasons. It happened instead because severe adverse supply shocks wracked the

7. At this writing, Google Scholar records only 273 citations to Blinder (1988).

United States and other economies. Adding supply-shock variables—food and energy shocks—patched the Phillips curve up quickly. But that's a story for chapter 5.

The important point for present purposes is that by about 1972 the strong consensus among macroeconomists was that neither monetary nor conventional forms of fiscal policy had permanent effects on employment or output.[8] There was a short-run trade-off between inflation and unemployment but no long-run trade-off. In practice, this meant that policy makers could shorten recessions and make them shallower, but at the cost of leaving the inflation rate permanently higher. Thought of a bit differently, expansionary monetary or fiscal policies could put the economy on a short-term "sugar high." But the sugar would dissolve, leaving inflation somewhat higher in its wake. That quickly became the canonical view in academia, and it still is. It also seems to have been the view embraced by President Richard Nixon and his handpicked Federal Reserve Chair, Arthur Burns, as we shall see in the next chapter.

Chapter Summary

A. W. Phillips discovered his famous curve in 1958 in much the same way that Alexander Fleming had discovered penicillin thirty years earlier—serendipitously. But the curve stood up for decades and had profound effects on the way monetary and fiscal policy were conceptualized. Intellectually, the Phillips curve provided the missing link in the old-fashioned Keynesian model, the so-called inflation equation. In terms of policy, the curve was thought at first to offer decision makers a menu of choices for where the economy could sit in inflation-unemployment space.

But Milton Friedman and Edmund Phelps argued persuasively that there could be no such menu in the long run. On basic theoretical grounds, money had to be neutral in the long run regardless of

---

8. By "conventional forms" I mean to allow for permanent incentive effects from, say, changes in marginal tax rates. Such possibilities were well known at the time, even though the term *supply-side economics* had not yet been coined.

what estimated Phillips curves of the day seemed to say. Within a few years, empirically estimated Phillips curves using lagged inflation as proxies for expected inflation were agreeing with Friedman and Phelps's theoretical proposition, although Sargent had argued that the coefficients on lagged inflation were irrelevant anyway. In any case, practical macroeconomic thinking soon congealed around the idea that policy makers could trade more inflation for less unemployment in the short run but not in the long run. That view remains largely intact today, although even a short-run Phillips curve is hard to find in U.S. data since the late 1990s.

4

Nixon, Burns, and the Political Business Cycle

No one has tried harder to help you.
—ARTHUR BURNS TO RICHARD NIXON, JUNE 1971

The complex personal relationship between Richard Nixon and Arthur Burns, which dated back to at least 1953, had profound effects on the nation's monetary and fiscal policies in the 1970s.[1] And its legacy lingers on. Nixon needs no introduction. Burns was an esteemed professor at Columbia University and one of the nation's foremost experts on business cycles when President Dwight D. Eisenhower tapped him to become his first chair of the Council of Economic Advisers in 1953. Nixon and Burns served together in the Eisenhower administration until the end of 1956, when Burns returned to teaching at Columbia.

But the sometimes tumultuous relationship between the two men was hardly over. Burns remained active in Republican Party circles, and in March 1960 he came to see Nixon with a warning: a recession

---

1. The epigraph is quoted in Meltzer (2009b, 793). The source is a White House tape.

looked likely. If it were allowed to occur, the economy would hit bottom around October 1960, Burns predicted, and that would gravely damage Republicans' prospects in the November election. He urged an increase in federal spending and an easing of credit conditions to try to ward off the incipient recession. Notice the conjoining of monetary and fiscal policy here. Strong belief in central bank independence was yet to come.

Burns didn't quite nail the timing to the month; the National Bureau of Economic Research (NBER) dates the 1960–1961 recession as starting in April 1960 and bottoming out in February 1961. But broadly speaking his forecast was excellent, far better than his powers of political persuasion. Eisenhower discussed Burns's idea to stimulate the economy with his cabinet but rejected it, much to the chagrin of then Vice President Nixon, the presumptive Republican standard-bearer in the 1960 election. Nixon (1962, 310) lamented a few years later that "in supporting Burns' point of view, I must admit that I was more sensitive politically than some of the others around the cabinet table." No doubt he was.

Nixon subsequently blamed the recession for his narrow defeat by John F. Kennedy in the popular vote (Kennedy's electoral college margin was far larger). Although his five o'clock shadow and nontelegenic performance in the nation's first televised presidential debate may have been just as important, Nixon certainly had a point. Recessions hurt incumbents.[2] In any case, he would not forget the bitter lesson of 1960 or the wise prophet who had warned him of the electoral peril.

Fiscal and Monetary Stimulus before the 1972 Election

Nixon's loss to Kennedy in 1960 did not, of course, end his political career. Nor even did his humiliating subsequent defeat by Edmund "Pat" Brown in the 1962 California gubernatorial race, after which Nixon famously told the assembled press "You won't have Dick Nixon to kick around anymore." It turned out that they would. A scant

---

2. A voluminous literature in both economics and political science supports this point, though virtually none of it predates 1960. See, for example, Fair (1978).

six years later he secured the Republican presidential nomination again and went on to defeat Vice President Hubert Humphrey in the 1968 election. Ironically, that election ended much like the Kennedy-Nixon election: with a razor-thin margin in the popular vote but a much more comfortable victory in the electoral college.

Burns was immediately appointed counselor to the president, a newly created position with cabinet rank. It was widely believed at the time that this was just a place for Burns to hang his hat while Nixon awaited the end of William McChesney Martin's last term as chair of the Federal Reserve Board, at which point Nixon would elevate Burns to the Fed chairmanship. That is indeed what happened.

When Nixon assumed the presidency in January 1969, both fiscal policy and monetary policy were in the later stages of the anti-inflation policy that Lyndon Johnson had belatedly begun in 1968, and which the Fed had started two years before that. Nixon's initial fiscal policies were appropriate to that end. Between fiscal years 1968 and 1970, what was then called the "full-employment deficit" shrank from about 4 percent of GDP to about 0.5 percent of GDP—a sizable fiscal contraction. With the economy near full employment at the time, those numbers meant that the federal budget was close to balanced. Eisenhower presumably would have approved. Monetary policy was also still tightening in 1969. The federal funds rate moved up from about 6 percent when Nixon was elected to about 9 percent in May 1969, but only half of that 300 basis point increase represented a higher real federal funds rate since inflation had risen from 4.4 percent to 5.9 percent.

For these and other reasons, the twelve-month Consumer Price Index (CPI) inflation rate peaked in early 1970 at 6.4 percent and then began to decline—albeit slowly (figure 4.1). Falling inflation was, of course, precisely the intended effect of the tighter monetary and fiscal policies. But those same forces also produced—as an unintended but unsurprising consequence—a short and shallow recession that began in December 1969 and ended in November 1970. Real GDP declined only about 0.6 percent in the 1969–1970 recession. The unemployment rate did rise by about 2.5 percentage points, but that still put it only around 6 percent.

FIGURE 4.1. Inflation in the Nixon-Ford years.
Source: Bureau of Labor Statistics.

No president relishes a recession on his watch. However, the timing was all but perfect for a president eager to engineer a political business cycle, as Nixon surely was. When a recession bottoms out two years before an incumbent president's next election, it's an extremely good bet that he will enjoy an expanding economy throughout his reelection campaign. And Nixon did. Nonetheless, with the memory of 1960 vivid in his mind, he didn't want to take any chances. In January 1971, Nixon famously described himself as "now a Keynesian in economics" (Reuters 1971), which was a very un-Republican thing to say at the time—and still is.[3] But he was signaling something. What?

As a matter of positive (that is, descriptive) economics, one of the central tenets of Keynesian economics is that short-run fluctuations in real GDP are dominated by changes in aggregate demand, some of which emanate from monetary and fiscal policy. These changes in demand show up mainly in real output rather than in inflation in the short run because inflation responds only with a long lag. That's precisely what empirical Phillips curves of the day showed.

As a matter of normative (that is, prescriptive) economics, being a Keynesian sometimes means worrying more about unemployment than about inflation. This relative weighting of the two major

---

3. Nixon is often incorrectly quoted as saying, "We are all Keynesians now." In fact, those words were Milton Friedman's, and Friedman's full statement was "In one sense, we are all Keynesians now; in another, nobody is any longer a Keynesian." See *TIME* (1965).

macroeconomic maladies may be why many conservatives shun the label "Keynesian" to this day. They may be positive Keynesians, but they are not normative Keynesians. Nixon was both.

Due mostly to increases in government spending, the full-employment budget deficit rose by about 1 percent of GDP in 1971 and another 0.5 percent of GDP in 1972. The first Social Security checks reflecting a huge 20 percent increase in benefits engineered by Nixon arrived in retirees' mailboxes in October 1972. Now, that's timing! These generous checks were accompanied by a none-too-subtle covering letter stating that "your social security payment has been increased by 20 percent, starting with this month's check, by a new statute enacted by the Congress and signed into law by President Nixon on July 1, 1972."[4] The checks must have brought smiles to the faces of many seniors—and votes to Republicans.

Meanwhile, Arthur Burns, who had taken over the helm of the Federal Reserve in February 1970, was also pushing monetary policy hard in the stimulative direction. By January 1972 the federal funds rate, which had peaked above 9 percent in 1969, was down to 3.5 percent—roughly equal to the inflation rate and thus about zero in real terms. It was still only 5.3 percent in the election month.

In those days, however, more attention was paid to the money growth rate than to the federal funds rate. Unfortunately, money growth numbers get revised constantly, and even the definitions of the Ms have changed many times since the early 1970s, including several changes made during Burns's chairmanship. For what it's worth, today's data on M1 growth display a go-stop pattern similar to that of the funds rate. The twelve-month lagging M1 growth rate was a mere 2.9 percent when Burns became chair of the Fed. By June 1971 it was up to 7.7 percent and then to 8.2 percent in November 1972. A year later, M1 growth was back down to 5.9 percent (see figure 4.2). M2 growth displayed a similar but even more exaggerated pattern, rising from 2.5 percent in February 1970 to 13.1 percent in June 1971 and 12.7 percent in November 1972 and then falling to 6.9 percent in November 1973. It sure looked like the monetary leg of a political business cycle.

4. A facsimile of this letter appears in (Tufte 1978, 32).

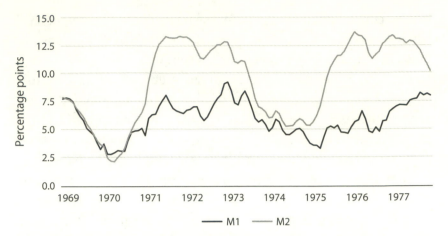

FIGURE 4.2. Growth rates of M1 and M2, from twelve months previously, 1969–1977.

Source: Board of Governors of the Federal Reserve System.

For decades there was much speculation, but no hard proof, that Burns was doing all this to help get his friend, Nixon, reelected. Burns vigorously denied the charge, claiming years later that "the election of 1972 had absolutely no influence on anything I did at the Fed."[5] But after the infamous Watergate tapes were released to researchers in stages, Burton Abrams (2006) published a number of quotations from Nixon-Burns conversations that left little doubt. Here is one excerpt from Abrams's paper pertaining to a phone call between Nixon and Burns just four days before the December 1971 Federal Open Market Committee (FOMC) meeting:

> Burns states that "I wanted you to know that we lowered the discount rate . . . , got it down to 4.5 percent." "Good, good, good," replies Nixon. Burns indicates that the announcement of the discount rate reduction would be accompanied by . . . an added statement that it was done to "also further economic expansion." Burns exclaims that he also lowered the rate to "put them [the Federal Open Market Committee] on notice that through this action that I want more aggressive steps taken by that committee on next Tuesday." "Great. Great," replies Nixon. "You can lead 'em. You

5. The quote is from Burns's obituary (*New York Times* 1987).

can lead 'em. You always have, now. Just kick 'em in the rump."
(Abrams 2006, 181)

The Nixon-Burns program of significant fiscal and monetary stimulus succeeded, with superb timing from Nixon's perspective. The
growth rate of real GDP, which had averaged a sluggish 2.1 percent
per annum over the final three quarters of 1971, leaped upward to
6.9 percent over the first three quarters of the election year 1972.
Very nice for the incumbent president. But there was more to the
exquisite timing than that.

Imagine yourself in Nixon's shoes in 1971 and with about as many
scruples. You will be running for reelection in 1972. The economy is
growing, though not rapidly, and the unemployment rate is about
6 percent, far higher than the roughly 3.5 percent when you took office.
Meanwhile, inflation is still stubbornly hanging around 4.5 percent per
annum, which is high enough to displease the American electorate.

Here's the temptation to which Nixon readily succumbed: Suppose
we boost GDP growth with fiscal and monetary stimulus in the election
year (remember, Nixon had a friend at the Fed) but then reverse field
after the election. To keep inflation at bay while all this is going on, we
can use the authority Congress gave us on a dare in 1970 to invoke wage-
price controls.[6] Such a combination of policies should get us through
the November 1972 election with the economy growing fast and inflation low. We can worry about cleaning up the inflationary mess later.

The August 1971 Surprise

That, in a nutshell, is precisely what Nixon did. Specifically, in a dramatic August 15, 1971, presidential address to the nation, he announced
comprehensive wage-price controls, beginning with a startling ninety-
day freeze on most wages and prices. It was America's first and only
experiment with economy-wide wage-price controls in peacetime.

---

6. A few years later George Shultz and Kenneth Dam, who were there at the
time, wrote, "The Congress had earlier, as a political dare, granted the President
sweeping authority to impose controls on the American economy" (Shultz and
Dam 1977, 141).

Coming from a Republican president who had denounced price controls as "a scheme to socialize America" less than a month earlier (Abrams and Butkiewicz 2017, 64), the controls came as quite a shock. Furthermore, the "conservative" chair of the Fed supported this "socialist" policy intervention.[7]

And the price controls worked, at least politically for Nixon. The twelve-month lagging inflation rate dropped from 4.4 percent in August 1971 to just 2.9 percent a year later, despite a booming economy (see figure 4.1). It was like a favorable supply shock that, given monetary policy, would be expected to boost real GDP growth. Of course, wage-price controls also brought with them the usual panoply of distortions, shortages, difficulties in enforcement, and the like. So, after the election the administration began to dismantle the controls in stages, starting in January 1973. Price controls were reimposed briefly when inflation flared up in the summer of 1973, but decontrol resumed in earnest in August 1973, and the last remnants of the Nixon wage-price controls were lifted by April 1974.

How did the controls affect the inflation rate? William Newton and I constructed a time series on the fraction of the CPI that was subject to price controls, month by month (figure 4.3) and used that to estimate two different econometric models of the effects of controls on core CPI inflation, that is, inflation excluding food and energy prices (Blinder and Newton 1981).[8] According to one model, the controls reduced the price level by about a cumulative 3 percent between July 1971 and February 1974 (the month of their peak effect), but the postcontrols bounce-back erased this effect entirely by October 1974. Notice that this estimate implies a huge positive impact of decontrol on inflation between February and October 1974. According to the other model, the peak effect of controls on the price level also came in February 1974, but it was larger: about 4 percent. However, the estimated bounce-back after controls

7. The *truly* conservative George Shultz, who was director of the Office of Management and Budget at the time, strongly opposed them. See, for example, Garten (2021, chap. 8).

8. The two models employed different measures of demand pressure.

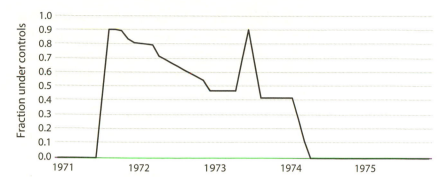

FIGURE 4.3. Blinder-Newton estimates of the fraction of Consumer Price Index under price controls.
Source: Blinder and Newton (1981).

were lifted is much more modest in this second model and was never complete. Thus, the two models agree that price controls reduced the annual inflation rate between August 1971 and February 1974 by roughly 1.5 percentage points on average.[9] But they disagree sharply over how much decontrol raised inflation after that.

The announcement of wage-price controls was not the only news President Nixon made on August 15, 1971. In fact, outside the United States it was not even the biggest news. Rather, the headline story around the world was that the United States was "temporarily" suspending the convertibility of the dollar into gold, thereby unilaterally ending the Bretton Woods system of fixed exchange rates. In truth, the United States had been running out of gold for years and was therefore nearing the end of its ability to peg the value of the dollar to the yellow metal in any case. With whatever remaining discipline from the Bretton Woods system thus removed—and there was not much left by 1971—the major countries of the world stumbled through a period of almost two years without quite knowing what to do about exchange rates. Eventually almost all of them turned to true—well, make that *managed*—floating in 1973.

Ending the Bretton Woods system was neither fiscal nor monetary policy, of course. But it was highly relevant to the latter, especially

9. The Blinder and Newton (1981) estimates of the depressing effects of controls on inflation are close to those of Gordon (1975).

in other nations but even in the United States. In simple textbook models, fixing the exchange rate removes monetary policy from the toolbox of *domestic* stabilization policy because the central bank must dedicate its monetary policy instruments to fixing the exchange rate, much as under the gold standard.

The reality is not quite that stark for a dominant economic power such as the United States, so Arthur Burns and the FOMC had some freedom to pursue conventional monetary policy even under Bretton Woods. Nonetheless, fixing exchange rates did impose constraints on central banks in every country that was party to the Bretton Woods agreement—hard constraints for many, a more pliable constraint for the Fed, but constraints nonetheless. It was therefore convenient for Nixon and Burns to get rid of those constraints in August 1971.

When the Bretton Woods system collapsed, those constraints on monetary policy all but disappeared.[10] In fact, a number of economists have blamed the worldwide upsurge of inflation after 1973 on the end of Bretton Woods.[11] The end of fixed exchange rates certainly played a role. But I am inclined to place much more weight on the supply shocks discussed in chapter 5. One reason is simple: if dollar depreciation leads to higher inflation in the United States, the corresponding currency appreciations of the currencies of America's major trading partners should produce lower inflation there. But the 1970s surge in inflation was a worldwide phenomenon; it hit virtually every country, albeit in different amounts.[12] Between August 1971 and August 1973, the CPI inflation rate rose from 3.4 percent to 8.1 percent in Canada, from 5.6 percent to 7.6 percent in France, and from 5.7 percent to 7.3 percent in Germany.[13]

---

10. "All but" because most countries still cared about their exchange rates.

11. See, for example, Bordo and Eichengreen (2013), who concentrate on a somewhat earlier period, when Bretton Woods was limping along, but taken more seriously. Others have expressed similar sentiments.

12. But it can be argued (and has been!) that the demise of Bretton Woods allowed U.S. monetary policy to become much more accommodative while foreign monetary policies became somewhat more accommodative, thus contributing to worldwide inflation. I thank Barry Eichengreen for pointing this out.

13. I end this comparison period in August 1973 because OPEC struck that September. The CPI data cited are from the Organisation for Economic Co-operation and Development.

Still, when all was said and done, the end of the Bretton Woods system destroyed what then passed as the world's best nominal anchor, flawed though it was. Floating exchange rates offered no substitute. The demise of Bretton Woods also freed the Fed from worrying about gold flows and the dollar exchange rate. The Fed could focus its full attention on inflation and unemployment in the United States.[14]

The Great Reversal of 1973

Of the two main macro variables, inflation commanded center stage in 1973. After the 1972 election, the unemployment rate drifted slowly downward, making it less salient both economically and politically. But the inflation rate soared, from just 3.4 percent in the twelve months ending November 1972 (with price controls in effect) to a startling 8.3 percent in the twelve months ending November 1973, the highest inflation rate in the United States since 1951. With the election now in the rearview mirror, the Burns Fed reacted strongly to higher inflation, boosting the federal funds rate from 5.1 percent in November 1972 to 10.8 percent in September 1973. Dwell on that for a moment: the Fed's main policy rate rose 570 basis points in just ten months. But inflation rose by 400 basis points over that same period, making the real tightening just 170 basis points.

Spurred on by the Arab-Israeli War, the Organization of the Petroleum Exporting Countries (OPEC) struck the following month, sending the price of oil soaring and pushing the United States and other economies into the unhappy combination of stagnation and inflation that the media dubbed *stagflation*.[15] Stagflation presents a central bank with an unpleasant policy dilemma that, though

14. In a famous June 23, 1972, conversation captured on the White House tapes, Nixon's chief of staff, H. R. Haldeman, reported to Nixon that Burns was worried about speculation against the Italian lira. Nixon famously replied, "Well, I don't give a shit about the lira" (Nixon 1972, 13).

15. The term *stagflation* was apparently first coined by Iain Macleod (1965, col. 1165), a British politician who later became chancellor of the exchequer, in 1965. But it was not widely used before 1973. This initial oil shock would later be dubbed OPEC I.

now well understood, had a lot of central bankers—not just Arthur Burns—scratching their heads at the time. If a central bank eases monetary policy to fight stagnation, that would exacerbate the inflation problem. Alternatively, if it tightens monetary policy to fight inflation, the stagnation problem would get worse. No central bank can mitigate both ills at once. So, what should monetary policy do?

As it turned out, the Burns Fed vacillated. It reacted first by easing monetary policy through February 1974, dropping the federal funds rate as low as 8.8 percent (against an inflation rate of 10%) to spur growth. But then it reversed field and raised interest rates again to fight inflation. The funds rate peaked at almost 13 percent in June 1974. Inflation was on the rise too, however. So, that seemingly sky-high funds rate was only about 2 percentage points above the 11 percent inflation rate. According to Holston, Laubach, and Williams's (2016) estimates, the neutral real federal funds rate at the time was slightly over 3 percent, so monetary policy was still expansionary. But of course, the Holston-Laubach-Williams estimates were not available at the time. Indeed, the very concept of the neutral real rate did not play a prominent role in the Fed's vocabulary or its thinking back then. Furthermore and shockingly, the chair of the Fed at the time was dubious about monetary policy's ability to move the inflation rate (more on this below)!

Fiscal policy was also tightening as the OPEC shock wracked the economy. The full-employment deficit, which had peaked at about 5 percent of GDP in the election quarter of 1972:4 (quite a coincidence!) was whittled down to about 2 percent of GDP by 1974:3. In a word, the preelection stimulation of the economy by both monetary and fiscal policy rapidly gave way to double-barreled restraint. It was a picture-perfect political business cycle.

Maybe too perfect. The obviously made-in-Washington character of the boom and bust of 1971–1974 coupled with the virtually universal condemnation of wage-price controls may have marked the undoing of the political business cycle in the United States. Nixon's political manipulation of the economy was so extreme and so shameless that his two more principled successors, Republican Gerald R. Ford and Democrat Jimmy Carter, seemed to avoid political manipulation like the plague. This attitude prevailed even though each president had ample opportunities and even plausible rationales for applying fiscal stimulus: the deep recession of 1973–1975 in Ford's case and the stagflation after OPEC II in Carter's case. And no American president since Nixon has even flirted with wage-price controls, not even when inflation rose back into double digits.[16] All this was Nixon's legacy for macroeconomic policy.

The Legacy of Arthur Burns

Burns's legacy at the Fed has two main components: his failure to control inflation in the 1970s and his willingness to surrender the central bank's independence to Nixon. Both were soon—and decisively—reversed by the staunchly independent and devoted inflation fighter Paul Volcker. But that's a story for chapter 7.

Sticking with Burns, it is unfair to pin the entire blame for rising inflation on him and his colleagues on the FOMC. The supply shocks just mentioned (and discussed more fully in the next chapter) deserve a large share of the blame. Yet the Burns Fed certainly deserves some of the blame, and for several reasons the Nixon-Burns episode is rightly viewed as a black mark on the Federal Reserve's history.

First, Burns was one of the advisers closest to Nixon who urged the unscrupulous president to invoke wage-price controls and then applauded when he did so (Nelson 2020, 321–31). Doing that will not endear you to many economists or to history.

Second, the Fed's loose monetary policies of 1971 and 1972 certainly contributed to the inflation of 1972–1974, even as Burns regularly railed against the evils of inflation. That made him look not just political but also hypocritical in the extreme.

Third, while there is room for debate on this point, Burns has been accused of turning the monetary spigots on again in 1976–1978. Over those three years, M1 growth averaged 7.6 percent per annum and M2 growth averaged 10.4 percent. Nelson writes that "the period

---

16. President Carter did, however, force Paul Volcker to impose credit controls briefly in 1980 (Volcker 2018, 110–12). For more on that episode, see chapter 7.

from 1976 to 1978—the final two years of Burns' tenure—arguably witnessed even greater monetary policy ease [than in 1970–1972] and was followed by a higher peak of inflation" (Nelson 2013, 2).

Fourth and more in the intellectual than the policy realm, Burns actually claimed that the Fed had little ability to control inflation. For example, he told the Senate Banking Committee in March 1971 that "I don't think that our fiscal policy and our monetary policy are sufficient to control inflation. Experience indicates that pretty clearly in our own country and even more dramatically in other countries, particularly in Canada and Great Britain."[17] Really? Milton Friedman, Burns's onetime student, and Anna Schwartz, among others, certainly thought otherwise.

Maybe Burns was just new at his job then. But in his famous Per Jacobsson lecture at the September 1979 meetings of the International Monetary Fund in Belgrade, well after he had left the Fed, Burns (1979) seemed to look everywhere but at the central bank for explanations of high inflation.

Burns blamed "the philosophic and political currents that have been transforming economic life in the United States and elsewhere since the 1930s," by which he meant the New Deal, the Great Society, and the like, noting that "the Federal Reserve was itself caught up" in these currents (Burns 1979, 9, 15). He complained that "as the Federal Reserve . . . kept testing and probing the limits of its freedom to undernourish the inflation, it repeatedly evoked violent criticism from both the Executive establishment and the Congress" (16). He concluded that central bankers' "practical capacity for curbing an inflation that is continually driven by political forces is very limited" (21).

Was it really social liberals and obdurate politicians who stayed the Fed's anti-inflation hand? To monetarists such as Friedman, that was apostasy. To Paul Volcker, it was a dangerous fantasy. As Volcker recalled in his autobiography, Burns "(infamously) expressed doubt that central banks were even capable of controlling inflation anymore" (Volcker 2018, 107). In the eyes of Volcker then and virtually all economists now, Burns was dead wrong. Supply shocks are sometimes important determinants of inflation; I argue in chapter 5

17. U.S. Senate Committee on Banking, Housing, and Urban Affairs (1971, 19).

that they were in fact far more important than demand shocks in explaining the rise and fall of inflation in the 1970s and early 1980s. In the long run, however, monetary policy is a—many would argue *the*—principal determinant of inflation, despite Burns's efforts to blame inflation on the welfare state. It is hard to see how a country gets sensible monetary policy when its central bank chief doubts that monetary policy affects inflation.

Arthur Burns (1904–1987)

Distinguished Scholar Turned Political

Arthur F. Burns was a consequential figure in both the study of business cycles and the history of U.S. business cycles from the 1950s through the 1970s. His attitudes and actions left strong marks on the Eisenhower administration, the Nixon administration, and after—including, of course, at the Federal Reserve, which he chaired from 1970 to 1978.

Burns was born in Austria in 1904, the son of a paint contractor. His family immigrated to the United States ten years later, and Burns grew up in New Jersey. He attended Columbia University, where he earned his bachelor's degree and, in 1925, his master's degree. For some years thereafter he taught at Rutgers—where, you may remember, he had Milton Friedman as a student—while working toward his PhD at Columbia.

There Burns encountered Wesley Clair Mitchell, the research director of the NBER who was then America's foremost authority on business cycles. It changed both their lives; the team of Burns and Mitchell subsequently became almost synonymous with business cycle research. Years later, Burns succeeded Mitchell as the NBER's research director.

Burns moved from Rutgers to Columbia in 1945, where, among other things, he met its president, Dwight D. Eisenhower. When Eisenhower became president of the United States in 1953, he invited Burns to chair his Council of Economic Advisers. In that capacity Burns urged Eisenhower, who was a dyed-in-the-wool fiscal conservative, to cut taxes and reduce spending to reduce the severity of the 1953–1954 recession. It was pure Keynesianism.

In 1956, Burns returned to both Columbia and to the NBER as its president. Though once again an academic, he remained politically connected, making him a natural choice for a position in the new Nixon administration in 1969. Burns was elevated to the chairmanship of the Fed in February 1970 and, as related in this chapter, had a tumultuous eight years there. As his *New York Times* obituary noted, "he was an unmistakable presence to millions of Americans, with his bushy gray hair parted down the middle, wire-rimmed spectacles, jutting pipe and precise, slightly nasal voice that maintained its soft-spoken tone under the most scathing questioning" (*New York Times* 1987, 1).[18]

In 1981, President Ronald Reagan appointed Burns ambassador to West Germany, a post at which he apparently excelled. Completing his term there in 1985, Burns returned to Washington as a private citizen, where he died in 1987. As a tribute to his historical importance, the *New York Times* carried his obituary as a page one story.

---

18. Much of the information in this profile comes from the *New York Times* (1987).

Chapter Summary

Richard Nixon and Arthur Burns illustrated the potential power of fiscal and monetary policy, working in tandem, to manipulate an economy—in this case for political ends. It was an idea they both understood as early as 1960. And when history gave them a chance to turn this idea into action in 1972, they did not squander the opportunity. Prior to the election, Nixon and Congress applied sizable fiscal stimulus, mostly in the form of spending, while Burns and the Fed applied strong monetary stimulus. While this was going on, Nixon invoked wage-price controls to hold inflation in check temporarily. The formula worked and then was quickly reversed once Nixon was reelected.

Ironically, the political business cycle they caused in 1971–1973 turned out to be an example of what is sometimes called catastrophic success. The preelection stimulus and postelection restraint were so blatant and so obvious—and got such a bad name—that no American president has tried it since.

Furthermore, as we shall see in chapter 7, Burns's notion that inflation was beyond the control of the central bank—perhaps a product of the welfare state—did not last long.

5

Stagflation and Its Aftermath

'Tis all in pieces,
All coherence gone,
All just supply
—JOHN DONNE, 1611

If one picture is worth a thousand words, figure 5.1 should be worth several thousand. It traces the behavior of inflation, as measured by the Consumer Price Index (CPI) in both its headline and core versions, from 1965 to 1985 and thereby vividly illustrates three important points.

First, this twenty-year slice of inflation history is dominated by two big "hills," one peaking around 1975, the other around 1981. (There is also a much smaller hillock around 1970.) Each of these inflation hills looks remarkably symmetric, suggesting—though certainly not establishing—that something happened to push inflation up for a while and then mostly disappeared, allowing inflation to fall back approximately to where it had been before. I argue in this chapter that those "somethings" were not mysterious forces but rather readily observable, even obvious, events: a series of supply shocks that hit the U.S. economy (and other nations, too). Each such shock came, crested through the economy, and disappeared, leaving just a trace on core inflation.

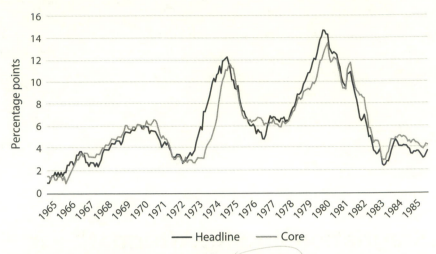

FIGURE 5.1. Headline and core inflation, 1965–1985.
Source: Bureau of Labor Statistics.

Second, figure 5.1 illustrates that headline inflation was more volatile than core inflation over this period, another crucial fact that points the finger of guilt in the direction of food and energy prices. Notice in particular that headline inflation exceeded core inflation in most of the years between 1972 and 1982 and by sizable margins in the years of truly high inflation (e.g., 1974 and 1980). Unless that is a coincidence, it provides further evidence that supply shocks drove the inflation rate over that critical decade.

Third, all that said, there is a visible upward trend in core inflation over the two decades depicted in figure 5.1. Initially, that trend was likely attributable to the failure of policy makers to rein in demand during the Vietnam War, as argued in chapter 2. Later, the upward trend in core inflation can perhaps be blamed on Arthur Burns's monetary policy—as argued in chapter 4—and perhaps also on inflationary monetary policy in 1976–1978. Inertia in the inflation process almost certainly played a meaningful role as well: once a supply shock pushes core inflation higher, it drifts back only very slowly.

This chapter focuses on the supply shocks of the 1970s and early 1980s descriptively, analytically, and especially in terms of the dilemma they posed for monetary and fiscal policy makers. There is a simple reason for this focus. In addition to the high inflation rates depicted in figure 5.1, the U.S. economy suffered through recessions in 1973–1975, 1980, and 1981–1982. Two of those three recessions were long and deep. Fighting that combination of maladies, which we call *stagflation*, was the central challenge for monetary and fiscal policy makers during this period.

Something New Under the Sun?

The supply shocks of the 1970s and early 1980s were large—large enough to make them the dominant economic events of the period. Figures 5.2 and 5.3 offer quick visual summaries of these shocks.[1]

Figure 5.2 displays the behavior of the real price of oil (deflated by the CPI) from 1970 to 1988. Both the first Organization of the Petroleum Exporting Countries (OPEC) shock in 1973–1974, which nearly tripled the real price of crude oil, and OPEC II in 1979–1980, which roughly doubled it again, are clearly visible. But there is an interesting difference. OPEC I looks like a permanent increase in the relative price of oil: the oil price rises substantially and then remains roughly on that higher plateau until 1979 (when it leaps

1. This section borrows heavily from Blinder and Rudd (2013).

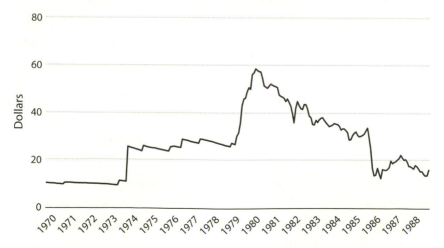

FIGURE 5.2. Real price of oil, 1970–1988 (in constant December 1988 dollars).
Source: Energy Information Administration and Bureau of Labor Statistics.

volatil opposite of stable.

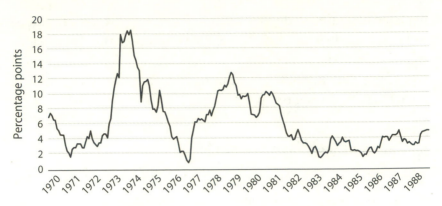

FIGURE 5.3. Inflation rate for food and beverages, 1970–1988.
Source: Bureau of Labor Statistics.

upward again). OPEC II, by contrast, though larger in real dollar terms, dissipated after 1981 (partly because of the global recession) and was basically gone by the end of 1985. Producers in the oil patch need no reminder that 1986 was a terrible year.

While oil was undoubtedly the star of the show, food price shocks were also notable during the period, especially in 1973–1974 and 1978–1980 (figure 5.3). Food accounts for a much larger share of GDP (and of the CPI) than energy does, so food prices, when volatile, matter a great deal for headline inflation. Yet for the most part, macroeconomists seem to have forgotten about the food shocks, perhaps because they have not recurred since 1980. Future historians certainly should not forget about them.

The first food shock, which predated OPEC I, was large. But inflation and unemployment really soared simultaneously in countries all over the world when OPEC jacked up the price of oil in the fall of 1973. Policy makers in the United States and elsewhere were initially puzzled by this conjunction of maladies. Statistical Phillips curves had shown that inflation and unemployment typically moved in opposite directions. Historical data displayed a clear, if imperfect, negative correlation. Yet, now the two were both moving up together. What was going on?

The puzzlement didn't last long. In short order, both Robert Gordon (1975) and Edmund Phelps (1978) published scholarly papers

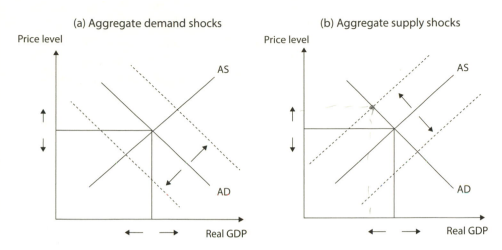

FIGURE 5.4. Demand shocks versus supply shocks.

explaining how and why, on basic macroeconomic principles, a "supply shock" (a term not previously in the economist's lexicon) should push prices up and real output down, to wit, cause stagflation. Even sooner than that—though it was, of course, not published—I had asked my Princeton PhD students in the core macroeconomics course to answer that very same question on a final exam in January 1974, just months after OPEC struck. The question wasn't that hard—either for me to write or for them to answer. Nowadays, freshmen answer it routinely in Economics 101. But in 1973–1974, stagflation was something new and puzzling. It wasn't supposed to happen.

The straightforward logic of supply versus demand shocks is depicted in the two panels of figure 5.4. For a generation or more, economists had become accustomed to the idea that macroeconomic fluctuations emanated primarily from demand shocks, whether positive or negative, as depicted in panel (a). In such cases, the price level and output should move in the same direction. Adapting these simple static diagrams to reality, this meant that inflation and the real growth rate should move in the same direction. And the data from say, 1947 to 1973 were broadly consistent with this prediction.

But now look at panel (b). If macroeconomic fluctuations are driven primarily by supply shocks instead, prices and output should move in opposite directions; the data should then display a negative correlation between inflation and growth—that is, stagflation. To get a little ahead of a story I'll tell more completely in this chapter, critics in the 1970s and 1980s who claimed that stagflation either contradicted Keynesian economics or was a mystery should have been embarrassed (but apparently were not). The "mystery" lasted for perhaps a few weeks. No contradiction was ever present.

There was, however, an intellectual puzzle. According to basic microeconomic theory, an exogenous increase in the price of any factor input (either food or energy, in this case) should reduce potential GDP, as both Gordon (1975) and Phelps (1978) made clear. And, of course, actual GDP did decline significantly during the 1973–1975 recession. Sounds good at first blush: unfavorable supply shocks reduce aggregate supply. But there were two gigantic loose ends.

First, if the recession was induced by declining supply (real shocks) rather than by declining aggregate demand, why did employment fall so much? In a strictly neoclassical world, there is no reason to think that a pure supply shock should push employment down—output, yes, but not employment. To see why, think about the aggregate production function as $Y = F(L,K,E)$, where L is labor input, K is capital input (which is fixed in the short run), and E is energy input, which is where the supply shock shows up. Suppose each factor gets paid its marginal product. If a higher oil price pushes E down, then Y will decline even with L and K fixed. Output and real wages should drop, but employment should not. In fact, if there is any ability to substitute labor for energy, L should rise. (Incidentally, the clear policy implication in this unrealistic case is that monetary policy should contract demand to match the reduced supply. More on this later.) But, of course, employment fell sharply in the United States and everywhere else after OPEC I. The neoclassical view must be missing something important.

Second, the magnitudes don't come close to adding up. Bruno and Sachs (1985) observed that on basic neoclassical principles, if all energy is imported (an exaggeration), then the three-factor production function above implies a domestic value-added (GDP) function $Q = Y - \rho E$. They show that the elasticity of Q with respect to ρ, the real oil price, is $s/(1-s)$, where s is the energy share in Y. That's a pretty small number. For example, if $s = 0.07$, then $s/(1-s) = 0.075$. Blinder and Rudd (2013, 129) used precisely this type of analysis to calculate that the pure neoclassical effect of OPEC I on output should have been a drop in GDP of just over 1 percent. But the actual decline between 1973:4 and 1975:1, relative to the roughly 3.5 percent annual trend prevailing at the time, was closer to 8 percent. Once again, the pure neoclassical analysis comes up far short.

What's missing from the picture? Many economists have suggested a variety of demand-side effects. Most prominently, observers have likened the oil shock to an "oil tax" imposed by OPEC on importing nations. The idea is simple. If imported oil becomes more expensive, the real incomes of Americans decline, just as if they were being taxed by a foreign entity. This "tax" hits people harder the less elastic the demand for energy, and we know that the price elasticity is quite low in the short run. So, not much of the tax would be shifted back to producers. (Long-run incidence is another matter entirely.)

In the case of OPEC I, the nation's bill for imported petroleum rose by about 1.5 percent of GDP by the end of 1974. With a multiplier somewhat above 1, the maximal hit from this "tax" would have been somewhat under 2 percent of GDP, or almost twice the size of the neoclassical supply-side effect.[2] But that still leaves us with just 3 percentage points of the GDP decline explained, far short of what actually happened. What else was going on?

For one thing, there was an internal redistribution within the United States as purchasing power was transferred from energy users to energy producers. To the extent that the latter group (e.g., oil companies and their shareholders) had lower marginal propensities to consume than the average consumer, aggregate demand would have been reduced further. Though true, it is hard to believe that this effect was very large.

2. By comparison, Blinder (1979, 84–85) cited two econometric studies—by Perry (1975) and Pierce and Enzler (1974)—that used an early version of the Fed's macroeconometric model to attribute approximately a 3 percent decline in real GDP to OPEC I.

A quantitatively more important effect may have come from the negative wealth effect on consumer spending as both equity values and the real values of other financial assets declined. People nowadays tend to forget that calendar years 1973 and 1974 were, in real terms, the next to worst two-year period in the history of the Dow Jones Industrial Average. (Remember, the price level declined sharply in the early 1930s but rose substantially in 1973–1974.)

Furthermore, with the unindexed tax system we had in 1973–1974, the upward shock to the price level led, via bracket creep, to higher income taxes. Perhaps more important quantitatively, higher inflation also raised the effective tax rate on capital because it is nominal, not real, interest rates and capital gains that are taxed—and depreciation allowances are imputed on a historic-cost (nominal) basis. These two automatic effects of an unindexed tax system amounted to implicit, unlegislated fiscal tightenings.

Everything we have discussed up to now was already on economists' radar screens by the mid to late 1970s. It is highly doubtful, however, that all these other demand-side effects combined come anywhere close to explaining an additional 5 percent drop of real GDP, which is what we need to complete the story. There are, however, at least two novel stagflationary channels that few people were talking about at the time but could be quantitatively important.

One derives from a now-famous article by a promising young scholar at the time named Ben Bernanke (1983). He offered a hypothesis that could conceivably explain a large deleterious effect on output from OPEC I because no one knew what to make of this new phenomenon. Specifically, the huge uncertainties created by the oil shock and the subsequent puzzling stagflation may have led both business investors and purchasers of consumer durables to pause until the fog lifted. Notice that this hypothesis is about delaying spending, not reducing it forever. In a similar vein, the increased uncertainty may have induced consumers to hunker down and increase their precautionary saving (Kilian 2008), subsequently creating more wealth that they presumably spent—but later.

The second novel idea involves the impact of lagging perceptions of productivity growth. In principle, there is no reason to expect a systematic link between inflation and productivity growth. Along any steady growth path, the growth rate of real wages should equal the growth rate of labor productivity (g), making the trend growth rate of nominal wages (w) equal to g plus the rate of inflation, π. If $w = g + \pi$, workers receive a constant share of national income regardless of the inflation rate. And in this rational world, any decline in g would show up immediately as a decline in the growth rate of real wages, with no particular implications for inflation.

In practice, however, there are at least two perceptual channels through which a surprise decline in productivity growth—which the United States experienced in 1973—could push the inflation rate up. The first stems from the possibility that the productivity slowdown is not promptly and fully reflected in slower real wage increases. Suppose workers and firms don't realize at first that productivity growth has slowed. They may then agree on real wage increases that are higher than those warranted by actual increases in productivity. That in turn would put upward pressure on unit labor costs and hence on inflation. Those "excess" wage increases would also reduce employment and therefore tend to raise the level of unemployment consistent with stable inflation, the nonaccelerating inflation rate of unemployment (NAIRU). In short, we would get stagflation.

The second channel through which a productivity slowdown might raise inflation arises if policy makers fail to recognize the slow-down on a timely basis. If the central bank fails to recognize that g has fallen, it will overestimate the growth rate of potential output and therefore target a growth rate of aggregate demand that is too high, leading to higher inflation. Furthermore, since the abovementioned mistakes by workers and firms will raise the NAIRU, policy makers may aim for a level of labor market tightness that is also inflationary (more on this shortly).

Arguably, both of these channels were at work during the Great Stagflation, especially the first episode in 1973–1974. Productivity growth actually began to slow down in the late 1960s as the expansion of the preceding decade came to an end. By the time OPEC I hit, trend productivity growth had moved about a percentage point below the rate that had prevailed over the preceding twenty years. But hardly

FIGURE 5.5. Labor's share of income, corporate business sector, 1961–1980. Total compensation divided by nominal corporate output.
Source: Bureau of Economic Analysis.

anyone noticed. The failure of real wage growth to adjust downward can be seen in the behavior of labor's share of income over this period, which spiked during the 1969–1970 recession (figure 5.5). But rather than moving back down thereafter, it remained high over the 1970s and even appears to have trended upward slightly. (Notice that each successive cyclical peak was higher than the preceding one.)

The monetary policy errors idea was advanced by Orphanides (2003), who argued persuasively that contemporaneous estimates of the output gap in the 1970s (and, by extension, estimates of the NAIRU) were far too optimistic. In addition, the natural rate of unemployment was drifting upward at the time, partly as a result of normal labor market frictions due to the entry of large numbers of young baby boomers and women into the labor force. Policy makers appear to have been slow to catch on to these demographic developments, and their misestimates of the output gap may have resulted in an inflationary monetary policy. Those same poor estimates may also have raised the perceived cost of reducing inflation. If policy makers see little prospect of reducing inflation despite what they perceive to be a large amount of slack, they may erroneously conclude that the sacrifice ratio is higher than it really is. That mistake, too, appears to have been made at the time.[3]

3. For example, Otto Eckstein (1981, 59–62) estimated that the unemployment rate would have to average about 8.7 percent for a decade to bring core inflation down from about 9 percent to about 5 percent.

In sum, when actual productivity decelerated in the early 1970s, sluggish adjustment of beliefs about productivity growth probably became a source of stagflation both in its own right and because it led to errors in monetary policy. Indeed, those errors may have been another reason—in addition to Richard Nixon—why Arthur Burns turned out to be such an inflationary Fed chair.

The Dilemma for Monetary Policy

Even once the Federal Reserve had figured out the nature and effects of supply shocks, what to do about them was far from obvious. Remember, the Fed was (loosely) targeting nominal money supply growth back then. So, any upward shock to the price level would automatically induce a monetary tightening by reducing real balances. Was that the correct policy response for an inflation-fighting central bank? Or should the Fed have eased policy in response to OPEC in order to mitigate the recession? Clearly, no central bank can do both.

To some economists and financial market participants at the time, the answer was obvious. Milton Friedman's famous dictum— "Inflation is always and everywhere a monetary phenomenon"—was held dear by monetarists. It denies that an economy can produce high inflation without rapid growth of the money supply. Never mind the price of oil; that's a relative price. In this view, which I'd classify as naive or even ideological monetarism, supply shocks could not have been the main culprit behind the surge in inflation in 1973–1974. It must have been excessive money growth.

Monetarists therefore gave short shrift to the Fed's dual mandate, insisting instead that the central bank should tighten monetary policy to stand steadfastly against both rising inflation and rising inflationary expectations. For example, Friedman wrote in *Newsweek* in September 1974 that "recent rates of monetary growth are not too low. If anything they are still too high to bring inflation to an end in a reasonable period of time" (Friedman 1974a, 82).

In part, this attitude stemmed from the classical dichotomy: the belief that real shocks (such as a rise in the relative price of energy) cannot affect inflation. The simplest version of the argument, which was raised immediately after OPEC I, holds that it is logically fallacious to believe that a change in a relative price can be a source of general inflation. Instead, a rise in the relative price of energy (P_E/P) will be achieved through a combination of higher nominal prices for energy products (P_E) and lower nominal prices for a variety of other things (call these P_O, for "other" prices). There is no reason for the overall price level, $P = \omega P_E + (1 - \omega)P_O$, to rise unless the money supply does. In Friedman's words, this time from a much-quoted June 1974 *Newsweek* column, "Why should the *average* level of all prices be affected significantly by changes in the prices of some things relative to others?" (Friedman 1974b).[4]

One important answer, of course, was that ever since the Keynesian revolution, most (though not all) economists have believed that nominal price and wage rigidities are pervasive. With nominal rigidities, relative price increases can and do lead to higher price levels, such as when P_E rises and P_O won't fall. As discussed earlier, if one of the sticky nominal prices is the nominal wage, real wages will get stuck "too high" for a while, causing higher unemployment.

One way to conceptualize this debate is to recognize that, with sticky wages and prices, the causation between inflation and relative price changes flows in both directions. On the one hand, when some prices are stickier than others, an inflationary demand shock will induce changes in relative prices. On the other hand, a supply shock that requires a large change in some relative price(s) can be a source of overall inflation because other prices will not fall easily. The empirical question then becomes which direction of causation is quantitatively more important in practice. The answer was obvious during the 1970s and early 1980s: supply shocks "caused" higher inflation, Milton Friedman and M1 notwithstanding.[5]

Another important issue for monetary policy makers at the time (and still) is how much second-round inflation gets induced by the

4. But in the very next sentence—which is never quoted—Friedman provided a partial answer: "Thanks to delays in adjustment, the rapid rises in oil and food prices may have temporarily raised the rate of inflation somewhat" (Friedman 1974b). As with so many strong monetarist positions, the question boils down to one of degree, not direction.

5. See, for example, Taylor (1981).

initial first-round effects of supply shocks on the price level, such as when higher energy costs creep into the prices of other goods and services or when cost-of-living clauses raise nominal wages. Regarding the price channel, Nordhaus (2007, 223) used an input-output model to estimate that the long-run pass-through of energy costs into other consumer prices (such as airfares, apartment rents, and so on) is 80 percent as large as the direct effect of energy prices on the index. That's sizable.

A more top-down approach to estimating second-round effects is to examine the impacts of supply shocks on measures of core inflation, which by definition remove the mechanical first-round impacts of energy and food prices on headline inflation but leave in the second-round effects. Blinder and Rudd (2013) used standard price-price Phillips curves to perform precisely this sort of calculation for three different types of stylized supply shocks: an energy price spike that disappears quickly (such as OPEC II), a rise in the relative price of energy to a permanently higher plateau (such as OPEC I), and a permanent increase in the energy inflation rate. The last of these is an implausible extreme case, of course, included only to provide a comparison. In each simulation we held the path of the unemployment rate constant, thereby tacitly assuming an accommodating monetary policy that prevents the supply shock from causing a slump. But we found that allowing for the "stag" part of stagflation did not reduce the estimated inflationary impacts substantially.

In the case of persistently higher energy price inflation, persistently higher core inflation naturally follows, although the nonenergy second-round effects are small. In this highly unrealistic case, a monetary tightening is likely the appropriate policy response. Without it, inflation will be left permanently higher.

In the case of a short-lived spike in the price of energy, we estimated that second-round effects on core inflation, while notable at first, would disappear after about eighteen months. Thus, core inflation displays a sizable blip that vanishes by itself without any need for the central bank to tighten. Such behavior of inflation might justify a policy decision to accommodate the supply shock, even though the accommodative increase in the money supply might lead to somewhat higher inflation.

The case of a permanent rise in the level of energy prices also leads to a blip in core inflation but one that does not disappear entirely of its own accord because of second-round effects on other prices. In this case, a central bank that does not want to tolerate a persistent rise in core inflation would have to tighten—eventually.

The second pass-through mechanism comes when (if?) higher inflation "gets into" wages. Blinder and Rudd (2013) examined that mechanism too, using a two-equation Phillips curve model and concentrating on the case that resembles OPEC I: a permanent level change in the relative price of energy. In the model, wage inflation responds to lagged headline CPI inflation, and core CPI inflation responds to trend unit labor costs. Our estimates imposed several "accelerationist" restrictions; for example, the coefficients on trend unit labor costs and lagged inflation in the markup equation were constrained to sum to 1. As a result, the implied pass-through of higher food and energy prices into core inflation follows the same qualitative patterns as in the simpler price-price model: headline inflation spikes immediately but quickly recedes. The estimated magnitudes are larger, however.

Monetary Policy Reactions to the Supply Shocks

All this is (or should be) far clearer to policy makers now than it was in real time in the fall of 1973. Back then, there was a lot of confusion about how the Fed should respond to what were not yet labeled "supply shocks." Indeed, I still remember one prominent monetarist (who shall remain nameless) arguing against any increase in money growth on the grounds that the additional U.S. inflation caused by such a monetary expansion would induce OPEC to raise the oil price equiproportionally. It doesn't take deep thought to see that this idea, even if true, is ridiculous quantitatively.

Here's the arithmetic. Suppose the OPEC shock would raise the U.S. price level by 5 percent if it was fully accommodated by expansionary monetary policy. If OPEC then reacted by raising the oil price by an additional 5 percent—a dubious proposition, to be sure—the second-round effect on the U.S. price level would, with an 8 percent energy share in the price index, be about $0.08 \times 5\% = 0.4\%$.

The implied inflationary cycle is pretty strongly damped! But these were the kinds of attitudes expressed by some anti-inflation monetarists at the time.

How did the Burns Fed react to OPEC I? Schizophrenically. Recall that the Fed had boosted money growth in advance of the 1972 election, probably for political reasons, and then reversed course shortly thereafter. None of this had anything to do with OPEC. Despite high inflation, M2 growth declined from double-digit rates to about 5 percent per annum by June 1974, where it remained (roughly) through January 1975. With inflation running sky high at the time, this meant that real money growth was substantially negative in the face of a deep recession—a very tight monetary policy. Early in 1975, with the recessionary consequences clear, the Fed reversed course sharply. The M2 growth rate started rising and was up to 14 percent by February 1976—a very loose monetary policy.

The federal funds rate, though less closely watched at the time, told a similar story. It rose, of course, after the November 1972 election but then actually eased back a bit after OPEC I (from September 1973 to February 1974). After that, however, inflation fighting was foremost on the Fed's mind, and the funds rate shot up from about 9 percent in February 1974 to about 13 percent in July 1974. (Although no one knew it at the time, that would be Richard Nixon's last full month in office.) At about that time, the Fed shifted its focus from fighting inflation to battling the burgeoning recession. By March 1975 the funds rate was down to about 5.5 percent, where it remained (roughly) for the next two-plus years.

All this would change dramatically when Paul Volcker became Fed chair. But that is getting ahead of our story.

Fiscal Policy Reactions to the Supply Shocks

Fiscal policy, broadly conceived, was similarly schizophrenic in the aftermath of OPEC I. Gerald Ford, who was never elected to the presidency, assumed the office in August 1974 under trying circumstances. ("Our long national nightmare is over.") Within two months, with inflation raging, he announced his comical Whip Inflation Now

(WIN) program. Millions of WIN buttons were handed out (I still have mine), and Ford's anti-inflation campaign asked Americans to sign and mail back a coupon that read "Dear President Ford: I enlist as an Inflation Fighter and Energy Saver for the duration." (I did not enlist.)

The idea, I suppose, was to exhort patriotic citizens to spend less (without asking them to pay higher taxes) and to conserve energy (without raising its price) via such brilliant voluntary "policies" as starting your own vegetable garden and giving your dog less time to enter and exit the house. Things like that, someone must have supposed, would help whip inflation. Really?

Milton Friedman and other monetarists were not impressed by this approach. A bit over a year later, he wrote that the WIN campaign "was a program that had some good things and some bad things, but *taken as a whole it was a pretty silly program.*"[6] Neither was Alan Greenspan, who was then Ford's CEA chair. Greenspan (2007, 66) wrote much later that he was thinking at the time that "this is unbelievably stupid." (One wonders, however, whether he said anything remotely close to that to President Ford.) I was a twenty-eight-year-old assistant professor at the time, and I recall that most economists thought the WIN campaign was a laugh line.

The U.S. inflation rate did tumble rapidly in 1974–1975, however, though not because of the WIN campaign. Nor was it because of monetary policy. Rather, both the supply shocks and the end of price controls simply ran their course and disappeared. The deep recession probably had an effect too, albeit with long lags. By December 1975, the twelve-month CPI inflation rate, which had peaked at 12.3 percent in December 1974, was down to 6.9 percent; a year later it was down to 4.9 percent. But the recession worsened during 1974, and the economy experienced its worst quarter in 1975:1 (a 4.8% annual rate of decline of real GDP).

Ford and other politicians saw the economy imploding, of course, and Ford withdrew his October 1974 call for a tax hike to fight inflation. Instead, in January 1975 he called for a temporary tax cut. Acting with unusual speed, Congress passed a comprehensive tax cut

6. Reprinted in Friedman (2017).

plan by the end of March 1975, featuring a 10 percent onetime rebate on 1974 tax liabilities. The bill also included an increase in the standard deduction and an increase in the investment tax credit, both of them also temporary.

Ironically, the National Bureau of Economic Research dates March 1975 as the last month of the recession. So, was this a case of too little too late? I think not.

First, we should not rule out the possibility that the 1975 tax cut hastened the end of the deep recession or helped invigorate the recovery or both. After all, 1975:1 was the last quarter of decline; growth resumed in 1975:2. The economy was near the trough of the business cycle when the tax cut passed. Fiscal stimulus was welcome, you might even say timely, then.

Second, although the tax cut was temporary, which presumably undermined its power,[7] it was large relative to the size of the economy. Contemporaneous estimates pegged the 1975 tax cuts, which were packed into a single quarter, as $46 billion at an annual rate. Some $31 billion of this was the rebate.[8] For the crucial quarter of 1975:2, Congressional Budget Office numbers record a decline in what would then have been called the high-employment surplus of 3 percent of GDP, making it the largest quarterly change in the fiscal stance in the entire historical series through 2019.

So, did the fiscal response come too late? I don't think so. It came in plenty of time to cushion the blow to the real economy, which then mounted a strong, quick recovery, growing more than 6 percent from 1975:1 to 1976:1. Was it too little? Certainly not. By the standards of the day, it was huge.

Last Word

One final point must be made because the study of economic history entails both economic events and economic ideas. The supply shock explanation of the stagflation of the 1970s and 1980s is obvious. The

---

7. Not all of it. Raising the investment tax credit should be more powerful if temporary rather than permanent.

8. Blinder (1981b, 39).

conceptual framework, outlined early in this chapter, is straightforward, and the triggering events detailed here were painfully obvious even at the time. There was no need to appeal to any mysterious unobserved variables. I and others told the supply shock story early on in a book (Blinder 1979) and in a series of papers (Blinder 1981a, 1982). Yet there was still enough intellectual resistance to the supply shock explanation that Jeremy Rudd and I (Blinder and Rudd 2013) were asked to revisit the issue in a paper for a conference held in 2008, thirty-five years after OPEC I!

What we found in that paper can be summarized in two simple statements:

1. The supply shock explanation of the inflation of the 1970s and 1980s holds up remarkably well to several decades of subsequent events, multiple data revisions, and several new intellectual developments in macroeconomics.
2. When you fill the simple conceptual framework with numbers, the data actually overpredict the rise in inflation. This is not to deny any role to aggregate demand; point estimates do, after all, have standard errors. But it does suggest that those who deny that supply shocks played a central role must be thrusting their heads pretty deeply into the sand. That some economists still do so reflects poorly on economics as a science.

Chapter Summary

Stagflation in the 1970s mystified both monetary and fiscal policy makers at first. Were they supposed to fight inflation or recession? This confusion led to some outright silliness—such as President Gerald Ford's WIN campaign—and to considerable policy vacillation. For example, Ford first requested a tax hike in October 1974 to fight inflation and then asked for a tax cut in January 1975 to fight recession. (He got the latter.) The Federal Reserve also vacillated between easing and tightening monetary policy.

Soon after OPEC I, several economists conceptualized the sharp increase in the relative price of oil as an aggregate supply shock, something that should raise inflation and reduce real economic activity at the same time. Monetarists resisted that conclusion, however. A relative price change, they insisted, could never induce generalized inflation unless it was accommodated by monetary expansion. The monetarist version told the Fed exactly what it should do: reduce money supply growth to fight inflation. The Keynesian version gave no such clear advice. Rather, it pointed to a genuine dilemma. Monetary policy could support the sagging economy or stand against inflation. But it could not do both.

Which side had it right? One important clue for policy makers, though hardly a decisive one, was that accounting for the magnitudes of the impacts of the two oil shocks required looking well beyond purely neoclassical supply effects, which were not nearly large enough to explain what the data showed. There must also have been some large demand-depressing components. The damage to aggregate demand, unlike OPEC's actions, could be partially offset by fiscal and monetary policy.

The oil shocks, especially firms' adjustments to them, also caused the growth rate of labor productivity to slow down. The logic was simple: using less energy and more labor should reduce labor productivity, other things being equal. Although the post-1973 productivity slowdown lasted a long time and eventually became obvious, it was not perceived immediately. And this misperception—the belief that productivity growth was higher than it actually was—probably had several deleterious effects. It likely led the Fed to pursue easier monetary policy than it would have under full (correct) information. It probably also led to more unemployment by keeping real wages "too high," that is, above their neoclassical equilibrium levels.

Wait. Am I hinging the argument on misperceptions? The rational expectations hypothesis, which was brewing in academia at the time, denied that systematic misperceptions such as those are even possible. I turn to that next.

6

Inflation and the Rational Expectations Revolution

The task which faces contemporary students of the business cycle is that of sorting through the wreckage.
—ROBERT LUCAS AND THOMAS SARGENT (1978)

As noted in the introduction, this book concentrates on the history of macroeconomic policy, not the history of economic doctrine. Nonetheless, as also mentioned there, the two get intertwined as theoretical developments influence (or fail to influence) policy and as real-world events influence (or fail to influence) theory. The rational expectations revolution offers prime examples of each, and it has had profound intellectual impacts on economic thinking about monetary policy. So a brief digression on rational expectations is appropriate at this point in the narrative.

In stark contrast to the Keynesian revolution, which had tremendous—and, I would argue, mostly salutary—influences on practical policy making, the rational expectations revolution created a deep intellectual chasm between the majority of academic macro-economists and almost all real-world policy makers. And I include in the latter category the many professional economists serving in government. It is true that rational expectations left major and lasting impacts on the ways central bank economists think about, talk about, and model monetary policy making. But what was truly a revolution in the thinking of PhD economists left only small traces in the world of practical policy making.

Furthermore, the essence of that deep chasm between theory and practice, as we shall see in this chapter, inhered not in the assumption of rationality, but rather in a number of auxiliary ideas (like rapid market clearing) that got attached to rational expectations like barnacles.

In my perhaps biased view, the so-called rational expectations revolution would have set back monetary policy making by decades were it not for a simple fact: Actual policy makers in central banks had the good sense to (mostly) ignore it.

Acorns Quickly Grow into Oak Trees

Intellectual revolutions, like political revolutions, sometimes start quietly, almost unnoticed. The seeds are sown long before open rebellion breaks out. So it was with the rational expectations revolution. In 1961 John Muth, then a young economist at Carnegie Mellon University, published a profoundly important scholarly paper titled "Rational Expectations and the Theory of Price Movements" (Muth 1961). Although the paper was published in one of the leading economic journals, *Econometrica*, its initial impact was minimal. As Robert E. Lucas Jr., the acknowledged leader of the revolution that came later, recalled, "Of course we knew about [rational expectations]. Muth was a colleague of ours at that time. We just didn't think it was important. The hypothesis was more or less buried during the '60s" (Klamer 1984, 38). But it rose like Lazarus during the 1970s.

What became a tremendously successful intellectual revolution started slowly. Lucas, who was another young economist at Carnegie Mellon at the time, presented a short paper at a 1970 Federal Reserve conference in Washington titled "Econometric Testing of the Natural Rate Hypothesis" (Lucas 1972a). Being published in an obscure conference volume, the paper was not widely cited. Indeed, it is hardly ever cited even today. Nor was it well understood at the time. Lucas's paper argued that simple models of inflationary expectations such as adaptive expectations, which assumed that people corrected their expected inflation rate by a fraction of their most recent forecasting error, were inconsistent with the Friedman-Phelps natural rate theory. The rational expectations model, on the other hand, was consistent with that theory. But testing the theory with rational expectations required more complicated econometric techniques than estimating conventional Phillips curves, which was the practice at the time.

If Lucas's 1970 conference paper was not widely read and under-appreciated at the time, his follow-up paper in the *Journal of Economic Theory* (Lucas 1972b) was simply baffling. (Try reading it.) The opening paragraph is worth quoting in full, however:

> This paper provides a simple example of an economy in which equilibrium prices and quantities exhibit what may be the central feature of the modern business cycle: a systematic relation between the rate of change in nominal prices and the level of real output. The relationship, essentially a variant of the well-known Phillips curve, is derived within a framework from which all forms of "money illusion" are rigorously excluded: all prices are market clearing, all agents behave optimally in light of their objectives and expectations, and expectations are formed optimally (in a sense to be made precise below). (Lucas, 1972b, 103)

Notice the amazing irony here. Lucas offered his *Journal of Economic Theory* paper as a rigorous foundation for the Phillips curve—micro foundations that he later deemed lacking if not impossible—in a model economy in which the existence of such a link between nominal and real variables seems most unlikely. The key assumptions that made the link unlikely were instantaneous market clearing and continuous optimization, not the rationality of expectations. These are the features that really separated what would come to be called new classical models from traditional Keynesian models. But it took quite a while for the economics profession to realize this.

The central contribution of Lucas (1972b) is elucidated in his footnote 7, where he dwells on the assumed efficiency of markets in the model but then adds, almost as an afterthought, the following pregnant remark: "It will also be true that price expectations are rational in the sense of Muth" (Lucas 1972b, 110). I think it is fair to say that Lucas's densely mathematical treatment of an age-old idea—the neutrality of money—had relatively little impact at the time. But it was destined to become a classic. In the 1980s and 1990s while teaching macroeconomic theory to PhD students at Princeton, I used to joke that graduate students in top economics departments were being brought up to believe that Bob Lucas invented the neutrality of money in 1972! David Hume? Who was he?

What Lucas actually accomplished in his *Journal of Economic Theory* paper was to bring Muth's idea of rational expectations, meaning that subjective expectations matched the mathematical expectations implied by the model, from obscurity into the mainstream and soon into a dominant intellectual position.

But the revolution was still incipient at that point. The Lucas paper that really called attention to rational expectations and to its potentially stunning implications for monetary policy came a year later in the much more widely read *American Economic Review*. It was an instant sensation. In a sense, Lucas (1973) "publicized" the idea of rational expectations and demonstrated its power in monetary models.

That 1973 paper also reemphasized what would soon come to be called "the Lucas supply function,"[1] the notion that the deviation of actual from potential output depends on the price level "surprise," that is, on the amount by which p_t exceeds its (rationally) expected value:

$$y_t - y_t^* = \beta(p_t - {}_{t-1}p_t) + \varepsilon_t, \qquad (1)$$

where y is the log of real output, y* is its potential (full information) value, p is the log of the price level, and ${}_{t-1}p_t$ is the mathematical expectation of p_t given all the information available up to time $t-1$.

In Lucas's (1973) specific model, such surprises were based on agents' confusion between changes in relative prices and changes in the absolute price level. Rational expectations, of course, implied that the "surprise" term had to have mean zero, implying that $y_t - y_t^*$ also had to have mean zero. No one—certainly not Lucas—paid

---

1. I say "reemphasized" because the Lucas supply function had been introduced in the Lucas (1972a) paper.

much attention to the fact that price level surprises could not be large with *monthly* data on the Consumer Price Index unless the annual inflation rate was gigantic. And these surprises could not last long. Each month's Consumer Price Index was publicly announced with only a short time lag.

In stark contrast to his *Journal of Economic Theory* model, Lucas's *American Economic Review* model was straightforward, easy to understand, and easy to teach to students. The paper also purported to offer supporting empirical evidence, though the "good fit" of Lucas's cross-country regression turned out to depend almost entirely on two outlier countries with very high inflation rates: Argentina and Paraguay. If Lucas's two papers published in 1972 were like subversive whispers in Fraunces Tavern, his 1973 paper was like Lexington and Concord: the intellectual shot heard 'round the world. Soon the Lucas (1973) model was a staple of teaching in graduate macro courses all over the world. The rational expectations revolution was truly launched.

And also like Lexington and Concord, Lucas (1973) was just the beginning of something much larger. Notice that the Lucas supply function (1) implies that only price level surprises, and therefore only monetary policy surprises, can move output. That point, which was not heavily emphasized in Lucas (1973), was brought to the fore in a celebrated 1975 paper by Thomas Sargent and Neil Wallace.

Sargent and Wallace (1975) originally set out to extend Poole's (1970) simple analysis of interest rate versus money supply rules in a variety of ways. But it turned out that only one change really mattered: modeling price expectations as rational rather than autoregressive. Soon Poole's question—should the central bank base its monetary policy on M or r?—was forgotten because, as Sargent and Wallace (1975, 242) put it, if expectations are rational, "one deterministic money supply rule is as good as any other," which is to say not good at all. This revolutionary idea was soon branded "the policy ineffectiveness result" because, under rational expectations, it is pretty much impossible for a central bank to engineer unanticipated movements in the money supply regularly.

Robert E. Lucas Jr. (1937—)

Leader of the Rational Expectations Revolution[2]

Robert ("Bob") Lucas, who followed Milton Friedman as the acknowledged leader of the Chicago School of macroeconomics, was born in Yakima, Washington, to parents who admired Franklin Roosevelt and the New Deal. The Lucas family ran a small restaurant that fell victim to the 1937–1938 recession. But Robert E. Lucas Jr., a baby at the time, was far too young to take notice. His interest in business cycles came later and had other sources.

Lucas was an excellent math-science student in high school. He recalls getting his "first taste of real applied mathematics, and an exciting one," by helping his father, who had not attended college, with a calculus problem. When it came time for college, MIT did not offer Lucas a scholarship, but the University of Chicago did. (The invisible hand at work, perhaps?) So, he matriculated there. Lucas intended to study mathematics but was quickly caught up in the college's unique liberal arts curriculum, which drew him to both history and an academic career. After a brief stop at Berkeley, where he was exposed to economics, he returned to Chicago for graduate study.

Ironically, it was the "confident and engaging style" of Paul Samuelson's *Foundations of Economic Analysis* (1947) that captured Lucas intellectually in graduate school. He recalls "working through the first four chapters, line by line, going back to my calculus books when I needed to," and winding up "as good an economic technician as anyone on the Chicago faculty. Even more important, I had internalized Samuelson's standards for when an economic question had been properly posed and when it had been answered."

The rest, as they say, is history, including being taught price theory by the persuasive Milton Friedman. Lucas recalls that he "tried to hold on to the New Deal politics I had grown up with," but Friedman's influence made that difficult. Few of Lucas's fellow economists think of him as a New Deal liberal today.

Lucas began his illustrious academic career in 1963 at what was then called the Carnegie Institute of Technology (now Carnegie-Mellon University). There he became acquainted with, among others, Leonard Rapping (his close friend and coauthor), Allan Meltzer, Tom Sargent, Ed Prescott, and, of course, John Muth. In 1974, when Lucas returned to the University of Chicago, he was already an academic superstar likely to win a Nobel Prize, which he did in 1995. The revolution that he and colleagues spawned left a deep and lasting intellectual imprint on academic macroeconomics.

The essence of the policy ineffectiveness result is straightforward: only "unanticipated" monetary policy shocks can cause price level surprises, and therefore under the Lucas supply function, only they can move real output. That left counterrevolutionaries only two ways out.

2. Much of this material and all the quotations come from Lucas's Nobel Prize autobiography (Lucas 1995).

You could dispute the rationality of expectations. But what was the alternative, irrational expectations?[3] That route did not seem promising in a discipline built around the hyperrational concept of *homo economicus*.[4] Or you could find fault with the Lucas supply function. Defenders of monetary policy effectiveness naturally concentrated their energies there. Stanley Fischer (1977) embraced rational expectations but noted that with long-term contracts, expectations that were rational at the time contracts were written might no longer be rational given current information. John Taylor (1980) took this idea, added staggering of wage contracts, and produced an ingenious model that generated realistic business cycles even with rational expectations. And there was much more.[5]

Sargent and Wallace's (1975) argument for policy ineffectiveness was based entirely on a priori reasoning—on theory, not on facts. But Robert Barro (1977) soon offered what he claimed to be strong empirical evidence in support of their hypothesis. To do so, he had to devise a way to divide data on money growth into anticipated and unanticipated components and then to show empirically that only the latter moved unemployment. This is precisely what he did. Five years would pass before Frederic Mishkin (1982) and Robert Gordon (1982) effectively debunked Barro's findings. But it took very long distributed lags to do so, leaving many believers in the Sargent-Wallace proposition unconvinced.

One more academic preliminary is important to our story—very important—though I have barely mentioned it up to now.

At the inaugural Carnegie-Rochester conference in April 1973 (but not published until 1976), Lucas presented one of the most

3. Years later, behavioral economists would argue that many aspects of human behavior are not rational in the strictly economic sense.

4. The assumption of rationality in expectations is not easy to test. Nonetheless, as the years went by more and more evidence mounted against it. Two of the many such papers are Lovell (1986) and Fair (1993). None of this was known in 1975, of course.

5. The simple Lucas supply precluded serially correlated deviations of output from potential. That was noticed immediately and spawned a cottage industry of more complicated models that provided a wide variety of reasons for serial correlation. See, for example, Kydland and Prescott (1982) and Blinder and Fischer (1981).

celebrated and influential scholarly papers of the second half of the twentieth century, "Econometric Policy Evaluation: A Critique." What would soon simply be called the "Lucas critique" was that standard econometric models and methods ignored the fact that changes in policy could cause changes in econometrically estimated parameters through expectational channels. So, adopting a different policy rule might change the quantitative dimensions of the policy's effects, thereby making the econometric evidence on which it had been based misleading.

We have met one such example already, in chapter 3. Sargent (1971) noted that a change in the autoregressive model generating actual inflation would change how rational agents use past data to forecast future inflation and therefore change the coefficients in an empirical Phillips curve of the form $\pi_t = \alpha(L)\pi_{t-j} + f(U_t) + \varepsilon_t$, where $\alpha(L)\pi_{t-j}$ is a distributed lag of past inflation rates, used as a proxy for expected inflation.

Lucas (1976) showed that the same idea applied to the analysis of the investment tax credit (ITC) and to temporary versus permanent changes in income taxes. All three examples—the Phillips curve, the ITC, and temporary income tax changes—were known prior to Lucas's 1976 paper. But his demonstration of the underlying unity of the three examples, plus the potential application of the same ideas elsewhere, made the paper an intellectual tour de force. More important, the Lucas critique is absolutely correct. Changes in expectations can render conventional econometric estimates of policy effects misleading. As Lucas (1976, 279) noted in that famous paper, "The argument is, in part, destructive."

Indeed it was. Lucas's observation quickly became an understatement, as the verb *can* got ignored in the academic frenzy—or rather turned into the verb *do*. Rather than viewing the Lucas critique as one among many pitfalls in doing empirical work with nonexperimental time series data, rational expectations revolutionaries elevated it to primus inter pares without question—and without any evidence of its practical importance. No one stopped to ask, for example, whether Lucas critique problems were more important in practice than, say, bias from omitted variables or endogeneity of right-hand variables.

Rather than serving as a well-founded warning that could have (and should have) improved econometric practice, the Lucas critique led to what might be called econometric nihilism on a grand scale.[6] Many rational expectations revolutionaries simply asserted that all "old-fashioned" models then being used for policy analysis were systematically misleading and should therefore be ignored. In their place, they offered what? Well, mainly a priori reasoning—and reasoning that struck many mainstream economists as wrongheaded.

In chapter 3, I mentioned a virtually unknown paper of mine, published in 1988, that cast doubt on the empirical importance (not on the intellectual coherence) of the Lucas critique in the Phillips curve context. In a 1984 paper that is perhaps even more unknown, I used three of those "old-fashioned" giant macroeconometric models to appraise the early effects of Reaganomics. After presenting a bevy of estimates, I observed that "there is no doubt that the . . . models are vulnerable to the Lucas critique" (Blinder 1984, 223). But then I went on to investigate something the rational expectations revolutionaries never did: whether the models displayed large errors in the places and times where we would expect expectational effects to be most important.

For example, the 1981 Reagan tax cuts accelerated depreciation allowances but promised even more accelerated depreciation rules a few years down the line. Standard Lucas-style (1976) reasoning therefore predicts that businesses should have postponed investments until the more generous depreciation schedules went into effect. If that expectational effect was quantitatively important, it should have led models that ignored it to overpredict investment spending in 1981 and 1982. But they didn't. There were several other such examples, leading to the overall conclusion that "my investigation does not suggest that the Lucas critique is of great empirical importance" (Blinder 1984, 226).

6. This statement is not fair to Sargent, Lars Hansen, and others who attempted to devise methods of estimating "deep structural" parameters that would not change when policy changed. These methods, however, relied on so many dubious and restrictive assumptions that many economists found the work technically demanding but ultimately unconvincing.

So here was the state of play in academia circa 1977:

- Academic economists were madly in love with rational expectations, barely recognizing that the term really meant "model consistent" expectations, no matter how silly the model was.
- Sargent and Wallace's policy ineffectiveness result had convinced many (though not all) academic macroeconomists that central banks that tried to mitigate business cycles were wasting their time because systematic monetary policy reactions to, say, unemployment could never cause unanticipated money shocks.
- The rational expectations revolutionaries completely ignored the supply shocks discussed in chapter 5. Rather, they sought to convince everyone that the high inflation the United States had experienced in the early 1970s was evidence that Keynesian economics had failed. To a disconcerting extent, they succeeded in undermining Keynesianism.
- And on top of all this, they insisted, no one should pay attention to results generated by models that fiscal and monetary policy makers had used for years to plan and appraise stabilization policies, for they all ran afoul of the Lucas critique. All you had to do to stop the show in those days was shout "Lucas critique" in a crowded seminar room.

The aphorism of the day was that "there are no Keynesian economists under the age of 40" (Blinder 1988, 278). I know that was untrue because I turned thirty-two in 1977. But in any case, citizens of the real world were fortunate that decisions on monetary and fiscal policy were firmly in the hands of people over forty.

Against this anti-Keynesian backdrop, the Federal Reserve of Boston convened a high-level conference on Martha's Vineyard in June 1978, giving it the provocative title "After the Phillips Curve." After? Robert Gordon, who was not among the attendees, would certainly have called the year 1978 during the Phillips curve era, not after it. He was busy patching up the traditional Phillips curve to account for supply shocks.

The most famous or infamous paper delivered at that memorable conference was coauthored by Lucas and Sargent and titled "After Keynesian Macroeconomics" (Lucas and Sargent 1978). There's that provocative word again, *after*, but now applied more broadly to the entirety of Keynesian economics. Their attack was broad and highly polemical—and not by accident. Lucas and Sargent (1978, 81) wrote after the conference that "since both of us are on record as rather severe critics of Keynesian macroeconometric models, we assumed that we were included in the program to express this dissenting view as forcefully and as accurately as possible." And they sure did.

Lucas and Sargent (1978, 49) declared that the "predictions" of Keynesian economics "were wildly incorrect, and . . . the doctrine on which they were based is fundamentally flawed." Furthermore, they asserted, these criticisms of Keynesianism "are now simple matters of fact, involving no novelties in economic theory. The task which faces contemporary students of the business cycle is that of sorting through the wreckage." And that was all on the first page. There was more to come.

According to what you might call the Lucas-Sargent critique, the prevailing Keynesian models, particularly their Phillips curve implications, were guilty of "econometric failure on a grand scale" (Lucas and Sargent 1978, 51) for missing the stagflation of 1973–1974 (something that is explained fully by supply shocks). Furthermore, patching up the models—as Keynesians had already done before the Boston Fed conference—was useless because "the difficulties are *fatal*: . . . modern macroeconomic models are of *no* value in guiding policy" (50). Fightin' words, you might say. Naturally, mainstream Keynesians fired back. Benjamin Friedman and Robert Solow were the official discussants of the Lucas-Sargent paper at the conference, and their remarks displayed a level of disdain that matched that of Lucas and Sargent. More important and less polemically, Gordon (1977) subsequently showed that his vintage 1972 Phillips curve, once modified for supply shocks in straightforward ways, fit the data quite well. But no matter. The Lucas critique was interpreted as telling economists to ignore all such evidence.

The battle was truly joined, lasted for years, and was often less than friendly. (I know; I was among the foot soldiers.)[7] It was a tumultuous time in academic macroeconomics. Many of the protagonists initially acted as if the rationality of expectations was the key dividing issue. It was not. Fischer (1977), Taylor (1980), and others showed that the true dividing line was rapid (instantaneous in the models) market clearing. Naturally, of course, if all markets clear instantly, you don't need government actions to fix things up. But in retrospect, it seems a waste of intellectual resources that academic economists expended so much pen and ink arguing over whether all markets—including the aggregate labor market—cleared virtually instantly. But that's what they did.

Meanwhile, Back in the Real World . . .

The 1970s and 1980s were also tumultuous times in the real world of monetary policy but for very different reasons. Broadly speaking, around 1980 or so it seemed as though the major industrial nations of the world looked around at the high inflation rates, decided they had had enough, and took actions to get rid of them. With variations in timing, Paul Volcker in the United States, Margaret Thatcher in the United Kingdom,[8] the Bundesbank in (West) Germany, and inflation fighters in other nations declared all-out war on inflation. If the rational expectations revolution, in particular the policy ineffectiveness result, had any influence on these policy makers' thinking, it sure didn't show. Central banks brought inflation down the old-fashioned way: by using tight money to cause deep recessions.

The justly celebrated Volcker disinflation in the United States worked well, but that's because it drove the unemployment rate to a high-water mark of 10.8 percent in November and December 1982, at the time the highest reading since the 1930s. Given the unending

---

7. See, for example, Blinder (1987b). Lucas was present at that American Economic Association session and took great umbrage at my remarks.

8. The Bank of England was not independent in those days. Monetary policy was governed from Whitehall.

debates in academia over the channels of monetary policy, I once asked Volcker after he had left the Fed how he thought monetary policy worked to crush inflation. His answer surprised me: by causing bankruptcies.[9]

In the United Kingdom, real GDP tumbled 5.3 percent between 1979:2 and 1981:1, and the Thatcher slump raised the unemployment rate from 5.4 percent in 1979 to 11.5 percent by 1983. Just as in the United States, that was the highest reading since the 1930s. But there too, the bitter medicine worked: consumer price inflation crumbled from over 15 percent to under 5 percent. Like Volcker in the United States, Thatcher pledged allegiance to monetarism. And like the experience of the Volcker Fed, money growth in the United Kingdom was far from stable.

Though the details and timing varied, it is hard to make a case that the Volcker and Thatcher recessions, as well as others in other countries, were consequences of unanticipated monetary contractions. Indeed, the iron-willed central banker in the United States and the Iron Lady in the United Kingdom practically shouted their attentions from the rooftops—and then followed through on their promises. True believers in Sargent-Wallace could, I imagine, argue that no one believed Volcker, Thatcher, and others. But that doesn't seem likely, given Volcker's reputation as a determined inflation hawk. Rather, the disinflations of the early 1980s look like clear cases of anticipated monetary tightenings causing deep recessions.

Notice the great historical irony here. One main reason why rational expectations macroeconomics, in particular its implication that the Phillips curve for anticipated changes in money is vertical even in the short run, caught on was the allegation that the incumbent Keynesian tradition had failed to either control or explain high inflation. "Failed to control," I suppose, was true, though the cost of stabilizing inflation in the face of huge supply shocks would have been devastating. But "failed to explain" was clearly a false charge

---

9. Not that Volcker relished driving businesses into bankruptcy. He just thought that was how the medicine worked.

once you gave Keynesian economists a few months to extend their framework to include supply shocks. That's all it took.[10]

Did the rational expectations approach, especially what would soon be called "new classical economics" because of its resemblance to pre-Keynesian thinking, offer a superior alternative? I don't think either Volcker or Thatcher thought their tough monetary contractions were "unanticipated." They certainly didn't intend them to be. But tight money in the United States and the United Kingdom seemed to have powerful effects on real output and employment— Keynesian effects, you might call them. I think both Volcker and Thatcher expected that too.

The fact that the rational expectations revolution swept the academy while all this was going on in the real world stands as a testament to academics' ability to closet themselves away in ivory towers at times. Had they peeked outside, they would have seen the real effects of anticipated monetary tightenings right before their eyes. Even the Phillips curve worked well, at least in the United States, as we shall see in chapter 8.

Chapter Summary

The storming of the Bastille in 1789 marked neither the beginning nor the end of the French Revolution, but it sure shook up the status quo. The same could be said about the 1970s salvos of the rational expectations revolution lobbed by Lucas, Sargent, and others. In the academy their effects were profound, questioning the very basis—never mind the details—of stabilization policy, especially of monetary policy.

But in the world of actual policy, it is hard to find more than a trace of influence of the rational expectations revolution on policy making. That trace—the idea that policy makers should pay closer attention to expectations formation, including expectations about future policy—was no doubt salutary. And it has (deservedly) lasted. But if rational expectations reasoning made policy makers anywhere

---

10. See, for example, Gordon (1975).

believe they could move real variables only through monetary surprises, they sure kept that belief to themselves.

During the notable disinflations of the late 1970s and early 1980s, real-world central bankers in the United States and elsewhere certainly didn't act as if they were looking to engineer monetary surprises. They looked and acted as if they believed that monetary stringency would beat inflation, and they were glad to announce their intentions. In short, rational expectations and new classical economics rode to academic victory on the backs of inflation just as actual policy makers were conquering inflation the old-fashioned way—with tight money and high unemployment. Ironic.

7

Carter, Volcker, and the Conquest of Inflation

At a certain point in the inflationary process, public opinion will support strong policies to restore stability even though those policies seem to entail a harsh short-term cost.

—PAUL VOLCKER, "THE TRIUMPH OF CENTRAL BANKING" (1990)

Chapter 6 was a sojourn into the history of doctrine, which is sometimes necessary to understand the history of policy. But the history of politics typically has far more bearing on economic policy.

Jimmy Carter took office as president of the United States in January 1977. When he moved into the White House, the U.S. economy had recently come through the rough stagflationary episode detailed in chapter 5, but it was clearly heading uphill. The U.S. body politic had perhaps come through an even rougher patch, given the disquieting Watergate hearings, Richard Nixon's resignation (to avoid impeachment) in August 1974, and Gerald Ford's controversial pardon of Nixon a month later.

So, when Americans went to the polls in November 1976, the country was ready for change and for someone who seemed both placid and honest—not for a continuation of the Nixon administration, which is how Carter tried to paint Ford in the campaign. Carter filled the I'm-not-Nixon bill superbly. His campaign mantra, "I'll never lie to you," was perfect for the times, and he won in a tight race: by about 2 percentage points in the popular vote and by a 297–240 margin in the electoral college.

Economic Tumult Begins

When Carter arrived in Washington, inflation as measured by the Consumer Price Index (CPI) on a twelve-month basis was down to 5.2 percent, which looked pretty good compared to the double-digit readings that had prevailed from February 1974 through April 1975. Inflation jumped above 6 percent in February 1977, however, and remained in the 6–7 percent range for the remainder of the year. No one knew it at the time, but inflation and Iran's Ayatollah Ruhollah Khomeini would prove to be the two banes of Carter's presidential existence.

In terms of real growth, the recovery from the deep recession of 1973–1975 was proceeding apace, with a robust 4.5 percent growth rate of real GDP between 1976:1 and 1977:1. Nonetheless, many Americans still felt like their economy was in recession.[1] The unemployment rate in January 1977 remained high, at 7.5 percent. It would never dip much below 6 percent during Carter's presidency.

To lead his economic team, Carter chose W. Michael Blumenthal, a prominent and highly successful corporate CEO—one of the few CEOs of the day who was a Democrat—as his secretary of the treasury and Charles Schultze, a deeply respected economist from Brookings, as his Council of Economic Advisers chair. Both had PhDs in economics and substantial prior Washington experience, but they were destined to clash. Like most professional economists, Schultze was data- and model-driven; Blumenthal, an experienced businessman, worried more about psychological factors that models

---

1. For example, a Harris poll conducted from September 18 to September 26, 1977, found 54 percent of people answering "Is" to the question "Do you think the country is in a recession or not?" (Louis Harris & Associates 1977).

ignored. He was also more hawkish on inflation than Schultze was. For director of the Office of Management and Budget Carter tapped Bert Lance, a businessman buddy from Georgia. That appointment raised eyebrows at the time,[2] and Lance did not last a year.[3]

Carter's most unconventional economic appointment, however, came about a year later when he nominated G. William Miller to replace Arthur Burns as chair of the Federal Reserve. Like Blumenthal, Miller had been a successful CEO. But unlike Blumenthal, he had no training in economics. Nor, it soon became apparent, did Miller have much understanding of how the Federal Reserve operates, a handicap Miller himself understood and had warned Carter about (Meltzer 2009a, 923). Miller's tenure as Fed chair was destined to be brief and less than successful.

Early in his presidency, Carter proposed and Congress passed a modest fiscal stimulus—amounting to roughly 1 percent of GDP—that was focused on job creation. It included several hundred thousand public service jobs and a novel tax credit for expanding employment (see just below). Carter's original stimulus proposal had been larger, including a $50 per capita rebate of 1976 taxes. But the rebate proved to be a political loser, derided by, for example, Senator Russell Long (D-LA), then chair of the Senate Finance Committee, as "throwing $50 bills off the top of the Washington Monument" (Eizenstat 2018, 292).

One reason the stimulus package was trimmed was that the federal budget deficit was already running at about 2.5 percent of GDP, which seems puny given what happened once Reagan succeeded Carter. But the balanced budget ideology was alive and well in 1977, at least at the level of lip service. The slimmed-down stimulus bill passed both the House and the Senate by overwhelming votes of 326–87 and 63–15, respectively, and Carter signed it into law on May 13, less than four months into his presidency.

2. The *New York Times* noted on December 4, 1976, that Lance "faces a formidable challenge in attempting to master the far greater complexities of the Federal bureaucracy with which he has had no previous experience" (Mohr 1976).

3. He resigned as a result of a banking scandal but was later acquitted.

One interesting historical footnote was buried in the 1977 stimulus bill: the New Jobs Tax Credit. Doubtless reflecting economists' desires to provide incentives at the margin rather than waste money subsidizing activities that would happen anyway, the tax credit offered firms a wage subsidy of 50 percent of the first $4,200 in wages for increases in employment of at least 2 percent over the previous year, the latter being a crude but practical way to focus the subsidy on marginal hiring.

Though it was a small-scale policy innovation, the New Jobs Tax Credit is generally considered to have been a success (Perloff and Wachter 1979). When I served on President Bill Clinton's Council of Economic Advisers in 1993, we convinced him of the virtues of making investment incentives marginal in a similar manner, but Congress rejected the idea. The New Jobs Tax Credit idea popped up again in 2009 when the Obama administration was searching for ideas to boost job creation, and something resembling it became part of the Hiring Incentives to Restore Employment Act of 2010.

But Carter's efforts to apply expansionary fiscal policy did not end with the 1977 stimulus package. Later that year the new president, who had (accurately) dubbed the existing tax code "a disgrace to the human race" in his campaign, was back to Congress with another tax bill. This one was intended to be more tax reform than tax cut, but as it worked its way through Congress the former morphed into the latter. Remember, the chair of the Senate Finance Committee at the time was the aforementioned Russell Long, whose famous aphorism for tax reform was "Don't tax you; don't tax me; tax that fellow behind the tree."

Long greatly admired many of those trees. So, by the time the bill passed the House and Senate by overwhelming majorities in October 1978, almost all of Carter's reform proposals had been stripped out. Instead, tax rates were trimmed, brackets were widened, the standard deduction was increased, and the maximum tax rate on capital gains was cut from 35 percent to 28 percent. By sheer coincidence, I imagine, the net tax cut in the Revenue Act of 1978 was roughly the same magnitude as the original 1977 stimulus, so the fiscal stimulus was effectively doubled. Carter, a fiscal conservative, was tempted to veto the bill, but his advisers and members of Congress talked him out of it (Eizenstat 2018, 316). Looking back on those two bills forty years later, Stuart Eizenstat, Carter's domestic policy guru, wrote that "given what we knew as we came into office early in 1977, it is difficult to argue that we were mistaken in putting forward a stimulus plan for the stalled economy. But it is equally difficult to defend the second jolt that we proposed late in the same year" (Eizenstat 2018, 314). In brief, there is something to the charge that fiscal policy became too expansionary in 1977–1978. The economy, growing nicely, didn't need it.

The year 1977 also saw the beginnings of what came to be seen as a "dollar crisis." Floating exchange rates were still new then and not entirely trusted. Since the U.S. dollar remained the linchpin of the international monetary system (as it still is), a falling dollar was considered a very big deal at the time both in the United States and abroad.

At an Organisation for Economic Co-operation and Development meeting in June 1977, Secretary Blumenthal made a mild remark that exchange rate adjustments should "play their appropriate role" in international macroeconomic adjustments. Under floating exchange rates, that thought comes close to being a tautology. Nonetheless, Blumenthal was accused of trying to boost U.S. growth and simultaneously slow down foreign growth by "talking down" the dollar, a charge he denied (Solomon 1982, 346). Regardless, secretaries of the treasury from then on studiously avoided saving anything that might evoke memories of "the Blumenthal dollar"—until Secretary Steven Mnuchin broke the taboo in January 2018 by stating, quite forthrightly, that a weak dollar was good for U.S. trade (Ball 2018). In fact, President Donald Trump had gone there before him (Chandler 2017).

Inflation was rising in 1977, and the Federal Open Market Committee's (FOMC) comparatively easy monetary policy may have weighed more heavily on the dollar than Blumenthal's banal remark did. Regardless of the cause(s), the dollar continued to fall into 1978. By October it was down 14 percent from its January 1977 level, as measured against the Fed's trade-weighted average of major foreign currencies. Its declines against the deutsche mark and the Japanese yen were particularly dramatic. A deutsche mark was worth just under 42 cents in January 1977 but cost over 54 cents by October 1978. The Japanese yen went from 291 to the dollar to just 184.

The Carter administration responded with a comprehensive "dollar rescue package" that included emergency sales of gold and borrowing from the International Monetary Fund for the only time in U.S. history. Even more drastically, the U.S. Treasury sold some debt securities denominated in deutsche marks and Swiss francs. They were dubbed "Carter bonds," a nickname not meant as a compliment. (The Treasury never issued foreign currency denominated bonds again.) It all looked a bit panicky.

The falling dollar was not the big problem, however. Rising inflation was.[4] The twelve-month CPI inflation rate rose from 5.2 percent in January 1977 to 9 percent in December 1978 and eventually to over 14 percent in 1980. Some of that increase, especially in 1979 and 1980, was due to the Organization of the Petroleum Exporting Countries' "OPEC II" shock, as detailed in chapter 5. But even core inflation, after hovering in the 6–6.5 percent range during 1977, was up to 8.5 percent by December 1978 and topped 13 percent for a few months in 1980.[5] Inflation was clearly the major problem of the day, topping even unemployment. And that, not the cheap dollar, was the big blot on the reputations of Carter and Miller.

Origins of the Dual Mandate

Another sequence of events in the early Carter years gets far less attention, but it is worth noting here for its importance to U.S. monetary history and to monetary policy even today. The little-known Federal Reserve Reform Act of 1977 was signed into law by President Carter in November 1977. Its focus was on increasing the Fed's accountability, including a legal requirement to report to Congress "concerning the ranges of monetary and credit aggregates for the

4. Only a small share of the rising inflation could be traced to the falling dollar.

5. A quirk in the CPI—later fixed—exaggerated inflation by counting rising mortgage interest rates as rising prices.

upcoming 12 months"[6] and beginning to hold separate Senate confirmation hearings for the Federal Reserve Board's chair and vice chair. Prior to that, while all Fed governors had to be confirmed, the president simply designated one of them as chair and another as vice chair.

Most significantly, however, the 1977 act established what we now call the Fed's *dual mandate*: to "promote maximum employment, production, and price stability." This mandate, which distinguishes the Federal Reserve from most other central banks by placing employment on an equal footing with inflation, is often falsely attributed to the Humphrey-Hawkins Act (the Full Employment and Balanced Growth Act), which Congress passed and Carter signed about a year later.

The Humphrey-Hawkins Act gets far more attention because it set a (probably unrealistic) numerical goal for the unemployment rate (4%) and established semiannual Humphrey-Hawkins hearings at which the Fed chair would explain the central bank's actions to Congress. The act also made a modest change to the wording of the monetary mandate to "maximum employment, stable prices, and moderate long-term interest rates." Because economists consider the last of these three to be redundant (if prices are stable, nominal interest rates will be low), this is called the Fed's dual mandate. But that mandate dates from the 1977 act, not the 1978 act.

Prior to 1977, the entire U.S. government was, of course, committed by the Employment Act of 1946 to pursuing "conditions under which there will be afforded useful employment for those able, willing, and seeking to work." This vague but important commitment was passed with the memory of the Great Depression still fresh in legislators' minds. However, Congress was not yet willing to embrace the title that had been proposed earlier, "Full Employment Act." Importantly, the Employment Act was not directed at the Fed; people in 1946 simply did not think the Fed was that important. In fact, the act, which also created the Council of Economic Advisers

---

6. This provision basically codified into law what Congress had directed the Fed to do in Concurrent Resolution 133 in 1975.

in the White House, required an annual Economic Report of the President. It asked for no such report from the Federal Reserve.

So, the 1977 and 1978 amendments to the Federal Reserve Act really were landmarks for monetary policy even if that was not realized at the time. I find it amazing that Allan Meltzer's monumental *A History of the Federal Reserve* (2009a, b), which leaves out approximately nothing, barely mentions the 1977 act and does not even mention its dual mandate provision.

Supply Shocks Strike Again

While all this was happening legislatively, food prices began to climb all over the world, and inflation once again became economic issue number one. In the United States, the growth rate of the food and beverages component of the CPI, which had dropped to a low of 1 percent (seasonally adjusted annual rate) in December 1976 began rising, eventually peaking at about 13 percent in February 1979 (figure 7.1). With a relative importance in the index of about 18 percent, these rising food prices alone contributed 2 percentage points to overall CPI inflation in 1978 and 1.75 points in both 1979 and 1980 (Blinder and Rudd 2013, 141).[7] Carter and Miller absorbed much of the blame even though, as Blinder and Rudd remarked, "we are deeply skeptical that agricultural diseases, bad weather, and the hog cycle were lagged effects of monetary policy" (142).[8]

That said, oil prices, not food prices, dominated the headlines in 1979 and 1980. What we now call OPEC II struck when the Iranian Revolution of 1978–1979, followed by Iraq's invasion of Iran, sent crude oil prices skyrocketing. The pass-through into consumer prices was quick and dramatic. The CPI energy component, which registered just 7 percent inflation (seasonally adjusted annual rate)

---

7. In addition, a measurement error, discussed later in this chapter, exaggerated inflation in 1978–1981.

8. More than two decades earlier, Blinder (1982, 270) had observed that a remarkably large proportion of the food inflation in 1978 and 1979 was actually "meat price inflation," the result of a sharp reduction in cattle herds followed by severe winter weather and rising feed costs.

FIGURE 7.1. U.S. food price inflation, 1975–1980.
Source: Bureau of Labor Statistics.

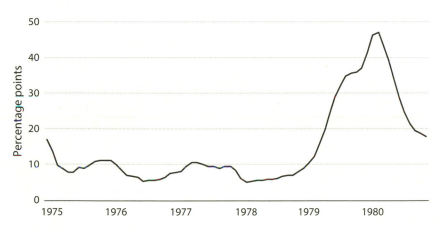

FIGURE 7.2. U.S. energy price inflation, 1975–1980.
Source: Bureau of Labor Statistics.

in November 1978, soared to 47 percent by March 1980 (figure 7.2). No, that is not a typo. Forty-seven percent.

Once again, as Rudd and I observed, "it should be obvious that both OPEC shocks were set in motion by geopolitical events that cannot possibly be attributed to, say, money growth in the United States or even to world economic growth" (Blinder and Rudd 2013, 140). Nonetheless, monetarists seem not to have found this obvious at all at the time. For example, Milton Friedman's rhetorical question in a 1975 *Newsweek* column—"Why should the average level of prices be affected significantly by changes in the price of some things relative to others?"—was supposed to answer itself (Friedman 1975b, 73). Some of Friedman's intellectual heirs remain unconvinced even to this day.[9] One reason, of course, is that core inflation soared at the same time—up from the 6 percent range in early 1978 to as high as 13.5 percent in mid-1980. Why?

Part of the explanation is that supply shocks, even temporary ones, leave some pass-through into core prices in their wake. Blinder and Rudd (2013, 146) estimated that this pass-through amounted to about 2 percentage points of additional core inflation in the 1978–1980 period. Nonetheless, even with this addition, the entire inflation story of 1978–1980 cannot be pinned on supply shocks.

One obvious additional cause of higher inflation was excessive growth of aggregate demand that pushed the economy beyond full employment. Indeed, the growth rates of real GDP over the four quarters of 1977 and 1978 were 5 percent and 6.7 percent, respectively—both well above trend. Consistent with that, the unemployment rate tracked downward steadily, with only small exceptions, from its recession high of 9 percent in May 1975 to a low of 5.6 percent in May 1979.

This rapid growth was due in part to the aforementioned fiscal stimulus. But monetary policy also played a role. For example, the growth rate of M2 (from twelve months earlier) remained in double digits from mid-1975 until the start of 1978. You don't have to be a monetarist to wonder whether money growth rates such as that might be inflationary. In any case, the combination of rapid money growth, rapid GDP growth, and rising inflation led many critics to blame the Miller Fed for losing control of inflation. They had a point. The Fed's official history website put it this way: "Unlike some of his predecessors, Miller was less focused on combating inflation, but rather was intent on promoting economic growth even if it resulted in inflation. Miller believed that inflation was caused by

9. See, for example, several of the chapters in Bordo and Orphanides (2013).

many factors beyond the Board's control."[10] That last sentence is redolent of Arthur Burns.

Many of Miller's critics on Wall Street were far less measured. For example, journalist Steven Beckner wrote (slightly hysterically perhaps) that "if Nixon appointee Burns lit the fire, Miller poured the gasoline on it during the administration of President Jimmy Carter" (Beckner 1996, 22). But before we embrace the excess demand explanation too uncritically, we should note that the unemployment rate never dropped below 5.8 percent during 1977 and 1978. Given the Congressional Budget Office's current estimate of the natural rate of unemployment at that time, which was around 6.2 percent (contemporaneous estimates were a bit lower), the overshoot was modest. You don't get much of an increase of inflation by overshooting the natural rate of unemployment by just 0.4 percentage point. As mentioned in chapter 5, however, Orphanides (2003) has argued that overestimation of the output gap, largely due to a failure to recognize the productivity slowdown that began in earnest in 1973, played a meaningful role in making monetary policy too loose under both Burns and Miller. In that case, the excess demand pressures had been building for some time, so looking just at 1977–1978 is too myopic.

Finally, a measurement issue with the CPI exaggerated the inflation rate. Until the Bureau of Labor Statistics (BLS) fixed the problem in 1983, the interest rate on home mortgages was counted as a "price" in the CPI. But since nominal interest rates in general and the mortgage rate in particular depend on the inflation rate, this measurement error created a positive feedback loop that exaggerated the rise (or fall) of inflation. Whenever inflation rose, the announced CPI level would get an extra boost from rising mortgage rates.[11] This was no trivial matter when interest rates rose sharply. The BLS now publishes a historical research series, dating back to 1978, that

10. Board of Governors of the Federal Reserve System, "G. William Miller," *Federal Reserve History*, Federal Reserve Bank of St. Louis, https://www.federalreservehistory.org/people/g_william_miller.

11. Among the many references that could be cited complaining about this error, see (Blinder 1980).

corrects this and some other problems. By that measure, the CPI inflation rates for 1978, 1979, and 1980 were 7.8 percent, 10.9 percent, and 10.8 percent, respectively; each well below the official CPI readings of 9 percent, 13.3 percent, and 12.4 percent for those years. But no one saw numbers like that in real time.

Enter Paul Volcker

By the summer of 1979, there was no doubt in Carter's mind that reducing inflation was both an economic and a political imperative of the first rank. He had famously, if rather awkwardly, labeled the energy crisis—one major source of the high inflation—"the moral equivalent of war." On July 15, Carter delivered to a nationwide TV audience what came to be called his "malaise speech," even though he never used that word (Carter 1979). Despite getting good initial reviews, the speech soon came to be widely panned for its negativity. It was viewed as being symptomatic of a failed presidency.

Within days of that fateful speech, Carter was cleaning house—firing, among others, Secretary Blumenthal and the first secretary of energy, James Schlesinger. (Carter had established the Department of Energy in 1977.) Miller, who was clearly a misfit at the Fed in any case, quickly replaced Blumenthal at the Treasury, leaving the Fed chairmanship vacant—but not for long. Carter moved almost immediately to nominate Paul Volcker, the well-known and iron-willed inflation hawk who was then president of the Federal Reserve Bank of New York, to replace Miller. The Senate confirmed Volcker within a week.

Volcker took over at the Fed on August 6, 1979, with little doubt about what would happen next. No more Carterite ad hoc approaches to fighting inflation, like naming anti-inflation czars and flirting with wage-price guidelines. No more Burns- or Miller-like excuses that the Fed was overwhelmed by stronger societal forces that rendered it unable to control inflation. It was going to be tight money—period. Carter harbored no illusions about what he was in for when he placed Volcker in charge of monetary policy, up to and possibly including defeat in the 1980 election. In Eizenstat's words,

"Carter courageously appointed Paul Volcker to head the Federal Reserve in full knowledge that this determined public servant would deploy the blunt instrument of tight money and high interest rates. This ultimately squeezed inflation out of the economy at the cost of high unemployment and helped squeeze him [Carter] out of a second term" (Eizenstat 2018, 278). The contrast with Nixon's appointment of Burns could hardly have been more stark.

Volcker reports being surprised when Miller first called to ask him to come to Washington to meet Carter. "I had never met the president. I had voted against Miller in Open Market Committee meetings. But, of course, I got on the [air] shuttle" (Volcker 2018, 108). After telling Carter that he felt strongly about both Fed independence and fighting inflation, Volcker returned to New York, telling his friends that "I just blew a chance of becoming Fed chair" (108). He was wrong. Early the next morning Carter called to offer him the job and, as Eizenstat observed, perhaps to doom his own reelection prospects. But Carter had at last found an effective weapon against inflation: a resolute Fed chair.

A long-standing controversy rages to this day over whether expectations of tighter monetary policy in the future should raise or lower long-term interest rates. On the one hand, if the market deems the news credible, inflationary expectations should decline, thereby lowering nominal interest rates. On the other hand, however, expected future short rates should rise. According to the standard expectations theory of the term structure, which holds that long rates are the appropriate weighted average of expected future short rates, that should boost longer-term interest rates. Keynesians tended toward the latter prediction. Monetarists tended toward the former, as did Volcker.[12] But as he put it in his autobiography, "No such luck" (Volcker 2018, 108).

The appointment of Volcker in the summer of 1979 might have offered an acid test of one hypothesis against the other, but apparently

---

12. There are probably hundreds of possible references on this debate. For the monetarist view, see, for example, Wray (1993). For the Keynesian view, see, for example, Mishkin (1995).

it didn't. The ten-year Treasury rate, which stood at 8.99 percent on the day Carter nominated Volcker (July 25, 1979), was 8.91 percent on the day Volcker took over at the Fed (August 6, 1979).[13] Could the mighty Volcker have been worth only 8 basis points? That seems implausible.[14] But the action on interest rates came later, when the Fed raised short rates. Long rates went up. The thirty-year Treasury rate, for example, rose more than 100 basis points between late September and late October 1979.

In late September Volcker few to Belgrade, in what was then Yugoslavia, for the annual meetings of the International Monetary Fund and the World Bank. There, among other things, he sat through what should really be called Arthur Burns's malaise speech (described in chapter 4). Before leaving Washington, Volcker had left instructions with some top Fed staffers to think about a new approach to monetary policy that would amount to "practical monetarism," that is, to paying more attention to growth in the monetary aggregates as opposed to (in Volcker's words) "the more extreme and mechanistic monetarism that Milton Friedman had advocated" (Volcker 2018, 106).

Remember, monetarists were then the strong anti-inflation constituency in the intellectual world. With assistance from Lucas, Sargent, and other rational expectationists, they had successfully, though unfairly, branded Keynesian economics as inflationary. So, cloaking a new approach to monetary policy in the garb of monetarism made a certain amount of public relations sense. Regardless of whether or not it was Keynesian, the old approach to controlling inflation had plainly not worked.

Volcker left the Belgrade conference early to fly back to Washington and get to work on the Fed's new monetarist-style policy. Then on October 6, 1979, he did something that Fed chairs virtually never do: he called an impromptu press conference—on Saturday

13. Federal Reserve Bank of St. Louis, Federal Reserve Economic Data.

14. In case you're thinking that Volcker's nomination was anticipated by the markets in advance, the long rate did not move much in the days prior to July 25 either.

night yet! Reporters who cancelled their entertainment plans for the night and attended en masse were not disappointed. Volcker told the assembled press corps that the FOMC had decided, at an unscheduled meeting earlier that day, to shift its focus away from day-to-day management of the federal funds rate and toward the growth rate of bank reserves (and thus of the money supply). As he put it at the press conference, "By emphasizing the supply of reserves and constraining the growth of the money supply through the reserve mechanism, we think we can get firmer control over the growth in money supply in a shorter period of time. . . . But the other side of the coin is [that] the daily rate in the market . . . is apt to fluctuate over a wider range than had been the practice in recent years" (Volcker 1979, 4).

A "wider range" indeed. As figure 7.3 shows, Treasury rates became much more volatile after October 1979. And it wasn't just more volatility; they headed upward. The three-month Treasury bill rate, which was 10.7 percent on the day before Volcker's press conference, leaped to 12.8 percent by October 22.[15] The effective federal funds rate, which averaged 11.4 percent in September 1979, averaged 13.8 percent in October 1979 and was up to 17.6 percent by April 1980.

Republicans, Democrats, and ordinary citizens alike were alarmed by such unprecedentedly high rates. They made their displeasure known to the Fed in a variety of ways, ranging from pointed criticism in congressional hearings to two-by-fours mailed in by home builders to death threats. By the end of 1980, Fed security personnel insisted that Volcker get armed protection (which the Fed chair retains to this day). Their judgment was not wrong. A year later, an armed intruder somehow got into the Fed's headquarters building and threatened to take the Federal Reserve Board hostage. Those were trying times indeed. But Volcker was a man on a mission, not easily deterred—a tower of strength and always true to his word.

---

15. By the middle of June 1980, amid the sharp recession discussed below, it was down to 6.2 percent.

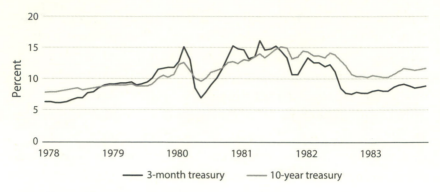

FIGURE 7.3. Selected U.S. interest rates, 1978–1983.
Source: Board of Governors of the Federal Reserve System.

Paul Volcker (1927–2019)

The Babe Ruth of Central Banking

Paul Anthony Volcker Jr. will forever be known as the man who conquered inflation in the United States. He did it the old-fashioned way: with excruciatingly tight money. More important, he did it at a time when many people thought the task was either impossible or vastly more costly than it turned out to be. Beating inflation required an iron will. Paul Volcker had one.

Volcker was born in Cape May, New Jersey, and attended Princeton University, where his senior thesis criticized the Federal Reserve's recent (ca. 1949) monetary policy. Princeton's motto at the time was "Princeton in the nation's service," an ideal Volcker exemplified. That attitude was instilled in him by his father, who was a city manager, and lasted a lifetime.

After Princeton, Volcker studied economics at what we now call the Kennedy School at Harvard and then at the London School of Economics. Returning to the United States in 1952, he took a job as an economist at the Federal Reserve Bank of New York, thus beginning a lifetime of public service. After a detour at the Chase Manhattan Bank, Volcker's career in government began in earnest when he joined the U.S. Treasury in 1962. Within two years, he had risen to the rank of deputy undersecretary for monetary affairs. Then after a second stint at Chase, he returned to the Treasury in 1969 as the undersecretary for international monetary affairs, a position he held for five tumultuous years. Notice that this quintessential technocrat, though a Democrat, was appointed by President Richard Nixon.

As undersecretary, Volcker was present at the destruction of the Bretton Woods system of fixed exchange rates in August 1971, which must have pained him, for he was to the end a believer in the importance of stable exchange rates. But he soldiered on as the Western world stumbled toward floating exchange rates.

Leaving the Treasury in 1974, Volcker spent a year teaching at his alma mater before being appointed president of the Federal Reserve Bank of New York, where among other things he established strong anti-inflationary credentials. When President Carter needed a new tough-on-inflation Fed chair in 1979, Volcker was the heir apparent.

A pillar of strength, probity, and integrity, Volcker remains a legend at the Federal Reserve. When rumors (which proved true) arose that President Ronald Reagan would not reappoint Volcker as Fed chair in 1987, I penned a column in *BusinessWeek* lauding him as "the Babe Ruth of central banking." I wrote then that "I reacted to the idea of replacing Volcker as the Boston Red Sox should have responded when the Yankees requested a trade for Babe Ruth: out of the question" (Blinder 1987c).

Volcker's devotion to public service did not end when his term as chair of the Fed did. Never one to say no to a good cause, he went on to, among other things, chair committees or commissions investigating Swiss bank reparations to Holocaust survivors, the United Nations tarnished Oil-for-Food Programme, and internal problems at the World Bank. Every major organization with a knotty problem on its hands, it seemed, wanted a "Volcker commission" to set things right.

The value of the Volcker imprimatur continued into the Obama administration. When the new president was looking to garner support for strict limits on proprietary trading by banks, an idea Volcker had championed, he named it "the Volcker rule." The name carried weight, just like Babe Ruth's does.

What about those money growth rates? Did they stabilize? Well, you be the judge. Figure 7.4 shows the growth rate (from twelve months previously) of what the Fed now measures as M1 and M2 (the definitions of the Ms have changed many times since 1979) from 1978 through 1983, just after the monetarist experiment ended. I find it hard to see less volatility after October 1979, and monetarists complained bitterly about that. As Volcker put it in his autobiography, "The monetarists, led by Milton Friedman, instead of claiming victory that the Fed was finally adopting a more monetarist approach, insisted we weren't doing it just right" (Volcker 2018, 109). Here's one example, from a Milton Friedman *Newsweek* column: "The Fed's targets for monetary growth have been reasonable. The problem is with the failure to achieve them. If a private enterprise's actual production deviated from plan as frequently and by as much, heads would roll" (Friedman 1980, 62).

It wasn't just a matter of some technicalities such as lagged reserve accounting, which monetarists disliked and which made precise control of money growth harder than need be.[16] Rather, the combination of high inflation, vestigial controls on nominal interest

16. As practiced at the Fed, lagged reserve accounting meant that required reserves were based on deposit volumes two weeks earlier.

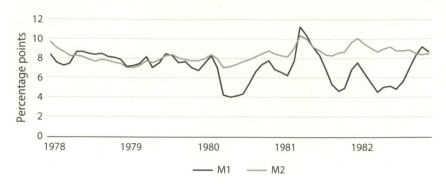

FIGURE 7.4. Growth rates of M1 and M2, 1978–1983.
Source: Board of Governors of the Federal Reserve System.

rates (which were subsequently removed), and a rash of financial innovation—itself largely a consequence of high inflation—wreaked havoc on the Fed's ability to come anywhere close to hitting its targets for M1, M2, or any number of other definitions of "money" that the Fed staff tried.[17]

Even Allan Meltzer, as devout a monetarist as you'll find, admitted that "monetary innovation added to the difficulty of choosing a path [for money growth] and announcing it to the public" (Meltzer 2009a, 1039). Put simply and without econometric detail, when you don't know what is happening to the demand for money, it is hard to formulate sensible targets for the supply of money, much less to hit them. The Fed had fits trying to do either.

One interesting question in monetary history lingers to this day: Did Volcker truly convert to monetarism as a better policy approach, or did he just view the pretense of focusing on money growth as a convenient political heat shield for what he knew was to come, excruciatingly high interest rates? More Fed watchers lean toward the latter explanation. So do I.

Volcker himself is a bit cagey on the question in his autobiography. After quoting Friedman's well-known dictum that "inflation is always and everywhere a monetary phenomenon," Volcker

17. Among many sources on the instability of money demand, see Goldfeld (1976).

immediately notes, first, that "the simplicity of that thesis helped provide a basis for presenting the new approach to the American public" and, second, that the avowedly monetarist approach "enforced upon the Federal Reserve an internal discipline that had been lacking" (Volcker 2018, 118). So, perhaps the monetarist experiment was really about public communication and private commitment, about tying the FOMC to the mast, not about any belief in the stability of velocity.

Stuart Eizenstat, who watched the monetarist experiment from the Carter White House, viewed it differently. After acknowledging Volcker's credibility arguments, Eizenstat added that "Volcker was no political babe in the woods. He also knew that this method provided more political cover than directly jacking up interest rates" (Eizenstat 2018, 345). Eizenstat quotes Volcker as saying in an interview that "this was certainly an easier way to get public support. You can say that we've got to keep the money supply under control; that's what we're doing; we're not directly aiming at interest rates" (345). A few years later when asked by a friend whether he really was a monetarist back then, Volcker replied directly, "Nah, I just wanted to shake 'em up" (345).

And shake 'em up he surely did. Yet through the first quarter of 1980, both inflation and interest rates remained sky-high, and there was no recession. Weak growth, yes, but no actual decline in real GDP. According to current data, the real GDP growth rate was just 1 percent (seasonally adjusted annual rate) in 1979:4 and 1.3 percent in 1980:1. Observers both inside and outside the Fed were growing impatient. But remember, the lags in monetary policy are long. Then in 1980:2, the anvil dropped.

The Credit Controls Catastrophe

Ironically, it was not Volcker who dropped the anvil. It was Carter, using the Federal Reserve as his chosen instrument.

The president and his inflation czar, Alfred Kahn, had become convinced that excessive growth of consumer credit was fueling inflation rather than, say, inflationary expectations, business spending, or

excess money growth. The Fed did not share this view.[18] However,
Carter had legal authority, left over from the Nixon years, to ask the
Fed to impose credit controls and he used it in March 1980. Looking
back on that decision, Eizenstat termed it "a monumentally bad idea"
(2018, 347). It was. Volcker and his colleagues at the Fed certainly
thought so, though even they were probably surprised at just how
bad it turned out to be.

Volcker later recounted that the Fed saw credit controls as "a
transparently political ploy" at a time when "excessive credit wasn't
the problem" and so "quickly designed 'controls' that we hoped
would lack real teeth" (Volcker 2018, 110). But the politically astute
Fed chair felt that the central bank, though independent, could not
just turn Carter down flat. After all, the president was supporting
their tight-money policy despite evident political peril to himself. So,
the Fed staff designed credit controls that, for example, exempted
borrowings to finance automobile and home purchases. Leaving a
toothless tiger, right?

Well, actually not. It turned out that Carter's well-publicized
emphasis on restricting credit resonated strongly with an American public that was sick and tired of high inflation. The response
was entirely unlike what had followed Gerald Ford's fruitless Whip
Inflation Now campaign in 1975. This time, "people were so desperate to do their part to fight inflation, they tore up their credit cards
as a patriotic act and sent the pieces to Kahn and the White House,
accompanied by letters saying: 'Mr. President, we will cooperate'"
(Eizenstat 2018, 348).

Those were apparently not empty gestures. Consumer spending crumbled, taking GDP growth down with it. The second quarter of 1980 stands out as one of the worst quarters in postwar U.S.
history, with an annualized growth rate of −8 percent (figure 7.5).
Consumer spending, normally one of the most stable components
of GDP, led the way, dropping at an incredible 8.7 percent annual

18. There is a long-running doctrinal dispute, which will not detain us here,
over whether monetary policy works mainly through the money supply channel
or mainly through the credit channel.

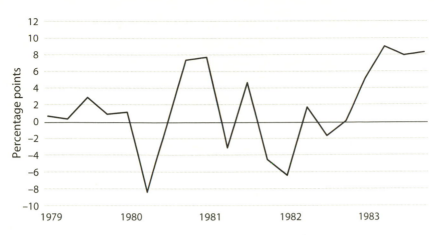

FIGURE 7.5. Annualized growth of real GDP, quarterly, 1979–1983.
Source: Bureau of Economic Analysis.

rate. Patriotism apparently trumped both interest rates and money growth.

The National Bureau of Economic Research dates the short but sharp recession of 1980 as starting in January and ending in July. For a president seeking reelection, that timing is about as bad as it gets. (Carter was also dealing, unsuccessfully, with the Iran hostage crisis at the time.)

The controls also held bad news for the monetarist experiment, since the flip side of less credit card lending was a sharp decline in money supply growth. Monthly M1 growth plummeted to –5 percent (seasonally adjusted annual rate) in March 1980 and to an astounding –13 percent in April. Even on a twelve-month basis, M1 growth fell from 8.3 percent in February 1980 to just 4.1 percent in April. Those were big changes for a central bank that was putatively stabilizing money growth. (Would a truly monetarist Fed have juiced up the money supply?) Yet despite the abrupt decline in money growth, interest rates plunged, and as Volcker put it, "we had to backpedal fast" (2018, 111).[19]

By August–September 1980, with credit controls gone, both money growth and the economy perked up, and the Fed felt

19. This backpedaling may have cost the Fed some credibility. See Bordo et al. (2017).

compelled to tighten once again. Its discount rate hike in late September came with the election barely more than a month away. Not surprisingly, this was not well received at the White House; Carter termed it "ill-advised" (Volcker 2018, 111). Yet progress against inflation was grudging. (Remember the long lags.) Core CPI inflation did plunge to 5.5 percent briefly during the third quarter of 1980, but it was back above 14 percent by the fourth quarter.[20]

Running Away from Monetarism

Things did not get much better for Volcker and his band of fledgling (or was it pseudo?) monetarists in 1981 and 1982. Ronald Reagan had replaced Jimmy Carter in the White House, but both interest rates and money growth rates remained volatile. Core CPI inflation was still almost 12 percent as late as September 1981 (but just 9.4% according to the BLS's research series), and then it plunged. The soaring dollar at the time no doubt played some role in this disinflation. The economy grew strongly during the snap-back from the artificial recession of 1980, but a real and very deep recession began in 1981:2. By 1981:4 and 1982:1, it was clear to the Fed that this was no garden variety recession; it was a whopper. At the time, it was the deepest recession since the 1930s.

The Reagan tax cuts, which will be discussed in the next chapter, had not kicked in much by the summer of 1982. So, it was clear to Volcker and his colleagues at the Fed that they had to ease up on monetary policy quickly lest the deep recession turn into something even more ugly. By the fall of 1982 monetarist doctrine stood in the way of doing so, which made it clear that monetarism had to go. The doctrine had not worked anyway. At the October 5, 1982, FOMC meeting, Volcker told the committee that "following a mechanical operation because we think that's vital to credibility and driving the

---

20. The latter was heavily affected by the measurement error mentioned earlier. The BLS research series records a 7.9 percent CPI inflation rate in the fourth quarter of 1980.

economy into the ground isn't exactly my version of how to maintain credibility over time" (FOMC 1982). To Volcker and his colleagues on the FOMC, monetarism had served its purpose. Inflation was, at last, heading down.

In October 1982, Volcker announced that "I do not believe that . . . we have any alternative but to attach much less than usual weight to movements in M1 over the period immediately ahead" (*American Banker* 1982). This was an understatement. The "temporary" suspension of money growth targeting turned out to be permanent. Monetarists were not pleased, but the Fed's monetarist experiment was over. It was not until July 1993, however, that Alan Greenspan officially abandoned any semblance of money supply targeting by the Fed, telling a Senate committee that "the relationship [between money growth and economic growth] has completely broken down" (Greenhouse 1993). Greenspan was right, of course. But that "news" came more than a decade after the fact.

Chapter Summary

Jimmy Carter came into office in January 1977 viewing the economy as still weak, probably weaker than it actually was. Appropriately, given that belief, he recommended and Congress passed a modest fiscal stimulus. However, the year 1977 was perhaps most notable in the history of stabilization policy for the formalization of the Fed's dual mandate in the Federal Reserve Reform Act of 1977.

In retrospect, Carter's fiscal policy in 1977–1978 and the Fed's monetary policy under G. William Miller appear too expansionary, although both food shocks and OPEC II deserve much more blame for the alarming rise in inflation in 1979–1980. Seeking a solution, Carter turned to the well-known inflation hawk, Paul Volcker, who emphatically rejected the idea that inflation was beyond the central bank's control. Leaving aside his flirtation with monetarism, Volcker knew what to do, and he had the iron will necessary to do it. Tight monetary policy, in conjunction with the passing of the supply shocks, brought inflation down, though not quickly and certainly not painlessly.

Credit controls, which are not part of the usual monetary-fiscal canon, caused a short but deep recession in 1980. That was followed by a more traditional recession, caused by tight money, in 1981–1982. Together, those dual recessions broke the back of core inflation. By October 1982, with the war on inflation well on its way to victory, Volcker and the Fed were ready to abandon any pretense of monetarism. And they did.

8

Reaganomics and the Clash between Monetary and Fiscal Policy

> *[O]ur kind of tax cut will so stimulate our economy that we will actually increase government revenues*
> —RONALD REAGAN, JULY 1981

There is probably no episode in U.S. history that illustrates better what can happen when monetary and fiscal policy clash than the Reagan years. A combination of the terrible stagflation and tight money discussed in previous chapters, the wrath of Ayatollah Ruhollah Khomeini in Iran, and the genial appeal of Ronald Reagan as a candidate combined to produce an electoral landslide in November 1980, ushering Jimmy Carter out of office. Reagan's victory opened the door to an abrupt turn in fiscal policy toward far lower taxes and much bigger budget deficits. Carter fretted about fiscal deficits but didn't do much about them. Reagan had pipe dreams about deficits (see the epigraph above) and pursued policies that made them explode.

But before getting enmeshed in the details, we should pause to consider two important antecedents to what became known as Reaganomics.

Setting the Stage

One of those antecedents was the doctrine that came to be called "supply-side economics," in particular the Kemp-Roth tax cut proposal, named for its two sponsors, Congressman Jack Kemp (R-NY) and Senator William Roth (R-DE). Their plan, which was first announced and promoted during Carter's presidency, called for a 30 percent reduction in personal income tax rates phased in at 10 percent per year over three years. Kemp-Roth garnered a great deal of attention. After all, tax cuts always have political allure, and this one was massive. But President Carter, a believer in fiscal responsibility, steadfastly opposed the drastic Kemp-Roth tax cuts. They were budget busters.

The tide of history, however, was flowing toward lower tax rates, whipped up by high inflation that had turned bracket creep into bracket gallop. In 1978 Carter reluctantly agreed to a substantial reduction in the tax rate on capital gains, proposed by Congressman William Steiger (R-WI), that dropped the top rate on gains from 40 percent to 28 percent. But the Steiger amendment just seemed to whet tax cutters' appetites. That same year witnessed a full-scale tax revolt in California—not coincidentally, Reagan's home state—that led to the famous/infamous (take your pick) Proposition 13, which slashed property taxes to the bone.

While all this was going on, and related to it of course, economist Arthur Laffer and journalist Jude Wanniski, among others, were promoting a stunning new doctrine called supply-side economics. Their argument, in brief, was that reducing income tax rates would have such powerful incentive effects on decisions to work, save, and invest that the tax base would grow so fast that tax revenue would actually rise, not fall, despite lower rates. The government could add by subtracting!

It was a seductive vision, first explained by Laffer to Wanniski in 1974 by sketching what came to be called a "Laffer curve" on a napkin in a Washington, DC, restaurant.[1] Wanniski became Laffer's publicist, using the editorial pages of the *Wall Street Journal* unrelentingly and effectively to spread the word. In 1978, he even published a book with the immodest title *The Way the World Works* (Wanniski 1978).

To economists, there was just one big problem: supply-side economics did not describe the way the world works; its extreme claims were never backed up by evidence. Yes, it is true that higher income taxes dull incentives to earn income. It is also true that tax rates can be set so high that cutting them actually produces more revenue. That's a simple matter of mathematics that any beginning student of calculus can prove for you. But Laffer, Wanniski, and others never offered any serious evidence that the income tax rates then prevailing in the United States were in or even near that prohibitive range. It was that gross exaggeration that induced Charles Schultze, Carter's top economic adviser, to quip in 1980 that "there's absolutely nothing wrong with supply side economics you couldn't cure by dividing its claims by a factor of ten."[2] Incentive effects from taxation? Sure. A free lunch? No.

But did Reagan or his team ever make the preposterous claim that the U.S. tax system was on the downhill side of the Laffer curve? This question may seem ridiculous on its face given, for example, this chapter's epigraph.[3] The answer is clearly yes. But in August 1991, I was forced to engage in a "debate," if you want to call it that, in the pages of the *Wall Street Journal* over exactly that point with Martin Anderson, who had been Reagan's top domestic and economic policy adviser in both the 1980 campaign and the early years of the Reagan presidency.[4] Anderson insisted that Reagan never made the extreme supply-side claim. Really?

---

1. The Laffer curve showed the tax rate on one axis and tax revenue on the other and took the shape of a hill, rising as comparatively low tax rates rose but then falling as high tax rates went even higher.

2. This remark has been cited and repeated in numerous places. I take these exact words from Schultze (2011, 13).

3. Quoted in Feldstein (1994, 21n).

4. "Forced" may be an exaggeration. In a 1991 op-ed in the *Wall Street Journal*, Anderson (1991, A16) had accused me of making an "unexpectedly reckless" attack on Reaganomics in my 1987 book *Hard Heads, Soft Hearts* (Blinder 1987a).

I beat this seemingly dead horse for a simple reason: the horse never died. To this day, some Republicans—alas, it's a political doctrine, not an economic one—insist that Laffer and Reagan were right all along: you can raise revenue by cutting tax rates. President George W. Bush used a Lafferite argument, among many others, to support his Reaganesque tax cut proposals in 2001. To cite just one example, looking back on the 2001–2003 tax cuts in a February 2006 speech, he asserted that "you cut taxes and the tax revenues increase" (Bush 2006).

Later in history, President Donald Trump's secretary of the treasury, Steven Mnuchin, claimed in 2017—apparently with a straight face—that "not only will this tax plan pay for itself, but it will pay down debt" (Davidson 2017). Of course, the Trump tax cuts of December 2017 did not pay for themselves and certainly didn't pay down the national debt. On the contrary, the federal budget deficit exploded into the trillion-dollar range well before the pandemic hit in early 2020. Nothing new there. The Bush tax cuts in 2001–2003 had also ballooned the deficit, as had the Reagan tax cuts years before them. While it is certainly possible to favor large tax cuts, raising revenue is not a valid reason.

The second antecedent to Reaganomics was discussed extensively in chapter 7: the excruciatingly tight monetary policy engineered by Fed Chair Paul Volcker to break inflation's back. Remember, Volcker's anti-inflation crusade began in October 1979, more than a year before the 1980 election. By the time Reagan took the oath of office in January 1981, the Fed's tight monetary policy was in full force, and a severe recession was likely in the cards. (The National Bureau of Economic Research dates the 1981–1982 recession as starting in July 1981.) Contemporary forecasters, however, did not see it coming. For example, the Congressional Budget Office observed many years later that it had "failed to anticipate the start of the 1981–1982 recession, and after it had begun, how deep it would be" (CBO 2017a, 17).

I could have ignored him, but I thought even then that history should be written accurately. See Blinder (1991, A13).

The Reagan-Volcker policy mix, at least in its initial years, combined loose budgets with tight money. Elementary economic reasoning says that such a mix should produce high real interest rates—and it did, as we shall see. But the important point for now is that Volcker's strongly contractionary policies came first. It is almost inconceivable that fiscal policy in 1981 could have headed off a recession even if it tried. Furthermore, supply-side doctrine actually embraced the use of tight money to fight inflation. In an odd blend of ideology and economics, supply-siders believed that monetary policy could be assigned to reducing inflation while tax cuts stimulated real economic growth at the same time (more on this belief shortly).

Reaganomics

This brings me back to Reaganomics. The supply-side vision of a free lunch was politically alluring in 1981, as it has been several times since. Furthermore, the idea that cutting the tax rates of rich people was the route to economic salvation was especially seductive to the rich, many of whom were enthusiastic Republican political donors. Who cared that virtually no mainstream economists signed up for supply-side economics (even though a number of them favored cutting taxes)? Republican politicians signed up in droves. One of them was the former governor of California, Ronald Reagan.

Candidate Reagan portrayed the Carter economy—not to mention the Carter budget deficit—as far worse than it actually was. Reagan scored what was seen as a virtual knockout punch in a televised debate in October 1980 by posing the famous rhetorical question "Are you better off now than you were four years ago?" It was a wonderful example of how bad economics often makes good politics. The fact was that real GDP per capita had risen about 8.5 percent over the four Carter years (1976:4 to 1980:4), so the answer for most Americans was undoubtedly yes. But Reagan's cleverly posed question strongly suggested that the answer was no. And with inflation raging and the short but sharp 1980 recession fresh in peoples' minds, many voters probably saw it that way. Perceptions lag behind realities. What we know for sure is that late-deciding voters broke overwhelmingly for Reagan (Dionne 1988).

The challenger campaigned on sharp cuts in income tax rates—basically the Kemp-Roth proposal—and won easily. Once installed as president, Reagan quickly pushed through a slightly slimmed-down version of Kemp-Roth. Instead of 10%–10%–10% over three years (which amounts to 27% in total), it was 5%–10%–10% in October 1981, July 1982, and July 1983 (which amounted to 23% in total). Top earners were not asked to wait that long, however; their need was apparently urgent. The highest bracket rate, which was 70 percent at the time, was dropped to 50 percent all at once in October 1981.[5]

The Economic Recovery Tax Act (ERTA) of 1981 also indexed individual tax brackets for inflation, a provision that had little effect on revenue in the short run but huge effects in the long run. Economists generally support indexing the tax code. After all, why should the rate of inflation, rather than the U.S. Congress, decide the tax rate? But arithmetic matters: if nothing was done to make up the lost revenue, indexing would add to future deficits.

Finally, although largely forgotten by now, ERTA also included truly massive reductions in corporate taxes, achieved mainly by accelerating depreciation allowances under the Accelerated Cost Recovery System, which was so generous that had it been allowed to go into effect with interest expenses remaining tax deductible, effective corporate "tax rates" on many types of equipment would have turned negative, that is, turned into subsidies. In fact, some of those subsidies would have been so large that the overall effective tax rates on these types of capital, including now corporate and personal taxes, would have become negative (Fullerton and Henderson 1984). Amazing! But it never happened. In the calmer atmosphere of 1982, Congress looked back at its 1981 handiwork and decided to repeal most of the corporate tax cuts in the Tax Equity and Fiscal Responsibility Act (TEFRA) of 1982.

---

5. Because October 1981 was near the end of the tax year, the 50 percent rate actually became fully effective only in 1982.

The sharp tax reductions embodied in ERTA, even net of the TEFRA increases, should have been expected to blow a big hole in the federal budget deficit. And they did. The U.S. Treasury subsequently estimated the revenue loss from ERTA in the fourth year after enactment to be 4.15 percent of GDP and the revenue gain from TEFRA in its fourth year to be 1.23 percent of GDP (Tempalski 2006). But Reaganite rhetoric denied that obvious piece of arithmetic. Led by its young and ideologically driven budget director, David Stockman, the Reagan economic team cobbled together budget numbers that projected massive tax cuts, a huge military buildup, and a balanced budget by fiscal year 1984 (White House 1981). (By way of contrast, Carter's last budget, for fiscal year 1981, had projected a deficit of 2.5% of GDP.) It looked like smoke and mirrors. And it was.

Unfortunately for the budget, though not for Reagan's political fortunes, magic tricks based on sleight of hand are illusions. That was the case for Reagan's original budget numbers. Stockman later confessed as much:

> Designing a comprehensive plan to bring about a sweeping change in national economic governance in forty days is a preposterous, wantonly reckless notion. . . . I soon became a veritable incubator of shortcuts, schemes, and devices to overcome the truth . . . that the budget gap couldn't be closed except by a dictator. . . . My expedients saw to it that critical loose ends were left unresolved everywhere. They ensured that the whole fiscal plan was embedded with contradictions and booby-trapped with hidden pressures. (Stockman 1986, 80, 105, 123)

As it turned out, the contradictions and booby traps prevailed, and the federal budget deficit ballooned from 2.5 percent of GDP in fiscal year 1981 to 5.7 percent of GDP in fiscal 1983. The latter was the largest figure since 1946, a time when demobilization from World War II was still in progress.

Table 8.1 displays the major budget categories in fiscal years 1981 and 1984, all as shares of GDP, plus, in italics, the Reagan team's February 1981 projection for fiscal 1984. The table makes a few things

TABLE 8.1. Federal Budget (as percent of GDP)

Fiscal Year	Receipts	Total Outlays	Defense	Interest	Other	Deficit
1981	19.1	21.6	5.0	2.2	14.4	2.5
1984 (actual)	16.9	21.6	5.8	2.6	13.2	4.7
1984 (projected)	*19.3*	*19.3*	*8.0*	*2.8*	*8.5*	*0.0*
Change 1981–1984	−2.2	0.0	0.8	0.4	−1.2	2.2

Source: White House (1981) and Office of Management and Budget.

obvious. First, the increase in military spending (0.8% of GDP) was more than offset by decreases in civilian spending (1.2% of GDP), so total noninterest spending fell a bit as a share of GDP. The drop in civilian spending was what Reagan and the Republicans wanted, though the magnitude was too small to truly "starve the beast." Maybe just put him on a diet.

Second, the explosion of the deficit is more than accounted for by sharply reduced tax revenue (2.2% of GDP) and correspondingly higher interest payments (0.4% of GDP), the latter being an arithmetical consequence of the larger budget deficits in the intervening years. Thus, the tax cut explains more than 100 percent of the deficit explosion under Reagan. In rhetoric, the Reagan revolution was supposed to spur so much growth that the deficit would shrink despite massive tax cuts, with some help from reductions in civilian spending. In reality, the tax cuts ballooned the deficit while the military buildup offset most of the civilian cuts. Incidentally, economic growth was about the same as under Carter, giving the lie to supply-side economics. One consequence of all this was that the deficit rose to levels unheard of in the United States since World War II.

This straightforward numerical comparison might be thought unfair, however, because one cause of the widening deficit was the severe recession, a by-product of Volcker's tight money, not Reagan's tax cuts, which were surely expansionary. That is true and quantitatively important for the fiscal 1982 and 1983 budgets. But the effect of the recession on the budget was already fading by fiscal 1984, which was a year of rapid growth. In fact, Congressional Budget Office

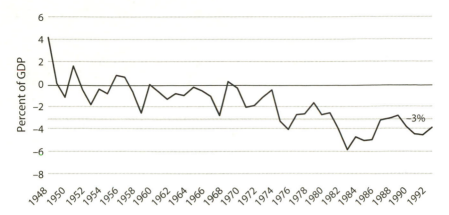

FIGURE 8.1. Federal budget deficit (or surplus) as percent of GDP, 1948–1993.

Source: Office of Management and Budget.

numbers show almost the same cyclical effect on the budget in 1984 as in 1981, which is hardly surprising since the unemployment rates of those two years were nearly identical (CBO 2019, 134, table C-1). Reaganomics created a deficit problem that remained at or near the top of the national agenda until Bill Clinton's second term.

Figure 8.1 illustrates just how unprecedented the Reagan peacetime deficits were. Between fiscal year 1948 and fiscal year 1981 (Carter's last budget), the federal budget deficit exceeded 3 percent of GDP only twice, in the recession-plagued fiscal years 1975 and 1976. The deficit over this time span averaged just 1.7 percent of GDP, and the debt-to-GDP ratio fell steadily even though the period included both the Korean War and the Vietnam War. Then came the Reagan budgets, starting in fiscal 1982, and the deficit-to-GDP ratio peaked at 5.9 percent in fiscal 1983 and came in under 3 percent of GDP only once over the next twelve fiscal years. The debt-to-GDP ratio rose sharply.

The Reagan budgetary episode also illustrates an important asymmetry in fiscal policy. It is easy, politically, to cut taxes or raise spending, a lesson that was not lost on Presidents George W. Bush and Donald Trump. But it is difficult, politically, to raise taxes or cut spending. Thus, while expansionary fiscal policy may be useful in fighting slumps, contractionary fiscal policy will probably not be

FIGURE 8.2. Quarterly growth of real GDP, 1981–1989.
Source: Bureau of Economic Analysis.

deployed to limit booms. The latter job was left, by default, to the Federal Reserve.

Unlike Richard Nixon, no one has accused Reagan of deliberately orchestrating a political business cycle to win reelection in 1984. But the ups and downs of the U.S. economy were just about ideal for that purpose, as shown in figure 8.2). As mentioned earlier, a deep recession began early in Reagan's first term, which from a crassly political perspective is exactly when an incumbent president would like to "take" his recession. Simple economics tells you that the sharp Volcker-Reagan clash between contractionary monetary policy and expansionary fiscal policy should have pushed up real interest rates, as it did. But it does not tell you to expect the dramatic bust-boom cycle that the United States experienced in the 1981–1984 period. Why did that happen?

The answer, in a word, is timing. Specifically, tight money and loose budgets were out of synch, with the former coming well before the latter. Volcker's tight monetary policy, it will be recalled, started late in 1979, was shelved for a while by the blowback from the credit controls disaster in 1980, and then took some time to gather steam once it resumed later that year. Allowing for the usual lags, we would expect the resulting drag on the economy to have begun in 1981 and to have been much stronger in 1982. The phased-in Reagan tax cuts had barely started by then, but they gathered steam in 1983 and 1984. So, while the tax cuts came too late to prevent the Volcker slump, they were perfectly timed to help slingshot the economy out of the recession in 1983 and 1984. Remember, monetary policy also turned expansionary around October 1982.

Figure 8.2 shows that the growth rate of real GDP over the final quarter of 1981 and the first quarter of 1982 averaged a miserable −5.2 percent (seasonally adjusted annual rate), while growth over the four quarters beginning 1983:2 averaged an astounding 8.6 percent. That remarkable turnaround was trumpeted effectively in President Reagan's famous "It's morning in America again" reelection commercial, and he annihilated his Democratic opponent, Walter Mondale, in the 1984 election.

Did the Reagan tax cuts spur growth? Certainly, but mainly from the demand side. No one seemed to notice or care at the time—or know even today—that the growth rate over Reagan's entire first term (3.26%) was almost exactly the same as during Carter's four years (3.19%). The United States experienced a bust followed by a boom in 1981–1984, producing a quadrennium of growth rates that was just about average. There was no supply-side miracle. But critically for Reagan's landslide victory, the demand-driven boom was going full steam when voters went to the polls in November 1984.

The Policy Mix

According to the standard mainstream view, contractionary monetary policy (à la Volcker) raises real interest rates, though perhaps only transitorily, and slows the growth of aggregate demand. According to that same mainstream view, expansionary fiscal policy (à la Reagan) raises real interest rates and speeds up the growth of aggregate demand. Put them both together at the same time, as Reagan and Volcker did, and you should expect real interest rates to rise sharply while the net effect on real output depends on how the tug-of-war just sketched works out. The rise in real interest rates will in turn dull incentives to invest. So, the Reagan-Volcker policy mix should hurt investment.

But supply-siders, led intellectually by the godfather of their doctrine, economist Robert Mundell, did not buy into this logic.

Rather, they claimed, tax cuts would fuel an acceleration of real economic growth, while tight money held inflation in check. The argument leaned on a rump version of the classical dichotomy asserted by Mundell, a brilliantly creative thinker who would later win the Nobel Prize (though not for supply-side economics). He had put it this way in a 1971 paper: "Monetary acceleration is not the appropriate starting point from which to initiate the expansion [in 1971], because of the risk of igniting inflationary expectations. Tax reduction is the appropriate method. It increases demand for consumer goods, which reverberates on supply. . . . Because of the idle capacity and unemployment, in many industries increased supply can be generated without causing economy-wide increases in costs. Tax reduction is not, therefore, inflationary from the standpoint of the economy as a whole" (Mundell 1971, 25).

Keynes thought he had demolished the classical dichotomy, which holds that the money supply alone controls the price level while other "real" factors (but not money) determine real output, in 1936. Apparently not. Mundell brought the classical dichotomy back as part of the supply-side revolution, thereby contradicting his own previous work on monetary and fiscal policy in the 1960s, seminal work that did win him the Nobel Prize (Mundell 1960). Under this new/old view, policy makers could simultaneously aim one weapon (tight money) at inflation and another (tax cuts) at growth.

Mundell communicated this unconventional view of the policy mix to Jack Kemp in 1976 (Wanniski introduced them), and it quickly became part of the supply-side canon. Largely on this basis, the Reagan team claimed that its hugely expansive fiscal program would not be inflationary. There was, they asserted, no policy-relevant trade-off between inflation and unemployment; anti-inflation monetary policy would take care of that. The Reagan-Volcker policy mix was thus a bold experiment though certainly not a controlled experiment (many other things were going on at the same time). How did the experiment work out? Which side of the policy mix debate came out looking better?

The answer is the conventional side, by a country mile. Figure 8.3 shows what happened to the real interest rate on ten-year Treasury

Robert A. Mundell (1932–2021)

Intellectual Father of Supply-Side Economics—and of Much Else

The brilliantly original and eccentric Robert "Bob" Mundell was born in Kingston, Ontario, Canada, in 1932 and earned his PhD in economics in 1956 from MIT. (Notice his age at the time.) After stints at Stanford University and Johns Hopkins University and on the staff of the International Monetary Fund, his academic career truly flourished at the University of Chicago, where in a scant five years (1966–1971) he influenced many of the top international monetary economists of the next generation.

But it was at the International Monetary Fund in the 1960s that Mundell and J. Marcus Fleming penned a pair of classic articles on monetary and fiscal policies under fixed versus floating exchange rates, forever known as the Mundell-Fleming model. That work, plus Mundell's pioneering analysis of optimum currency areas, won him the Nobel Prize in 1999. Ironically, Mundell is sometimes called the "father of the euro" because of his work on optimum currency areas even though his research clearly points to the opposite conclusion: that the countries that constitute the eurozone are almost certainly not an optimum currency area.

Mundell's Princeton essay on the supply-side policy mix, cited in the text, was far less noteworthy academically. But it turned out to be extremely noteworthy in the policy arena. There, Mundell suggested the policy mix of tax cuts to spur real growth plus tight money to fight inflation, a recipe later incorporated into supply-side economics.

securities from 1979 to 1989.[6] It clearly rose sharply in 1981–1983 as the Reagan program was first being proposed, then legislated, and then promulgated. Standard macroanalysis suggests that an upward leap in real long rates should reduce the investment share in GDP and push up the dollar exchange rate. The investment share did indeed fall, from 13.6 percent in 1981 to 12.1 percent in 1982 and 12.6 percent in 1983. But that's far from a clean comparison because recessions always take a toll on investment.

The impact on the dollar exchange rate perhaps offers a cleaner comparison (figure 8.4).[7] The trade-weighted value of the U.S. dollar against a basket of other major currencies soared by 54 percent between September 1980 and March 1985, with only a few minor interruptions. By 1985, pressure was mounting on the U.S. government to

6. There were no Treasury Inflation-Protected Securities in the 1980s, so the monthly real interest rates shown here are calculated by subtracting the CPI inflation rate (over the past twelve months) from the nominal ten-year Treasury rate.

7. The exchange rate shown is the Federal Reserve's old index of the trade-weighted dollar against major foreign currencies.

FIGURE 8.3. Real Treasury bond rate, 1979–1989.
Source: Board of Governors of the Federal Reserve System and Bureau of Labor Statistics.

do something about the overvalued dollar, which was, among other things, hollowing out the manufacturing base in the Midwest. (The term "Rust Belt" became common parlance in the early 1980s.) This pressure eventually led to the September 1985 Plaza Accord, named after the location of the negotiations at the Plaza Hotel in New York City. There the G5 nations (the United States, West Germany, the United Kingdom, Japan, and France) agreed to intervene in the foreign exchange markets to push the dollar down, something the market had been doing anyway since March 1985. When you give a push to a snowball that is already rolling downhill, the odds are with you. And the Plaza Accord succeeded. The dollar fell 10 percent between September 1985 and April 1986.

This Reagan-era experience with exchanges rates and the trade balance reminded American economists, who often lapse lazily into a closed-economy frame of mind, that large government budget deficits are likely to crowd out net exports as much as or more so than they crowd out domestic investment. As a share of real GDP, the trade deficit rose from roughly zero in 1980–1982 to about 2.4 percent of GDP in 1984, wreaking havoc on U.S. manufacturers and on exporters in general.

The response of policy makers was, as just noted, to knock down the value of the dollar via the Plaza Accord. In principle, the pressure

FIGURE 8.4. Trade-weighted value of the U.S. dollar, 1978–1988.
Source: Board of Governors of the Federal Reserve System.

on the dollar could have been alleviated instead by pairing tighter fiscal policy with the far easier monetary policy that the Volcker Fed began to pursue in October 1982. But by then there was a deep recession to fight, and the administration was not at all inclined to repeal the centerpiece of Reaganomics.[8] Income tax rate cuts took place in 1983 and 1984, right on the schedule that had been legislated in 1981. Fiscal expansion was in full force.

The Great Disinflation

I mentioned earlier that the Reagan team came to Washington promising near miracles on both the budget side (a balanced budget by 1984) and the growth side (a sharp acceleration of real GDP growth). They also came to town promising to slay the inflationary dragon, adopting the Mundellian dichotomy as their model. So, most supply-siders firmly supported the Federal Reserve's war on inflation, at least initially. According to supply-side doctrine, inflation would fall without a recession. In fact, it would fall while growth accelerated and unemployment fell. Or so it was claimed.

8. Except that, as noted earlier, much of the corporate cut that Congress had passed in 1981 was repealed in 1982.

Mainstream economists were highly skeptical of this halcyon view; I presume that Volcker was, too. Instead, many (including myself but probably not including Volcker) placed their bets on what I used to call the "Brookings rule of thumb," named mainly for Robert Gordon's series of Phillips curve papers published in the *Brookings Papers on Economic Activity* in the 1970s and 1980s (Blinder 2021).

Suppose the Phillips curve takes the simple form introduced in chapter 3, which, in the linear case, is

$$\pi_t = \theta + \pi_t^e - \beta U_t + \varepsilon_t. \tag{1}$$

If we use lagged inflation as a reasonable empirical proxy for expected inflation, equation (1) becomes

$$\Delta\pi_t = \beta(U^* - U_t) + \varepsilon_t, \tag{2}$$

where U^*, the natural rate of unemployment, is $U^* = \theta/\beta$. With β around ½, equation (2) says that each point year of additional unemployment reduces the inflation rate by about 0.5 point. That is the Brookings rule of thumb.

How well did this rule of thumb work in the Great Disinflation of the 1980s? Using 5.8 percent (the actual unemployment rate of 1979) as the estimated natural rate at the time, the Volcker disinflation featured 13.9 point years of "extra" unemployment during the six years 1980–1985, inclusive. And it brought the core Consumer Price Index (CPI) inflation rate down by 6.2 percentage points over that same period.[9] The ratio of the two implies a Phillips curve slope, β, of $6.2/13.9 = 0.45$. Not bad unless you were a believer in either the separation between the real and nominal sides of the economy advanced by Mundell or in the rational expectations view of the (vertical) Phillips curve of Lucas and Sargent.

As I emphasized in chapter 6, it is hard to understand how rational expectations triumphed in the academy while such a painful and pre-announced disinflation was proceeding in the real world. Blissfully,

9. The research CPI discussed in chapter 7 measures the decline in core inflation as 5.6 percentage points.

however, supply-side economics never made serious inroads in the academy. It was and remains to this day a political doctrine.

The Legacy of Reaganomics

Ronald Reagan left a multifaceted legacy. His military spending spree surely helped win the Cold War by crippling the Soviet Union, which tried like a drunken sailor to match the big spending of the much-richer United States but failed. He also pulled the Republican Party sharply to the right, compared to more moderate predecessors such as Gerald Ford, Richard Nixon, and Dwight Eisenhower. Reagan deserves to be viewed as a major historical figure (Wilentz 2008). But I will stick to macroeconomics here. What difference did Reaganomics make?

A naive answer might start with inflation, which was 11.8 percent (on a twelve-month CPI basis) when Reagan was inaugurated and 4.5 percent eight years later. That sounds like a big victory. But as we saw in chapter 7, that disinflation was largely the handiwork of Volcker and his colleagues at the Federal Reserve. Apart from giving the Fed verbal running room early in Reagan's first term, which was important, nothing the Reagan administration did was actually anti-inflationary.

On the growth front, nothing notable happened under Reagan. Yes, the sharp bounce-back from the 1981–1982 recession was impressive, and the tax cuts no doubt gave it extra strength. Incentives do matter. But in terms of real growth, the eight-year Reagan period looks about the same as the four Carter years that preceded it and is slightly worse than the eight Clinton years that followed it. Supply-siders promised a growth miracle, but they did not deliver one.

The biggest economic impacts of Reaganomics were probably on tax policy and the budget. Before the Reagan presidency, there was a bipartisan understanding that tax cuts—which everyone likes—had to be constrained by deficit considerations. There was also an unspoken consensus that the federal budget deficit should not exceed 3 percent of GDP (see figure 8.1). Reagan's political success blew both of those norms out of the water. As Vice President Dick Cheney would later put it, "Reagan proved deficits don't matter"

(Suskind 2004, 291). I'm pretty sure he meant they don't matter *politically*.

In any case, federal budget deficits averaged 3.3 percent of GDP from Reagan until the coronavirus pandemic struck, a period that includes Clinton's string of budget surpluses. By comparison, deficits averaged just 0.9 percent of GDP from fiscal year 1947 until the Reagan presidency. Furthermore, two of the three Republican presidents since Reagan have pushed massive tax cuts through Congress. And the third, George H. W. Bush, may have lost his 1992 reelection bid because he broke his "no new taxes" pledge in order to shrink the deficit. Republicans after Reagan forgot about fiscal prudence and became the party of tax cuts.

That said, the need to reduce the budget deficit via what Jude Wanniski had derisively called "root canal economics" (tax hikes and spending cuts) became the central economic policy concern of the next three presidential terms (Bush, Clinton, Clinton). If fiscal policy is focused on reducing the deficit regardless of whether the economy is booming or slumping, the job of stabilization policy is ceded to the central bank, which, of course, is precisely what happened in the United States.

Last but certainly not least, the desirability of tax cuts, whether the budget is near balance or showing a big deficit and regardless of whether the economy is soaring or sagging, has become the central tenet of Republican economics. For example, when Trump came into office, the federal government already had a large budget deficit (about 3.5% of GDP), and the nation had a low unemployment rate (4.7%). These preconditions do not obviously militate for a tax cut. But Trump proposed a large tax cut anyway, and the Republican-controlled Congress gleefully passed it. Would that have happened without Reagan's legacy?

Chapter Summary

When Ronald Reagan took office in January 1981, Paul Volcker's excruciatingly tight monetary policy was in the pipeline, but the severe recession of 1981–1982 was not yet in sight. Furthermore, the supply-side doctrine that the Reagan team embraced held that tax cuts could expand the economy while tight money fought inflation. So, there was no conflict between Reagan and Volcker at first. The new president supported tight money.

This uneasy peace fell apart, however, as the Reagan-Volcker policy mix of loose fiscal policy and tight monetary policy met up with reality. The huge Reagan tax cuts, which were largely accomplished by cutting personal income tax rates, ballooned the federal budget deficit (as a share of GDP) to levels not seen in the United States since 1946. Meanwhile, the Federal Reserve's allegedly monetarist policy sent both interest rates and the dollar exchange rate through the roof and, not incidentally, made Volcker and the Fed politically unpopular.

Higher interest rates took a toll on domestic investment, though perhaps not as large a toll as expected. More sizable effects were seen on U.S. net exports, which taught U.S. economists to be more open-economy minded when it comes to thinking about crowding out. Meanwhile, inflation disappeared rapidly as a consequence of two back-to-back recessions, the dwindling effects of supply shocks, and the rising dollar. Conventional Phillips curves of the day, which had been modified to account for supply shocks, tracked the disinflation quite well.

There are two lasting and important legacies of the Reagan-Volcker episode on monetary and fiscal policy. First, the traditional aversion to budgets deficits disappeared, at least within the Republican Party.[10] Deficits have been systematically larger (as shares of GDP) since Reagan than before him, and the attraction of "supply-side" tax cuts to Republicans has never died. Second and related, the job of stabilization policy was essentially delegated to monetary policy for over a quarter century. After all, if one party promotes tax cuts regardless of the macroeconomic situation and the other party is bent on reducing the deficits it inherits, fiscal stabilization policy has essentially been thrown out the window.

---

10. Bill Clinton would later dedicate part of his presidency to deficit reduction. See chapter 11.

9

The Long Expansion of the 1980s

The reports of my death are greatly exaggerated.
—MARK TWAIN, 1897

No one knew it at the time, of course, and after two recessions within three years, no one dared assume it, but the expansion that began in November 1982 was destined to last into 1990, making it the second longest in U.S. business cycle history at the time. (The expansion from June 2009 to February 2020 would later shatter all records.) Just like the 106-month expansion of the 1960s, the long cyclical upswing of the 1980s eventually reignited breathless claims that the business cycle was dead[1] (which it wasn't) and ushered in what came to be called the Great Moderation (which it was).[2]

The Great Moderation

Figure 9.1 offers one depiction of the Great Moderation, which was indeed great. The name refers to the sharp reduction in the volatility of real GDP growth from quarter to quarter or year to year that

---

1. For one example, see Kilborn (1987a).
2. The term seems to have been coined by James Stock and Mark Watson (2003) but was popularized by Federal Reserve governor Ben Bernanke (2004).

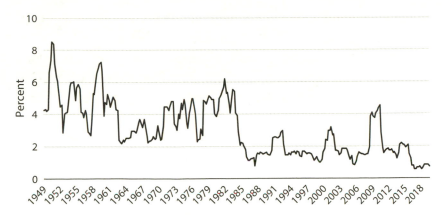

FIGURE 9.1. Standard deviation of real GDP growth rate, 1949–2019.
Source: Author's computations from Bureau of Economic Analysis data.

began around 1984. (Inflation was also low and reasonably stable for most of this period.) The specific measure shown here is the eight-quarter, moving-average standard deviation of real GDP growth. But except for details and timing, four-, twelve-, or sixteen-quarter windows would show a similar pattern. The particular volatility measure shown in figure 9.1 dropped from an average of 4.5 percent over the quarters spanning 1949:1 through 1983:4 to just 0.8 percent from 1983:4 through 2019:4, after which no one thought much about "moderation" of any kind. As can be seen in the figure, the decline in volatility was abrupt, and not even the Great Recession of 2007–2009 brought it back to its previous level except for a few fleeting quarters.

Once this phenomenon was noticed by scholars, a cottage industry developed to explain what had happened. Was the decline in volatility due to improved stabilization policy, to structural changes in the economy (e.g., better inventory management or the shift from goods to services), or just to better luck in the form of smaller shocks (e.g., less volatile commodity prices)? Stock and Watson's (2002) thorough, though early, analysis of multiple time series covering the period from 1959:1 through 2001:3 concluded that the reduction in variance—which was smaller in their shorter sample than in figure 9.1—could not be attributed to structural changes. Rather, they estimated that it stemmed from a combination of improved monetary policy (10–25%), identifiable good luck in the form of smaller productivity and commodity price shocks (20–30%), and unidentifiable good luck in the form of smaller stochastic shocks. Better fiscal policy, they concluded, played a trivial role. In short, monetary policy helped a little in producing the Great Moderation, but it was mainly a long streak of good luck.

Subsequent research suggested a somewhat larger role for countercyclical monetary policy, but essentially no one has attributed much (if any) of the Great Moderation to improvements in fiscal policy (Gali and Gambetti 2009; Benati and Surico 2009). And no wonder. As hinted already and as this and coming chapters will show, one main reason why fiscal policy played such a small role in moderating the business cycle is that it was not used much for stabilization purposes after Ronald Reagan's first term. Rather, over the years 1984–1997, federal tax and spending policy turned almost exclusively toward one overriding goal: reducing the budget deficit, which is definitely not what Walter Heller meant when he spoke of fiscal policy serving as a "balance wheel."

As noted in chapter 8, the Reagan tax cuts ballooned the deficit into the 4–5 percent of GDP range beginning in fiscal year 1982, and it remained above 3 percent of GDP virtually every year through fiscal year 1993. Whether the economy was weak or strong and whether monetary policy was easing or tightening, fiscal debates in this period invariably revolved around cutting spending or (more rarely) raising taxes. None of this talk sounded much like "fine-tuning," or any kind of "tuning" for that matter. In fact, current Congressional Budget Office data show only one fiscal year (1987) between 1984 and 2002 in which the standardized budget deficit or surplus moved by as much as 1 percent of GDP. Fiscal stabilization policy—in the sense of using timely changes in spending or taxes to manage aggregate demand—went into hibernation.

Tax Reform: The Impossible Dream Becomes Possible

I will deal with the focus on the budget deficit in more detail in chapter 10. For now, it is worth mentioning that the one big fiscal policy action of President Reagan's second term was tax reform rather than either lowering taxes (as in 1981) or raising them (as in 1982). The Tax Reform Act of 1986 was also, in the view of many economists (including me), the finest tax law Congress has passed in the postwar era and maybe ever. But its passage required a bit of a political miracle.

Like seemingly all presidents, Reagan bemoaned the complexity of the Internal Revenue Code. In his January 1984 State of the Union address, he called upon the Treasury Department to deliver a comprehensive tax reform plan by December—that is, after the November 1984 election, thank you. But tax reform was far from a major point of emphasis in Reagan's speech. His now-famous "clarion call" for reform actually consisted of exactly one paragraph:

> Let us go forward with an historic reform for fairness, simplicity, and incentives for growth. I am asking [Treasury] Secretary Don Regan for a plan for action to simplify the entire tax code, so all taxpayers, big and small, are treated more fairly. And I believe such a plan could result in that underground economy being brought into the sunlight of honest tax compliance. And it could make the tax base broader, so personal tax rates could come down, not go up. I've asked that specific recommendations, consistent with those objectives, be presented to me by December 1984. (Reagan 1984a)

The Treasury's nonpolitical professional staff was brimming with ideas for reform and now had their marching orders: Simplify the tax code. Don't use reform as a way to raise revenue. Don't touch the mortgage interest deduction (though that instruction was not in the speech). And please don't report back until after the election.

These skilled technocrats made good use of their newfound freedom. When the Treasury's initial handiwork was published in November 1984 (U.S. Department of the Treasury, Office of the Secretary 1984), political hair started catching on fire all over Washington. "Judging by the anguished squeals that greeted what came to be called 'Treasury I,' you might have thought the document proposed repealing the bill of rights, reinstituting slavery, and outlawing motherhood" (Blinder 1987a, 161). It didn't do any of these things, of course. Rather, the Treasury careerists had behaved like the well-trained professional technocrats they were and had proposed sending a large herd of sacred cows (not including the mortgage interest deduction) off to the slaughterhouse.

Corporate investment incentives, some of which had originated in the 1981 tax cuts, would be slashed. So would tax breaks that the oil and gas, real estate, finance, and defense-contracting industries had enjoyed for years. A variety of fringe benefits for workers would lose their tax-exempt status. Perhaps most audaciously, capital gains would be indexed and then taxed like ordinary income, ending a politically sensitive tax preference that dated back to 1921. The list went on, with virtually every item sounding an alarm bell in some lobbyists' offices.

It's a good bet that most of these reform ideas came as surprises to Secretary Donald Regan, a former CEO of Merrill Lynch, who introduced the plan by emphasizing that it "was written on a word processor" and thus easily changed (Wicker 1985b). This was not exactly a ringing endorsement of the Treasury staff's handiwork! Changes came quickly as the political class discovered what the proposal included, and lobbyists descended on the Treasury and White House to get much of it excised. When the next draft, called "Treasury II" (U.S. Department of the Treasury, Office of the Secretary 1985), was submitted to Congress in May 1985, it had been politically scrubbed. Nonetheless, it was still identifiably a tax reform bill, not a tax cut. Paul Samuelson gave it this half-hearted endorsement in a newspaper column: "The present mishmash is a bit worse than the new rigamarole" (Samuelson 1985). He was ungenerous. The "rigamarole" was a big improvement over the "mishmash."

Tax reform next met up with the U.S. Congress, where fairness is in the eye of the beholder, concern with economic efficiency is hard to find, and rigamarole is beloved as a wonderful way to dispense favors. The first stop on the Hill was at the House of Representatives, where the Committee on Ways and Means was chaired by the old-school (and very effective) congressman Dan Rostenkowski (D-IL) of Chicago. By the time a bill emerged from Ways and Means, many loopholes had been restored, a bunch of new ones had been added,

Rostenkowski was admitting that "we have not written a perfect law" (Wicker 1985a), and few were disputing his assessment.

The scene then shifted to the Republican-controlled U.S. Senate, where prospects for reform looked even bleaker. Senate Finance Committee Chair Bob Packwood (R-OR) had already declared his opposition to tax reform. It was therefore no surprise that as the committee set out to craft its own bill, the proceedings were dominated by senators who seemed to have a lot of friends who deserved loopholes. As Senator Daniel Patrick Moynihan (D-NY) memorably put it, "We commenced to overhaul the tax code . . . and with the best of intentions made things steadily worse. On the day we voted the depreciation life of an oil refinery to be five years, something told us our immortal souls were in danger" (Moynihan 1986). Tax reform looked dead.

But it wasn't. Persuaded by some combination of Senator Bill Bradley's (D-NJ) substantive arguments in favor of reform, some serious reelection difficulties back home in Oregon, and the allure of a superlow 27 percent top income tax rate,[3] Packwood executed a complete 180-degree turn in April 1986, announcing a radical plan to eliminate most itemized deductions in return for sharply lower tax rates. It was the economists' age-old dream: broaden the base, lower the rates. But this time it had real political force behind it, not just advocacy from a bunch of eggheads with no political clout. Before the lobbyists could effectively man the battlements, Packwood jammed an amazingly clean reform bill through his committee and then through the whole Senate on an astonishing 97–3 vote.

At that point, Congress had two very different bills on its hands: a loophole-laden House bill and a comparatively clean Senate bill. Compromising the many differences between the two looked to be a difficult and delicate political task. But the action in the Senate had changed the political dynamic dramatically. Rostenkowski's astute antennae had picked that up, and he surprised everyone by joining forces with Packwood. The two chairs then fashioned a compromise that passed both houses easily and was signed into law by

3. That top rate was subsequently raised to 28 percent to get a bit more revenue.

President Reagan. One committee staffer, who watched in astonishment as the two chairs batted down one proposed amendment after another in the House-Senate conference, penned the following bit of doggerel:

> Here's to the tax-reform conference,
> Home of low rates and high drama
> Where Rosty speaks only to Packwood
> And Packwood speaks only on camera.
>
> (BIRNBAUM AND MURRAY 1987, 281)

The act of political jujitsu that got the Tax Reform Act of 1986 (TRA86) passed is an interesting story in and of itself.[4] But this book concentrates on economics, not politics, and in particular on macroeconomics. And macroeconomically, the act was not a big deal. It is far too simple just to count up projected revenue gains and losses and net them out. In terms of impact on GDP, not to mention allocative effects, one tax dollar is not the same as every other. Nonetheless, the net effect of tax reform on the budget is a reasonable place to start. Reagan wanted the reform to be revenue neutral, and Congress delivered approximately that (CBO 1998b, 25, table 10).

Allocative effects are an entirely different matter, however. Most obviously, the tax sheltering industry—which had enjoyed major outposts in real estate and oil and gas for decades—was decimated. "There is little doubt that investments in tax shelters have all but disappeared since the enactment of TRA86," wrote one tax expert a decade later (Samwick 1996, 194). Resources flowed out of rental housing and other tax-favored investment activities. Relative to the status quo ante, the reform also favored equity financing over debt, dividend payouts over retention (which generates capital gains), S corporations (which are pass-throughs taxed at the owners' personal rates) over conventional C corporations, and much more. The tax changes were complicated and comprehensive. But on balance they did not have major effects on aggregate demand.

---

4. It is told, among many places, in Birnbaum and Murray (1987).

Monetary Policy in the Great Moderation

On the monetary front, the Volcker Fed had eased up in the closing months of 1982, as noted earlier, and interest rates began to fall. Though interrupted by occasional increases—due to Federal Reserve policy moves, the business cycle, or both—the drop in both real and nominal interest rates would turn out to be a major phenomenon of the Great Moderation and after. It is an exaggeration, but one that does little violence to the facts, to say that the ten-year Treasury rate has been basically falling since the fall of 1981 (when it peaked just below 16%), a period of about forty years.

Many factors underpin this stunning development. The most obvious reason for lower nominal interest rates is, of course, the decline of expected inflation. But real rates also fell, and that development presumably traces to changes in the worldwide balance of saving and investment. One clear element is the rise of China, with its huge saving rates. Another may be that newer technologies require less investment than older ones did. Compare Facebook with the Grand Central Railroad. All that said, a full answer is not yet in, and economists will be wrestling for years with the question of why interest rates fell so much and for so long.

There were, however, a few times during those decades in which rates rose, and one of them is of particular interest here. As figure 9.2 shows, the ten-year Treasury rate declined steadily and sharply from its September 1981 peak into the 10 percent range by the spring of 1983. But then, with the economy rapidly picking up steam (the average annual growth rate over the six quarters from 1983:1 through 1984:2 was a jaw-dropping 7.8%), interest rates began to climb. By May–June 1984, the ten-year rate was back up to nearly 14 percent.

These large rate increases were natural and certainly not a product of any deliberate Federal Reserve tightening. In fact, one might more legitimately attribute them to Reagan's expansionary fiscal policies than to anything the Volcker Fed did. But the unemployment rate was still high in July 1984 (7.5%), and the Reagan White House, thinking mainly about the November election, did not relish higher interest rates.

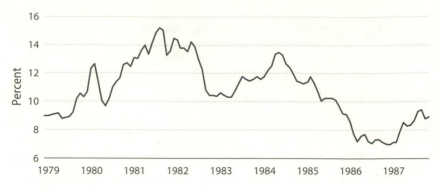

FIGURE 9.2. Ten-year Treasury yield, 1979–1987.
Source: Board of Governors of the Federal Reserve System.

One day that summer, Volcker was summoned to a White House meeting with the president. On arrival, he found Reagan sitting with his chief of staff, the formidable James Baker, and looking "a bit uncomfortable" (Volcker 2018, 118–19). While Reagan remained silent, Baker delivered a simple and direct message: "The president is ordering you not to raise interest rates before the election." Notice the commanding verb here—*ordering*. That, of course, vastly eclipsed the president's authority. Volcker reports being "stunned," and he was not one to take orders. But he was not planning to raise rates anyway. So he merely "walked out without saying a word" (119), which must have left Baker nonplussed. In any event, monetary policy was essentially unchanged through the 1984 election.

For most of the remainder of Volcker's second term, the central bank's attention was focused more on a series of banking crises and near-crises, including the savings and loan (S&L) fiasco discussed below, and international issues, such as the Latin American debt crises and the Plaza Accord, than it was on conventional monetary policy. The funds rate never rose much above 8 percent or fell much below 6 percent during that time.[5] All part of the Great Moderation, you might say.

Inside the Fed, however, Volcker had to quell what he called an "attempted coup" by the four Reagan appointees: Vice Chair

---

5. In those days, the federal funds rate target range was about 400 basis points wide (e.g., 8–12%), and the FOMC took its target ranges for the Ms seriously.

Preston Martin and Governors Manuel Johnson, Wayne Angell, and Martha Seger. At a routine Federal Reserve Board meeting on Monday, February 24, 1986, "Martin made an out-of-the-blue proposal to cut the Federal Reserve's discount rate" (Volcker 2018, 142), which passed on a 4–3 "party line" vote. Volcker felt ambushed and threatened to resign. Angell and Martin offered Volcker a second vote, which the chair won. Had the coup worked, the stock market might have crashed that very day. Instead, it waited until October 19, 1987.

As mentioned in chapter 8, the value of the U.S. dollar also became a major issue for the administration, the Fed, and other nations in the 1984–1987 period. The Plaza Accord of September 1985 helped push the dollar down from its dizzying heights, and the Louvre Accord of February 1987 subsequently tried (less successfully) to arrest its fall. But exchange rate issues were still in the air as the expiry of Volcker's second four-year term (August 1987) approached. The biggest questions in the world of monetary policy in the United States and abroad became whether Reagan would reappoint Volcker, who had by then acquired Olympian stature but had shown himself to be less than pliant, and whether Volcker would accept another four-year term.

Had the decision been up to the financial markets, there is no doubt that Volcker would have been reappointed by acclamation—and chained to his desk. But the decisions belonged to Reagan and Volcker. Motivated in part by his wife's ill health, Volcker had been thinking (and talking to his wife) about leaving for years. He was torn between his personal obligations and his strong attachment to public service. Reagan's top aides, including James Baker, who by then was secretary of the treasury, presumably wanted Volcker out (Woodward 2000, 19–21). But Reagan himself either equivocated or was inscrutable.

Volcker reports that Baker "told me that, in effect, it was my responsibility to stay" at a meeting in late May 1987. Yet "my overall impression [was] that he would not be personally heartbroken by my decision to leave" (Volcker 2018, 149–50). When Volcker informed Reagan on June 1 that he did not want to continue in office, "Jim Baker was delighted. 'We got the son of a bitch,' he told a New York friend" (Woodward 2000, 24). So, the answer to the classic question "Did he jump or was he pushed?" may have been both.

In any case, Reagan—or perhaps Baker—had a replacement ready: Alan Greenspan. Greenspan subsequently became as much of a monetary god as Volcker. But in the summer of 1987 Greenspan was new to the Fed, untested, and viewed as suspiciously political. He had, after all, been closely associated with the disgraced Richard Nixon, who had appointed him chair of the Council of Economic Advisers shortly before resigning in August 1974.

The Savings and Loan Debacle

To last as long as it did, the Great Moderation had to survive a number of hazards that imperiled it. One such hazard was the S&L debacle. The relevant events are sometimes called the S&L crisis, but that seems a grave misnomer for something that took years to develop and then years to fix. It was more like a slow-motion train wreck followed by an agonizingly slow repair job.

While the details are complex, the basic source of the debacle was simple: S&Ls, or more generally thrift institutions, were designed to lend long and borrow short. That sounds like the normal sort of maturity transformation that banks and other financial intermediaries perform routinely. But there was an important quantitative difference: S&Ls concentrated on loans that were very long, such as thirty-year fixed-rate mortgages, and financed themselves with deposits, which can turn over quickly. When the maturity mismatch is that extreme, rising interest rates can do more than just drive the market value of a thrift institution's assets (mainly mortgages) below the market value of its liabilities (mainly time deposits, which remain at par), thereby leading to economic (but not regulatory) insolvency. If rates rise sharply enough, they can even push the cash outflows from interest payments on deposits (which adjust relatively quickly) above the cash inflows from preexisting fixed-rate mortgages (which do not), thereby causing operating losses and, potentially, acute illiquidity.

Both of these feared events occurred when the Federal Reserve jacked up interest rates sharply under Volcker's post-1979 monetary

FIGURE 9.3. Interest rates on thirty-year fixed-rate mortgages and three-month certificates of deposit, 1975–1985.
Source: Board of Governors of the Federal Reserve System.

policy (figure 9.3). In the summer of 1977, the thirty-year mortgage rate was almost 9 percent and the rate on three-month certificates of deposit was a bit over 6 percent, leaving S&Ls a comfortable net interest margin. By early 1980 that margin was gone or had turned negative, leaving quite a few thrifts either insolvent on a mark-to-market basis or headed there. In 1978, a mere 1.4 percent of thrift assets were held in institutions that were operating in the red, a sign of a healthy industry. By 1980, that figure was over 30 percent, a sign of a sick industry. And by the second half of 1981 it was over 90 percent, a sign of a virtually dead industry (White 1991, 70, table 5.3).

But these zombie thrifts were allowed to stagger on for years. Because S&Ls did not keep their books on a mark-to-market basis, they remained technically solvent for both Generally Accepted Accounting Principles and regulatory purposes long after they were economically insolvent. The huge gap between regulatory capital (which looked fine) and true economic capital (which in many cases was gone) allowed regulators and Congress to keep these institutions alive rather than shut them down. The latter would have required paying off the insured depositors, something legislators were less than eager to do.

Staying alive, however, meant continuing to lend, and many thrifts gambled for redemption by making increasingly risky loans. In consequence, the industry grew rapidly during the years 1983–1985 even though it was in its death throes, a case of backwards capitalism. After 1985, however, declines in real estate values, especially in Texas, hammered the final nails into the thrifts' coffins as did the Tax Reform Act of 1986, which devastated real estate tax shelters. So, most of the S&Ls that had gambled for redemption lost their gambles. On top of all that, there was a disgraceful amount of fraud personified by but not limited to Charles Keating and the infamous Keating Five.[6]

Congress and the Reagan administration also made a gamble but one of a different sort: that they could keep the lid on the problem until after the 1988 election. That gamble paid off, though it required such devices as irresponsible deregulation (e.g., allowing expanded lending powers), regulatory forbearance, and even allowing or encouraging accounting chicanery plus, of course, closing down some of the worst thrifts, which drained the deposit insurance fund.[7] Through such legerdemain, the Potemkin village managed to remain standing even as the underlying problem worsened. But the public's anger mounted along with the banks' losses. There was anger at the industry, anger at the regulators who had failed to prevent the debacle, and anger at politicians for "bailing out" the ill-behaved banks.

It was left to the new Bush administration, elected in November 1988, to finish the job, which it did starting with passage of the Financial Institutions Reform, Recovery, and Enforcement Act in August 1989. The act tightened regulation of S&Ls, recapitalized the deposit insurance fund (though inadequately), raised insurance premiums on both thrifts and banks to bring more revenue into

6. Among many sources that could be cited on Keating and other S&L crooks, see Mayer (1990).

7. In those days, S&Ls had their own insurance fund, run by the Federal Savings and Loan Insurance Corporation, which was later merged into the Federal Deposit Insurance Corporation.

the fund, and established the Resolution Trust Corporation (RTC) to dispose of the assets acquired from insolvent thrifts, a task that took years.

In the end, about one-third of the nation's three thousand S&Ls failed. The budgetary arithmetic was unpleasant. Taking over an institution with negative net worth left a financial hole that the RTC—which is to say, the taxpayers—were obliged to fill. Slightly hysterical early estimates of the costs ran as high as $500 billion,[8] which was over 8 percent of GDP at the time, a daunting figure. In the end, however, the cleanup efforts themselves plus a strong economy helped raise real estate values and, commensurately, reduce the RTC's and thus the taxpayers' bill to "only" about $130 billion, or 2 percent of GDP (GAO 1996).

There was an important if obvious lesson here. But it was somehow lost on members of Congress who, years later, refused to support the Troubled Asset Relief Program in 2008. If the government steps in to buy bad assets on a large scale, whether directly or indirectly, the prices of those assets will rise, which will reduce the cleanup bill. The S&L cleanup presented a large bill nonetheless, one that contributed both to continuing large federal budget deficits and to political anguish.

The Stock Market Crash of 1987

The stock market crash of 1987 presented a second potential hazard to the Great Moderation. It was also Alan Greenspan's baptism by fire as Fed chair. Greenspan's first day in office was August 11, 1987. The stock market, which had been on an almost uninterrupted climb for five years, began to swoon that very month, and it got worse in October. Then on a single frightening day—Black Monday, October 19, 1987—the Dow Jones Industrial Average shed almost 23 percent of

---

8. For one example, see Thomas (2000), who wrote that "the public did not realize the monster Congress had created until taxpayers got the roughly $500 billion bill for bailing out the thrift industry."

its value, nearly matching the percentage drop on Black Tuesday, October 29, 1929. Market participants were shell-shocked, as was the Reagan White House. And both turned to the Fed for salvation. Hardly anyone, it seemed, gave a thought to using fiscal policy to cushion the impending blow to aggregate demand.[9]

As luck would have it, Greenspan had been scheduled to travel to Dallas that day to address the American Bankers' Association. He and his colleagues decided it would look panicky if he cancelled the speech. So, Greenspan boarded the plane for the three-hour flight from Washington to Dallas that morning, even though the Dow was already down about 200 points (roughly 9% at the time). There were no telephones on airplanes in those days, so the rookie Fed chair must have had quite a nerve-racking flight. When he landed, he immediately asked one of his Federal Reserve Bank of Dallas greeters where the market had closed. The answer seemed reassuring at first: "It was down five oh eight." Thinking that meant a mere 5.08 Dow points, Greenspan breathed a sigh of relief: "Great, what a terrific rally." But the pained expression on his colleague's face suggested anything but relief. The Dow had actually fallen an amazing 508 points.[10] At 2021 levels of stock prices, that would be over 8,000 points on the Dow—in one day!

What caused the great stock market crash of 1987? Despite volumes of study, we still don't know[11] and probably never will. Some commentary at the time blamed James Baker's not-very-veiled threat to depreciate the dollar, which came on the Saturday just before Black Monday. But that explanation always seemed thin to me. Others blamed "portfolio insurance," a new-fangled way to automate trading, in this case leading to heavy computerized selling into a falling market. In the end, Robert Shiller's survey-based

9. The Congressional Budget Office's time series on the budget deficit/surplus as a share of GDP shows virtually no change between fiscal 1987 and fiscal 1988.

10. This story is told in many places. My source is Greenspan (2007, 105).

11. See, for example, the multivolume Brady Report (Presidential Task Force on Market Mechanisms 1988).

nonexplanation may provide the best explanation: the main "news" that motivated selling that day was reports that other people were selling (Shiller 1989, 379–402). Panicky selling induced more panicky selling, and portfolio insurance accelerated that.

When a nation's stock market crashes, there are two sorts of possible reactions by its central bank, each with many variants:

Wrong decision. You can prop up the stock market any way you can to prevent further losses and maybe even to restore some of the destroyed wealth. In 1987, that would have meant slashing interest rates despite the strong economy.

Right decision. You can make it clear—both by words and by actions—that you stand behind the financial system, especially the banks, and will serve as the lender of last resort as much as necessary to confine the damage.

The Greenspan Fed made the right decision. The next day, it issued a statement that was short but to the point: "The Federal Reserve, consistent with its responsibilities as the Nation's central bank, affirmed today its readiness to serve as a source of liquidity to support the economic and financial system." In plain English, or at least as plain as the Fed was willing to be at the time, the discount window was now wide open to any banks—and maybe even to any brokerage houses—that might need it. Those reassuring words did the trick. Hardly any banks actually showed up looking for loans, the Fed accommodated a sharp but brief surge in demand for excess reserves, and the threat of a general financial panic dissipated quickly. The stock market even made up over half of its Black Monday losses within days and all of them (remember, it was almost a 23% drop!) in less than two years.

The response to the crash wasn't really a hard call, but Greenspan had clearly done the right thing. He had also displayed calm under pressure and proven that he could handle a financial crisis as well as Volcker could. No one at the time talked about a "Greenspan put"

TABLE 9.1. Annualized real GDP growth rates, quarterly, 1987–1988

	Q1	Q2	Q3	Q4
1987	3.0%	4.4%	3.5%	**7.0%**
1988	2.1%	5.4%	2.4%	5.4%

Source: Bureau of Economic Analysis.

under equity values; that talk would come later. Rather, everyone seemed happy and relieved at the new Fed chair's stellar performance. The Greenspan legend had begun.

Monetary Policy after the Storm: The Nearly Perfect Soft Landing

Most important to macroeconomic history, the October 1987 stock market crash made nary a dent in the strong recovery. Table 9.1 shows the annualized growth rates of real GDP over the eight quarters of 1987 and 1988. Not only was there no recession, but you can't even detect an impact of the crash—which happened early in the bold-faced fourth quarter of 1987—in these numbers.

Neither could the Federal Open Market Committee (FOMC) as it watched the data unfold in real time. Immediately after the crash, the committee provided more reserves to the banking system, and the federal funds rate, which was then managed in a very wide range (5–9% before the crash and 4–8% after), drifted down by about 100 basis points. After that, the funds rate did not change much for months, as shown in figure 9.4.

As 1988 progressed, however, sighs of relief at the Fed gave way to concern about potential overheating and a consequent rise in inflation. Remember, memories of high inflation and of the pain the Volcker Fed had inflicted to end it were still fresh in central bankers' minds. From early 1987 to early 1988, the unemployment rate trailed down gradually from 6.6 percent to 5.7 percent, a number that was at or below most economists' estimates of the natural rate at the

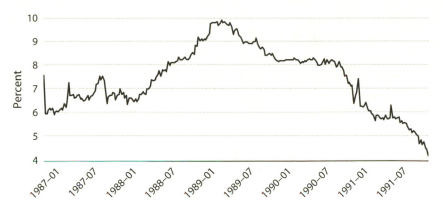

FIGURE 9.4. Effective federal funds rate, weekly, 1987–1991.
Source: Board of Governors of the Federal Reserve System.

time. That view of the natural rate of unemployment was supported by the performance of inflation: core Consumer Price Index inflation crept up from 3.8 percent in the year ending December 1986 to 4.4 percent in the year ending March 1988. Not much, but the Fed did not want to get "behind the curve." So, the FOMC decided at its March 1988 meeting to "increase slightly the degree of pressure on reserve positions." Those words were code for a rate hike of 25 basis points, but the FOMC was saying nothing in public back then. America's secretive central bank stuck to code words—even for internal purposes!

The 1988–1989 tightening cycle lasted about a year, during which time the Fed raised the funds rate by about 3.25 percentage points and then, importantly, stopped (see figure 9.4). Real GDP growth slowed down commensurately from an average of about 3.8 percent in 1988 to an average of 2.8 percent in 1989, a modest deceleration. Consistent with that, inflation, which had been creeping up slowly in 1987 and the first half of 1988, basically flatlined at around 4.5 percent in the second half of 1988 and throughout 1989. The episode had all the makings of a perfect soft landing at the so-called NAIRU (nonaccelerating inflation rate of unemployment), the holy grail of monetary policy. Then another oil shock hit.

This time it was not from the Organization of the Petroleum Exporting Countries (OPEC) but instead from Saddam Hussein, whose army invaded oil-rich Kuwait on August 2, 1990. The price of a barrel of crude oil (West Texas intermediate) skyrocketed from around $16 in July to over $40 in October. While the 1990 oil shock was short (it was over by February 1991), it was not sweet. The violent spike in oil prices was enough to push the country into the short recession of 1990–1991 and to destroy the Fed's hopes of a soft landing. GDP growth, which had averaged about 3 percent during the first half of 1990 (a nice pace for a soft landing), plummeted to an average of –1.7 percent over the next three quarters. The National Bureau of Economic Research dates the business cycle trough as March 1991, but the unemployment rate kept rising until the middle of 1992, leading journalists to dub the 1991–1992 period "the jobless recovery." The long expansion of the 1980s was over.

On the price front, core Consumer Price Index inflation rose from a low of 4.3 percent in the fall of 1989 to a high of 5.6 percent in early 1991. Headline inflation rose more, of course, because of oil prices, topping 6 percent in the final four months of 1990. The FOMC responded to this inflationary uprising by raising the federal funds rate sharply (by 100 basis points) but only briefly (for about a month in January 1991), despite the recession (see figure 9.4). After that, the FOMC reverted to its previous policy of bringing the funds rate down to help the economy recover. At its last meeting in 1991, a December 20 conference call, the Board of Governors slashed the discount rate by an eye-catching 100 basis points, and the FOMC, in the tortured prose of the day, voted to allow "part of the reduction in the discount rate to be reflected in the federal funds rate." The funds rate ended the year at around 4.25 percent, as compared to a 3 percent inflation rate.

The U.S. economy had finally run out of good luck, and so had President George H. W. Bush. At first, the military response to the Persian Gulf War (1990–1991) shot his presidential approval ratings into the stratosphere—to as high as 89 percent in a February 1991 Gallup poll. But then the economic response to the oil shock pulled that rating back down to 61 percent in October 1991 and eventually to as low as 29 percent in July 1992. Bush blamed his electoral defeat on

Greenspan's monetary policy, which he deemed insufficiently expansionary (*Wall Street Journal* 1998). The president had a point, though a more accurate villain would have been Saddam Hussein.

Alan Greenspan (1926—)

Maestro of the Federal Reserve

Life is full of ironies. As a dyed-in-the-wool conservative, Alan Greenspan, the Federal Reserve chair with the second-longest tenure in office,[12] would steadfastly deny that policy makers have the ability to fine-tune the national economy. Yet that's just what he did, with amazing success, for more than eighteen years. Greenspan's Olympian reputation as a monetary policy maker was tarnished late in his career by his neglect of the Fed's regulatory duties in the years leading up to the financial crisis of 2008–2009. But as a monetary policy maker, his record is hard to match.

Greenspan was born in New York City to parents who divorced, leaving him to be raised by his mother, with whom he remained close until her death. An intellectually gifted and musically talented student, he studied first at the Juilliard School in New York but then gave up on a potential musical career in favor of economics. Greenspan earned his bachelor's degree (1948), master's degree (1950), and PhD (1977), all in economics, from New York University. Notice the date of his PhD. It came long after he had established himself in both business and government.

Greenspan's first career was as a business economist heading his own small firm, Townsend-Greenspan. He interrupted that to serve as chair of the Council of Economic Advisers for President Gerald Ford from 1974 to 1977 but then returned to his firm. President Reagan tapped Greenspan to replace Paul Volcker in 1987.

By the time Greenspan took over the leadership of the Fed, inflation had been vanquished, and the Great Moderation had begun although no one knew that at the time. It seems fair to say, however, that Greenspan's monetary policies contributed to that moderation. In particular, as described in this chapter, the Fed nearly achieved a "perfect soft landing" in 1989 and then actually succeeded in executing one in 1994–1995 (see chapter 11).[13] Shortly thereafter, Greenspan made what has been called his "great call" (Meyer 2004) by recognizing—before almost anyone else—that rapid growth in productivity in the late 1990s would enable the economy to grow faster without igniting inflation.[14]

Over his long and successful tenure as Fed chair, Greenspan became a kind of national guru on all things economic. He had a blind spot, however, when it came to financial regulation, where his deep belief in laissez-faire led him to place excessive faith in financial markets' ability to assess and handle risk. The Fed's regulatory neglect in the 2004–2006 period left a blemish on Greenspan's overall record. But his record on monetary policy was stellar.

---

12. Martin edges out Greenspan by a few months.

13. Full disclosure: I was vice chair at the time.

14. Greenspan saw this coming before it showed up in the data. More disclosure: I was among the many skeptics. See chapter 11.

Chapter Summary

One might argue that monetary policy had done its job well by 1984. Inflation had been vanquished, the economy was roaring back from a terrible recession, and the Great Moderation was just beginning. Had the Fed not been forced to deal with two calamities—the 1987 stock market crash and the oil price spike of 1990–1991—Alan Greenspan and Company might have lived the quiet life for a decade. But that was not to be.

Fortunately, the 1987 crash left essentially no trace on the macroeconomy. But the 1990–1991 oil shock caused yet another bout of stagflation, albeit of a smaller magnitude and much shorter time frame than either OPEC I or OPEC II. The Fed, of course, understood well by 1990 that it could not fight both the *stag* and the *flation* components of stagflation at once. Its compromise allowed a short spike in inflation and a modest recession. Reasonable choices, it seemed to many.

Where was fiscal policy in all this? Apart from the 1986 tax reform, which was micro policy not macro policy, approximately nowhere. Or, to be more precise, it was totally preoccupied with the budget deficit, which is the subject of the next chapter.

10

Deficits Crowd Out
Fiscal Policy, 1982–1998

*For three decades, six Presidents have come before you to warn
of the damage deficits pose to our nation. Tonight I come before
you to announce that the federal deficit, once so incomprehensibly
large that it had 11 zeros, will be, simply, zero.*
—BILL CLINTON, STATE OF THE UNION ADDRESS, JANUARY 1998

As noted at the end of the last chapter, once the large Reagan budget
deficits were firmly in place, all thoughts of using fiscal policy as a
stabilization tool vanished into the political sands. Instead, discussions of federal spending and taxation focused almost exclusively on
how to bring down the yawning budget deficit. One consequence of
this fixation on deficit reduction was that monetary policy became,
quite literally, "the only game in town" when it came to stabilizing
the macroeconomy.

The political consensus to reduce the federal deficit was shared by
both parties, at least at the level of lip service. But bipartisan agreement ended right there. Democrats and Republicans battled incessantly over budget priorities for about a decade and a half, with the
Democrats arguing for lower defense spending and resisting civilian

budget cuts while the Republicans wanted to trim social spending and defend the Defense Department.

To illustrate how the fiscal norm changed after Reagan, figure 10.1 displays data for the thirty-two years prior to 1982. Panel (a) shows the federal deficit as a share of GDP. Deficits clearly outnumber surpluses, but the average deficit over this period was only 1.1 percent of GDP, and the deficit exceeded 3 percent of GDP only during the deep recession that spanned fiscal years 1975 and 1976.[1] As panel (b) shows, the debt-to-GDP ratio was mostly declining during that era. In brief, the budget norm prior to the Reagan presidency was clearly to run deficits but small enough to keep the debt-to-GDP ratio declining.

Figure 10.2 displays the same sort of data over the years of partisan wrangling over the deficit that are the focus of this chapter, 1982 through 1998. The differences are stark. In particular, over the twelve fiscal years from 1982 through 1993, the deficit averaged 4.1 percent of GDP and fell below 3 percent of GDP only in one boom year (fiscal 1989). The debt-to-GDP ratio naturally rose during those years, as did political attention to the deficit.

Economists, editorial writers, and politicians alike all railed against large federal budget deficits over the decade that spanned the early 1980s to the early 1990s. Deficits would be a burden on our children and grandchildren (an inchoate claim). Deficits threatened the nation with insolvency (silly). Deficits could crowd out business investment (a real possibility). But it was all to no avail. Not that anyone in America thought deficits of 4 percent, 5 percent, and 6 percent of GDP represented sound public policy. It was just that politics seemed to block any path toward smaller deficits. The conventional wisdom was that cutting the deficit—which meant raising taxes, reducing spending, or both—was a political loser. "Root canal economics," supply-sider Jude Wanniski had called it.[2]

The political logic was simple and apparently compelling. The pain from deficit reduction is visible and immediate. Voters don't

---

1. In those years the federal government's fiscal year ran from July 1 to June 30. Thus, fiscal year 1975 spanned July 1, 1974, through June 30, 1975.
2. See, among other possible sources, Safire (1984).

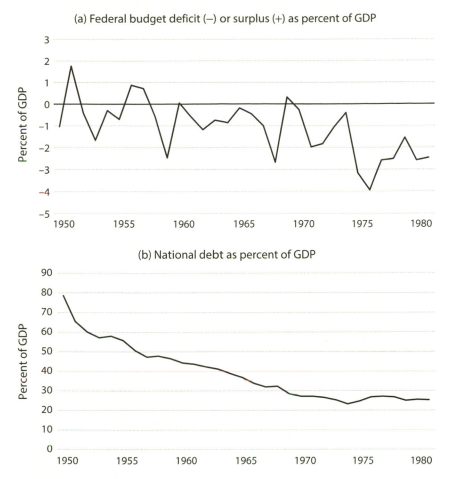

FIGURE 10.1. Federal budget deficit and the national debt as percent of GDP, 1950–1981.

Source: Congressional Budget Office.

want to see their taxes raised or their favorite government expenditure programs cut, and politicians understand that. Besides, what would elected officials gain in return? According to conventional economic thinking, lower deficits would reduce real interest rates and, by dint of that, lead to higher levels of business investment and thereby (eventually) to higher real wages via improvements in productivity. But that chain of reasoning is a bit subtle for politics, and the benefits accrue gradually over a protracted period of time. They are unlikely to be apparent by the next election.

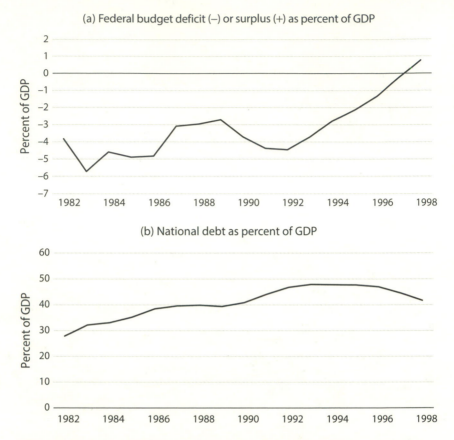

FIGURE 10.2. Federal budget deficit and the national debt as percent of GDP, 1982–1998.
Source: Congressional Budget Office.

Policies that produce subtle—and probably unnoticed—benefits years in the future hardly constitute a recipe for political success. For years, public opinion polls consistently showed that the public wanted lower deficits in principle but opposed virtually anything that might actually get them there in practice, such as higher taxes or cuts in spending programs. For example, "a 1981 Harris Survey found that in no instance were a majority of respondents willing to reduce spending on any domestic program rather than unbalance the federal budget" (Blinder and Holtz-Eakin 1984). Ronald Reagan, it appeared, had discovered a winning political formula: offer the voters tax cut goodies right away and worry about the consequences of budget deficits later. Doing the opposite risked incurring immediate political pain in return for distant, abstract, and uncertain gains.

For a long time, Reagan's assessment looked exactly right, and the problem festered. The federal budget deficit had ballooned to an average of about 5 percent of GDP in the first five fiscal years after the Reagan tax cuts, and it was still 4.7 percent of GDP in 1992. Zero progress. Economists and other advocates of fiscal prudence despaired that nothing would be done. Not that there weren't numerous false starts.

The first manifestation of serious concern about future deficits came already with the aforementioned Tax Equity and Fiscal Responsibility Act, which President Reagan signed into law, probably reluctantly, in September 1982. The act basically repealed most of the corporate tax cuts that had been passed amid the frenzied euphoria of 1981. Its aim was clearly to ameliorate the huge budget-busting consequences of the 1981 tax bill. Further to this end, the president also exacted a pledge from Congress that it would enact three dollars of spending cuts for every dollar of tax increase. That pledge was not redeemed, however, and the combination of the Reagan tax cuts that were not repealed (about three-quarters of the total) and the deep recession of 1981–1982 ballooned the deficit to almost 6 percent of GDP in fiscal year 1983. By fiscal 1985, with the economy recovering strongly from the recession, the deficit was still a whopping 5 percent of GDP.

False Starts: Gramm-Rudman-Hollings

Back in those days, politicians in general, especially conservative politicians, were appalled by such large budget deficits, which, of course, the Reagan team had promised would not occur. In the context of one of the many squabbles over raising the national debt ceiling—something Congress was forced to do early and often because of the large Reagan deficits—Senators Phil Gramm (R-TX), Warren Rudman (R-NH), and Ernest "Fritz" Hollings (D-SC) cobbled together a bipartisan majority in the Senate to pass the Balanced Budget and Emergency Deficit Control Act of 1985, which became known as Gramm-Rudman-Hollings (GRH) or sometimes just Gramm-Rudman. The bill passed the House too, and President Reagan signed it into law in December 1985.

The central idea behind GRH was simple—far too simple, in fact. The law created a series of allegedly binding annual targets for the federal budget deficit over the next five fiscal years. These targets laid out a sequence of declining deficits that, if followed, would lead to a balanced budget by fiscal 1991. If the GRH deficit targets were not met by congressional actions, a series of across-the-board spending cuts (called *sequestration*) would come into effect automatically in the form of equiproportional reductions in most categories of spending. At least that's what the law said. However, there were three titanic sets of problems.

The biggest problem was clear to economists immediately, and it eventually became clear to members of Congress as well. GRH set annual targets for an endogenous variable—the budget deficit—that Congress cannot control any more than King Canute could control the tides. What Congress can control are the volume of discretionary spending on the programs that receive annual appropriations (a minority of the budget), the rules governing eligibility for and generosity of entitlement programs, and tax rates and other provisions of the tax code. Wisely, these were precisely the three items on which the Budget Enforcement Act of 1990 would eventually focus congressional attention. But that came years later.

Notice also that had the letter of the GRH law actually been followed, it would have not just short-circuited the automatic stabilizers but also set them in reverse as automatic *de*stabilizers. Weaker economies breed larger deficits, mainly via lower tax receipts but also via increased spending on a variety of entitlement programs, unemployment insurance being the most obvious example. We call that *automatic stabilization* because fiscal policy becomes more expansionary automatically, without any need for congressional action. But if Congress actually adhered to fixed deficit targets, members would have had to cut government spending anytime the economy slumped. That's automatic destabilization: fiscal austerity at just the wrong time.

Rudman himself labeled GRH "a bad idea whose time has come" (Romano 1986, C2). I wrote shortly thereafter that "the idea's magnificent simplicity was matched only by its simplemindedness" (Blinder 1987a, 102). Many others shared that sentiment. Nonetheless, "somehow an unholy alliance of Republicans and Democrats took utter nonsense and treated it like gospel" (Blinder 1987a, 103). GRH passed the House by a vote of 272–154 and the Senate by an overwhelming 61–31 margin.

The second set of problems with GRH was political: the act ignored two well-known facts about American government, perhaps about any democratically elected government. First, no Congress can bind a succeeding Congress. In fact, future Congresses failed to take the actions necessary to meet the 1985 GRH targets, even though they had mostly the same members. Second, most senators and representatives, then as now, liked to preach fiscal discipline without practicing it. So, when push came to shove, the House and Senate either set aside the GRH targets or postponed them.

The third set of problems was legal. The U.S. Supreme Court ruled in 1986 (in *Bowsher v. Synar*) that the sequestration mechanism in GRH was unconstitutional because the process it created to enforce budget cuts gave executive authority to an agency of Congress, the General Accounting Office (GAO), thereby violating the separation of powers. To fix this legal problem, Congress passed GRH II (officially the Balanced Budget and Emergency Deficit Control Reaffirmation Act) in 1987. This version had a revised sequestration process that passed constitutional muster by making the White House Office of Management and Budget (OMB), rather than the GAO, the enforcer of sequestration. GRH II also offered revised— less strict, of course—deficit targets and pushed back the target date for budget balance to 1993.

While the legal change satisfied the courts, the other two problems remained. King Canute had not learned how to control the tides, and Congress did not abide by its own rules. As a result, the annual budget deficit hung around the $150 billion range in fiscal years 1987–1989 and then moved up to over $200 billion. Those numbers were far above the annual GRH targets. GRH had failed.

First Landmark: The 1990 Budget Agreement

The election of 1988 elevated Reagan's vice president, George H. W. Bush, to the presidency. While vying for the Republican nomination in 1980, Bush had derided supply-side economics as "voodoo economics," and as president he took the deficit problem more seriously than Reagan ever had. Bush was hemmed in, however, by both the potentially harsh spending limits mandated by GRH (even though they were typically ignored) and by his famous (or infamous, in Republican circles) campaign pledge: "Read my lips, no new taxes."

Perhaps more important operationally, the Democrats maintained their majorities in both the House and the Senate in 1988 despite Bush's landslide victory over Democrat Michael Dukakis, the governor of Massachusetts. Hard negotiations between the White House and Congress were inevitable, and they did not bear fruit in Bush's first year in the White House. By the summer of 1990 after many failed attempts, Bush was growing desperate to cut the Gordian knot because sequestration under GRH would have reduced fiscal 1991 spending drastically and indiscriminately (by 35% for nondefense spending and 31% for defense). Given that the Persian Gulf War had just started, that was intolerable.

Against this background, Bush agreed to hold a September 1990 budget summit with congressional leaders from both parties at what was then Andrews Air Force Base (now Joint Base Andrews). The idea was for everyone to leave Capitol Hill and start afresh. Since everything was on the proverbial table at Andrews, even tax increases were within the realm of the possible, although they were anathema to Republicans. Their majorities in both Houses of Congress gave Democrats an important advantage in the bargaining, but President Bush had his veto pen.

Skeptics saw the summit as a futile exercise. Like so many budget negotiations before it, they believed, Andrews would end in failure and acrimony.[3] The skeptics were proven wrong, however, and a bipartisan agreement emerged. The 1990 budget agreement naturally

3. See, for example, the satirical tone in Yang (1990).

included a variety of spending cuts, including some to Medicare. But the most salient aspect politically was Bush's agreement to some tax increases in violation of his well-known 1988 campaign pledge. The so-called Bush tax hikes had many components, including an increase in the top bracket rate from 28 percent to 31 percent (although the capital gains rate was capped at 28%), a limit on item-ized deductions for high-income taxpayers, a phase-out of personal exemptions for even higher-income taxpayers, and more. All told, the tax hikes agreed to at Andrews amounted to roughly 0.5 percent of GDP—not that much.

Nonetheless, this obvious retreat from the "no new taxes" pledge enraged many Republicans. According to the *New York Times* on October 2, 1990, "Civil war broke out among Republicans today as dozens of House members insisted that White House lobbying would not stop them from seeking to thwart the budget package announced on Sunday" (Berke 1990). One of those rebels was the firebrand congressman from Georgia, Newt Gingrich. About two years later, the Cato Institute's Stephen Moore dubbed the Andrews agreement "the crime of the century" (Moore 1992). (A bit polemi-cal, perhaps?) He suggested, as did many other observers, that it might cost President Bush the 1992 election.

Whatever your opinion then or now, it is certain that the 1990 tax hikes garnered far more media attention than any other aspect of the budget agreement. The Congressional Budget Office (CBO) estimated in December 1990 that the tax increases amounted to just under one-third of the total deficit reduction in the Andrews pack-age (CBO 1990). But measured by column inches in newspapers, it must have been at least 95 percent.

Economically, however, the most important item to emerge from the Andrews summit was not the tax hikes but rather the Budget Enforcement Act of 1990. In this act, Congress gave up its futile attempts to legislate overall deficit targets as in GRH and enacted instead what it was actually capable of legislating: caps on discre-tionary spending. The caps excluded revenues and spending on entitlements, two obviously endogenous variables that are sensi-tive to the state of the economy. Instead, the Budget Enforcement

Act instituted a pay-as-you-go rule to cover these two categories. This meant, in practice, that any proposal to reduce tax receipts or raise entitlement spending had to be paired with an accompanying proposal to recoup the lost revenue or pay for the increased spending. In short, any changes in taxes or entitlements had to either leave the projected budget deficit unchanged or decrease it. PAYGO, as it came to be called, did not post a target path for deficit reduction, a path Congress could not achieve in any case. Instead, it created a major procedural asymmetry: policy actions could reduce the deficit but not increase it.

The early judgment on PAYGO was negative but decidedly wrong. As Janet Yellen and I wrote some years later,

> The 1990 budget agreement was much maligned at the time, and proved to be a political albatross around the neck of President Bush. . . . Despite its bad press, the agreement marked the first giant step down a path that would eventually lead the federal government to sizable budget surpluses. Unfortunately, contemporary observers did not see it that way. What they saw, instead, was a budget deficit that was on the rise despite the so-called deficit reduction package. That simple arithmetic made the 1990 budget agreement look bad, and it was prematurely and unfairly pronounced a failure. (Blinder and Yellen 2001, 5)

The critics were mistaken for two main reasons. First, and to Bush's great credit, the government finally decided to bite the bullet and shoulder the inevitable costs of cleaning up the savings and loan mess discussed in the previous chapter. That decision alone added about $60 billion to the budget deficits of fiscal years 1990 and 1991. Second, a recession began in July 1990 and lasted until March 1991. Though it was a mild one, the CBO estimated that the slump raised the deficit by about $160 billion between fiscal years 1991 and 1993. These events conspired to increase the deficit despite the roughly $100 billion per year in deficit reduction negotiated at Andrews. That apparently perverse budget behavior plus the hostility to tax hikes conspired to give the 1990 budget agreement a bad name.

It was a bad rap, however. In particular, PAYGO proved to be the sleeper in the Budget Enforcement Act. Though it was ignored by many and derided by others as a meaningless gesture, the new approach worked. Even I, then writing a column in *Business Week* magazine, expressed skepticism that Congress would stick with "this giant step toward rationality" (Blinder 1990, 29). The right-wing press was much harsher. For example, Heritage Foundation economist Daniel Mitchell later opined in the *Wall Street Journal* that "Mr. Darman [Bush's budget director] is either ignorant of the budget law or is deliberately being deceptive" (Mitchell 1992, A16).

However, unlike the uncomfortable and politically impossible budget corsets created by GRH I and II, the Budget Enforcement Act established rules with which Congress could and did live. As long as PAYGO remained the law of the land—a period that covered the rest of the Bush I years and all eight Clinton years—Congress generally abided by the rules it had written in 1990, and the deficit mostly fell. In fact, it turned into a surplus in fiscal years 1998–2001. Then when Congress abolished PAYGO to pave the way for the Bush II tax cuts, the deficit ballooned in fiscal year 2002 and thereafter. Coincidences? I don't think so.

Given the themes of this book, it is noteworthy that barely any prominent voices at the time suggested using fiscal stimulus to ameliorate, much less end, the 1990–1991 recession. On the contrary, "It's no secret that many of the President's economists, along with much of the economics establishment, fear that economic stimulus of any kind is as likely to harm as help" (Passell 1991). Harm? If Keynesian ideas weren't dead at the time, they were certainly moribund, replaced by the rantings of a large herd of "bond market vigilantes," as they were called then, who drove interest rates higher at the slightest whiff of a larger fiscal deficit.[4]

The 1990–1991 recession may have marked the nadir of fiscal stabilization policy in America. The Fed fought the recession hard but

4. "Higher" interest rates must be assessed against the long-term downward trend in interest rates discussed earlier.

fought it alone (see the next chapter). In the intellectual world, it is amazing that a large 1986 National Bureau of Economic Research conference volume titled *The American Business Cycle: Continuity and Change* (Gordon 1986) did not even include a chapter on countercyclical fiscal policy. In its place was a long essay by Robert Barro (1986) titled "The Behavior of United States Deficits" that focused on his tax-smoothing hypothesis (Barro 1979). Imagine that: a big, thick volume on the business cycle with no mention of fiscal stabilization whatsoever. Walter Heller could never have imagined that.

Interestingly, although the budget battles of the 1980s and 1990s were more about politics than economics, they were nonetheless reflected in the academic thinking and writing of the day. Scores of papers appeared on the effects (or lack thereof) and the sustainability (or lack thereof) of government budget deficits. One empirical finding got less attention than it should have, however: it proved to be surprisingly hard to find a reliable econometric link from larger deficits to higher interest rates.[5] The seeds of the idea that the government could run large deficits without sending interest rates through the roof were sown. But in the hostile climate of the 1980s and 1990s, they didn't germinate.

Second Landmark: The Clinton Budget of 1993

Bill Clinton left his biggest mark on U.S. fiscal policy by turning large, chronic budget deficits into surpluses, although those surpluses did not outlive his presidency. It is therefore easy to forget that candidate Clinton did not run on a platform of thoroughgoing deficit reduction in 1992. Rather, Clinton's campaign slogan, "Putting People First," stood for a detailed economic program that included a variety of new spending proposals (he liked to call them "investments") and a middle-class tax cut (Clinton 1992). Nonetheless, Clintonomics wound up turning a large and growing fiscal deficit into a sizable budget surplus.

5. Many references could be cited. Two are Evans (1987) and Kliesen (2002).

Prior to the Clinton presidency, including during the 1992 campaign, fiscal frugality was not what people typically associated with the Democratic Party. Rather, fiscal prudence and railing against the evils of budget deficits were deeply ingrained Republican traditions back then. (Remember Dwight Eisenhower?) Ronald Reagan's budget-busting policies changed all that. But before Reagan, it was the Democrats who were thought of as the big spenders. Their traditional motto, which dated all the way back to Harry Hopkins in the New Deal, was "Tax and tax, spend and spend, elect and elect." Clinton's presidency flipped the script, suddenly and dramatically. Why? What happened? Several things.

First and perhaps foremost, the surprising electoral success of the gadfly third-party candidate, billionaire Ross Perot, in the 1992 election was sobering and, to a politician with antennae as finely tuned as Clinton's, enlightening. Perot ran almost as a one-issue candidate: the supposedly urgent need to balance the budget and then to start paying down the national debt. Although this novice politician did not win any states, his popular vote count was impressive:

Clinton: 43.0%
Bush: 37.4%
Perot: 18.9%.

To be sure, Clinton defeated Bush decisively. But Perot's 19 percent vote share was the best by a third-party candidate since Theodore Roosevelt in 1912. Remarkably, Perot garnered about half as many votes as Bush! Furthermore, for several months during the summer of 1992, Perot actually led both Clinton and Bush in the polls. To Clinton, the political message must have been clear and sobering: there was more grassroots support for deficit reduction than he and other political "experts" had imagined.

Second, during the 1992–1993 transition period, Clinton was apparently convinced by his economic advisers—somewhat to the dismay of his political advisers—that reducing the deficit was an urgent national priority that could not wait. Coupled with the stunning Perot vote, Clinton may have concluded that he should and could turn good policy into good politics, despite the electorate's well-known aversion to both tax increases and spending cuts.[6] He knew it was risky—I was among those who told him so—but he took the gamble.

Clinton's original economic team was led de facto by Robert Rubin, who had left his position as a prince of Wall Street (cochair of Goldman Sachs) to become the first director of the National Economic Council, a Clinton creation.[7] I was part of that team, as a member of Clinton's first Council of Economic Advisers, and I distinctly remember Rubin citing, time and time again, possible dire consequences that might occur in the financial markets if the federal government didn't curb its borrowing. Rubin was always careful to hedge his wording, and he delivered his message with far more sobriety than Perot's high-pitched rants. But it carried the authority of (in Rubin's pet phrase) "my 26 years on Wall Street." That said, the warning was substantively similar to what Perot had claimed: if the deficit was not reduced, something terrible might happen in the financial markets. Rubin was always careful not to forecast Armageddon or to spell out what Armageddon would look like. But he not-so-subtly suggested that the danger was palpable. The bond market vigilantes had, after all, often shown their teeth during the Bush I years.

For OMB director Clinton chose Leon Panetta, an affable (and funny) career politician from northern California who had previously chaired the House Budget Committee. Panetta knew the budget inside out, both substantively and politically, and both he and his knowledgeable deputy, Alice Rivlin, were self-declared deficit hawks. I got to know Panetta well, and I came to believe that he saw deficit reduction as at least in part a moral issue. Congress had

6. To be sure, public opinion polls typically found support for less government spending in the abstract. But when offered cuts in specific programs, respondents rejected almost all of them.

7. Previous presidents had something analogous to the National Economic Council. But Clinton's clear intent was to elevate economics to the same status as national security, hence the name National Economic Council to give it parity with the National Security Council.

shirked its solemn duty by letting the deficit grow so large. In sharp contrast, Clinton's political team could be characterized as deficit doves who were not eager to pursue root canal economics. They viewed Panetta and Rivlin as adversaries, competing for the mind and soul of the newly elected president.[8]

The top economic official on the Clinton economic team, at least de jure, was the secretary of the treasury, Lloyd Bentsen, a wily Texan who had chaired the Senate Finance Committee. Those of us (like me) who were excluded from the innermost loops of the administration learned later, from Bob Woodward's *The Agenda* (1994), that Bentsen had opened an active back channel to his long-time friend, Fed Chair Alan Greenspan, who was urging strong deficit reduction. Even before inauguration day, Bentsen had informed Greenspan that Clinton and his economic team supported deficit reduction. "The Fed chairman, first among deficit hawks, smiled at the news" but offered no deal on interest rates (Woodward 1994, 98). Yet Greenspan participated in formulating the fiscal plan from a distance, using Bentsen as a conduit. It was an odd form of coordination between monetary and fiscal policy.

Although Greenspan promised nothing, his involvement went well beyond mere moral support for smaller deficits. The new president gave his economic team just four weeks to redo the entire federal budget, line by line. To make this Herculean task manageable, we decided to focus our attention on fiscal year 1997. The other years could be filled in by spreadsheet. The budget numbers that the outgoing Bush administration left us suggested a whopping deficit of $346 billion in fiscal year 1997, roughly 4 percent of GDP, if current policies were continued. With Clinton participating actively in every decision, we decided, after much internal debate, on an ambitious but attainable target: to reduce that number by $140 billion.

Why 140? To me (and others), that particular number just popped up one day, seemingly out of the blue, at one of our endless series of budget meetings. Prior to that day, an active debate had raged over what the 1997 target should be, a debate informed and given texture

8. This is a major theme of Woodward (1994).

by the specific cuts necessary to reach any particular target. Yet all of a sudden, the debate was over; the target was $140 billion. We later learned from Woodward's book that the magic number had come not out of the blue but instead out of the Fed, passed on from Greenspan via Bentsen.

There were opposing, more dovish voices but not many in the top economic positions. As just noted, the political crowd (James Carville, Paul Begala, George Stephanopoulos, and others) were never keen on proposing politically perilous spending cuts and tax hikes. Carville famously quipped that "I used to think that if there was reincarnation, I wanted to come back as the President or the Pope or as a .400 baseball hitter. But now I would like to come back as the bond market. You can intimidate everybody" (Wessel and Vogel 1993, A1).

Robert Reich, a longtime Clinton buddy who was secretary of labor, worried out loud that we were overdoing it and, in the process, threatening many of the "putting people first" initiatives on which Clinton had campaigned. Reich didn't argue against deficit reduction, only for less of it. He battled Rubin early and often at National Economic Council meetings and elsewhere. But ensconced as he was a mile and a half away at the Labor Department, Reich scored precious few victories over the clever Wall Streeter whose tiny office was just feet from the Oval Office. Proximity matters.

As part of my job as the incoming CEA's "macro member," I had delivered at a transition-period briefing in Little Rock the conventional message that tighter fiscal policies reduce aggregate demand and could therefore slow down or even destroy growth. Backed by Laura Tyson, the incoming CEA chair, I displayed numerical estimates showing that too much deficit reduction could produce "a recession similar to the Bush recession." As Woodward reported, "the effect on Clinton was electric"—and not joyful (Woodward 1994, 95). The president-elect knew full well what the recession of 1990–1991 had done to President Bush's popularity.

My briefing hastened to add, however, that either the Fed or the bond market could obviate this danger by pushing interest rates sufficiently lower. That thought brought a scowl to Clinton's face. "You mean to tell me that the success of the program and my reelection hinges on the Federal Reserve and a bunch of f___-ing bond traders?" (Woodward 1994, 84). Everyone around the table nodded in agreement. As we know now, the bond traders came through big-time. But nobody knew that in January 1993.

Looked at broadly, however, the internal disagreements on the Clinton economic team were minor. The difference between deficit hawks such as Panetta and deficit doves such as Reich was, roughly, between reducing the deficit by $140 billion or $120 billion four years later. Twenty billion over four years? That wasn't even rounding error in macroeconomic terms. In the end, the president surprised many of us by opting for the larger number. Clinton announced his new budget plan in his first major speech as president on February 17, 1993. The date chosen for this address was interesting, by the way. Reagan's first budget plan was unveiled on February 18, 1981. We would beat them by a day!

After years of being handed phony plans built with noncredible numbers and laden with gimmicks, the budget Clinton proposed in February 1993 made the fearsome bond market vigilantes practically delirious with joy. The numbers were judged to be highly credible (more on this shortly), and the thirty-year Treasury rate, which was then the benchmark, dropped from 7.3 percent on Clinton's inauguration day to just below 5.9 percent in early September 1993. This remarkable bond market rally had major implications for both the economy and monetary policy, which I'll get to in the next chapter. For now, let's stick with the fiscal policy.

Clinton's economic advisers shared the young president's belief that the 1990–1991 recession and the "jobless recovery" that followed had probably cost George H. W. Bush the election. (Bush certainly thought so.[9]) We did not want a repeat performance. Furthermore, the U.S. economy in early 1993 did not look nearly as strong as it would look a few years later. The unemployment rate, which had peaked at 7.8 percent in June 1992, was still 7.3 percent in January 1993. Not much progress. The GDP growth rate had stumbled to

9. In a TV interview years later, Bush lamented that "I reappointed him and he disappointed me" (Greenspan 2007, 122).

0.7 percent in the first quarter of 1993, though no one knew that in January because of data lags. Finally, Clinton's economists, Keynesians all, were worried about stifling aggregate demand by cutting spending and raising taxes.

This macro concern affected the budget plan in two main ways. First, the original February 1993 budget proposals tacked a small short-run fiscal stimulus—around $30 billion over two years—onto a substantial deficit-reduction program of nearly $500 billion over five years. This strategy of one step backward, five steps forward proved to be too clever by half, however, and the stimulus part was quickly rejected by Congress. Instead, Congress subsequently passed, albeit barely and without a single Republican vote,[10] a deficit-reduction package somewhat larger than Clinton had originally proposed. Thus, the initial stages of Clintonomics turned out to be fiscal prudence without fiscal insurance. Just reduce the deficit, period.

Well, sort of. When you looked at the details, the five-year deficit reduction plan was heavily back-loaded to ease both the expected economic pain from reducing aggregate demand and the expected political pain of getting the plan through Congress. Specifically, the five-year deficit reduction targets for fiscal years 1994–1998 were

1994: –$39 billion
1995: –$54 billion
1996: –$92 billion
1997: –$140 billion
1998: –$148 billion

Even in the much smaller (than today) economy of 1993, $39 billion was not much—about 0.5 percent of nominal GDP.

Selling the Clinton Budget

But back to the credibility issue. During the 1980s and early 1990s, bond traders had seen, chewed over, and rejected as nonserious one deficit-reduction plan after another. They had come to believe

10. Vice President Al Gore had to break a 50–50 tie in the Senate.

that Rosy Scenario ran macroeconomic forecasting in the White House. We on the Clinton team were determined not to let that happen again. So, several features of the budget plan were specifically designed to make it highly credible.

First and perhaps foremost, Clinton's first budget designated several sacred cows for ritual slaughter. Most prominently, Social Security benefits were reduced by making some of them taxable for upper-income (though not rich) individuals. Whoever thought a Democrat would advocate that?[11] It was a real head-turner.

Second, the deficit-reduction plan included significant new revenues from both higher income taxes on the rich and a brand-new BTU tax, designed to raise revenue while reducing carbon emissions. The latter, a pet policy of Vice President Al Gore, was quickly eviscerated by Congress. The former survived, although its inclusion probably ensured that the overall plan would get zero Republican votes. Both of those tax proposals, however, demonstrated to the bond market that the new administration was willing to take political hits in order to bring the deficit down. The vigilantes, who remembered the political reception accorded the 1990 Bush tax hikes, liked that.

Third, the initial Clinton budget plan, covering five years, was remarkably free of the gimmicks and accounting subterfuges that the markets had come to expect but also detest after years of Reagan and Bush budgets. No blue smoke and mirrors for us. The document we produced looked (and was) sober and serious.

Fourth, the one "gimmick" that Clinton himself ordered (thereby ending a heated internal battle within the staff) actually cooked the books against him. Far from embracing Rosy Scenario as his forecaster, the new president directed the OMB to score the budget proposals by using the CBO's more pessimistic economic forecast rather than his own administration's more optimistic one.[12] A less

---

11. Confession: I made a small bet with another economist on the Clinton team that the president would not accept that recommendation. I lost.

12. Another confession: I was in charge of the administration's five-year forecast, which while more optimistic than the CBO's proved to be far too pessimistic.

robust economy in the future naturally meant that tougher policies would be required to reach the $140 billion deficit-reduction target. Clinton understood that, but he insisted on using the CBO forecast anyway.

Selling deficit reduction to Carville's feared bond market was one thing. Selling it to the public—and hence to the politicians whom Clinton wanted to vote for it—was quite another. For years, many Americans had shared an uneasy feeling that the federal budget deficit was too large. But precious few understood the benefits that could be expected to flow from smaller deficits.

In 1993 just as before and since, most mainstream economists would have told you a story that ran something like this: Smaller federal deficits should lead to lower real interest rates, which should in turn spur greater private investment spending. Since the larger capital stock spawned by higher investment is one of the mainsprings of worker productivity, which is in turn the central source of higher real wages, shrinking the budget deficit is an indirect way to boost real wages and living standards. That, not our Puritan heritage, is the main reason to seek lower deficits. Clinton's economists told him precisely that.

But that is not how the president sold deficit reduction to the American public. For Clinton, deficit reduction, like everything else, was a jobs program—a vehicle for redeeming his campaign pledge to create eight million new jobs in four years. This message made most of us economists cringe. It was possible, of course, that lower deficits would so reduce interest rates that economic activity would actually be stimulated. But at the time that seemed like betting on a long shot.[13] To stay on message without destroying our integrity, the Clinton CEA (consisting at the time of Laura Tyson and myself) insisted that we claim that the economy would create eight million jobs *with* our deficit reduction program, not *because of* our deficit

---

The economy did vastly better than we dared imagine. But no one ever criticized me for the terrible forecast!

13. The long shot came in. Long-term interest rates plummeted while the Clinton plan was being debated and enacted.

reduction program. It was the truth though perhaps not quite the whole truth.

Clinton saw things differently, however, and with far greater political sensibility. The issue of the day in early 1993 was not real wages; it was jobs. America had been struggling with a sluggish "jobless recovery" for almost two years, and the public wanted their new president to do something about it. The intellectual argument leading from lower deficits to higher real wages, though logically tidy, was abstract, hard to follow, and out of touch with what the people wanted most at the time: more jobs. Had we tried to sell deficit reduction on those grounds, the effort would probably have failed.

Bill Clinton, the master politician, understood that and insisted that we sell deficit reduction as a way to create jobs, not as a way to boost real wages. ("Don't ever say our program could cost jobs in the short run," he warned us [Woodward 1994, 124].) History will record him right on both counts. The deficit-reduction program made it through Congress, though barely. And interest rates dropped like a stone, which helped jump-start the economy and throw the great American jobs machine into high gear. Clinton was amply rewarded for his perspicacity and risk taking. Total job creation during Bush's four years had been only 2.6 million. During Clinton's first term that total rose to above 11.6 million, greatly exceeding his pledge of 8 million jobs.

With this fine record to run on, Clinton smashed Republican Bob Dole in the 1996 election, winning the electoral college vote by a margin of 379 to 159. And that Clinton's job approval rating remained high right through the end of his presidency, despite the Monica Lewinsky scandal, was due in no small part to the economic success. The American people were rewarded with another 11.6 million net new jobs in Clinton's second term. The unemployment rate fell to its lowest level in a generation.

So, was Clinton wrong to sell deficit reduction as a job creator? Would anyone have been better off if instead he had tried to sell deficit reduction as the route to more investment and higher real wages (the economists' answer) and the package had failed in Congress? Clearly not. This seems to be a case in which some arguably misleading rhetoric produced stellar substantive results whether judged on economic or political criteria.

Revisionist Thinking on Fiscal Policy

It did do some intellectual harm though. The fact that the Clinton boom began shortly after Congress passed a deficit-reduction package gave rise to some revisionist thinking—some of it serious, much of it muddled—on even the sign of the fiscal policy multiplier. Among politicians and media types, the notion that raising taxes or cutting spending, or both, would expand (rather than contract) the economy took hold rapidly and uncritically, with seemingly little thought about the mechanisms by which this was supposed to happen.

Quicker than you could say "Robert Rubin," the idea that reducing the budget deficit was the way to grow the economy—even in the short run—came to dominate thinking in Washington, in the media, and even in the financial markets (where many people had degrees in economics). Such thinking was, of course, profoundly anti-Keynesian. Maybe it wasn't thinking at all. But it still had a strong following in Congress years later when President Barack Obama tried to get a large fiscal stimulus bill through Congress in 2009 (more on this in chapter 15).

How could such thinking have been right? How could raising taxes or cutting spending increase output and create jobs, which requires a negative fiscal multiplier? I wondered about that a lot during the early Clinton years and after. The argument that Rubin and other deficit hawks made was that if nothing was done to curb the deficit, something terrible might happen. If reducing the deficit decreased the probability of that implied catastrophe and if that catastrophe would kill many jobs, you could argue that deficit reduction was a (net) job creator in a probabilistic sense. Clinton, Rubin, and others did precisely that.

But what was the feared catastrophe? In some nations, it could be a currency crisis in which capital flees the country, the exchange rate plummets, interest rates soar, and everything heads south. That indeed has happened in a number of times and places. But it seemed an implausible scenario for the United States of America in 1993—or now for that matter. Alternatively, "it" could mean that investors start thinking that the government might default on its enormous debt, interest rates would spike, and the country would fall into recession. Default by the U.S. Treasury? On debt denominated in U.S. dollars? How could that happen? A weaker version, I suppose, might envision not a default but rather a mass movement by investors away from U.S. government debt as foreign portfolios got saturated with treasuries, an interest rate spike, and a recession. Well, maybe. But that seems a weak reed to stand on.

Are there better arguments? In the academic world, some earlier theorizing by Stephen Turnovsky and Marcus Miller (1984) and by Olivier Blanchard (1984) was dusted off to explain how a credible reduction in expected future budget deficits could increase aggregate demand today. Their basic idea was that convincing investors that the national debt will be lower in the future would reduce long-term interest rates today, thereby stimulating current demand. Their models did not claim, however, that a reduction in the current budget deficit would be expansionary today, that is, that the fiscal multiplier was negative. Still, the Turnovsky-Miller-Blanchard analysis offered a theoretically coherent explanation of the Clinton boom that was decidedly superior to the many incoherent ones.

After the fabulous success of Clintonomics, few people stopped to ask whether the lessons of those glory years could be generalized. One exception was Janet Yellen and I in a small book published years later. Our conclusion was that "this is not a formula that can be repeated at will" (Blinder and Yellen 2001, 23). Why not? One obvious reason is that a fiscal announcement can precipitate a major bond market rally only if bond yields start high, as they did in 1993. Another is that fiscal policy must surprise the bond market pleasantly and in large magnitude. This consideration almost requires a prior period of fiscal irresponsibility and then an election that brings in new leadership, as also happened in 1993. Finally, as emphasized earlier, the proposed fiscal changes must be highly credible. Could all that happen again? Certainly. But we should not expect it to occur frequently.

Chapter Summary

The long road to repairing the damage done to the federal budget in 1981 began in 1982 with the repeal of some of the Reagan tax cuts. But progress stalled right there for more than a decade. In the 1980s, three senators (Gramm, Rudman, and Hollings) tried twice to legislate a solution—and eventually a balanced budget—by threatening Congress with mechanical sequestrations of appropriated funds if deficit targets weren't met. But Congress called its own bluff each time, and both attempts failed.

The first successful steps toward genuine deficit reduction came under President George H. W. Bush in 1990. Despite a recession, he agreed with the Democratic majority in Congress to raise taxes and cut spending. By classroom definitions this was perverse, destabilizing fiscal policy. But the most important step taken in the 1990 budget agreement was to institute a pay-as-you-go requirement for any tax cuts or increases in entitlements, balancing the budget at the margin. PAYGO proved the naysayers wrong by working well until it was repealed in 2002 in order to allow President George W. Bush to bust the budget again. Thus, ironically, one of the good deeds of the father was repealed by the son.

PAYGO was in force when Bill Clinton came into office, and he bolstered it with a sizable five-year deficit-reduction package that included tax hikes, cuts in discretionary spending, and even some trims in entitlements. In Clinton's memorable phrase the Democrats became "Eisenhower Republicans," and a sharp bond market rally made it all work—amazingly well, in fact. Helped along by the Clinton boom of the late 1990s, the federal budget went from chronic large deficits to surpluses with amazing speed. Even Clinton's anti-Keynesian prophecy that deficit reduction could create jobs seemed to come true.

These developments were good news for the American economy but bad news for believers in Keynesian fiscal policy. Under George H. W. Bush, the government opted for fiscal contraction during a recession. Under Bill Clinton, a fiscal contraction seemed to precipitate a boom. Was the fiscal multiplier actually negative? No. But quite a few Americans, including many members of Congress, came to think so.

Ideas have consequences. The thought of what would happen the next time the U.S. economy needed a boost from fiscal policy left many economists uneasy. They didn't have to wait long.

11

The Long Boom of
the 1990s

CEA Chair Charles Schultze: *We cannot fine tune the economy,
and we do not intend to try.*

Congressman Henry Reuss: *Well, I think you have got to
fine tune the economy, and you should intend to try.*

—TESTIMONY TO THE JOINT ECONOMIC COMMITTEE, 1979

The 1990s are known, macroeconomically, for the long boom that
stretched from 1991 all the way into 2001. But the decade didn't start
out smoothly. According to National Bureau of Economic Research
(NBER) dating, a brief and mild recession began in July 1990 and
ended in March 1991. During that time span, real GDP fell for only
two quarters (1990:4 and 1991:1) and by a total of only 1.4 percent.
Then when the recession ended, the nation embarked on an unbro-
ken expansion that was destined to last ten years. At the time, it
was the longest expansion in U.S. history by far. (The 2009–2020
expansion would later eclipse that record.) This happy episode is
often referred to as "the Clinton boom" because Bill Clinton was
president for eight of those ten years.

The Bush Recession?

In fairness, however, it all began under President George H. W. Bush. Ironically, the words "fairness," "Bush," and "business cycle" do not join together easily because the business cycle was patently unfair to the first President Bush. As discussed in chapter 9, the 1990–1991 recession is more accurately blamed on Saddam Hussein and the brief but sharp oil shock he engendered by invading Kuwait in August 1990. It certainly cannot be attributed to the tax hike to which Bush reluctantly agreed in November 1990 but which went into effect only in January 1991. By that time, the recession was almost over.

Nonetheless, Bill Clinton and the Democrats hammered the incumbent president on the weak economy during the 1992 campaign even though the growth rate of real GDP over the first three quarters of 1992 averaged a robust 4.5 percent. Voters, however, didn't understand that when they went to the polls in November 1992—perceptions lag behind realities. For example, as late as September 1992, some 80 percent of respondents told a Gallup poll that they thought the economy was in decline (CNN/Knight Ridder 1992).

What went wrong for Bush? Quite a lot. Part of the story was political. He gained the enmity of many members of his own party when he agreed to raise taxes after pledging not to do so. As the *New York Times* reported at the time, "A civil war broke out among Republicans today as dozens of House members insisted that White House lobbying would not stop them from seeking to thwart the budget package." One of the leading warriors was Newt Gingrich (R-GA), who would go on to become Speaker of the House when Republicans gained control in January 1995. According to Gingrich, the Andrews agreement "will kill jobs, weaken the economy" and "the tax increase will be counterproductive" (Berke 1990).

In addition, the nation normally grows weary of one-party rule after twelve years or even eight. In this case it was Republican rule, and three "Reagan terms" were probably enough for the electorate. Finally, the young governor of Arkansas proved to be a formidable

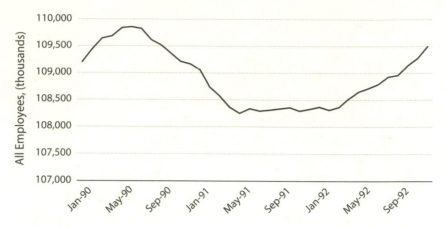

FIGURE 11.1. Payroll employment, monthly, January 1990–December 1992.
Source: Bureau of Labor Statistics.

campaigner, a remarkably intuitive politician, and a debater who could "feel your pain" in a way the patrician Bush could not. One famous incident encapsulated this difference poignantly. During an October 1992 debate in town hall format, the TV camera caught Bush looking longingly at this watch—seeming to hope the ordeal would soon be over—while Clinton, oozing sympathy, waded into the crowd enthusiastically.

Other parts of Bush's electoral problem were macroeconomic, however. The recovery from the 1990–1991 recession was "jobless" at first. The national unemployment rate, which had hovered in the neighborhood of 5.5 percent from Bush's January 1989 inauguration through the NBER business cycle peak in July 1990, rose to 6.8 percent in March 1991, the month of the NBER trough. That's not a huge increase. But then unemployment kept climbing during the "recovery," hitting a high of 7.8 percent in June 1992. In the election month, it was still 7.4 percent. To many Americans, it didn't feel like a recovery at all.

Job growth was sluggish throughout the period, as figure 11.1 shows. About 1.6 million jobs disappeared during the recession. Then they came back at a snail's pace during the early stages of the recovery, averaging essentially zero net new jobs per month until early 1992 and then just 56,000 per month over the eighteen months from June 1991 through November 1992. This behavior of employment differed from historic norms only in degree, not in kind. It is normal for the decline in the unemployment rate to lag behind the recovery in GDP. As luck would have it—bad luck for George Bush, good luck for Bill Clinton—the pace of job creation accelerated smartly right after the election, to 226,000 jobs per month over the next twelve months. The unkindness of the business cycle was one big reason why Clinton defeated Bush handily in the 1992 election.

A White House at War with the Fed

Bush blamed his electoral defeat on Alan Greenspan's monetary policy, which Bush himself, his treasury secretary, his Council of Economic Advisers (CEA) chair, and other administration figures claimed was too tight.[1] This blaming, in fact, started well before the recession. Richard Darman, the brilliant but abrasive Baker protégé who was Bush's budget director, took the lead in attacking the Fed. In a September 1989 appearance on *Meet the Press* (note the early date), he opined that the Fed "may have been a little too tight" and suggested that "if we do have a recession," it would be the Fed's fault (Woodward 2000, 62). Greenspan was watching on TV that morning, and as he put it, "I nearly spilled my coffee. . . . Listening to his argument, I thought it made no economic sense. . . . [I]t was political rhetoric" (Greenspan 2007, 119). Darman didn't relent, however. He subsequently peppered Greenspan with memos and faxes, none of which endeared the brash budget director to the reserved Fed chair. When the recession finally did arrive, Darman blamed Greenspan (Woodward 2000, 89).

Secretary of the Treasury Nicholas Brady, a Bush chum from Yale days, followed Darman in urging Greenspan to cut interest rates more aggressively. Brady did so both privately and in the media. After hearing his fill of this, an exasperated Greenspan at one point challenged Brady to call members of the Federal Open Market Committee (FOMC) on the phone and see if he could persuade them. (Brady in fact called a few FOMC members, to no avail [Woodward

1. See Greenspan (2007), especially chap. 5.

2000, 90].) By March 1992, things had gotten so testy that Brady cancelled his weekly breakfast meetings with Greenspan. After that, in the Fed chair's words, "The 'Greenspan account,' as they called it in the White House, shifted to CEA Chair Mike Boskin and the president himself" (Greenspan 2007, 121).

Bush was his usual cordial self, and Greenspan felt that the president of the United States was entitled to an explanation of the central bank's decisions. But by a June 1992 interview with the *New York Times*, Bush was saying that "I'd like to see another lowering of interest rates" (Woodward 2000, 91). He had a point. But with the election just months away, the usual lags in monetary policy meant that June 1992 was already too late politically. A looser monetary policy earlier would presumably have led to faster growth in 1992, which would have helped the incumbent president's reelection bid. There are at least three important "buts," however.

First, the major macroeconomic problem of 1992 was not laggard GDP growth. As just noted, real GDP grew nicely. The problem was that even robust growth in output did not produce many new jobs—for reasons that are still not well understood. But monetary policy influences the growth rate of GDP, not the way GDP growth translates into jobs. Had Brady somehow convinced Greenspan that the Fed should boost the number of jobs per billion dollars of GDP, it's unclear what Greenspan and his colleagues could have done to make that happen.

Second, there is really no case that Greenspan was playing politics with the economy in 1990–1992. Without a doubt, this longtime— and highly political—Republican Fed chair favored Bush over Clinton, a Democrat who was far from certain to reappoint Greenspan to a new term in 1996. Yet by all appearances, the Fed chief played it straight. From early 1988 until the spring of 1989, the FOMC raised the federal funds rate by about 300 basis points because it was worried about an overheating economy (figure 11.2). Then it eased as the economy slowed, cutting rates well before the recession began and then cutting them more during the recession and still more after the recession had ended. In total, the FOMC cut the funds rate by

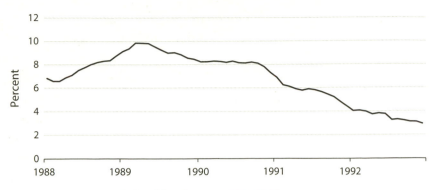

FIGURE 11.2. Target federal funds rate, 1988–1992.
Source: Board of Governors of the Federal Reserve System.

almost 700 basis points between April 1989 and the November 1992 election, the last few cuts being aimed squarely at the "jobless recovery." That sure didn't look like tight money to tilt the election away from Bush.

Finally, if you are grading the central bank's performance, it should be remembered that as mentioned in chapter 9, the Greenspan Fed came close to achieving a perfect soft landing in 1989–1990. Indeed, it might have achieved that elusive goal had Saddam Hussein not thrown a monkey wrench into the operation. Thus, in a sense both Bush and Greenspan were victims of the Persian Gulf War but with an important difference: only Bush had to stand for reelection.

The Budget Battle of 1993

Bill Clinton assumed the presidency in January 1993, and his initial budget submission about four weeks later kicked off an epic political battle that lasted six months. Putatively, the Democrats controlled the White House and both Houses of Congress at the time. The door to passing legislation thus seemed wide open, and Clinton had come to Washington with a long agenda. But the Democrats are a famously fractious bunch, prone to forming circular firing squads. As Will Rogers had astutely observed almost sixty years earlier, "I am not a member of any organized party—I'm a Democrat" (O'Brien 1935, 162).

Apparently, nothing much had changed in the interim. Congressional Democrats were not about to defer to the young newcomer from Arkansas.

Though much beloved by the financial markets and by many economists, Clinton's 1993 budget did several things that looked "wrong" from a political perspective. Most hateful to Republicans, it raised income tax rates on upper-bracket taxpayers from the 31 percent top rate established under George H. W. Bush all the way up to 39.6 percent. Never mind that the top tax rate under Dwight Eisenhower had been as high as 92 percent. To the post-Reagan Republican Party, raising marginal tax rates was a mortal sin, as Bush had learned the hard way. Many Republicans bravely or foolishly (take your pick) predicted a recession if taxes were raised.

They also bridled against several of Clinton's proposed spending programs, the things he liked to call "investments." For example, Gingrich declared on February 2, 1993 (less than two weeks into the Clinton administration), that "we have all too many people in the Democratic administration who are talking about bigger Government, bigger bureaucracy, more programs, and higher taxes. I believe that that will in fact kill the current recovery and put us back in a recession" (U.S. Congress 1993, 1642).

On the Democratic side of the aisle, most members were less concerned about the income tax hikes but quickly rallied against Clinton's proposed BTU tax. The idea was first eviscerated with numerous exceptions (What? Make aluminum more expensive? Or coal? Or fertilizer?) and eventually whittled down to a puny 4.3 cents per gallon increase in the federal gasoline tax. Even Clinton's "investments" got a decidedly mixed reception from Democrats on the Hill. The politics of cutting back old programs to make room for new ones ran into a classic political roadblock: old programs have all sorts of entrenched interests and lobbyists lined up to protect them; new programs do not. On top of all that, some Democrats in Congress were true deficit hawks who insisted on even more deficit reduction than Clinton had proposed. That attitude left little room for new programs.

When the 103rd Congress opened for business in January 1993, the Democrats held seemingly comfortable majorities of 57–43 in the Senate and 258–176 in the House. That looked good on paper, but a naive body count failed to reckon with both the need for sixty votes in the Senate on most bills (though not on the budget) and the lack of discipline in Will Rogers's old party. As the budget debate dragged on, with Republicans just saying no to everything and Democrats asking the White House for one change after another, a kind of bazaar developed within the Democratic caucuses of both Houses. Member after member refused to promise their votes unless they got X. Different members, of course, had different choices of X. And quite a few seemed willing to hold the whole budget hostage to their own pet idea.

In the end, the Clinton budget barely squeaked through the House. As freshman member Marjorie Margolies-Mezvinsky (D-PA), who had won her seat in a traditionally Republican district, strode down the aisle to make the vote 218–216 in favor, Republicans jeered her with the chant "Goodbye, Marjorie!" And she was in fact defeated in the 1994 election. Over in the Senate, it took a full-court press to convince the maverick senator Bob Kerrey (D-NE) to cast the fiftieth vote for passage, thus enabling Vice President Al Gore to register the tie-breaking vote. Remember, there were fifty-seven Democratic senators at the time. For all his political skills, Clinton managed to get just fifty of them to vote with him. In sum, reducing the deficit in 1993 was extremely popular in principle but far less so in practice.

The new president signed the Omnibus Budget Reconciliation Act of 1993 into law on August 10, 1993. As macroeconomic events unfolded, it turned out to be the fiscal "contraction" that was not contractionary. Instead, the economy boomed. However, nobody knew that in August 1993 even though a strong bond market rally was already under way. All eyes on Clinton's economic team then turned toward the Fed. Would Greenspan help bail out the fledgling administration with interest rate cuts or at least with interest rate forbearance?

The White House–Federal Reserve Wars End

It is important to remember that when Clinton assumed the presidency in January 1993, there was a widespread feeling in the American populace that the economy had underperformed of late and that only three things mattered: jobs, jobs, and jobs. Indeed, that became the mantra of the new administration. Every policy was evaluated by its potential to create (or, God forbid, to destroy) jobs. I recall a hilarious cartoon that appeared in the *New Yorker* at the time. It showed Christopher Columbus importuning King Ferdinand and Queen Isabella to fund his voyage with a promise that it "will not only forge a new route to the spices of the East but also create over three thousand new jobs." While this book is not about trade policy, it is also worth remembering that former presidential candidate Ross Perot railed against the North American Free Trade Agreement on the grounds that there would be "a giant sucking sound" as American jobs moved south of the border.

By contrast with the salience of jobs, most voters paid no attention whatsoever to the Federal Reserve, much less understood its role. When I joined the Federal Reserve Board as its vice chair in June 1994, one of the incumbent governors joked to me that most Americans thought the Federal Reserve was a national forest! Yes, Smokey Bear was more famous than Alan Greenspan, who had not yet been anointed the national guru on all things economic.

Close observers of the Fed such as Clinton and his advisers were, of course, familiar with the charge that stingy monetary policy had cost Bush the election in 1992. And they did not want a repeat performance. Mindful of James Carville's famous election motto "The economy, stupid," Team Clinton watched Greenspan carefully and warily.

The back-channel discussions of deficit-reduction targets between the Fed chair and the incoming treasury secretary, Lloyd Bentsen, were discussed in the previous chapter. Greenspan smiled benignly at the deficit-reducing initiatives that Clinton would soon release but made no commitment to cut interest rates as a reward, just as he had made no such commitment to Bush in 1990.

Most of the Clinton economic team and, I believe, Clinton himself saw themselves as at the mercy of the Fed and the bond market. The team's acknowledged leader, Robert Rubin, had come from a successful bond trading house (Goldman Sachs) and repeatedly observed that bond market reactions were the crucial element. After all, with the federal funds rate already very low—roughly zero in real terms—the FOMC seemed unlikely to cut interest rates much if at all. It was going to be up to the bond market—which, as noted earlier, came through mightily—to prevent deficit reduction from being contractionary.

Unlike Bush and many presidents before him, Clinton understood, absorbed, and accepted something his economic team was telling him: that going to war with the Fed was a risky business, probably a loser's game. Better to seek a pax Washingtoniana. To that end, Clinton artfully invited Greenspan to sit in a front-row seat in the House gallery for the dramatic February 17, 1993, address to a joint session of Congress that introduced his economic plan. Seating Greenspan between First Lady Hillary Clinton and Second Lady Tipper Gore made for a great camera shot, which was viewed by millions on national TV. To many financial market players, it signaled that Greenspan was endorsing the Clinton budget plan. Right or wrong, that thought pleased Clinton.

Greenspan said later that he was "uncomfortable" with being "positioned up front for a political purpose." He had expected to be a backbencher (Greenspan 2007, 142). I wonder about that assertion, given Greenspan's astute political antennae and his well-known penchant for being at the center of things. (He rarely missed an A-list Washington party.) But regardless, after years of warfare with the Bush administration, a noteworthy truce had broken out between the White House and the Fed. This was important for both monetary policy and fiscal policy.

Less than a year later, that truce almost fell apart. Clinton had battled his big deficit-reduction package through Congress, finally getting it passed in August 1993 after many changes, numerous compromises, and considerable political bloodletting. The president correctly viewed that victory as a signal achievement both politically and economically. He breathed a sigh of relief when he saw the bond market smiling at his handiwork by driving down long-term interest rates. But then on February 4, 1994, the FOMC voted to raise interest rates for the first time in five years. The rate hike was just 25 basis points, but it took markets by surprise, bond yields leaped upward, and the stock market fell by about 2.5 percent in a matter of hours. Within a few months as the Fed kept raising rates, the thirty-year Treasury yield was up about 120 basis point from its February 4 level.

We later learned that Greenspan had held back a more hawkish FOMC that wanted to raise rates even more that day. After listening to a majority of the committee express a preference for going up by 50 basis points, not 25, he interjected, "Well, I've been around a long time watching markets behave and I will tell you that if we do 50 basis points today, we have a very high probability of cracking these markets. . . . To go more than 25 at this point I think would be a bad mistake" (FOMC 1994b, 53). Later in the meeting, in a most unusual step, the Fed chair called for the FOMC equivalent of a whipped vote: "I would request that, if we can, we act unanimously. It is a very potent message out in the various communities with which we deal if we stand together. If we are going to get a split in the vote, I think it will create a problem for us, and I don't know how it will play out" (57). After this plea, the FOMC voted unanimously for 25 basis points.

Because this was the Fed's first rate hike in five years, Greenspan also took the unprecedented (at the time) step of issuing a press statement, under his own name, explaining that "the decision was taken to move toward a less accommodative stance in monetary policy in order to sustain and enhance the economic expansion" (FOMC 1994a). Yes, you read that right. Greenspan declared that the Fed was tightening monetary policy in order to enhance growth! It was Fedspeak extraordinaire, and that sentiment continued in subsequent statements.

But the most remarkable aspect of that February 4 statement was that it existed at all. Prior to that day and even after, Greenspan was known for being tight-lipped and inscrutable, much like Paul Volcker before him. The Fed's unspoken motto seemed to be "say very little, and say it cryptically." Although Greenspan may not have realized it at the time, that first short statement would prove to be the proverbial camel's nose under what would prove to be a large Federal Reserve transparency tent. But that development was years in the future.

At the White House, Clinton viewed the rate hike of 25 basis points as neither progrowth nor a friendly gesture. He was livid, but only in private. Insiders at the time (I was still one of them) witnessed his anger; he literally turned red. In the president's view, he had done exactly what Greenspan wanted right down to the deficit reduction number ($140 billion) and at considerable political peril. Yet here was the Fed stabbing him in the back.

His economic team, led by Rubin, managed to talk Clinton down from his anger using two main arguments. The argument that failed was straight economics. We pointed out that the real federal funds rate had been zero for almost a year and a half, which was an unsustainably low level. So, it was not so terrible if interest rates rose a bit; indeed, it was inevitable.

The argument that succeeded came more from the realm of political economy: if the president berated the Fed in public, his rhetoric might get the central bank's back up and induce it to demonstrate its independence by raising rates even further, as it had perhaps done under President Bush. Furthermore, renewing the war between the White House and the Fed would spook the markets. Bond and stock traders preferred peace; if war broke out instead, stock prices would probably fall, and interest rates would probably rise. Clinton bought into that argument. Most important, he smartly kept his displeasure with the Fed hidden within the White House walls.

The radio silence was deafening. Markets heard virtually nothing from the administration about the Fed other than Rubin's oft-repeated phrase "We don't comment on the Fed." All of us on the Clinton economic team learned to repeat this new mantra in our sleep, especially when talking to the press. The wording was critical. If we praised the Fed after some decisions but not others, those latter cases would be read as veiled criticisms. So, it was always "we don't

Robert E. Rubin (1938—)

Successful on Wall Street and in Washington

There is a moderately deep tradition of highly successful Wall Street executives coming to Washington only to fail as secretary of the treasury. The two jobs require different skills and radically different mindsets. But a few succeed, and Robert Rubin was certainly one of them. There is no doubt that he had enormous influence on the thinking of President Bill Clinton. And when Rubin left office in 1999, he was being compared to Alexander Hamilton. Quite a compliment.

Rubin was born in New York City in 1938 but raised mostly in Miami Beach, Florida. From there it was on to Harvard, from which he graduated summa cum laude in economics, and then Yale Law School. Fresh with his law degree in hand, he joined a top New York law firm in 1964 but did not stay there long. Wall Street beckoned, and in 1966 he joined Goldman Sachs. From there it was off to the races. Rubin later ran Goldman's stock and bond trading departments and became cochair (with Stephen Friedman) in 1990.

While at Goldman, Rubin became heavily involved in Democratic politics and especially in the 1992 campaign of Governor Bill Clinton of Arkansas. Once Clinton was elected to the presidency, Rubin was a natural choice to become the first director of the National Economic Council—a Clinton creation—and thereby the tacit leader of the economic team. In that position, Rubin urged Clinton to reduce the deficit and then helped shepherd the resulting reconciliation bill through Congress.

When Lloyd Bentsen left the Treasury post in January 1995, Rubin was again the natural choice to become secretary of the treasury. Within a few months he was leading something almost unprecedented: a concerted international effort to prop up the sagging dollar via both rhetoric and intervention in the foreign exchange markets. "A strong dollar is in the national interest," he insisted. The effort to boost the dollar succeeded mightily, earning Rubin the nickname "Trader Bob." He also worked with the International Monetary Fund and others to ameliorate financial crises in Mexico, other Latin American countries, Russia, and Southeast Asia.

Rubin has been credited with much of the economic success of the Clinton administration, though some of that success was due to Alan Greenspan at the Fed. The biggest blemish on Rubin's sterling record may well have been his refusal to permit regulation of derivatives—again in partnership with Greenspan.

---

comment on the Fed." And we didn't.[2] After the contentious Bush years, Greenspan must have been thrilled beyond belief.

The broad public, of course, did not realize how unusual the "no comment" policy was. As we have seen in earlier chapters, Presidents John Kennedy, Lyndon Johnson, Richard Nixon, Ronald Reagan, and George H. W. Bush all had either tried to "coordinate" the

---

2. I left the Clinton administration in June 1994 to join the Fed.

Fed's monetary policy with their fiscal policy or berated the Fed for not going along. Clinton changed that—dramatically. This newfound respect for the Fed's independence would last until Donald Trump became president.

The Perfect Soft Landing

The FOMC continued to raise interest rates as the economy grew: 25 basis points each in March and April 1994, 50 in May, and then after a short pause another 50 in August.[3] In the press release following the August 16, 1994, meeting, the FOMC stated that its latest hike of 50 basis points was "expected to be sufficient, at least for a time, to meet the objective of sustained, noninflationary growth." The phrase "at least for a time" may sound innocuous, but it was a very big deal at the tight-lipped FOMC at the time. It was the first time the committee had ever given what we now call (and routinely expect as) "forward guidance." By breaking a long-standing taboo, those five words raised eyebrows in the financial markets.[4] Speculation about how long "for a time" was began immediately.

It turned out to be about three months. In November, with (unfounded) inflation fears running rampant, the Fed boosted the funds rate by another 75 basis points, the largest change in the entire Greenspan era. Then the FOMC finished the 1994–1995 tightening cycle with another 50 basis points in February 1995. That last rate hike came during Mexico's financial crisis, a fact that did not faze the FOMC. Neither did the concerned voices of Janet Yellen (then a Fed governor) and me (I was vice chair), who worried that the Fed might be overdoing it. Neither of us registered a formal dissent, however. Lodging a dissent poses a high bar for a member of the Federal Reserve Board and an even higher bar for its vice chair. (In fact, no

---

3. Full disclosure: I was vice chair of the Fed throughout this period.

4. More disclosure: I was instrumental in getting those words into the FOMC statement. Greenspan thanked me at the time, but I'm not sure he thanked me later as markets interpreted—and sometimes misinterpreted—the FOMC's words.

vice chair has ever dissented.) We didn't feel that our disagreement with Greenspan warranted jumping that high.

As the Fed raised the funds rate in increments, long rates backed up, starting with a flurry of activity (and volatility) at the first rate hike. By May 1994, the thirty-year Treasury yield (the benchmark at the time) was all the way back to where it had been on election day 1992, and it then kept rising through the Fed's notable rate hike of 75 basis point in November. By that time, market expectations of how high the FOMC would go were clearly exaggerated relative to expectations held inside the committee.[5] That exaggerated view didn't do any good to bond prices.

By the time the dust settled on the Fed's rate-hiking cycle, the federal funds rate had been raised from 3 percent to 6 percent in a year's time. With the inflation rate virtually unchanged over that period, the real federal funds rate had also gone up about 300 basis points, from about zero to about 3 percent. At that point, Greenspan and the FOMC stopped. The thirty-year bond rate, incidentally, rose by about 150 basis points on net over this period.

In getting to the 6 percent funds rate, the committee had agonized over each rate hike as well as several decisions to stand pat. At meeting after meeting, it was "Shall we do 50 basis points, 25, or zero today?" If that's not fine-tuning, I don't know what is. And it worked—perfectly. When the tightening cycle ended in February 1995, the unemployment rate was down to 5.4 percent, which was close to contemporary estimates of the natural rate, and the Consumer Price Index inflation rate (over the preceding twelve months) was 2.9 percent. Greenspan and the Fed would probably have been content to live with numbers like those forever, and they almost did.

When the economy weakened in 1995 to a sluggish 1.3 percent growth rate in the first half of the year, there was more fine-tuning. The FOMC inched the funds rate down to 5.25 percent in three baby steps of 25 basis points each, ending in January 1996. Then the FOMC held the rate there for more than a year except for one little

5. This I know for sure. I was there.

increase of 25 basis points in March 1997. The funds rate was thus sitting at 5.5 percent when the financial crisis struck in August 1998, precipitated by the dramatic collapse of the famous hedge fund Long-Term Capital Management and by Russia's stunning choice to default on its sovereign debt.

The Fed responded to the financial chaos that emerged by cutting the federal funds rate 25 basis points on September 29, 1998. Notably, that dramatic emergency action was not taken because the U.S. economy needed a boost; real GDP growth over the first three quarters of 1998 averaged a robust 4.3 percent. The rate cut was certainly not stabilization policy in the usual sense, at least not domestic stabilization policy. Rather, it was intended to help calm turbulent world financial waters, which it did wonderfully well.

In a magnificent piece of journalistic exaggeration, the media dubbed this "the 25 basis points that saved the world." *TIME* magazine (O'Neill 1999) later featured Greenspan, Rubin, and Lawrence Summers (then Rubin's deputy) on the cover of its February 15, 1999, issue as "The Committee to Save the World." Apparently, you could do that, if you were the magical Greenspan, with just 75 basis points of rate cuts (the total amount the Fed did between September 29 and November 17, 1998). Such was the belief in fine-tuning and in Greenspan at the time.

A Separate Peace

Peace also broke out over fiscal policy but not before another bout of fiscal paralysis. Politically wounded by both the epic budget battle of 1993 and the failure of his health care plan in 1994, Bill Clinton and the Democrats suffered a humiliating defeat in the November 1994 elections. While Clinton himself was not on the ballot, numerous Democrats were, and almost all of them lost. Democratic senators, congressmen, and governors fell in droves. Even the Speaker of the House at the time, Tom Foley (D-WA), lost his seat, the first time that had happened since 1862!

When Congress convened in January 1995, both the Senate and the House had Republican majorities; for the House, it was the first time in forty years. House Republicans promptly installed as Speaker Newt Gingrich, the firebrand congressman from Georgia who had led them to electoral victory. Gingrich, a political warrior at heart, teamed up with the far less bellicose Senate majority leader, Bob Dole (R-KS), on a new "just say no" strategy. No to everything.

The 1995 budget season (for fiscal year 1996) opened accordingly, with battle stations manned. The Gingrich Republicans demanded steep cuts in Medicare, Medicaid, and other civilian spending. Clinton and the Democrats refused. In retaliation, Gingrich threatened not to raise the national debt ceiling, which had it actually happened would have thrown the U.S. Treasury into technical default on its debt.

The rancorous "debate," if you want to grace it with that name, finally produced a continuing resolution to keep the government running until November 13. (Remember, the new fiscal year had already started on October 1.) But the budget war dissolved into acrimony, leading to two (partial) government shutdowns: one for six days in November and the other for a long twenty-two days, including both Christmas and New Year's Day 1996. From a political perspective, the shutdowns went badly for the Republicans, and Gingrich and colleagues eventually agreed with the White House on a seven-year plan to balance the budget through both spending cuts and tax increases.

The negotiations in 1997 over the fiscal year 1998 budget fared much better. Clinton had won reelection easily, and compromise became the order of the day. There were still major disagreements over budget priorities that ran along the usual party lines. Republicans wanted to shrink domestic spending in areas where Democrats wanted to increase it. Democrats favored defense cuts, which Republicans abhorred. But revenue was pouring into the Treasury from the higher tax rates acting in concert with a booming economy and a soaring stock market that produced bountiful capital gains.[6]

---

6. To cite just one dramatic example, the Internal Revenue Service took in $36 billion from taxes on capital gains in 1994. By 1998 that was up to $89 billion, and it topped out at $127 billion in 2000. See Tax Policy Center (2017).

And Clinton had probably convinced himself by then that deficit reduction accompanied by favorable bond market reactions created jobs, the negative fiscal multiplier once again. A bipartisan agreement seemed possible and was in fact reached in August 1997.

Politically, the Balanced Budget Act of 1997 was touted as a major achievement at the time. It established new spending caps (which were, however, subsequently violated), renewed the PAYGO provision from the 1990 budget agreement, and even made some cuts in Medicare, which were taken as a sign of seriousness. Economically, however, it was not a big deal. In fact, when you examined the details of the 1997 agreement, it actually increased the budget deficit a bit for the first few fiscal years (Blinder and Yellen 2001, 74–76). Nonetheless, the gusher of revenue emanating from the booming economy diminished the red ink rapidly and pushed the budget into surplus.

Table 11.1 displays the deficits projected in January 1997 before the Balanced Budget Act of 1997 passed, the deficits projected a year later after the act had passed, and the deficits actually recorded in subsequent years. Clearly there were some big, pleasant surprises for dedicated deficit reducers.

But the more important policy point is this: while the 1990 and 1993 budget agreements were major landmarks on the path to a sounder fiscal position, the 1997 agreement was, by comparison, small beer that garnered far too much credit at the time. In its December 1997 report, the Congressional Budget Office (CBO) credited it with just $127 billion worth of deficit reduction over five years. (The 1993 budget agreement was closer to $500 billion.) As table 11.1 shows, the budget was already close to balance by fiscal year 1997, before the 1997 agreement took effect.

The Productivity Boom and Greenspan's "Great Call"

As just noted, the roaring economy helped push the federal budget into the black with amazing speed. Just compare the January 1997 and January 1998 CBO projections for the fiscal year 2002 deficit shown in table 11.1, and remember that the putative goal was to

TABLE 11.1. Actual and projected budget deficits, 1997–2002 (in billions of dollars)

Fiscal Year	Projected deficit in January 1997	Projected deficit in January 1998	Actual deficit (−) or surplus (+)
1997	−124	−22	−22
1998	−120	−5	69
1999	−147	−2	126
2000	−171	−3	236
2001	−167	14	128
2002	−188	69	−158

Source: Congressional Budget Office.

TABLE 11.2. Macroeconomic indicators in the late 1990s

Year	Real GDP growth (Q4-Q4)	Unemployment rate (December)	Inflation rate (December)	Productivity growth (Q4-Q4)*
1996	4.4	5.4	3.4	2.1
1997	4.5	4.7	1.7	2.7
1998	4.9	4.4	1.6	3.3
1999	4.8	4.1	2.7	4.2
2000	3.0	3.9	3.4	3.0
Ave. 1996–2000	4.3	4.5	2.6	3.1

*Labor productivity in the nonfarm business sector.
Source: Bureau of Labor Statistics and Bureau of Economic Analysis.

balance the budget in five years. The budget outlook for fiscal year 2002 improved by $257 billion in a single year, and the CBO estimated that virtually none of that was due to policy changes from the 1997 budget agreement (CBO 1997, 1998a). The budget was nearly balanced while the negotiators were still negotiating.

The boom of the late 1990s also created millions of new jobs and drove the unemployment rate down to 3.8 percent, marking the first reading below 4 percent since January 1970. Table 11.2 offers a selective snapshot of just how great macroeconomic performance was in the late 1990s. Over the half decade shown there, real GDP growth averaged 4.3 percent per annum, and the unemployment rate dropped to a thirty-year low. Meanwhile, inflation averaged just

2.6 percent, defying predictions that tight markets would foment inflation.

I have already suggested that the Fed's expert fine-tuning played a role in this spectacular success. But it got a huge assist from another source. The last column shows the remarkable acceleration of (labor) productivity growth from an average of just 1.4 percent over the period 1973–1995 (not shown in the table) to an astounding 3.1 percent over the five years 1996–2000, presumably largely due to rapid advances in information and communications technology. A gain of 1.7 percentage points in the productivity growth rate is gigantic. It gave the economy additional running room that no one anticipated.

Well, almost no one. In fact, Alan Greenspan somehow saw it coming. Skillful monetary policy and rapid productivity growth interacted positively to produce what former Fed governor Laurence Meyer labeled Greenspan's "great call" (Meyer 2004, chap. 6). At the start of this period, an unemployment rate in the 5.5 percent range was considered a prudent estimate of the nonaccelerating inflation rate of unemployment (NAIRU). For example, the CBO's estimate of NAIRU in this period was 5.4 percent (CBO 2021; NROU data). Labor markets much tighter than that made inflation hawks— and even a few doves—nervous. Remember, the FOMC had been tightening monetary policy to ward off inflation as recently as February 1995, basing its decisions in part on a Phillips curve with a NAIRU in the 5.5–6 percent range. We thought we had managed a perfect soft landing at full employment.

But then growth accelerated, and unemployment fell even further. Yet Greenspan, the alleged inflation hawk, did not react by raising interest rates. Rather, as Janet Yellen and I put it later, "the best one-word description of the Fed's monetary policy from early 1996 to the summer of 1999 is *forbearance*" (Blinder and Yellen 2001, 35). The Fed watched and waited for a rise in inflation that never came. The FOMC's patience was remarkable on its face and even more remarkable when you remember that Greenspan had been praised in the financial press for acting preemptively against inflation in 1994, that is, for raising rates before inflation rose.

Yet in 1996–1999 with Greenspan unmistakably in charge, the FOMC abandoned preemption in favor of forbearance. As GDP sped along and unemployment fell, even dovish members of the Federal Reserve Board, such as Larry Meyer and Janet Yellen, grew increasingly nervous. (I had left the Fed by then.) Was the Fed already behind the curve? Was it sitting on an inflation pot that was about to boil over?

Shortly before the September 24, 1996, FOMC meeting (note the early date), Meyer and Yellen visited Greenspan in his office to express concern about the inflationary risks the Fed was taking by holding interest rates constant with resource utilization so tight. They told the chair that they thought it was time to start raising rates, albeit gently. Then at the FOMC meeting, they both stated out loud that they were prepared to support a rate increase of 25 basis points if the chair proposed it.[7] He didn't, however, and the funds rate remained where it was—at 5.25 percent. Two years later in September 1998, the funds rate was still 5.25 percent even though the unemployment rate was down to 4.6 percent.

Greenspan's forbearance derived from his belief that productivity was accelerating, a belief he held well before it appeared in the official data. The numbers in the last column of table 11.2 show that Greenspan's hunch was correct. But no one knew this in 1996 or 1997. It was an educated guess. Make that a well-educated guess because Greenspan devoured both numbers and anecdotes. He talked to businesspeople, he pored over data that went well beyond the standard macroeconomic aggregates, and at least in this case he saw things that others didn't.

The idea that faster productivity growth would allow the economy to grow safely—that is, without higher inflation—at a faster speed had been germinating in Greenspan's mind for a while. The public didn't hear his speculations on the subject for years. Instead, he posed artfully as an inflation hawk. But those of us on the inside heard him ruminate about the wonders of the "new economy" at several FOMC meetings. At the December 1995 meeting, he put

7. The story is told in Meyer (2004).

it all together in a lengthy peroration in which he broached what he called "a broad hypothesis about where the economy is going over the longer term." In his own words, "My idea was that as the world absorbed information technology and learned to put it to work, we had entered what would prove to be a protracted period of lower inflation, lower interest rates, increased productivity, and full employment" (Greenspan 2007, 166–67).

Greenspan later wrote that "this was all pretty speculative, especially for a working session of the FOMC. . . . Most committee members seemed relieved to return to the familiar ground of deciding whether to lower the fed funds rate by 0.25 percent" (which they did). But when the time for the vote came, I needled him slightly by saying "I hope you will allow me to agree with the reasons you've given for lowering the rate without signing on to your brave-new-world scenario, which I am not quite ready to do" (Greenspan 2007, 167). In his memoir, Greenspan referred to the person who made this cheeky remark as "one of our most thoughtful members." Thank you, Alan. But I was wrong.

In retrospect, I should have signed on to the brave new noninflationary world scenario right then and there. In December 1995, however, the data didn't show it—not even close. Nor did the data show it in 1996 and 1997. Unlike Greenspan, I didn't like to base decisions on hunches. Like Larry Meyer and Janet Yellen—all three of us academic economists—I wanted to see it in the data.

Figure 11.3, which depicts data from Blinder and Yellen (2001, 61), shows just how long we data guys had to wait. The lower line is the point estimate of the break in the upward trend of labor productivity in a series of conventional output-and-hours equations, each ending in a different quarter. These estimates bounce around a bit, but calling them all "about 1 percent" right through the end of the 1990s does not do great violence to the estimates. It's the t-ratios (for statistical significance of the break in trend), shown in the upper line, that are more interesting. Using the conventional benchmark of t > 2, an econometrician would not have been ready to declare an increase in trend productivity until the third quarter of 1998, if then. Greenspan was there years earlier, which is why Meyer

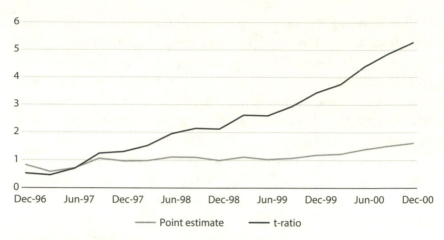

FIGURE 11.3. Estimated break in the productivity trend and its t-ratio (regressions ending in quarter indicated).
Source: Blinder and Yellen (2001).

called it Greenspan's "great call." Thanks to that call, millions more Americans found jobs in the late 1990s.

There was, however, at least one loose end in Greenspan's analysis. Faster productivity growth alone will raise the economy's speed limit, that is, the long-run growth rate that the economy can sustain without straining resources too tightly. Roughly, that's the sum of labor force growth plus productivity growth. However, when the economy grows at that rate, the unemployment rate should remain stable, which is far from what happened in the late 1990s. Rather, unemployment kept falling, indicating that resource utilization was tightening. Yet there were no inflationary consequences, just as Greenspan had speculated at the December 1995 FOMC meeting.

The Rise of Central Bank Independence

In addition to the wonderfully long-lasting boom, the 1990s witnessed an important and almost worldwide revolution in thinking about the respective roles of central banks and elected politicians in making monetary policy. It was in this decade that central bank independence came to dominate both thinking and practice.

The United States, of course, had an independent central bank well before the 1990s. But it is a myth to think that central bank independence had a long and illustrious history here. Nor is it enshrined in the U.S. Constitution. There are nations in which the independence of the central bank has constitutional protection, but the United States is not one of them. Rather, the Constitution gives Congress the power "to coin Money" and "regulate the Value thereof" (Article I, Section 8). In the Federal Reserve Act of 1913 and its many amendments since then, Congress has delegated that authority to the Fed, which has de facto independence. But those are just ordinary statutes that Congress can change at any time. Delegated power can be reclaimed.

We have seen early in this book (especially chapter 1) that there was far from uniform belief in Federal Reserve independence in the 1960s and 1970s. Economists with views as disparate as James Tobin and Milton Friedman opposed it. Even the Fed's longtime leader, William McChesney Martin, saw the Fed as part of the economic "team." Importantly, however, monetary policy decisions were in fact made by nonpolitical technocrats on the FOMC. Martin established some measure of de facto independence when he defied President Lyndon Johnson in 1966.

The 1970s probably marked the nadir of central bank independence in the United States. As we saw in chapter 4, President Nixon installed his friend Arthur Burns as chair of the Fed in February 1970. Unlike Martin, Burns had long-term relationships with Republican politicians in general and with Nixon in particular. He seemed to make monetary policy subservient to the political needs of Nixon, which is the antithesis of independence.

After the brief Miller interlude in 1978–1979, the indomitable Paul Volcker took over at the Fed and quickly reasserted the central bank's independence. Notice that there was no change in law. Nor was there even a change in the presidency; Jimmy Carter appointed Miller first and Volcker second. But there was a huge change in the personality and intestinal fortitude of the Fed chair and in his dedication both to fighting inflation and to asserting the independence of the central bank. As noted in chapter 8, both President Reagan, who inherited and then reappointed Volcker, and his right-hand man James Baker found Volcker's degree of independence annoying, to say the least. One suspects that they thought the more political Alan Greenspan would be more pliant.

If so, they were probably disappointed. As noted in this chapter, the George H. W. Bush administration and the Greenspan Fed were often at loggerheads. So, while the Federal Reserve acted independently during the Bush administration, the White House chafed at the Fed's independence and tried to undermine it with rhetoric.

The next watershed for central bank independence in the United States came in the early days of the Clinton administration when, as observed in this chapter, Bill Clinton held—or maybe bit—his tongue when the Greenspan Fed started raising interest rates in February 1994. Throughout his eight-year presidency, Clinton rarely deviated from the mantra "we don't comment on the Fed." While it is unlikely that a warm feeling ever developed between the back-slapping Democratic pol from Arkansas and the stiff Republican Fed chair from Manhattan, Clinton nevertheless reappointed Greenspan in 1996 and again in 2000. By then, Greenspan had become an institution. Years later in October 2007, Senator John McCain (R-AZ), who would become the Republican presidential standard-bearer in 2008, jokingly declared Greenspan to be indispensable: "If he's alive or dead, it doesn't matter. If he's dead, just prop him up and put some dark glasses on him, like 'Weekend at Bernie's'" (*Boston Herald* 2007).

If you looked around the world at the end of the 1980s, the Federal Reserve, the Deutsche Bundesbank, and the Swiss National Bank stood out as almost the only independent central banks on earth. (New Zealand would follow soon.) In other major countries, monetary policy was either made by (e.g., the United Kingdom) or heavily influenced by (e.g., Japan) the president or prime minister's office. But such arrangements changed rapidly and decisively in the 1990s. By the decade's end, all the advanced industrial countries of the world and many of the emerging market ones had made their central banks independent.

The reasons behind this highly consequential change in economic governance were numerous. Perhaps paramount was the high inflation rates of the 1970s and 1980s. Bodies politic and their elected officials everywhere grew unhappy with high inflation, saw that it did them no good (e.g., there was no long-run gain in employment), and searched for a way out. Looking at the German and Swiss (and, to a lesser extent, the American) examples, they saw lower inflation rates without higher unemployment rates. Some politicians may even have been acquainted with scholarly research establishing that same nonrelationship statistically.[8]

Geopolitical events also played major roles. When the Soviet Union collapsed in 1991, the former Soviet satellite nations suddenly found themselves without any "monetary policy," a job that had previously been handled from Moscow. These new nations needed to do something about monetary and financial policy, and establishing an independent central bank seemed an attractive option. Remember, one of them was East Germany, which had the successful West German model at its doorstep.

A year later, twelve member nations of the European Union signed the Treaty of Maastricht that, among other things, set them on a course toward a common currency and, of course, toward a single central bank. Establishing an independent national central bank was among the Maastricht requirements. (The Bundesbank was clearly the model.) France made its central bank independent in 1993, Spain followed in 1994, and so on.

The United Kingdom dropped out of the process that eventually led to the creation of the euro and the European Central Bank in 1992. But the UK government nonetheless freed the Bank of England to make monetary policy independently almost immediately after Labour's smashing electoral victory in 1997.[9] "Independent but accountable" was the United Kingdom's mantra. The Bank of Japan

---

8. Alesina and Summers (1993) was probably the best-known at the time. But others, such as Bade and Parkin (1988) and Grilli et al. (1991), had earlier found that more independent central banks were associated with lower inflation.

9. In return for gaining monetary policy independence, the Bank of England relinquished its traditional authority over bank supervision and regulation.

followed suit the next year. Thus, by late 1998 almost all major nations had independent central banks.

The intellectual currents of the day may also have played a role in the sharp turn toward central bank independence. The notion that political control of money produced too much inflation was hardly a revelation; sovereigns had been "clipping the currency," whether literally or figuratively, for centuries. If you followed that political economy logic a bit further, it led to the idea that it might be better (in the Pareto-dominating sense) to let technocrats make monetary policy rather than politicians.

Finn Kydland and Edward Prescott had dressed this old argument up in new rational expectations clothing in 1977. Their celebrated paper on "time inconsistency" in monetary policy (Kydland and Prescott 1977), the idea that central bankers might reach for short-term employment gains at the cost of higher long-term inflation, garnered a huge amount of attention in academia, eventually leading to a Nobel Prize for the pair. But all that fuss led some academics to give the Kydland-Prescott analysis far too much credit for the trend toward independent central banking. They forgot, for example, that both the Volcker disinflation in the United States and the Thatcher disinflation in the United Kingdom were entirely discretionary, not rules-based in the least. The latter was even accomplished by an elected politician, as the Bank of England was subservient to 10 Downing Street at the time. Kydland and Prescott's time-inconsistency analysis is one of the starkest examples of an idea that sweeps academia but makes barely a ripple in the real world of policy making.

Whatever the reasons or, more accurately whatever the weighting of the various reasons, central bank independence, which was rare in 1990, became the norm by 1998. In a world such as that of central banking, where change typically comes at a glacial pace, this was blazing speed.

Chapter Summary

The 1990s began with a recession but ended with the tightest labor markets the United States had seen since 1969.

The public was slow to recognize that the recession ended early in 1991. That misperception, enhanced by the fact that the recovery was "jobless" at first, contributed to George H. W. Bush's defeat at the polls by Bill Clinton in November 1992. Bush, however, blamed Alan Greenspan and the Fed for cutting interest rates too slowly. During the last two years of Bush's presidency, administration officials bashed the Fed incessantly and in public.

Relations between the White House and the Fed warmed dramatically during the Clinton presidency. Clinton's aggressive 1993 target for deficit reduction was actually suggested by Greenspan. The financial markets loved the program, and bond rates fell. But Republicans in Congress "just said no," and Democrats picked Clinton's budget proposals apart. In particular, they rejected Clinton's idea to shield the economy with a small short-term fiscal stimulus. Keynesian fiscal policy was deeply out of fashion at the time. Even without the stimulus, that first Clinton budget barely squeaked through Congress without a single Republican vote. It turned out to be wildly successful, however. The budget deficit melted away, and the economy grew strongly.

Clinton was enraged when the Fed began to raise interest rates in February 1994. But unlike Bush, he held his tongue: *We don't comment on the Fed*. Over the course of a year, the FOMC raised the federal funds rate by 300 basis points, which turned out to be exactly the right amount, leading to a perfect soft landing at about 3 percent inflation and about 5.5 percent unemployment. Economists at the time thought that was about as good as it gets. But then things got better.

The late 1990s were a period of above-trend growth, falling unemployment, and stable inflation. One key to this success was a sharp acceleration of productivity after 1995, presumably a result of the information technology revolution and of Greenspan's belief in that acceleration long before the data showed it. Trust in the Fed's ability to steer the economy with discretionary monetary policy reached fantastic heights during this time.

While Alan Greenspan's position in the United States may have been unique, one nation after another made their central banks independent in the 1990s, and none have gone back to political control of money. In stark contrast, the idea of using discretionary fiscal policy to manage aggregate demand continued its vanishing act. Instead, many Washington hands started to believe (and to say) that reducing the deficit was the way to "grow the economy." Those wonderful days for the U.S. economy were dark days for Keynesianism.

Then came the election of President George W. Bush, and everything changed.

12

The 2000s: The Job-Loss Recovery and the Bubbles

And the cornerstone of my economic policies, when I first got elected, was cutting taxes on everybody . . . who paid taxes.
—GEORGE W. BUSH INTERVIEW WITH LARRY KUDLOW, 2010

The productivity surge discussed in the previous chapter, in concert with what became known as the dot.com bubble in the stock market, were major drivers of the fabulous macroeconomic performance of the late 1990s. The productivity part was solidly based and lasted well into the 2000s.[1] You can see it in the data today, although as mentioned, Alan Greenspan perceived it well before it appeared in the data. There is also little doubt that the commercialization of the internet played a major role in the productivity surge.[2]

1. There is controversy to this day about the end point of the period of rapid productivity growth. I prefer 2010; others prefer a much earlier end date, such as 2004.
2. Among many sources that could be cited, see Oliner and Sichel (2002).

The Dot.com Boom and Bust

The stock market's infatuation with dot.coms in 1998–2000 took an underlying reality and ran wild with it. Even at the time, many observers believed that stock traders had lost touch with any semblance of fundamental values. Market valuations for companies with no current earnings, and in many cases poor prospects for ever having earnings, soared to incredible heights. Ordinary people who had no business doing so became day traders. That a bubble was inflating was obvious to almost everyone. The only questions were when it would burst and how hard. Brave (or foolish) investors decided to ride the bubble for as long as they could. As is common in such crazes, too many "investors" thought they could be among the first out the door.[3]

Figure 12.1 offers a highly subdued picture of the stock market bubble by comparing the performance of the Nasdaq index (where most of the new tech stocks were traded) with that of the Dow Jones Industrial Average (the bluest of the blue chips) over the decade 1995–2005. Though subdued, the picture is still dramatic. You can barely discern what was actually a sizable bubble in the Dow, which rose from just over 3,800 at the start of 1995 to a peak around 11,500 in January 2000 (thus tripling in five years) before tumbling to roughly 7,500 (approximately its November 1997 value) by October 2002, a decline of 34 percent.[4]

But this rise and fall was dwarfed by the wild ride of the Nasdaq, which skyrocketed from roughly 750 at the start of 1995 to over 1,900 in July 1998, up more than 150 percent in just three and a half years. The party was just getting started, however. The dot.com craze really took off late in 1998, driving the Nasdaq to a dizzying peak of over 5,000 on March 10, 2000, an additional gain of 157 percent in under two years. Do the math. It multiplies to a mind-boggling 567 percent rise in the Nasdaq in little more than five years. Of course, the truly insane valuations of March 2000 couldn't and

---

3. For many earlier historical examples, see Kindleberger (1978).
4. Stock market numbers in this and the next paragraph are monthly averages.

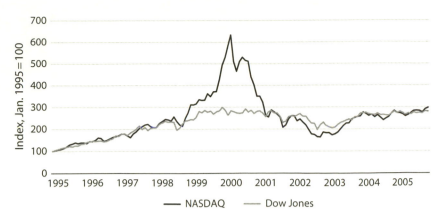

FIGURE 12.1. Two stock market indexes, 1995–2005.
Source: S&P Dow Jones Indices and NASDAQ OMX Group.

didn't last. By September 2001 the Nasdaq was back down to about 1,600, right where it had been at the start of 1998. It continued to fall, however, bottoming out at 1,242 in October 2002, thus making the peak-to-trough decline about 75 percent! The index did not return to the 5,000 range until the summer of 2016.

The Nasdaq is an average of many stocks. The ascents and subsequent declines of some of the individual dot.coms were far more spectacular. Priceline, which turned out to be one of the survivors, went public in March 1999 and saw its share price double in a month to over $900. At the time, all the company did was sell discounted airline tickets. The *New York Times* reported at the time that "Priceline, which lost $114 million last year selling $35 million worth of airline tickets, is now worth more than the United Airlines, Continental Airlines and Northwest Airlines combined" (Hansell 1999). A bit richly priced, perhaps? By the end of December 2000, Priceline shares had plummeted to $6.75, a drop of more than 99 percent. The company survived, however, and remains in business today as Booking.com.

Many other dot.coms simply vanished from the face of the earth. One well-publicized example was Webvan, which was founded in 1996 on a not-very-original idea: delivering groceries to customers' homes. That's a good idea, of course, but home delivery of groceries

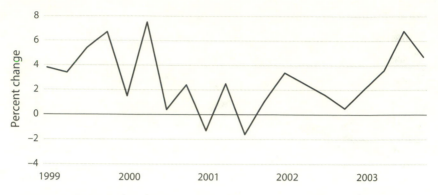

FIGURE 12.2. Annualized real GDP growth rates, quarterly, 1999–2003.
Source: Bureau of Economic Analysis.

had been going on for a century or so (Muller 2015). Could ordering over the internet really be so superior to ordering by telephone? Apparently not. Webvan began deliveries in the San Francisco Bay area in June 1999, investing heavily in warehouses, trucks, and advertising in an effort to "get big fast" (the celebrated Amazon model). At the time of its initial public offering in November 1999, Webvan had logged cumulative sales of $400,000 (yes, that's thousand, not million). Yet the initial public offering valued the company at more than $4.8 billion. Webvan filed for bankruptcy in June 2001.

When the stock market crashes as hard as it did in 2000–2001, it is not surprising if a recession follows—and it did. However, the 2001 recession was both short (only eight months long) and shallow, so shallow in fact that it disappears if you look only at annual data: real GDP was actually 1 percent higher in 2001 than in 2000. You have to peer closely at quarterly data to find two slightly negative quarters, 2001:1 (a −1.1% seasonally adjusted annual rate) and 2001:3 (−1.7%). Those two quarters are not even consecutive (figure 12.2). But the National Bureau of Economic Research (NBER) business cycle dating committee, which looks at a myriad of data series, not just GDP, decided to call it a recession anyway. I have long called it the recessionette.

The Election of 2000 and Tax Cuts

A soaring stock market, burgeoning federal budget surpluses, and a booming economy formed the economic backdrop of the 2000 presidential campaign. That election ended in a virtual tie between Vice President Al Gore and Governor George W. Bush of Texas.[5] Booming economies help incumbents, and as Bill Clinton's vice president, Gore was almost an incumbent, just as Bush's father had been in 1988. Yet Gore chose to run away from Clinton rather than toward him, presumably due to the taint of the Monica Lewinsky scandal. It was a costly political error; Clinton was extraordinarily popular at the time.[6]

Gore did, however, embrace the Clinton administration's signal achievement, which he called "balancing the budget." Curiously, Clinton, Gore, and other politicians of the day preferred to speak of balanced budgets rather than budget surpluses. Perhaps they thought that negative numbers were too complex for political discourse, or perhaps they just thought that "balancing the budget" had a nicer rhetorical ring. Political messaging aside, official budget projections in 2000 showed surpluses "as far as the eye could see." For example, the Congressional Budget Office's (CBO) ten-year projection issued in July 2000 envisioned budget surpluses not just continuing but actually growing larger through fiscal 2010 (CBO 2000). What to do with these surpluses became a major issue in the campaign.

Gore's platform included a plan to pay off the entire national debt by 2012. Given what happened thereafter, that sounds like a bad joke. But serious people at the time were ruminating about the problems that might arise if and when there was no longer any Treasury debt outstanding. One of those serious people was Alan Greenspan (Greenspan 2007, 217–18). Among the many novel questions was how the Federal Reserve would conduct monetary policy in a world

---

5. Full disclosure: I was principal economic adviser to Al Gore's presidential campaign.

6. Clinton's approval rating hovered near 60 percent throughout the campaign, according to the Gallup poll. See Gallup Organization (2001).

with no Treasury debt. As an early down payment on the eventual elimination of the national debt, Gore pledged to set aside funds for Medicare, Medicaid, and Social Security in a figurative "lock-box," a metaphor that apparently lent itself to political ridicule. Inelegant messaging aside, Gore clearly ran as the fiscal conservative in the race. True to Clinton's observation, the Democrats had become the party of Eisenhower Republicans.

In stark contrast, Bush and the Republicans of 2000 were not heirs to the Eisenhower legacy. Like Ronald Reagan twenty years earlier, George W. Bush campaigned on enacting large tax cuts, arguing, among other things, that the government should not take more money from people than it needed to pay its bills. As he opined in his August 2000 acceptance speech at the Republican National Convention, "The surplus is not the government's money. The surplus is the people's money" (Bush 2000). And it should go back to them.

Candidate Bush sometimes seemed to suggest that his proposed tax cuts would (almost?) pay for themselves with faster economic growth, thereby echoing the false assertions of the supply-siders of a generation earlier (Krugman 2001). When Gore attacked the tax cut proposal as a "risky scheme," Bush famously countered that Gore was using "fuzzy math." In sum, George W. Bush, like Reagan before him, ran on a highly expansionary fiscal plan despite a strong economy that did not need stimulus. They were perhaps Lyndon Johnson Republicans.

This sharp partisan difference in fiscal policy between Bush and Gore played a prominent role in the campaign, which ended in a virtual dead heat on election day. Initially Bush was declared the victor by the media, a call that was quickly withdrawn due to disputes over the vote in Florida. It took a harrowing thirty-six days to resolve the mess, which the U.S. Supreme Court finally did on December 13, 2000, by ordering a halt to a recount that was then in progress in Florida. Bush was thereby awarded Florida by a margin of 537 votes out of over 5.8 million cast in the Sunshine State. That slim margin was enough to give him 271 electoral votes and victory in the electoral college even though Gore had won the national popular vote by about 540,000 votes.

The days between the election and the January 2001 inauguration were tumultuous and unsettling, filled with huge political uncertainties and marred by a feeling among many Democrats that Gore had been robbed of the White House. This tumult may have contributed to the small decline in real GDP that took place in the first quarter of 2001 (−1.1% at an annual rate).[7] That's impossible to know. But a short, shallow recession began in March, although the NBER did not declare the start of the recession until November 2001, which was the month the recession ended.

The weak macroeconomic performance of early 2001 presented President Bush and his team with an entirely new rationale for a major tax cut: it would provide a Keynesian stimulus (though they abjured the adjective) for a sluggish economy. Never mind that Keynesianism was the antithesis of supply-side economics. "With the economy in a slump, a senior White House adviser said, the administration simply believes that the Keynesian rationale for a tax cut has the best chance of winning public support" (Leonhardt 2001).

The tax bill that Bush signed into law in June 2001 was comprehensive. It reduced income tax bracket rates (for example, the top marginal tax rate dropped from Clinton's 39.6% to 35%), doubled the child tax credit, phased in a repeal of the estate tax, reduced the so-called marriage penalty, and more. Bush's original request was scored by the CBO as losing $1.6 trillion in revenue over ten years, or almost 1.5 percent of GDP.

However, that sum was soon whittled down to $1.35 trillion over nine years by some creative accounting. To avoid a filibuster in the Senate, Republicans incorporated the tax bill into the congressional budget resolution; but that required it to include a sunset clause. The budget window then (as now) was ten years, so legislating tax cuts that would sunset after nine years reduced the CBO score substantially and did not carry the revenue loss over into the following ten years. Of course, neither Bush nor congressional Republicans intended the tax cuts to disappear, and that set the stage for future

---

7. Growth rates in the quarters just before and just after were 2.5 percent and 2.4 percent, respectively.

budget battles. Nor did the administration offer any pay-fors; the entire revenue loss went straight into the budget deficit.

Among the more interesting sidelights of the tax debate in 2001 was the active participation of Federal Reserve Chair Alan Greenspan. Greenspan, as we have seen, had gotten along famously with Bill Clinton. But Greenspan was a Bush Republican at heart. In congressional testimony just days after George W. Bush's inauguration, the Fed chair all but endorsed the new president's tax cut proposals, partly on the grounds that once the government had paid off the entire national debt, continuing budget surpluses would force it to buy private assets, something Greenspan found abhorrent.

Was he really so naive as to believe that Congress in the twenty-first century would allow surpluses that large to persist for years, as it had in the nineteenth century? Students of Congress rolled their eyes in disbelief, and we know that Greenspan had a keen political sense (Woodward 2000). Democrats opposed to the tax cuts were enraged at what they saw as rank partisanship from the Fed chief. Economists who valued the separation of monetary policy from fiscal policy winced at the idea that Congress might return the favor by interfering in monetary policy. Greenspan himself later admitted that his congressional testimony in support of tax cuts "proved to be politically explosive" even though (he claimed) "politics had not been my intent. . . . I'd have given the same testimony if Al Gore had been president" (Greenspan 2007, 220, 222). Many of us on the Gore team wondered about that claim.

Regardless, this overt involvement in fiscal decision making was something new for a Fed chief. Prior to the Clinton presidency, Federal Reserve chairs had grown accustomed to fending off attempted encroachments on their territory from the fiscal authorities. They didn't like White House interventions, though they expected them. Now Greenspan, taking full advantage of his exalted status as the nation's economic guru, seemed to be poaching into the territory of fiscal policy and on a hotly partisan issue to boot. Many observers of monetary policy felt that this was unwise.[8] President Bush, how-

8. See, for example, Sperling (2001).

ever, was delighted: "I was pleased to hear Mr. Greenspan's words. I thought they were measured and just right" (Berry 2001).

Curiously, the Fed chair eschewed what could have been a plausible Keynesian rationale for the 2001 tax cuts, even though the U.S. economy was weakening at the time and the Fed was reducing interest rates to bolster demand. The Federal Open Market Committee (FOMC) began a series of rate cuts on January 3, 2001, by lowering the funds rate from 6.5 percent to 6 percent. It then continued to cut rates aggressively throughout the year and then once more in 2002 and a final time in 2003, eventually pushing the funds rate all the way down to 1 percent by June 2003.

Fiscal policy was not passive during this period either. Not content with the 2001 tax cuts, which turned out to be exquisitely timed from a countercyclical perspective, the president followed with more tax cuts in 2003. The reductions in bracket rates that were scheduled to be phased in by the 2001 act were accelerated, as were depreciation allowances. Tax rates on capital gains and "qualified" dividends (which covered most of them) were lowered. The revenue losses from the 2003 act were smaller than their 2001 counterparts. And just as in 2001, the Bush administration did not propose any pay-fors. Doing so was made easier by the fact that the PAYGO law had expired in 2002.

The 9/11 Attacks and the Job-Loss Recovery

George W. Bush had been president for less than eight months when terrorists struck the World Trade Center in New York City and the Pentagon. Nearly three thousand lives were lost on September 11, 2001, and the nation, it is fair to say, was thoroughly traumatized. It was, after all, an attack on the American mainland, something Americans had not witnessed since the War of 1812. While accustomed to sending soldiers to fight overseas, U.S. citizens were not accustomed to defending the homeland. It was widely claimed at the time and since that 9/11 changed everything. In many respects it did. America has not been the same nation since, and 9/11 remains a searing memory to this day.

But from the narrow perspective of macroeconomics, 9/11 didn't change much. Figure 12.2 displays the growth rate of real GDP, quarter by quarter, from 1999 through 2003. The two negative quarters in 2001 stand out; the second of these (2001:3) is the 9/11 quarter. But remember that the terrorist attacks occurred late in the quarter, too late to have much of an effect on third-quarter data. By the fourth quarter, when you might have expected 9/11 to have its greatest impact, growth was positive again though barely so. And by 2002, the economy was clearly heading uphill. Taking a broader perspective, GDP growth over the ten quarters prior to 2001:3 averaged 3.25 percent. Over the ten quarters after 2001:3 it averaged 2.9 percent. That's lower but hardly a sharp break in trend.

Nor did 9/11 change fiscal or monetary policy much. The Fed, as noted earlier, was reducing interest rates aggressively before 9/11 and continued to do so thereafter. The Bush administration continued to promote tax cuts, just as it had before 9/11, and succeeded in getting more of them enacted in 2003. Real spending on national defense rose by about 15 percent over the two years following 9/11. But most of that was attributable to the ensuing war in Afghanistan (a direct response to the terrorist attacks) and, even more so, to the subsequent war in Iraq (which was a response to what?). Overall, however, the biggest changes in fiscal policy under President George W. Bush came on the tax side. The CBO's estimates of tax receipts without the effects of the automatic stabilizers (thus controlling for cyclical influences) fell from 19.7 percent of GDP in fiscal 2000 to just 15.8 percent of GDP in fiscal 2004. That huge swing dwarfed changes on the spending side, which were just 0.6 percent of GDP over those same four years.

In sum, neither monetary nor fiscal policy shows any major discontinuity around 9/11. What did change after 9/11, but probably not because of 9/11, was the behavior of the U.S. labor market. As we saw in the previous chapter, a "jobless recovery" plagued President George H. W. Bush in 1991–1992. It may well have cost him the election. Job performance was even worse for his son, President George W. Bush. After the 2001 recession, the economy embarked on what was at first a job-*loss* recovery. Output grew but employment fell. Output per hour grew instead.

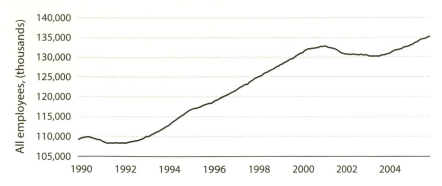

FIGURE 12.3. Payroll employment, monthly, 1990–2005.
Source: Bureau of Labor Statistics.

Figure 12.3 displays monthly data on payroll employment from 1990 through 2005. From March 1991 (the NBER trough) through March 1992, net job growth was essentially zero. Then the job market snapped back to life, and the economy added about 1.6 million net new jobs over the following year. After the minirecession of 2001, by contrast, the economy continued to lose jobs, albeit at a slow rate, for most of the next two years. Not until January 2005 did employment finally regain its March 2001 level. Huge uncertainties owing to, first, 9/11 and then the 2003 war in Iraq may have contributed to firms' reluctance to add to their payrolls.

Fiscal Indiscipline under Bush

George W. Bush's fiscal policies turned out to be among the most profligate in U.S. history to that point. His precedent of not "paying for" tax cuts in 2001 and 2003 was quickly extended to not paying for the wars in Afghanistan and Iraq and even to his expansion of Medicare to include prescription drugs. Medicare Part D was originally proposed by Bill Clinton in 1999 but rejected by congressional Republicans at the time. With drug prices rising sharply, Bush revived the idea in 2002 and 2003, and it received a far warmer reception from the Republican-controlled Congress. Medicare Part D became law in November 2003 and went into effect on January 1, 2006.

From a fiscal policy perspective, the unique thing about Part D is that unlike the rest of Medicare and most other entitlement programs, the law provided no source of funding. The costs for the new drug benefit would just be tacked onto the budget deficit. The CBO's original published cost estimate was about $400 billion over the ten fiscal years 2004–2013 (CBO 2004a), but that was a highly misleading figure because drug benefits did not start until the second quarter of fiscal 2006. Had the CBO started the count in fiscal 2007 instead, the projected ten-year cost would have topped $600 billion. (For reference, $60 billion a year in those days amounted to about 0.4 percent of GDP.) And, of course, the bill for Part D would keep growing over time (CBO 2014).[9]

When you put all the Bush fiscal policies together and remove the effects of the automatic stabilizers, the CBO estimates that the fiscal 2000 budget surplus of 1.1 percent of GDP was transformed into a budget deficit of 2.8 percent of GDP by fiscal 2008 (a fiscal year that ended just days after the Lehman Brothers bankruptcy). Of course, Bush and his advisers could not have known in 2001 or 2004 that huge fiscal stimulus would be necessary in 2008–2010 to fight the worst recession since the 1930s. Nonetheless, the burgeoning deficits of the 2000–2007 were ill-timed for reasons Al Gore had highlighted in his presidential campaign: the leading edge of the populous baby boom generation would start turning sixty-five late in 2010, making huge demands on both Medicare and Social Security. Nothing was more predictable than that: you just had to add 65 to 1945 to get 2010. Yet, this inexorable piece of demography was basically ignored by Bush and his administration's fiscal policy makers.

Monetary Policy and the House-price Bubble

Turning to monetary policy, the failure of jobs to return after the recessionette was probably the main reason why the FOMC continued to cut the federal funds rate (albeit only slightly) in 2002 and

9. That said, as projections turned into actual spending numbers in the ensuing years, Part D expenditures came in lower than expected. See CBO (2014).

2003 and then maintained it at the superlow level of 1 percent until June 2004. With Consumer Price Index inflation averaging about 2.5 percent during this time, the real federal funds rate was sharply negative.

The Federal Reserve has been subjected to withering criticism for being slow on the interest rate trigger as the house-price bubble inflated in 2003 and 2004.[10] However, the central bank had a good reason for being slow: the economy was not generating jobs. To cite just one example, at the January 2004 FOMC meeting when the committee held rates steady yet again, Vice Chair Roger Ferguson noted that the "good news [on aggregate demand] must be tempered by a clear understanding that firms are not yet creating jobs as quickly as we would like" (FOMC 2004, 158). Even later in 2004 when net new jobs finally started to appear, the (annualized) rate of job growth was a mediocre 1.6 percent.

Furthermore, the FOMC had used forward guidance to give market participants hints that rate hikes were on the way well before it started to raise rates on June 30, 2004. It was on March 19, 2003, that U.S. forces struck Iraq with their "shock and awe" campaign. On May 6, 2003, a concerned FOMC shifted its assessment of the balance of risks to "weighted toward weakness over the foreseeable future." But by the December 9 meeting, the risk assessment was once again balanced. That was already a subtle hint that rate hikes were likely once the fog of war lifted, and similar hints persisted until the FOMC actually raised rates on June 30, 2004, stating that "the Committee believes that policy accommodation can be removed at a pace that is likely to be measured."

Finally, hindsight is far clearer than foresight. As we look at the data today or indeed as people looked at them in 2008 or 2009, it is evident that a house-price bubble—fueled by irresponsible mortgage lending—began sometime around the year 2000. But what would become a big bubble was minor at first, and bubbles are hard to recognize in real time—especially when the fundamentals are improving, thereby justifying higher prices.

10. For one example, see Taylor (2009a).

In writing my book *After the Music Stopped* (Blinder 2013) on the financial crisis, I scoured both scholarly writings and media accounts for early alarms about a house-price bubble. I found only scant warnings in 2002 and virtually none before that. Even the celebrated bubble finder, Professor Robert Shiller of Yale, was not convinced in the fall of 2003 that the United States was experiencing a house-price bubble (Case and Shiller 2003). Bubble warnings became common only in 2004, the year the Fed started raising interest rates. As I wrote in my 2013 book,

> It is not hard to understand why most of us—including me— missed the early stages of the house-price bubble. America had witnessed comparable price increases in its history. Mortgage interest rates had fallen, which should boost house prices for perfectly conventional *fundamental* reasons.
>
> So, even with the magnificent wisdom of hindsight, it is not obvious that house prices were bubbly in 2002 or 2003. How much harder, then, must it have been to tell in real time?
>
> As late as October 2005, as keen an observer as Ben Bernanke, who was then Chairman of President Bush's Council of Economic Advisers, declared that while "house prices have risen by nearly 25 percent over the past two years . . . these price increases largely reflect strong economic fundamentals." While Bernanke was wrong . . . he was not alone in this judgment. (Blinder 2013, 33–35)

So, I am not inclined to fault the Fed for failing to raise interest rates in 2002 and 2003. (Its inexcusable regulatory failures, which it shared with other agencies, are another matter entirely.) And once the central bank started raising rates, it kept at it for a full two years. The initial liftoff from the 1 percent funds rate came at the end of June 2004. By the end of that year the rate was up to 2.25 percent. By the end of 2005 it was 4.25 percent, and it topped out at 5.25 percent in June 2006. All told, the FOMC pushed interest rates up by 425 basis points in two years. Was that enough? Did it come too late? Indeed, was the Fed's easy-money policy in 2001–2003 among the root causes of the bubble?

Those questions will be debated for years. John Taylor and others were highly critical of the Fed's "loose money" policy in this period (Taylor 2009a). My own view exonerates the Fed on the monetary policy side, though decidedly not on the regulatory side. It is based on four indisputable facts plus one assertion.

The first and most important fact was mentioned earlier: The recovery from the 2001 recession was not creating jobs in 2002 and 2003, despite meaningful fiscal stimulus. So the Fed, with its dual mandate, had good reason to keep interest rates low. Second, the house-price bubble was inflating well before the Fed dropped interest rates to the floor. That makes you wonder how important super-low interest rates were to feeding the bubble, though they certainly played some role. Third, the bubble continued to inflate for at least two years after the Fed started raising rates. So, do we really think the bubble would have been stopped by raising rates, say, a year earlier? And fourth, other countries such as the United Kingdom had house-price bubbles as big as or bigger than ours despite higher central bank interest rates. Those facts cast serious doubt on the notion that tighter money in, say, 2002 or 2003 would have curbed the U.S. house-price bubble.

My assertion is this: With popular expectations of house-price inflation running at 10–20 percent per annum,[11] a monetary tightening that pushed mortgage rates up by, say, 1 or 2 percentage points would not have been nearly enough to stop the bubble in its tracks. To accomplish that, much higher rates would have been needed, and that much tightening might have killed the economy. Instead, real GDP continued to grow in 2005, 2006, and 2007. The data shown in figure 12.4 suggest that the Fed's interest rate medicine in 2004–2006, which works with long lags, may well have slowed the economy moderately. But its effects on the bubble were more dubious. Should the Fed therefore have tightened by much more than it did and likely have precipitated a recession? I think not.

Regardless of where you stand on the Fed's culpability for the house-price bubble or what it might have done better, the central

11. For some examples, see Blinder (2013, 36–37).

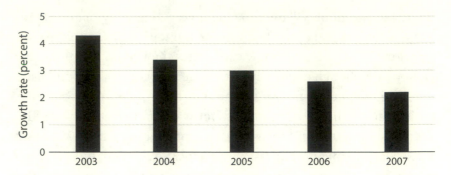

FIGURE 12.4. Real GDP growth rates, fourth quarter to fourth quarter, 2003–2007.
Source: Bureau of Economic Analysis.

bank's reactions (or lack thereof) to the bubble reignited a debate that had raged during and after the tech stock bubble a few years earlier: Should a central bank fight asset-price bubbles by raising interest rates?

On the "yes" side, there are two indisputable propositions. First, bubbles do eventually burst. History speaks with one voice on this point, although it also tells us that when any given bubble will burst is never predictable. Second, when bubbles burst, they do cause economic damage to families, investors, pension funds, homeowners (if they are housing bubbles) and, if they are big enough, to the entire economy. So, it follows that if the central bank can recognize bubbles in time and if it has weapons to deflate them without killing the economy, it should use them.

Those are two very big *ifs*, however. As we have just seen, the house-price bubble of 2000–2006 in the United States was not widely recognized until at least 2005. By then it was too late. Or think back to the dot.com bubble. When did stock prices become excessively bubbly? In 1998? Probably not. Sometime in 1999? If so, then when? In early 2000? By then it was far too late. And by the way, was there ever a serious bubble in nontech stocks anyway?

That last question shines a spotlight on the second big if. As a rule, the central bank does not possess well-targeted instruments that it can deploy against particularly bubbly assets even if it thinks it knows which ones to target. The rising stock market in 1999 provided a clear example. Suppose FOMC members had been convinced sometime in 1999 that there was a bubble in tech stock prices but not in non-tech stock prices, something they may well have believed. What could policy makers have done? Answer: Nothing. Or take the house-price bubble of the 2000s. Raising the funds rate would no doubt have pushed up mortgage interest rates. But how soon and by how much? Might a sharp tightening of monetary policy have broken the economy's back before it burst the house-price bubble?

If there is anything resembling a consensus on bubble bursting today, it runs something like this. When equity-financed bubbles burst, a great deal of wealth gets destroyed. But the damage may be contained within the stock market, where it is mostly limited to upper-income households who can weather the storm.[12] The legend of 1929 notwithstanding, even a severe crash of the stock market need not cause a deep recession.[13] As we saw in chapter 9, the devastating (to equity prices) crash of 1987 did not even slow the economy's forward momentum. The sharp stock market crash of 2000 may well have contributed to the 2001 recession, but, as noted, that recession was one of the gentlest on record.

The other, more dangerous, type of bubble is a debt-financed bubble involving lots of leverage, exactly the type that inflated alarmingly in 2005–2007. When debt-based bubbles burst, creditors of all types are hurt, and cascades of defaults and bankruptcies may follow. Such debt-based bubbles can in principle originate anywhere. But more often than not they come from the real estate sector, where high leverage is a way of life (Turner 2016). Falling real estate values lead to mortgage delinquencies and defaults and thereby to loan losses for banks that hold these mortgages and to capital losses for holders of mortgage-based securities.

---

12. In fairness, another class of victims would be pension funds, which are heavily invested in equities.

13. The notion that the stock market crash of 1929 caused the Great Depression is a vast exaggeration. Were it not for other factors, the crash probably would have caused a recession at most.

Furthermore, when the debt bubble burst violently in 2007–2008 (see the next chapter), we all learned that a complex and highly leveraged mountain of derivatives had been constructed atop these mortgage-based securities, thereby greatly magnifying the losses. Those frightening events imperiled banks and other financial institutions in a way that the stock market crashes of 1987 and 2000–2001 never did. Thus, the case for leaning against debt-financed bubbles is much stronger than the case for leaning against equity-financed bubbles. That said, such "leaning" probably means doing so with regulatory or macroprudential tools more than by raising interest rates. Blunt instruments cause collateral damage.

Chapter Summary

The 2000s up until 2008 was a period in which the idea of using fiscal policy as a countercyclical measure was basically shunned, just as it had been in the 1990s. However, in stark contrast to the Clinton years, when the focus on reducing the deficit turned chronic budget deficits into surpluses, the Bush II years saw the surplus quickly disappear and large deficits reemerge. Part of this fiscal transformation came because economic growth slowed and capital gains plummeted; both cut into tax receipts. But much of the fiscal deterioration stemmed from a series of policy decisions made in George W. Bush's first term, when tax receipts were slashed and budgetary outlays leaped upward. Here is one small indicator: As Bush took office in January 2001, the CBO's projection for fiscal year 2008 was for a surplus of $635 billion (CBO 2001). Three years later in January 2004, the projection for fiscal year 2008 was for a deficit of $278 billion (CBO 2004b). The fiscal picture had indeed changed mightily.

On the monetary policy side, by contrast, the main story of the 2000s was continuity. Alan Greenspan remained chair of the Federal Reserve through January 2006 and continued his policy of fine-tuning in deed though not in word. For example, the FOMC raised the federal funds rate by exactly 25 basis points at each of Greenspan's last fourteen meetings in the chair. Baby steps, you might call them. There was not a single 50 basis–point move or a single zero during that streak.

When Ben Bernanke assumed the chairmanship on February 1, 2006, he was an untested economics professor replacing a central banking legend. So, it was only natural for Bernanke to project continuity with the Greenspan era, which is precisely what he did. The Fed funds rate went up by 25 basis points at each of Bernanke's first three FOMC meetings too. Things would start to change dramatically at the Fed in 2007, but that is a story for the next chapter.

13

The Financial Crisis and the Great Recession

When the music stops . . . things will be complicated. But as long as the music is playing, we've got to get up and dance.
—CHUCK PRINCE, CEO OF CITIGROUP, JULY 2007

A truly strange sort of dance was in full swing in the financial world when Ben Bernanke replaced the legendary Alan Greenspan at the helm of the Federal Reserve in February 2006. "Things" were just starting to get "complicated" at the time, but I think it is fair to say that virtually no one anticipated the great unraveling that began in earnest in August 2007.[1]

Greenspan was a libertarian apostle of Ayn Rand. His attitudes toward the financial excesses of the day were not far from those of Chuck Prince in the epigraph. The Fed chair found it implausible that sophisticated financiers would take crazy risks they didn't even

---

1. This chapter and the next two borrow heavily from my 2013 book *After the Music Stopped*, including some excerpts therefrom scattered here and there. The epigraph begins that book and inspired its title.

understand with their own money and their companies' money on the line. Modern risk management techniques, he believed, were high-tech safeguards against that sort of negligence. As he confessed to the House Committee on Oversight and Government Reform in October 2008, "Those of us who have looked to the self-interest of lending institutions to protect shareholders' equity, myself included, are in a state of shocked disbelief" (Andrews 2008).

That see-no-evil attitude had led the Federal Reserve and other financial regulators to turn a blind eye toward the financial excesses and shenanigans of the day.[2] Like all central banks, the Fed had tacit responsibility for maintaining financial stability. But that responsibility was far from central to their thinking, which was a costly mistake—one that Bernanke inherited and, at least at first, did nothing to correct. In fairness to Bernanke,[3] he was taking over from a legendary figure whom some had suggested might be the greatest central banker in history.[4] It would have been asking a lot of a former professor with no financial market experience, upon assuming the leadership of the Fed, to announce major departures from Greenspan's policies. Those departures would come later.

Two Bubbles Burst

It is common to speak of the house-price bubble as bursting in 2006, and it did. But there was also a gigantic and multifaceted bond market bubble or, more accurately, a fixed-income bubble that burst in stages soon thereafter. In fact, it was more the latter, including the mountain of derivatives built atop mortgage-related securities, than

2. Some warnings of impending problems in the mortgage market were coming even from inside the Fed, notably from Governor Ned Gramlich. See, for example, Blinder (2013, 58–59).

3. Full disclosure: Bernanke and I were colleagues together at Princeton for many years and remain personal friends.

4. I was among them. See Blinder and Reis (2005, 13). In fairness to myself and to Reis, we were examining only Greenspan's monetary policies, not his regulatory policies, to which I had frequently objected when I was vice chair of the Fed. For one concrete example, see Goodman (2008).

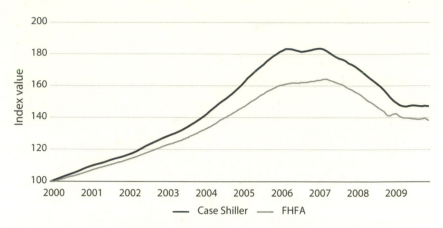

FIGURE 13.1. Two measures of the house-price bubble, 2000–2009.
Source: S&P Dow Jones Indices and Federal Housing Finance Agency.

the former that laid waste to the financial system in 2007–2009. Although the two bubbles were intertwined, let's take them up in turn.

Figure 13.1 offers two alternative depictions of the boom and bust in U.S. house prices that took place between 2000 and 2009. The two versions display similar (though not identical) timing, but they differ enormously in magnitude. The Case-Shiller index, originally created by Professors Charles "Chip" Case of Wellesley College and Professor Robert Shiller of Yale and now maintained commercially by Standard & Poor's, shows a far more dramatic bubble. It rises by a stunning 81 percent between January 2000 and January 2006 and then crumbles. A much less dramatic bubble can be seen in the official Federal Housing Finance Agency index, which rises by only 60 percent over that same time period and then, naturally, falls by much less.

Regardless of which index you select, there certainly was a house-price bubble, and it burst. Interestingly, the net change from the January 2000 starting point until 2009 is almost the same in the two indexes. The discrepancy is mostly about how large a bubble blew up in the interim. Which index is more accurate is not an easy question to answer, since the two measures differ in numerous ways.[5]

5. Blinder (2013, 18) discusses this divergence, noting reasons why the Case-Shiller index might overstate the runup in prices while the Federal Housing Finance Agency index might understate it.

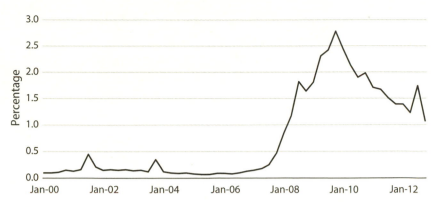

FIGURE 13.2. Loss rates on home mortgages, 2000–2012 (in percent).
Source: Board of Governors of the Federal Reserve System.

That's why figure 13.1 displays both. By either measure, house prices fell substantially from 2006 to 2009.

Declining house prices, of course, impair the collateral that underpins home mortgages. Worse yet, the irresponsible mortgage lending practices of the boom period—including disgracefully lax underwriting standards, low-to-zero down payments, and other grotesque practices—exacerbated this unavoidable problem. Figure 13.2 shows banks' loss rates on home mortgages from 2000 to 2012. The spike in 2008–2010 is enormous.

One thing this spike does not show is that many of these losses were incurred on young mortgages that were written during the boom years 2004–2007. In those bubble years, when seemingly nothing could go wrong, home buyers and speculators took out many mortgages that could be serviced and eventually repaid only if house prices continued their rapid ascent, which they did not. When the bubble started to burst, many reckless mortgages (and some nonreckless ones) went underwater, meaning that the mortgage debt exceeded the market value of the house that served as collateral.

If homes were just like financial assets, homeowners who found themselves underwater would have simply walked away, leaving their houses in the banks' hands. But houses are not like stocks and bonds; most homeowners who found themselves underwater tried mightily to hold on to their homes. In the end, the number of reported foreclosures over the years 2007–2010 was under 7.5 million, and the national foreclosure rate never topped 2.25 percent (per year).[6] These are terrible numbers, to be sure. For comparison, the foreclosure rate was closer to 0.5 percent per year late in the boom years. But foreclosures never got as bad as would be necessary, under fundamental valuations, to justify the massive flight from mortgage-backed securities. Later, a great deal of money was made by investors who were brave enough to buy mortgage-based securities (MBS) low and sell them high.

The mention of MBS leads naturally to the fixed-income bubble. Here no simple graphs analogous to figures 13.1 and 13.2 can capture the story in a picture or two. The markets for fixed-income securities ("bonds" for short) are numerous, diverse, in some cases hideously complicated, and, when you add them all up, truly gigantic—vastly larger, for example, than the markets for houses or even for common stocks. During the bubble period of the 2000s, they all shared one common trait, however: risk premiums (relative to treasuries) shrunk to ludicrously low levels. It was as if investors somehow decided that the risks inherent in lending had disappeared. They hadn't, of course. They were just masked by the euphoria of the day.

Let's start with MBS, the financial assets most closely tied to the real estate bubble. Wall Street financial engineers took straightforward "plain vanilla" MBS—which were like mutual funds of home mortgages—and sliced them up into tranches of varying degrees of risk. Through the magic of tranching, they made risk disappear for many MBS investors—or so they claimed. It wasn't true, however. Risks can be transformed and moved around, but real economic risks cannot be eliminated by repackaging financial assets. And in this particular case, the underlying assets—mainly subprime mortgages, which were debts of borrowers whose credit ratings were less than stellar—were definitely risky unless house prices just kept on rising. In the eyes of gullible investors, the new financial instruments

6. The foreclosure numbers come from various news reports. The foreclosure rate comes from Statista (2021).

looked safe. This delusion, of course, got a major assist from rating agencies that were, to put it very charitably, incompetent.

An unrealistically simple example will illustrate how the process worked. Start with a large pool of home mortgages. Then, instead of dividing the pool into pro rata shares, as stock mutual funds do, create tranches ordered by risk. The most junior tranche, often colorfully called the "toxic waste," would absorb, say, the first 8 percent of losses in the entire pool. Next would come a "mezzanine" tranche (or, more likely, several) that would take, say, the next 2 percent of losses. If you imagined that losses on a pool of home mortgages would never exceed 10 percent, as both investment bankers and investors did at the time, then the upper senior tranche was essentially risk free. Buyers of senior tranches thought they were getting what amounted to ersatz Treasury bonds that offered higher yields than real treasuries. After all, these senior tranches were often blessed with the solid-gold AAA credit rating by compliant rating agencies.

Call the whole shebang, from the most junior tranche to the most senior, a collateralized debt obligation (CDO). The key merchandising idea was not to sell the entire CDO to any one investor—that would keep all the risks together—but rather to sell the tranches separately as distinct securities. Sell the junior tranche to investors willing to take risks to earn higher expected returns, the senior tranche to investors looking for safety, and the mezzanine tranches to people in between. This little example, by the way, is far simpler than the actual CDOs of the day. Those creatures often had eight or more tranches, and they sometimes threw nonmortgage loans into the mix too.

The complexity didn't stop there, though. Clever financial engineers soon figured out that you could gather up a bunch of toxic waste tranches from different CDOs, pool them all into a new, more complicated security called a CDO^2, and then tranche the CDO^2 just as in the previous example. Through this act of magic, the majority of the resulting CDO^2—all of which, please remember, came from toxic waste tranches of subprime mortgages—was transformed into supersenior securities on which the sleepy (or worse) rating agencies would bestow the coveted AAA rating: safe enough for grandma. And there was more, such as derivatives on CDOs and CDO²; credit default swaps, which were bets on whether or not one of these concoctions would go into default; and a variety of other ways to wager on various aspects of the mortgage market.

In truth, the CDOs and especially the CDO² were far riskier than Treasury securities. But the market spreads over treasuries implied that the additional risk was small. Bear Stearns fund manager Ralph Cioffi, who was charged with securities fraud but acquitted, told the Financial Crisis Inquiry Commission that "the thesis behind [his] fund [composed of MBS and CDOs] was that the structured credit markets offered yield over and above what their ratings suggested they should offer" (FCIC 2011, 135). That's a polite way of saying that ratings from the agencies were inflated. Had the ratings been lower, as they should have been, the risk spreads would have been higher.

Junk bonds, which are marketable debt instruments of companies below investment grade, participated in the dance too even though they never had the benefits of AA or AAA credit ratings bestowed upon them by the rating agencies. In the spring of 2007, the spread between yields on ten-year treasuries and CCC-rated (or lower) corporate bonds dropped below 4.5 percentage points for a while. By comparison, it had averaged 12.8 percentage points over the years 1997–2005.[7]

The story was similar with sovereign debt instruments issued by nations with credit ratings that you might (charitably) call "below investment grade." And you didn't have to go all the way to emerging markets to find them. My favorite example was Greek government bonds, which traded at yields about 25 basis points above German bunds during the first half of 2007, implying an annual expected loss from default of just 0.25 percent. One chance in 400 to default? As is well known, that 400-to-1 longshot came to pass in 2012. It should have come as no surprise. Reinhart and Rogoff had chronicled earlier that Greek sovereign debt had been in default about half the time

7. Federal Reserve Bank of St. Louis (2022).

since the country gained its independence in 1829 (Reinhart and Rogoff 2009, 30, table 7).

In sum, wherever you looked in the fixed-income markets of 2006 and early 2007, investors seemed willing to overlook risk as they reached for yield in an environment of low interest rates. What could go wrong? As it turned out, quite a lot.

The World Financial Crisis Begins

The house of cards began to crumble when house prices stopped rising in 2006. Remember, the viability of many subprime mortgages was predicated on ever-rising house prices. Many of those mortgages were actually "designed to default" if house prices stopped rising.[8] And stop they did. The national guessing game about the house-price bubble quickly gave way to two new questions: How fast and how far would home prices fall?

Optimists foresaw a flattening or perhaps just a small decline in house prices. After all, while housing bubbles had inflated and burst frequently in local markets over the years, there had not been a nationwide decline in house prices in the United States for decades. The brilliant financial market, which allegedly aggregates the collective wisdom of thousands of traders and prices risk, was looking for a house price decline of just 6.4 percent in early September 2006.[9] Pessimists were skeptical of the market's "genius." Some suggested that house prices might drop 20 or 30 percent—a catastrophic outcome, it seemed. But it turned out to be far closer to the truth.

House prices were one thing. The market values of mortgage-related securities were quite another, since they reflected among other things the poor credit quality and excessive leverage—both direct and indirect via derivatives—embedded in many of these securities. Our national system of housing finance began to crack

8. I believe the phrase is due to Gary Gorton (2010), an academic economist who was then a consultant to American International Group.

9. This number comes from prices of futures based on the Case-Shiller index traded on the Chicago Mercantile Exchange. Cited by Blinder (2013, 88).

in 2007, beginning with the bankruptcies of several nonbank mort-gage lenders and then massive downgrades of MBS and CDOs by the suddenly awake rating agencies. Those downgrades, of course, reduced the prices of the securities. The fixed-income bubble was starting to burst.

In July 2007 Bear Stearns, the nation's fifth-largest broker dealer and a major player in the subprime boom, told investors that one of its highly leveraged funds had "effectively no value left" because of large losses on mortgage-related assets. The dance was now over, but the ballroom had not yet caught fire.

The blaze started in earnest on August 9, 2007, when the giant French bank BNP Paribas halted withdrawals on three subprime mortgage funds. Their cited reason? "The complete evaporation of liquidity in certain market segments of the US securitization market has made it impossible to value certain assets fairly" (FCIC 2011, 250–51). Investors in those funds and similar assets read that state-ment (correctly) as saying *you've lost money, we don't know how much, and you can't get access to it anyway because we've shut the exit door.* Those with even a nodding acquaintance with the history of banking panics in the nineteenth-century United States conjured up pictures of bank runs following actual or feared suspensions of specie payments, that is, cases when banks would stop exchang-ing their notes for gold or silver. Whether you were a French or an American investor, the signal was clear: it was time to panic. And that is exactly what market participants did, all over the world.

The events leading up to the panic and, of course, the panic itself called into question the liquidity and even the solvency of top-tier financial institutions such as Bear and Paribas and, by inference, many others. Could you be sure your counterparty would pay up? We know that faith in even major counterparties started to wane that day because interbank lending rates spiked. The bellwether that everyone watched at the time was the London Interbank Offered Rate (LIBOR), which indicated what one big bank charged another for short-term lending. The LIBOR market was limited to the biggest players: Citibank, JP Morgan Chase, Barclays, HSBC, and the like. Was there actually a risk that one of these august financial giants might fail to repay an overnight loan? The risk premium reflected in LIBOR said yes. The spread over U.S. treasuries jumped by 30 basis points in just three business days. In the ultrasafe world of LIBOR, 30 basis points was an eye-opener. Fear was overtaking greed.

Once the seeds of doubt were sown, an epic scramble for liquidity ensued. Financial markets are fundamentally built on trust, in this case trust that the other guy will pay what he owes you in full and on time. As that trust faded, enormous "flights to quality" took place. Markets with even a little risk found buyers disappearing, and they began to seize up. Thus did the fixed-income bubble end with a bang, not a whimper, right after August 9, 2007.

However, the Fed and other central banks did not yet see the unfolding events as presaging a macroeconomic catastrophe. And that lack of vision was crucial. By sheer coincidence, the Federal Open Market Committee (FOMC) had held a meeting two days earlier, at which the committee's August 7 statement concluded that "although the downside risks to growth have increased somewhat, the Committee's predominant policy concern remains the risk that inflation will fail to moderate as expected." Their predominant concern was inflation, then running around 2.5 percent, not economic collapse? Many Fed watchers blinked in disbelief. I was one of them.

The day after Paribas Day, the FOMC hurriedly arranged another meeting, this one by telephone. Its August 10 statement assured the financial world that the Fed was "providing liquidity to facilitate the orderly functioning of financial markets," as it should. Free translation: Come in and borrow as much as you want. But the committee kept the federal funds rate right where it had been since June 2006— at 5.25 percent. Was inflation still the "predominant policy concern" for the Fed?

The answer came six days later after another telephonic meeting. The FOMC's August 16 statement noted that "the downside risks to growth have increased," thereby demoting inflation from its singular status as the predominant risk. That was a healthy step toward parity, but the committee still refused to cut the funds rate. How cutting rates could have been even mildly controversial at that point, with the financial system crumbling around them, is difficult to comprehend. Many Fed critics said so at the time.

But the FOMC did not touch the funds rate until its next regularly scheduled meeting, which came on September 18, 2007, a full forty days after Paribas Day. A lot of rain can fall in forty days and forty nights, and it had. The committee finally woke from its slumber by cutting the funds rate by a large 50 basis points that day, observing that "the tightening of credit conditions has the potential to intensify the housing correction and to restrain economic growth more generally." The Fed's attitudinal conversion was crucial. The cataclysmic failure of Lehman Brothers, which removed all doubt, was still a year away. In the fall of 2007, there were two competing narratives about what the financial crisis was all about.

In the narrower technical view, the financial world was experiencing a liquidity crisis, an acute one to be sure but still a liquidity crisis. Frightened investors and institutions were scrambling to get their hands on more cash than was available partly because of heightened counterparty risk, partly because allegedly safe assets no longer looked safe, and partly because banks and investment funds feared that their customers might show up at the electronic door one day requesting hefty withdrawals. Walter Bagehot had taught central bankers what to do under such circumstances back in 1873: lend freely, against good collateral, at a penalty rate. Central bankers in 2007 understood Bagehot's dictum and were adhering to it. But it was about providing liquidity to obviate financial instability, not about supporting the economy through monetary policy.

The darker view demanded different sorts of actions. It conceptualized what was happening in 2007 as the beginnings of a serious impairment of the economy's credit-granting mechanisms. In this broader view, the scarcity of liquidity was just the tip of the iceberg. The real problems lurked underneath in the forms of massive deleveraging, possible insolvencies of major institutions, gigantic losses of wealth, and severe damage to the financial system, including to banks regulated by the Fed and other central banks around the world. If all that came to pass—and remember, by September 2007 it hadn't happened yet—the whole economy would be in big trouble.

Economies that are starved of credit fall into recessions or worse. Businesses decline and fail. Workers lose their jobs.

Ben Bernanke, who had been a leading scholar of the Great Depression in his academic career, knew all that. One of his earliest acclaimed scholarly papers was on how the breakdown of the credit markets had "helped convert the severe but not unprecedented downturn of 1929–30 into a protracted depression."[10] But the Fed was not yet thinking hard enough about financial stability and its responsibility to preserve that stability. Along with other bank supervisors, the Fed had allowed the banks it putatively regulated to become, among other things, too leveraged (sometimes via off–balance sheet entities) and too willing to tolerate weak underwriting standards. Such safety and soundness concerns would subsequently crowd out other issues as financial stability concerns rose to the fore. But in September 2007, the hawkish-leaning FOMC was more focused on inflation and not yet ready to act to support the economy.

The Fed Goes All In

That said, history records that the Fed's monetary policy reactions came much faster than those of, say, the European Central Bank. That doesn't mean, however, that they came fast. In the fall of 2007, FOMC members still didn't know what they were dealing with. A number were far from convinced of the need to ease monetary policy. Wouldn't providing lots of liquidity, à la Bagehot, suffice? After its rate cut of 50 basis points on September 18, the Fed waited another six weeks—until its next regularly scheduled meeting—to cut rates again. By that time many mortgage-lending companies had failed, and Citigroup and other major banks and brokerages had announced large write-downs of subprime mortgages. But the Fed chipped in with just another 25 basis points on October 31, a

10. His "Nonmonetary Effects of the Financial Crisis in Propagation of the Great Depression" (Bernanke 1983) received a lot of attention and was published in what is probably the world's most prestigious economics journal, the *American Economic Review*.

baby step that it repeated at its next regularly scheduled meeting on December 11. There was clearly no sense of urgency. The FOMC was still a tortoise, not a hare.

After that, however, the Fed stepped up its pace. The next day it announced two new facilities to provide liquidity. The first was a series of currency swap lines with foreign central banks that had turned to the Fed for help after finding their own banking systems seriously short of dollar liquidity. The second was the Term Auction Facility (TAF), which was designed to do Bagehot-type lending to banks but for longer periods than usual, up to four weeks.

The Fed's earlier attempts to lend to banks had been stymied by American bankers' traditional fears of being stigmatized. In standard (U.S.) banking practice, coming to the central bank's discount window was something to be studiously avoided because it signaled that you were a weak bank. The TAF sought to overcome that stigma problem in two ways. First, it was set up as an auction to which all banks were invited. The bank didn't need to show it was in trouble, just come and bid for the available funds. Second, the TAF delayed the payment from the Fed to the banks; a borrowing bank would not receive the cash for a few days. That was a cleverly designed tweak in discount window practice because a loan that is delayed a few days will not save a bank that is teetering on the brink. The TAF was a resounding success. At its peak usage in March 2009, the facility had outstanding loans of $493 billion. A year later it shut down completely; it was no longer needed.

But the Fed was just warming up. Over the Christmas–New Year holidays, Bernanke must have been mulling over the Fed's passivity in the 1930s. These were not fond memories. On January 9, 2008, he convened the FOMC by conference call, ostensibly to review recent developments but probably to shake the committee out of its lethargy. The minutes of that meeting noted that "the downside risks to growth had increased significantly since the time of the December FOMC meeting," but the committee was not yet prepared to cut interest rates again. Undaunted, Bernanke got them all on the phone again twelve days later. The minutes of that call (on January 21) observe that "the outlook for economic activity was weakening." Indeed it was, and the FOMC was now ready to act decisively.

With just one dissenter, the members agreed to announce an almost unprecedented cut of 75 basis points in the federal funds rate early the next morning. In the entire eighteen and a half years of Greenspan's leadership, the FOMC had moved the funds rate by 75 basis points only once, and that was an increase. Furthermore, this move would come between regularly scheduled meetings, something the Fed rarely did. As if all this wasn't enough to get markets' attention, the federal funds rate announcement came at 8:30 A.M. rather than exactly at 2:15 P.M., which was the rule in those days. The Fed wanted to be heard on January 22, 2008, and it was. Eight days later at its next regularly scheduled meeting, the FOMC dropped the funds rate by another 50 basis points, down to 3 percent, leaving federal funds trading 125 basis points lower than they were just nine days earlier. The Fed was at DEFCON 1.

What had changed? By January 2008, the FOMC saw clearly that it was fighting a two-front war, and it was gearing up for battle on both fronts. It needed to provide massive amounts of liquidity, of course, for well-known reasons that Bagehot had enunciated in 1873. But the FOMC was also fighting an imminent recession, which was likely to lead to many insolvencies, and needed to cut interest rates sharply for well-known reasons that Keynes had enunciated in 1936. As noted earlier, Chair Bernanke was acutely aware of the Fed's failures in the 1930s and was determined not to repeat them.

Another 100 basis points of rate cutting followed in short order, and then in March 2008 the Fed threw the financial markets another kind of life preserver: the Term Securities Lending Facility (TSLF). The TSLF was designed to alleviate acute liquidity shortages then being experienced by the so-called primary dealers, a selective group of major banks and broker-dealers who make markets in Treasury securities. At the time, these firms were awash in less liquid securities but short on Treasury bills, which serve as the medium of exchange for large-dollar transactions. So, the Fed helped the primary dealers out by swapping T-bills, which the Fed owned in abundance, for some of these less liquid securities. Note that the TSLF's operations did not change the size of the Fed's balance sheet, just its composition. It was not monetary policy as construed at the time: it did not raise bank reserves, and it did not reduce the federal funds rate.

The TSLF opened for business on March 27, which was just a bit too late for Bear Stearns, the smallest and arguably the scrappiest of the Wall Street giants. More germane, however, Bear was deemed to be the proverbial slowest antelope in the herd at the time. Like its brethren, it had grown accustomed to living on overnight loans (largely repos). During the week of Monday, March 10, rolling those loans over became more and more difficult. As Wall Street veteran Henry "Hank" Paulson, then the secretary of the treasury, observed, when confidence goes, it goes, and Bear needed help from the Fed and from JP Morgan Chase just to make it to the weekend. Bear Stearns was at death's door. Potential counterparties were shunning exposure to Bear even when it posted treasuries as collateral.

That weekend, as the Fed sought a buyer for the firm, it quickly concluded that the only viable candidate was JP Morgan, which had both a fortress balance sheet and a desire to acquire Bears Stearns's business lines. As the only viable bidder, JP Morgan was in the driver's seat. To close the deal, the Fed agreed to take almost $30 billion in dodgy mortgage-related assets that JP Morgan's hard-driving CEO, Jamie Dimon, deemed too risky for his shareholders. Taking those assets onto its own balance sheet was a major step for the Fed, the first of what would eventually become a series of quasi-fiscal actions, that is, assuming risks that, if they went south, would result in taxpayer losses. To the tradition-bound Federal Reserve, this was venturing into alien territory. (No one at the time could imagine the events of 2020!)

In an ironic historical footnote to this episode, on the same day that the Fed and JP Morgan Chase announced the deal for Bear Stearns (March 16), the Fed's Board of Governors created the Primary Dealer Credit Facility to provide more credit to primary dealers. Bear had been one of those primary dealers. Its discredited CEO, Jimmy Cayne, later told the Financial Crisis Inquiry Commission that the Primary Dealer Credit Facility came "just about 45 minutes too late" to save his firm (FCIC 2011, 294). He probably exaggerated. But who knows?

In any case, the FOMC cut the federal funds rate twice more, on March 18 and April 30 (to 2 percent), and then paused to see what would happen. Was that enough monetary stimulus? Would the ship now right itself?

Fiscal Stimulus: Round 1

The Federal Reserve was not, of course, the only Washington institution that noticed the developing recession. So did the White House and the Democratically controlled Congress, which quickly agreed on the Economic Stimulus Act of 2008. (Notice the highly Keynesian name.) President Bush signed it into law in February 2008.

The centerpiece of the multipart stimulus program, which totaled about 1 percent of GDP, was sending checks to 130 million taxpayers: $600 to individuals and $1,200 to married couples. These transfer payments were called "tax rebates" for what I suppose were public relations reasons. But they were not refunds of past taxes paid. In fact, the "rebates" were not tied in any way to the taxes people had paid in 2007 or to what they would owe for 2008. That said, you did have to be a taxpayer to receive a check, a restriction that left out millions of low-income Americans.[11]

According to standard economic thinking, a onetime transfer payment such as the 2008 rebate should have substantially less impact on consumer spending (but also less budgetary cost) than a permanent tax cut of equal magnitude. Under the pure permanent income hypothesis, for example, the $600 or $1,200 should have been spent out smoothly over each taxpayer's remaining lifetime, implying in most cases little spending in 2008. But that didn't appear to happen. Using a clever methodology based on the fact that checks

11. There is an irony here. The 2001 Bush tax cuts had taken many low-income Americans off the income tax rolls, a progressive step applauded by liberals at the time. But this meant that they did not receive "rebates" in 2008.

were sent to different people on different dates, Parker et al. (2013) and Broda and Parker (2014) estimated that consumers spent about 50–90 percent of their stimulus payments within three months of receipt. That's a pretty high marginal propensity to consume. Interestingly, insights from behavioral economics suggest higher, not lower, marginal propensities to consume from onetime windfalls.[12]

That said, sending out millions of checks is not a trivial administrative task, and it was late summer 2008 before the checks arrived, far too late to prevent a recession that the National Bureau of Economic Research (NBER) dates as beginning in December 2007. More important, the prospects for the financial system had deteriorated badly in the interim. As we have just seen, Bear Stearns had to be bailed out spectacularly in March 2008. By July, Fannie Mae and Freddie Mac, the two giant government-sponsored entities for housing finance, were nearing bankruptcy, and Congress authorized the Treasury to bail them out by in essence (though not in name) nationalizing them. On September 7, 2008, Secretary Paulson felt compelled to do just that. And, of course, the rout began in earnest just eight days later, when Lehman Brothers collapsed into the arms of the bankruptcy courts.[13] The economy started collapsing almost immediately, and a fiscal stimulus amounting to 1 percent of GDP was not nearly equal to the task.

The Great Recession

The deep recession that followed on the heels of the financial crisis was soon labeled the Great Recession. No one at the time, of course, anticipated the far deeper (though brief) recession that would befall the U.S. economy (and other economies) in 2020. The natural frame of reference at the time was the ten post–World War II recessions. And compared to those, the recession of 2007–2009,

---

12. For two examples, see Agarwal and Qian (2014) and Fuster, Kaplan, and Zafar (2021).

13. Much has been written about the decision of Paulson, Bernanke, and others to send Lehman Brothers to bankruptcy court rather than bail it out. For more on this, see the next chapter.

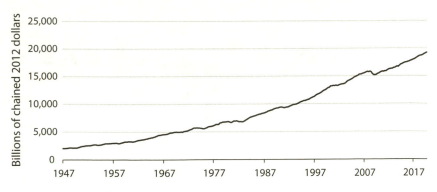

FIGURE 13.3. Real GDP, 1947–2019.
Source: Bureau of Economic Analysis.

while subsequently dwarfed by the recession of 2020, was indeed "great."

Figure 13.3 displays the broad historical perspective on U.S. recessions by charting real GDP, quarterly, since 1947. I end the graph in 2019 because if 2020 was included, the horrific drop in 2020:2 would make everything else look small. The figure lacks the traditional shading of NBER recessions, and without that aid the eye strains to see the ten recessions prior to 2007. With the possible exception of the back-to-back recessions of 1980–1982, you have to squint to see them. Not so for the 2007–2009 recession, which is clearly visible. Real GDP fell 4 percent, and the graph gives the unmistakable impression that we never made up the lost ground. Rather, the economy appears to have regained its previous growth rate but never to have returned to its prerecession trend. It looks like the level of real GDP was permanently reduced.

Figure 13.4 offers a closer look at the period just prior to, during, and just after the Great Recession. The sharp collapse beginning in 2008:3 is evident. That the collapse followed close on the heels of the Lehman Brothers bankruptcy in September is even more evident in figure 13.5, which displays monthly employment gains or losses during this period. The economy pretty much fell off a cliff in mid-September 2008.

I would not claim that the failure of Lehman Brothers and the cascading financial calamities that followed were the sole cause of

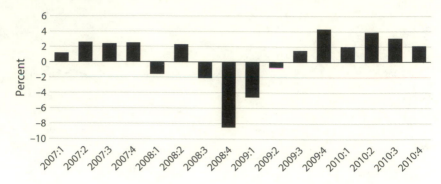

FIGURE 13.4. Annualized growth rate of real GDP, quarterly, 2007–2010.
Source: Bureau of Economic Analysis.

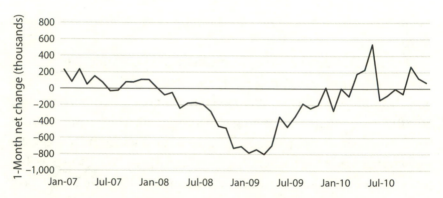

FIGURE 13.5. Change in payroll employment, monthly, 2007–2010.
Source: Bureau of Labor Statistics.

the terrible recession. There was, after all, a huge increase in the price of oil in the 2000s, culminating in June 2008 at over $175 per barrel (for West Texas Intermediate), an oil shock of sorts but a long, drawn-out one. Nonetheless, the economy still managed to limp along through 2007 and the first half of 2008 with positive growth. Then all hell broke loose after the Lehman Brothers failure; pretty much everything in the financial system rapidly started to come unglued in quick succession:

- American International Group (AIG), the giant insurance company that took enormous risks insuring the AAA-rated tranches of complex mortgage securities, was essentially nationalized by the Federal Reserve even though the Fed had never supervised AIG or any insurance company before.

- Merrill Lynch, America's best-known stockbroker, avoided oblivion only by selling itself hastily to the Bank of America.
- Even Goldman Sachs and Morgan Stanley, the bluest of Wall Street's blue-chip investment banks, looked shaky. Confidence in them was shored up when the Fed declared them to be bank holding companies and the firms demonstrated the ability to raise outside capital.
- The world's oldest money market mutual fund broke the buck when its shares fell under the sacred $1 mark, thereby precipitating both a run on money funds and a collapse of the commercial paper market.
- America's largest thrift institution, Washington Mutual, and its fourth-largest bank, Wachovia, crashed and burned. Each was sold for a pittance by the Federal Deposit Insurance Corporation.

And there was more. Nobody had ever seen anything like it. Finally, with seemingly everything collapsing around them, Secretary Paulson and Fed Chair Bernanke marched down to Capitol Hill to inform the congressional leadership that the world might end if they didn't quickly approve a $700 billion appropriation to buy "troubled assets."

Such stunning financial ructions do not leave the real economy unscathed. As just observed, both employment and GDP crumbled more or less immediately after Lehman Day. Any thoughts that the United States would avoid a serious recession were quickly dispelled. With the financial system cracking, thereby impairing normal credit channels, with homebuilding tanking, and with massive wealth destruction in the housing, stock, and bond markets, it was pretty clear the United States was in for a bad recession. In some quarters, talk turned to speculation about "Great Depression 2.0."

I remember well my own changing attitudes at the time. Prior to the Lehman Brothers failure I was a relative optimist, relative, that is, to the prevailing gloom and doom. While the economy was clearly limping along, somewhat wounded, and the S&P 500 had given up about 14 percent since January 1, I was not convinced that we were headed for a serious recession. After all, real GDP growth had averaged 2 percent in 2007 and zero in the first two quarters of 2008—not good but hardly catastrophic. On September 15, 2008, however, I turned deeply pessimistic. So did lots of others. Between Lehman Day and November 20, the S&P 500 dropped another 37 percent. The roof was caving in. Much more fiscal and monetary stimulus would clearly be needed.

Chapter Summary

The financial world went crazy in the mid–2000s, producing unsustainable bubbles in house prices and in a wide variety of fixed-income securities, especially but not limited to mortgage-related securities. While some critics have sought to place the blame on the Federal Reserve's easy-money policy in 2002–2004, I noted in the previous chapter that the charge will not stick. The Fed can be justifiably criticized, however, for not taking its responsibility for financial stability seriously enough. Fiscal policy is even more blameless than monetary policy unless you count lax regulatory policies and attitudes, which are not the focus of this book.[14]

Although the Fed raised interest rates gradually in 2004–2006, the Great Recession was certainly not caused by tight money. Nor was it caused by an oil shock, although the world experienced a sizable one between January 2007 and June 2008. The main cause, of course, was the massive and far-reaching collapse of the financial system. The full dimensions of the financial market shock were not apparent until Lehman Brothers filed for bankruptcy in September 2008. But it was already apparent that several national economies were headed for trouble more than a year earlier, when BNP

14. It's a stretch, but one might perhaps call the hybrid half-private, half-public status of Fannie Mae and Freddie Mac part of "fiscal policy." It was certainly part of the problem but was not part of the macroeconomic stabilization policy that is the focus of this book.

Paribas shocked the world by shutting the doors on some mortgage-related funds in August 2007.

The Federal Reserve reacted cautiously at first, wondering whether the financial system just needed a lot more liquidity or whether the real economy needed serious monetary stimulus. By January 2008, however, the Fed was on full macroeconomic alert, cutting interest rates sharply and opening the first of what would eventually be an alphabet soup of lending facilities. Fiscal policy quickly followed suit, with a stimulus package amounting to about 1 percent of GDP in February 2008, thus demonstrating once again that the White House and Congress could act expeditiously when the situation demanded it. The old attitude that fiscal policy was too slow and unreliable to be useful was dying.

None of these policy initiatives were sufficient, however, once the damn broke after the Lehman Brothers failure. The economy went into its worst tailspin since the 1930s. Unlike in the 1930s, however, Keynesian attitudes turned out to be deeply ingrained in policy makers' minds, at least for a while. Both fiscal and monetary policy swung into action in unprecedented ways.

14

All Together Now: The Fed and the Treasury Join Hands

Necessity is the mother of invention.
—WELL-KNOWN PROVERB

By the fall of 2008 the Bush administration was pretty much a spent force, beaten down mainly by the endless wars in Iraq and Afghanistan. The president's job approval rating in a Gallup poll stood at 31 percent just prior to Lehman Day and then dropped to an all-time low of 25 percent at the beginning of October 2008. The president himself seemed disengaged, delegating economic management almost completely to Secretary of the Treasury Hank Paulson. And, of course, a presidential election loomed on the near horizon, pitting the dynamic young Senator Barack Obama (D-IL) against the much older war hero Senator John McCain (R-AZ). It was not a propitious moment for activist fiscal policy—with one big and highly unusual exception: the Troubled Assets Relief Program (TARP).

Unfurling the TARP

The TARP was invented on the fly. As Paulson later put it, "frankly we had no choice but to fly by the seat of our pants, making it up as we went along" (Paulson 2010, 254). The impetus came after Lehman Brothers failed and then, just days later, American International Group (AIG) was nationalized in deed though not in word. The panic was on. Paulson, a former king of Wall Street, saw things spinning out of control so badly that "we couldn't keep using duct tape and bailing wire to try to hold the system together" (254). Chair Ben Bernanke at the Fed strongly joined in that judgment, telling Paulson "we can't keep doing this" (Sorkin 2010, 431). Bernanke was also eager for Congress to get the central bank off the hook by appropriating money for financial rescue missions.

Paulson and Bernanke had many motives in proposing what eventually became the TARP. First and foremost, the financial conflagration was spreading, not receding. Increasingly it looked like "the big one," the time to pull out all the stops. Second, despite (or perhaps because of) using the Exchange Stabilization Fund to stabilize the money market mutual funds after Lehman crashed, Paulson felt an acute need for a pot of money explicitly appropriated by Congress for financial firefighting.[1] Who knew what might come next? Third, the Fed had stuck its neck way out to save both Bear Stearns and AIG and in other ways too. With each ad hoc emergency rescue program, public money was being put at risk by the nonpolitical, unelected Federal Reserve System. Bernanke was highly uneasy about this development for reasons of democratic legitimacy. Such decisions, he believed, should be made by elected politicians. Finally, all the ad hockery had left financial markets confused about the rulebook. Was there one?

As the two financial leaders and their staffs planned for the TARP, a major difference of opinion emerged between the former

---

1. The Exchange Stabilization Fund was created in 1934 to stabilize the dollar exchange rate, which was certainly not the problem of the day.

economics professor and the former Wall Street mogul. The intellectual Federal Reserve chair, backed by the New York Fed, favored injecting capital directly into banks to bolster their weakened balance sheets. An expert on economic history, Bernanke knew that publicly provided capital almost inevitably follows in the wake of a banking crisis—sometimes sooner, sometimes later. Why wait for things to get worse? Besides, providing banks with new capital would leverage the government's money. Since banks typically operate with approximately ten-to-one leverage, each $1 of additional bank capital should support $10 or so of renewed lending, at least in theory.[2]

But the less cerebral, more action-oriented treasury secretary overruled Bernanke on both political and market grounds. Politically, any proposal to purchase bank shares, thus making the government a part owner of the country's largest banks, would be decried as socialism by Republicans and vilified as gifts to fat-cat bankers by Democrats. It wouldn't stand a chance in Congress. Furthermore, even a partial nationalization of the banks would scare off private investors, whom the Treasury and the Fed were still hoping to coax into buying equity in banks. (Bank stock prices were very depressed.) For these quite legitimate reasons, Paulson didn't want to inject capital directly into banks; he didn't even want to let anybody talk about it, lest the idea of purchasing bank shares leak into the public discourse.

When it comes to political matters and especially in dealing with Congress, the chair of the Federal Reserve generally defers to the secretary of the treasury, who after all represents the president and therefore carries implied political legitimacy. Besides, Paulson's read of the political environment was probably pretty good. So, when the pair trooped down to Capitol Hill to implore Congress to help, their plea was to fund Paulson's pet idea (buying toxic assets), not Bernanke's (injecting capital into banks).

---

2. Some people, myself included, found this belief naive under the circumstances. Why would banks be so venturesome? Wouldn't they use the new capital to bolster their ailing balance sheets rather than engage in more risky lending? For further discussion of this issue, see Blinder (2013, chap. 7).

The political drama began in earnest at a remarkable meeting on Thursday night, September 18, 2008, just three days after the Lehman bankruptcy. The Fed chair and the treasury secretary, having first conferred with President George W. Bush, sat down with congressional leaders of both parties, who had been hurriedly convened in the conference room of the Speaker of the House, Nancy Pelosi (D-CA). As they filed in, the pictures in the minds of members of Congress were nowhere near as bleak as those of Bernanke and Paulson. Members still saw the unfolding disaster as a Wall Street problem, not a Main Street problem. They were also viscerally hostile to bank bailouts. Both the Bear Stearns rescue and the AIG bailout had been extremely unpopular with their constituents. Senators and Members of the House were wary, to put it mildly, of putting massive amounts of taxpayer money at risk to salve banks' self-inflicted wounds. In their minds, this was akin to political suicide.

In stark contrast, using the Federal Reserve's ample balance sheet looked pretty attractive to those few politicians who understood the Fed's capabilities. Via the Fed, money could flow to banks in their districts without Congress appropriating a dime, Bernanke would take the heat if anything went wrong, and members of Congress could later berate the Fed for overstepping its authority or for anything else they didn't like. This last point—the Fed's acute political exposure—was, of course, exactly what Bernanke was trying to minimize.

By all accounts—and members of Congress do talk, so there were plenty of eyewitness accounts—the September 18 meeting was extremely tense. Paulson was seen by the Democrats as pleading to bail out the moneyed interests. As he had confided to Bernanke earlier, "They'll kill me up there. I'll be hung out to dry" (Wessel 2009, 203). In fact, before the treasury secretary left for Capitol Hill that evening, his chief of staff had warned him that "this is only going to work if you scare the shit out of them" (Sorkin 2010, 445). Though crudely put, it was probably sound advice. And Paulson took it.

Paulson and Bernanke apparently went well beyond merely outlining their vision of the financial Armageddon in store for the country if Congress didn't act with dispatch. According to some members of Congress present at the meeting, the two went much further and actually sketched a scenario in which civil order broke down and there was rioting in the streets. Apparently, there was much gulping around the big mahogany table. As Paulson later wrote, Bernanke's devastating assessment of what might happen to the economy "was enough . . . to leave the members of Congress ashen-faced" (Paulson 2010, 259). Bernanke himself later said, "I kind of scared them. I kind of scared myself" (Wessel 2009, 204).

In the less polemical moments of the meeting, one presumes, Paulson outlined the plan he wanted to introduce the next morning. The Treasury would buy troubled assets from the banks, thereby both raising the assets' market values and getting them off the books of troubled banks. The Treasury purchases would make banks healthier, thereby helping the economy avoid the worst. Unfortunately, doing that would require hundreds of billions of dollars, and Treasury wanted the legislation passed within days. Appropriating that kind of money that fast shocked the assembled legislators, who were accustomed to acting at a far more leisurely pace, especially in the Senate where, as Majority Leader Harry Reid (D-NV) quipped, "It takes me 48 hours to get Republicans to agree to flush the toilets" (Hulse and Herszenhorn 2008).

But the congressional leadership, stunned by the apocalyptic vision, reluctantly agreed. It was a rare moment of bipartisanship. The mere news that the meeting had taken place ignited a strong stock market rally the next morning. But Reid, McConnell, Pelosi, and most of all House minority leader John Boehner (R-OH) would soon learn that their members were by no means ready to stretch a protective TARP over the financial system.

The next morning, Paulson outlined his plan at a press briefing, defending the basic idea—"These illiquid assets are choking off the flow of credit that is so vitally important to our economy"—and declaring himself "convinced that this bold approach will cost American families far less than the alternative" (Paulson 2009), which was presumably a mammoth financial collapse of 1930s dimensions or worse. He did not, however, put a price tag on the TARP. That was no accident, for the Treasury had not yet decided how much money to seek. Paulson and some top aides wrestled with that question that very night. Here is journalist Andrew Ross Sorkin's version of how the conversation went:

> *"What about $1 trillion," [Neel] Kashkari said.*
> *"We'll get killed," Paulson said grimly.*
> *"No way," [Kevin] Fromer said, incredulous at the sum.*
>   *"Not going to happen. Impossible."*
> *"Okay," Kashkari said. "How about $700 billion?"*
> *. . . As he plucked numbers from thin air, even Kashkari laughed*
>   *at the absurdity of it all.* (Sorkin 2010, 450)

But who could blame them? No one knew how much would be enough. (As it turned out, $700 billion was more than was needed.)

Congressional passage proved difficult. Paulson originally submitted a three-page draft giving him virtually unlimited power, even precluding judicial review. This short and explosive document was greeted with a combination of derision and alarm, and Democrats in Congress—who held majorities in both Houses at the time—began working with the administration on their own version. Numerous changes were made along the way. Judicial review was, of course, restored. The TARP money was appropriated in tranches rather than all at once, thereby saving some for the next administration. Multiple layers of oversight were added including a Congressional Oversight Panel, which wound up being headed by a Harvard Law School professor named Elizabeth Warren. Warren proved to be both a zealous guardian of the public purse and a thorn in the side of first Secretary Paulson and then Secretary Tim Geithner. Her high profile later propelled her to the U.S. Senate and even to a run for the White House in 2020.

Perhaps most important, clear language directing the Treasury to use some of the TARP money to mitigate foreclosures was added in several places throughout the bill, including in the basic definition of what constituted a "troubled asset." Paulson had requested no such language. But there was no mistaking the intent of Congress. Members wanted some of the bailout money—maybe a lot—to go to distressed homeowners, not just to distressed banks.

The bill that ultimately passed, the Emergency Economic Stabilization Act of 2008, ran to 451 pages, of which 261 dealt with the TARP. But nowhere in those 261 pages can you find a single word about using TARP money to inject capital into banks, Bernanke's pet idea but one that Paulson failed to mention. There was, however, a catchall phrase under which the secretary of the treasury was authorized, after "consultation" with the chair of the Fed[3] and a written explanation to Congress, to purchase "any other financial instrument that the Secretary . . . determines the purchase of which is necessary to promote financial market stability." Language that broad allowed pretty much anything.

The House leadership believed they had the votes to pass the TARP bill on September 29, but the rank-and-file surprised them by rejecting it on a 205–228 vote. Opposition came from both Republicans and Democrats, though for starkly different reasons. The Right posed the bigger problem; more than two-thirds of House Republicans voted against the TARP. Apparently, Bernanke and Paulson hadn't quite "scared the shit out of them." But the stock market soon did. The S&P 500 fell almost 9 percent the next day, destroying about $1.25 trillion of wealth—almost twice the TARP request—in a single day. That sell-off made believers out of enough House members to pass the bill by a comfortable 263–171 margin four days later. The Senate had already passed it, and President Bush signed the legislation into law on October 3, 2008.

It was noteworthy that Chair Bernanke more or less disappeared from view as the political debate proceeded. Appropriating money, he properly believed, was a fiscal policy issue. The distinction was critical to him (and to others). The inability or unwillingness of the Treasury to take the lead prior to TARP had forced the normally reclusive Federal Reserve to step into the spotlight repeatedly. Although its emergency lending was clearly legal under authority granted by Section 13(3) of the Federal Reserve Act, a number of the central bank's actions had put taxpayer money at risk. And putting

---

3. Notice that the law did not require his approval, only that there be consultation.

money at risk is just a step away from spending money, a power reserved to Congress. Furthermore, the Fed had been pushed into both the political arena and the media spotlight and was eager to get out of both. As Don Kohn, a Fed careerist who was then the Fed's vice chair, put it with some relief, "As the Treasury stands up, the Fed stands down" (Wessel 2009, 205).

While this political drama was playing out in Congress, something else that would damage the TARP's image was brewing behind the scenes. Paulson became persuaded that Bernanke had been right all along: injecting capital into banks was a better salve for the financial system's wounds than purchasing troubled assets. Treasury staff work had apparently convinced Paulson that designing a program to purchase toxic assets was fraught with difficulties and would take too long.[4] Buying equity stakes in banks would be simpler and faster. When the treasury secretary informed his top press officer, Michelle Davis, of his decision, she reacted with stunned disbelief. "We haven't even gotten the bill through Congress. How are we going to explain this? We can't say that *now*" (Wessel 2009, 227). And Paulson didn't.

In consequence, the U.S. Senate and House of Representatives voted to inject capital into banks while thinking they were voting to purchase troubled assets and mitigate foreclosures. The TARP, which certainly did not need any more political baggage, got some anyway when Paulson announced his radical change of plans just nine days after Congress passed the new law. It looked like a classic case of bait and switch. Ironically, later in the crisis the Fed would step in to do something very close to what the TARP was originally designed to do,[5] with the Treasury kicking in money to shield the Fed from any possible losses (more on the Fed's actions below).

4. Though the technical problems required thought, they were not insoluble. Swagel (2009, 55) reported that "we had reverse auctions to buy MBSs essentially ready to go by late October 2008—including a pricing mechanism."

5. The words "very close" connote the fact that the Fed did not buy the troubled assets itself but rather made loans that enabled other entities to buy them. The legal distinction was important under the Federal Reserve Act. The economic distinction was far less clear.

Paulson was a man of action. As soon as he made the October 12 announcement, he was on the phone with the CEOs of America's nine largest banks telling them that he and Fed Chair Bernanke were inviting them to a meeting at the Treasury the next day. It was a euphemism. When the secretary of the treasury and the Fed chair "invite" you to an emergency meeting, you don't check your calendar; you pack your bags. And they all did, not knowing what to expect. As it turned out, they were going to be force-fed the initial installments of the brand-new Capital Purchase Program (CPP), Treasury's name for the capital injections from the repurposed TARP.

Technically, the government lacked the legal authority to compel banks to participate, but Paulson made it clear that their answers would all be yes (Wessel 2009, 238). "If you don't take it and you aren't able to raise the capital . . . in the market," he said, "then I'm going to give you a second helping [of capital] and you're not going to like the terms" (Sorkin 2010, 527). Banks that were teetering on the brink of survival (such as Citicorp) or were politically astute (such as Goldman Sachs) accepted with alacrity. After all, the Treasury had designed the terms to be attractive, not onerous.[6] But a few well-capitalized banks didn't welcome the partial nationalization and feared interference from Washington. The most vocal of these was Wells Fargo, which had already announced plans to raise $25 billion privately. Paulson's response to Wells Fargo's plea was unequivocal: "Your regulator is sitting right here. And you're going to get a call tomorrow telling you you're undercapitalized" (Sorkin 2010, 528). So much for voluntary acceptance. All nine bankers signed on the dotted line. Incidentally, the CPP included no commitments to mitigate foreclosures, none at all.

Paulson made the terms banker-friendly in order to get the big banks to sign up willingly. But his extreme generosity toward banks coupled with the stinginess toward homeowners was politically tone deaf; it fed the claim that this was a "bank bailout." Yes, the Treasury

---

6. Two examples: Restraints on executive compensation were minimal, and the dividend rate on the government's preferred stock would be a mere 5 percent, half of what Warren Buffet had just charged Goldman Sachs.

got the broad and rapid take-up it wanted, but the CPP's design had two sets of adverse consequences, one political and the other economic. Politically, because bankers were villains in the eyes of the public, the program's munificence made the CPP and therefore the entire TARP extremely unpopular. It was viewed as a giveaway to undeserving bankers while millions of homeowners struggled to avoid foreclosure. Economically, forcing capital on banks that didn't want or need it wasted a precious share of the $700 billion that Congress had appropriated. What if more funds were needed, perhaps for more rescues or for mitigating foreclosures or even for buying troubled assets?

The Election of 2008

While all this was happening on the financial front, the United States of America was in the home stretch of a historic presidential election pitting the preternaturally calm man who would become America's first black president against a mercurial war hero who would have been (at the time) the oldest president ever elected for a first term. In the days leading up to the Lehman Brothers bankruptcy, John McCain had pulled ahead of Barack Obama in a Gallup poll by about 4–5 points. But right after Lehman the lead flipped, with Obama surging ahead by roughly 4 points (figure 14.1). And Obama never looked back. Amid the turmoil, the voters preferred calm to mercurial.

On September 25 while TARP legislation was being debated, a somewhat panicky-looking McCain suspended his campaign, suggested calling off the upcoming president debate (which Obama refused to do), and dashed back to Washington for a crisis meeting at the White House, a meeting that he, not President Bush, called. I suppose the former naval officer hoped the operation would look like "John McCain to the Rescue." According to most participants, however, it turned out to be a waste of precious time—or worse.

McCain's performance put the spotlight on his reputation for being hasty and erratic at times, which was not what the electorate was looking for during the Panic of 2008. Calm, smart, and thoughtful were

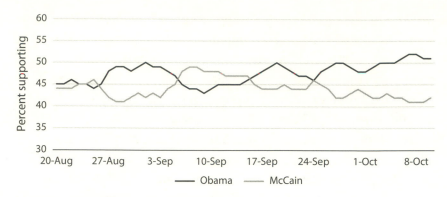

FIGURE 14.1. Obama-McCain opinion polling: Calm beats stormy.
Source: The Gallup Organization.

more like it. Immediately after the September 25 fiasco, Obama's Gallup poll lead widened to 8 points (see figure 14.1). No one knew it at the time, but for all intents and purposes the race was over. One Obama campaign aide later told journalist Noam Scheiber that "I believe we won the election in the ten days between the collapse of Lehman and the first debate. It created the sense that one guy was solid and had his feet on the ground, and the other guy was not" (Scheiber 2012, 15). Obama won the popular vote on November 4 by a convincing 7.2 percentage points and the electoral vote by a smashing 365–173 margin.

American law provides for a long transition between administrations. In this case, it was a long and agonizing transition. President George W. Bush appeared to have checked out. So, on any given day many Americans didn't quite know whether they had one president, two presidents, or none at all at the helm. Paulson also looked like a spent force, though he slogged through another two and a half months before President Obama replaced him as treasury secretary with Tim Geithner, who came over from fighting the crisis as president of the New York Fed. Geithner took charge of the remaining $350 billion in available TARP money late in January 2009, though he never deployed anywhere near the full $700 billion (U.S. Department of the Treasury 2021).

In the end, the TARP proved to be among the most successful but least understood economic policy innovations in our nation's history. For years, it had a terrible name with the body politic. For example, a Pew poll in February 2012 found that just 39 percent of Americans thought TARP's "major loans to banks and financial institutions to try to keep the markets secure" in 2008 were "the right thing . . . for the government to do," while 52 percent thought it was the wrong thing. The poll then quizzed Americans on "how much of the . . . money . . . has been paid back." Only 15 percent gave the correct answer at the time, which was either "all of it" or "most of it." By contrast, 72 percent chose either "only some of it" or "none of it" (Pew Research Center 2012). For years after TARP's passage, one of the surest ways to kill any proposal being considered by Congress was to brand it as being like TARP.

The Federal Reserve Gets Inventive

Monetary policy was busy during this period, too. The conventional part was simple and uncontroversial: the Federal Open Market Committee (FOMC) lowered the federal funds rate to the floor. As mentioned earlier, the committee had ceased cutting the funds rate at 2 percent in April 2008, when they paused to see what would happen next. On October 8, the committee resumed rate cutting and with a renewed sense of urgency. As the FOMC approached its December 16, 2008, meeting, the funds rate was down to 1 percent and virtually certain to be reduced further. But not even close Fed watchers anticipated what a landmark meeting was about to occur.

During the three months that had elapsed since Lehman Day, a frail U.S. economy had descended into disaster, and the Fed had taken numerous drastic actions, many of which the central bank's hawks didn't like. Prior to the December 16 meeting, market speculation was rampant about what more the Fed should, could, or would do. There were three main candidates.

The first was to apply more conventional expansionary monetary policy. While the federal funds rate was already down to a superlow 1 percent, the FOMC could reduce it further. The markets judged a cut of 50 basis points most likely. Second, the committee could try to reduce longer-term interest rates by committing to holding its overnight rate low for a long time. Some called that "open-mouth policy": talking the yield curve down. Nowadays we call it "forward guidance," and we expect it routinely from the Fed. Back then, however, it was a nearly revolutionary idea. Third, the FOMC could keep expanding its balance sheet, which had already soared from $924 billion the week before Lehman to $2,262 billion on December 11. (What would later be called QE1 had started in November.) Which option would the Fed choose?

In a stunning outcome that made it clear there were no hawks left on the FOMC, the answer turned out to be "all of the above." In the committee's own language, it decided to use "all available tools" to fight the recession. All available tools? Actually, the Bernanke Fed was inventing tools as it went along. For openers, the federal funds rate was slashed from 1 percent to a range between zero and 25 basis points. That marked the biggest rate cut in twenty-six years and was more than the markets expected. Over the next year the effective federal funds rate would average 16 basis points, dipping as low as 8–9 basis points at times.

As it turned out, the FOMC wound up maintaining that range of 0–25 basis points for seven long years. But it steadfastly refused to go all the way to zero, much less into negative territory—even years later, when many other central banks around the world had pushed their overnight rates below zero. Why not?

I was a prominent advocate of a negative federal funds rate during those years, urging several FOMC policy makers, including Chair Bernanke, to "go negative."[7] The Fed's counterarguments, which seemed to emanate mainly from the New York bank, looked flimsy to me and to others. Negative rates were not a panacea, they argued. Well, of course not; no one ever claimed they were. Fed economists also argued that a negative federal funds rate would damage money market mutual funds severely. I and other advocates retorted, "True, but so what?" The companies would not destroy their computer

---

7. One of these occasions was in front of a huge audience at the Economic Club of New York on November 20, 2012 (Bernanke 2012a, 24–26). There were many others, both in public and in private.

programs or their legal documents. When rates turned positive, they would be right back in business again. These arguments never persuaded a majority of the FOMC, however. In fact, even many years later when the economy collapsed in 2020 under pressure from the COVID-19 pandemic, there was no sentiment on the FOMC to go negative.

The Fed's second major departure at that fateful December 16, 2008, meeting was to add strong words of commitment to its post-meeting statement: "weak economic conditions are likely to warrant exceptionally low levels of the federal funds rate for some time." In plain English, the Fed was saying "We're going to keep the funds rate in the range of 0–25 basis points for quite a while." Two meetings later, the FOMC changed the phrase "for some time" to "for an extended period," wording it would maintain until August 2011 when it started referring to possible end dates (e.g., "at least through mid-2013"). The clear intent of each version of this evolving forward guidance was to flatten the yield curve. According to the well-known expectations theory of the term structure, reducing expected future short-term interest rates should bring down today's long-term interest rates.[8] The FOMC was trying to talk the yield curve down by managing expectations.

Over the coming years, the Fed would continue to experiment with various forms of forward guidance. Notably, in January 2012 it began offering market participants its now-famous "dot plot," showing where FOMC members expected (or was it wanted?) the funds rate to be over the next few years. In December 2012, the FOMC statement switched from using dates to using economic conditions as indicators of when it might start raising rates, following suggestions made earlier by Charles Evans, president of the Federal Reserve Bank of Chicago.

But by the January 2014 meeting, which was Janet Yellen's first in the chair, the FOMC was dissatisfied with that approach too. It

---

8. The theory is extremely well known and often taken as gospel even though virtually every empirical test has refuted it! See, for example, Campbell and Shiller (1991). Numerous other empirical studies have reached the same conclusion.

adopted instead purely qualitative forward guidance by declaring that "it likely will be appropriate to maintain the current target range for the federal funds rate for a considerable time after the asset purchase program ends." When would that end be? Nobody knew. As it turned out, QE3 ended in October 2014, and the "zero" interest rate policy continued until December 2015.

The third major departure on December 16, 2008, was an FOMC promise to expand its balance sheet further, in several dimensions. It would "expand its [QE1] purchases of agency debt and mortgage-backed securities" and was "evaluating the potential benefits of purchasing longer-term Treasury securities." That was classic Fedspeak; experienced Fed watchers knew those words meant that the FOMC would soon be buying Treasury notes and bonds for sure. Finally, the FOMC would also begin making nonrecourse loans to entities that purchased private assets under its new Term Asset-Backed Securities Loan Facility (TALF) "early next year." In fact, TALF lending operations began on March 3, 2009. (More on TALF just below. Suffice it to say here that none of these troubled assets were ever "put" to the Fed.)

Markets stood up and cheered the Fed's aggressive trifecta. The S&P 500 soared by 5 percent that day. The good news was that Bernanke, the expert on the Great Depression, and the FOMC doves were now firmly in control of monetary policy. The Fed's hawks went along reluctantly, the dire outlook having overwhelmed their usual conservatism.[9]

The Fed's Alphabet Soup

While the FOMC would not push the funds rate below the 0–25 basis points range, expansionary monetary policy didn't end there. Before the crisis was over, the central bank would create and in several cases generously fund an alphabet soup of new lending facilities

9. David Wessel (2009, 257–58) reported that Richard Fisher, president of the Federal Reserve Bank of Dallas, initially lodged a dissent but then withdrew it. The reported vote was therefore unanimous.

designed first to provide liquidity, then to prevent markets from collapsing, and finally to support asset prices. Three of these facilities have been mentioned already: the Term Auction Facility to make loans to banks, the Term Securities Lending Facility to ease liquidity strains at primary dealers, and the Primary Dealer Credit Facility to provide credit to those same dealers. But that trio was just the warmup act. The Fed really swung into action after Lehman Day.

The flurry of activity began with the Asset-Backed Commercial Paper Money Market Mutual Fund Liquidity Facility (AMLF)—quite a mouthful. When the AMLF opened for business on September 22, it was sorely needed. Shortly after Lehman went bankrupt on September 15, markets had learned that the Reserve Primary Fund, the world's oldest money market mutual fund, had invested heavily in Lehman's commercial paper, which was now worthless. As a result, the Reserve was forced to "break the buck," that is, to redeem shares at less than their $1 face value, specifically at 97 cents on the dollar. A 3 percent loss may not sound like much compared to other asset-market calamities that were happening at the time, but money funds were then and are now thought to be 100 percent safe. The Reserve's surprise announcement therefore precipitated a panic. Dominoes began to fall.

Other money market mutual funds were the first big domino, and I do mean big. In September 2008 these funds held $3.4 trillion in assets, roughly equal to half of all deposits held in banks secured by the Federal Deposit Insurance Corporation. Furthermore, investors thought of money market mutual fund shares as riskless, like bank deposits. So, seeing the Reserve Primary Fund's shares drop to 97 cents on the dollar felt like losing money in your checking account—but without any deposit insurance to make up the missing 3 cents. A run on money funds ensued, and within a week investors had withdrawn about $350 billion. That run, in turn, forced fund managers to liquidate an equal volume of commercial paper (CP), T-bills, or whatever else they owned. But after the Reserve's well-publicized losses on Lehman CP, not many buyers were eager to acquire CP. Prices for this formerly ultrasafe security dropped like a stone, and new issuance fell sharply.

Most ordinary citizens had never heard of commercial paper, but to financial aficionados these developments struck at the heart of the system. Many of America's biggest companies rely on CP for short-term borrowing to tide themselves over routine gaps between payments and receipts, such as large outflows on paydays. Stories arose that even blue-chip companies such as General Electric and IBM might be unable to make payroll.[10] Memories of those fears were probably what was on Ben Bernanke's mind when he later recalled that, "We came very close to a total financial meltdown" (FCIC 2011, 358).

Both the Treasury and the Fed reacted quickly to the impending disaster. As mentioned earlier, the Treasury raided the Exchange Stabilization Fund on the thin rationale that because some of the skittish money fund investors were foreign, "a collapse of the money fund industry could easily lead to a run on the dollar" (Paulson 2010, 253). The Fed pitched in by establishing the aforementioned AMLF to make nonrecourse loans at low interest rates to banks that were willing to purchase high-quality CP from money funds. By October 8, the AMLF had outstanding loans of almost $150 billion. Together, the Treasury's guarantee program and the Fed's AMLF successfully ended the run on the money market funds.

But the battles to save the money funds and the CP market did not end there. On October 7, the Federal Reserve Board invoked Section 13(3)—the emergency lending clause of the Federal Reserve Act—to justify creating the Commercial Paper Funding Facility (CPFF). In the Fed's words, its purpose was to "provide a liquidity backstop to U.S. issuers of commercial paper" (Federal Reserve System, Board of Governors 2008). The CPFF was followed just two weeks later by the announcement of the Money Market Investor Funding Facility to facilitate the sales of money market instruments in the secondary market, but that additional funding mechanism turned out never to be needed.

The CPFF marked a critical turning point in the Fed's thinking and actions. Providing a "liquidity backstop" and "facilitating" secondary

---

10. Sorkin (2010, 420) reports a conversation with GE's CEO, Jeffrey Immelt, to that effect.

market sales sound innocent enough, but the Fed was now prepared to purchase CP outright through special purpose vehicles created expressly for that purpose. In doing so, the central bank would cross a line by, in essence, buying corporate debt instruments that private markets were shunning, including even paper issued by nonfinancial companies such as General Motors and General Electric.

As things turned out, the Fed made a good bet, turning a profit of over $5 billion on its CP purchases. But profit wasn't the objective. The Fed was trying to stanch the bleeding, which it did. The market for CP stabilized and started functioning again. Investors who had refused to deal with even the bluest-chip counterparties returned to the CP market, reassured by the Federal Reserve backstop. Loan balances in the CPFF eventually peaked at $350 billion. But by February 2010 the market no longer needed life support, and CPFF loans fell below $9 billion.

Few people realized it at the time, but the successful effort to nurse the CP market back to health marked a crucial conceptual and operational turning point in the Federal Reserve's approach. Prior to the CPFF, the Fed's policy focus was—by necessity—on saving (or not saving) specific institutions: Bear Stearns, yes; Lehman Brothers, no; AIG, yes; and so on. Each intervention was ad hoc, and the markets had a hard time discerning any pattern or guiding principles. For example, why save Bear but not Lehman, a question that lingers even today? But with the CPFF, the Fed turned to saving markets. Commercial paper was the first test case, and it worked. Asset-backed securities would be the next.

The asset-backed securities (ABS) markets had all but shut down in the Panic of 2008. On November 25, the Fed announced its intention to establish the Term Asset-Backed Securities Loan Facility (TALF) to support the issuance of ABS collateralized by student loans, auto loans, credit card loans, and loans guaranteed by the Small Business Administration. By this time the TARP was in operation, so the Treasury put up $20 billion in TARP money to backstop any losses incurred by what would be a $200 billion Fed facility.[11]

11. Without TARP, the Treasury had refused to backstop the CPFF.

The lines between monetary policy—if you classified the TALF as monetary policy—and fiscal policy were blurring.

On that same day and back clearly within the domain of monetary policy, the Fed announced its first quantitative easing (QE) program: large-scale purchases of debt obligations of and mortgage-backed securities backed by the government-sponsored entities, mainly Fannie Mae and Freddie Mac. For a central bank that had long restricted its open-market operations to treasuries, QE1 was an adventurous foray into securities that while still quite safe could not be called 100 percent riskless. Since the Fed would be buying these securities outright, not making loans to help others buy them, losses—though very unlikely—were possible. The Fed's press release that day envisioned $600 billion in eventual purchases, but history records that after several subsequent rounds of QE, the Fed's ownership of mortgage-based securities (MBS) rose to a peak of about $1.75 trillion in 2015.

Importantly, both the Fed and market participants thought of the new program as rescuing the moribund MBS market or perhaps resuscitating it, since there were hardly any private-sector buyers left. Thus, the Federal Reserve was doing through TALF and MBS purchases something close to what Paulson and Bernanke had decided not to do with TARP money: purchase "troubled assets."[12] QE1 was clearly intended to reduce the interest rate spreads of MBS over treasuries, and it worked marvelously. MBS spreads plummeted from post-Lehman highs around 175 basis points back down to below their precrisis highs by May 2009 (figure 14.2). It was eye-opening to see what a deep-pocketed buyer could do to a dead market. Home mortgage interest rates naturally fell too.

When the Fed moved on to QE2 in late 2010, its large-scale asset purchases were limited to medium- and long-term Treasury securities. The clear intent was to push down longer-term Treasury rates

---

12. To be sure, these were among the least troubled of the "troubled assets." Fannie and Freddie MBS carried far less risk than, say, private-label MBS. Also, as noted above, in the TALF the Fed was just lending against troubled assets, not buying them.

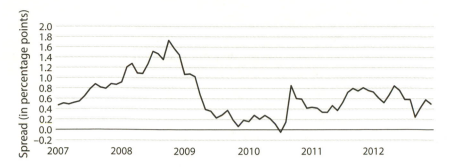

FIGURE 14.2. Interest rate spreads of mortgage-based securities over treasuries, 2007–2012. (Option-adjusted spread over a corresponding treasury.)
Source: Bloomberg Barclays U.S. Mortgage-Backed Securities Index.

and with them other long-term interest rates, that is, to flatten the yield curve. Curiously, even though no private assets were involved in QE2, it turned out to be the most politically controversial of all the QE programs. Bernanke and the Fed were attacked from directions as diverse as noted monetary policy experts, Sarah Palin (John McCain's 2008 running mate) and Texas governor Rick Perry, and the German finance minister Wolfgang Schauble, who should have known better.

When I defended Bernanke and the Fed in a *Wall Street Journal* column, I was myself attacked by Palin, who argued that "it's time for us to 'refudiate' the notion that this dangerous experiment in printing $600 billion out of thin air, with nothing to back it up, will magically fix economic problems" (Blinder 2010, A17; Palin 2010). It was as if Palin and others had just discovered that central banks have the power to create money and decided they didn't like it.

The furor over QE2 surprised and puzzled Fed policy makers. The policy was decidedly less radical than, say, QE1; after all, central banks have been buying (and selling) government bonds forever. It was telegraphed well in advance, so the markets barely moved when it was announced. Yet the political furor was loud and long. Some observers even believe that it made the Fed more timid in contemplating further rounds of QE, an idea supported by the fact that the Fed's next program of asset purchases, nicknamed Operation Twist, entailed buying long bonds but selling shorts in equal amounts, thus not expanding the Fed's balance sheet. Whatever the

Ben Bernanke (1953—)

The Right Man at the Right Time

Ben Bernanke is a brilliant but unassuming man whose intellectual background made him a perfect fit for the job of Federal Reserve chair when it fell to him to keep America from falling into Great Depression 2.0. But neither he nor anyone else knew that when he first assumed office on February 1, 2006.

Bernanke was raised in the small town of Dillon, South Carolina, where his father, uncle, and mother ran a pharmacy. A precocious child, Bernanke spent only two weeks in first grade before his teachers advanced him to second grade. At age eleven he won the state spelling bee but stumbled in the National Spelling Bee over the word "edelweiss." (The youngster from small-town South Carolina had never seen *The Sound of Music*.) That failure was probably his only one in nineteen years of schooling. Young Bernanke taught himself calculus, achieved the highest SAT score in the state, graduated as valedictorian of his high school class, and headed off to Harvard, which was a long way from Dillon both geographically and culturally.

Bernanke's stellar performance at Harvard easily landed him a spot in MIT's PhD program, the best in the world. There he again excelled, learning Keynesian economics and much else from the likes of Paul Samuelson, Robert Solow, and Stanley Fischer. The latter actually pushed Bernanke to read Friedman and Schwartz's *Monetary History of the United States*, and Bernanke was hooked. As a star PhD graduate in 1979, he had his choice of attractive academic offers and chose Stanford's Graduate School of Business before moving on to Princeton in 1985. There, over the next seventeen years, he became an academic superstar, chair of the economics department, and a member of the Montgomery School Board in New Jersey. The latter apparently clinched the deal when President George W. Bush was considering him for the Federal Reserve Board (Bernanke 2015, 50).

Bernanke left Princeton in 2002 to accept a position as a governor of the Federal Reserve System. After about three years there, he moved briefly to the White House as chair of President Bush's Council of Economic Advisers, from where as a Bush "insider" Bernanke was a natural choice when Alan Greenspan's term expired in 2006.

Bernanke's eight years at the Fed's helm were tumultuous, innovative, and controversial. Under his leadership, the central bank dropped interest rates to (almost) zero, created multiple new lending facilities that stretched the Fed's scope and capabilities, made major increases in transparency (including holding press conferences), and officially adopted a 2 percent inflation target. Most of all, Bernanke and his colleagues, with help from the fiscal authorities, averted Great Depression 2.0. All in all, a pretty consequential chairmanship.

---

rationale, when the FOMC announced QE3 in September 2012, it limited itself to MBS.

By the end of 2012, the Federal Reserve had stood up the TAF, TSLS, PDCF, AMLF, CPFF, MMIFF, TALF, QE1, QE2, and QE3 (and this list omits a few minor items). All in all, it was impressive display of central bank firepower and of the Fed's willingness to use it.

The Riverboat Gamble

Many economists, including this author, credit the end of the financial crisis and the Great Recession to a trio of important policy initiatives. The TARP was one. The 2009 fiscal stimulus program, which will be taken up in the next chapter, was another. The third member of the triumvirate was the bank stress tests. And unlike the other two, it neither busted the federal budget nor put taxpayers' money at risk.

The stress test initiative began inauspiciously on February 10, 2009, just twenty days into the new Obama administration, with what became known as Secretary Tim Geithner's "deer in the headlights" speech. Geithner is a man of many talents, but giving a speech is not one of them. To make things worse, he had been sandbagged the night before by President Obama, who had inadvertently announced in a nationally televised press conference that his treasury secretary would provide the details of the administration's new banking plan the next day. "*What?*," Geithner must have thought as he watched his TV. He knew the plan was not ready.

When he faced the press the following day, the rookie treasury secretary must have felt like a Christian thrown to the lions. He was, by necessity, painfully short on details, and he seemed a bit unsteady, even flummoxed. (Who wouldn't have been under those circumstances?) Geithner's speech was widely panned. The stock market reacted by falling 5 percent that day, not because of any bad news but instead because traders had not heard enough news. Worse yet, stock prices continued to drop for about a month after that, declining by a frightening 22 percent before they finally hit bottom. Welcome to Washington, Mr. Geithner!

The big irony about Geithner's much-decried February 10 speech is that he actually did announce (without details, of course) what turned out to be a decisive step in bringing the acute phase of the financial crisis to an end: the stress tests of nineteen major financial institutions,[13] which was a joint exercise of the four bank regulatory

---

13. These were not all banks. The list included GMAC, MetLife, Goldman Sachs, and Morgan Stanley. MetLife had become a bank holding company when

agencies, led by the Federal Reserve. Once the stress tests were complete and the results were announced publicly, it was mostly uphill from there for the financial system.

In announcing the stress test idea on February 10, Geithner said, "First, we're going to require banking institutions to go through a carefully designed comprehensive stress test, to use the medical term. We want their balance sheets cleaner, and stronger. And we are going to help this process by providing a new program of capital support for those institutions which need it" (U.S. Department of the Treasury 2009). Sketchy, for sure. But the last sentence, "we are going to help this process by providing a new program of capital support for those institutions which need it," was both a promise and a threat. Both aspects were vital. If a bank failed its stress test and could not raise enough fresh capital on its own, it would receive an infusion of capital from the Treasury using TARP money but with plenty of unpleasant strings attached.

Here is how the stress tests worked. Regulators designed an adverse hypothetical scenario lasting two years and then told banks what loan loss rates to assume under such stressful macroeconomic conditions. The banks were then allowed to net those projected loan losses against projected profits over the two-year period. The net result was an estimated increase or decrease in capital for each bank. Regulators then judged whether each bank's existing capital was enough to get it through the high-stress scenario. With its promise to be the capital provider of last resort, the U.S. government now stood solidly behind these nineteen institutions. They were all now too big to fail, which reassured markets. Moral hazard considerations could wait for calmer times.

Few people in February 2009 imagined how important the bank stress tests would prove to be. But many observers perceived the high-stakes nature of the gamble. If the capital needs estimated by the stress tests looked suspiciously low, as later happened with Europe's initial stress tests, markets might conclude that the government

---

it acquired a New Jersey bank in 2001.The other three, seeking shelter from the financial storm, had become bank holding companies hurriedly in 2008.

was covering up deeper problems or, worse yet, had lost its grip on reality—and therefore panic. On the other hand, if the stress tests generated capital needs that looked beyond banks' ability to raise new capital, markets might conclude that the banking system was headed for either oblivion or nationalization—and therefore panic. For the stress tests to ease market anxieties, the numbers would have to be, as in the tale of Goldilocks and the three bears, just right.

These risks were heavily debated inside the Obama administration, with National Economic Council director Larry Summers particularly concerned and Secretary Geithner and his lieutenant, Lee Sachs, pushing to go ahead (Scheiber 2012, 124–29). As it turned out, the administration and the Fed hit the jackpot. When the stress test results were made public on May 7, 2009, nine of the nineteen banks were found not to need any additional capital at all. In most of the other ten cases, the estimated capital shortfalls were small enough to fall well within the bank's capabilities. Aggregated across all nineteen institutions, the total capital shortfall was "only" about $75 billion, a number that didn't look big when stacked up against the $180 billion bailout for AIG, the $700 billion TARP, and the $787 stimulus bill. Of that $75 billion, about $34 billion belonged to one bank, the Bank of America. The message from the government was therefore clear: large U.S. banks could now be trusted; you could deal with them without fear.

Just as important as the bottom-line capital numbers, however, were the details that accompanied the report on the stress tests, including specifics on how the tests were conducted and a surprising level of detail about the financial condition of each bank. That bank-by-bank information was an eye-opener to aficionados because, prior to the stress tests, bank supervisory data were guarded like nuclear secrets. The bank-by-bank detail created a whole new level of transparency, and that transparency added immensely to the credibility of the whole operation. Yes, the regulators got the stress tests just right, and confidence began to return.

Few people realized it at the time, but the successful stress tests were a major turning point. They relieved a lot of stress. They also marked the end of the acute stage of the financial crisis and the beginning of the return to normalcy, albeit just the beginning. Most bank stocks rose after their test results were made public, and it wasn't long before everyone stopped worrying about the survival of America's biggest banks. "Monetary policy" had expanded both its reach and its grasp.

Chapter Summary

Just about everything regarding the U.S. economy and its financial system went south in the weeks that followed the Lehman Brothers bankruptcy in September 2008. It was then that the fiscal and monetary authorities really got serious and pulled out all the stops, grudgingly in some cases. Three big, creative, and highly successful initiatives head the list.

The first, which was started under George W. Bush's presidency and finished under Barack Obama's, was the Troubled Assets Relief Program (TARP), a misnamed (as it turned out) effort to get dodgy mortgage-related assets off the books of damaged financial institutions. The immense magnitude of the program, which was budgeted at $700 billion, was stunning at the time. And the purpose—which the media characterized as "bailing out" banks—was seen as politically poisonous. Congress balked at first but then, after the stock market tanked, passed the TARP bill with alacrity. Shortly thereafter, Secretary Hank Paulson announced that TARP money would not be used to buy "troubled assets" after all but rather to buy shares in banks. It turned out to be a bank bailout after all.

One interesting question for this book is whether the TARP constituted fiscal policy or monetary policy. In the conventional sense, it was neither. TARP was not about cutting taxes, spending money, or reducing interest rates. Rather, it was about putting taxpayer money at risk by purchasing assets that might decline in value, such as preferred stock in banks. The program was also designed jointly by the Treasury and the Federal Reserve. So, was it monetary policy then? No, though its firepower was squarely aimed at the financial system. Rather, the TARP was a hybrid that is best thought of as financial stability policy, something the U.S. government had not needed since the Great Depression (but would need again in 2020).

The second big initiative was the bank stress tests, which were announced in February 2009 and completed that May. Once again, this program was neither fiscal policy (though it could have had fiscal implications if Treasury payouts had proven necessary) nor monetary policy but rather financial stability policy. And once again, the stress tests were a joint product of the Treasury Department, which announced it, and the Federal Reserve, which carried it out (along with other banking agencies). Importantly, the transparency of the stress tests convinced markets that the capital hole in the U.S. banking system was of manageable size, and confidence returned.

These two major financial stability initiatives, each involving extensive cooperation between the Treasury and the Fed, helped restore the financial system to health. Coupled with the hundreds of billions of dollars in fiscal stimulus that will be discussed in the next chapter, the three aggressive policy interventions helped get the U.S. economy moving uphill again in June 2009. The downturn proved to be smaller and less long-lived than pessimists had assumed, and the expansion that began in June, though it started slowly, would eventually shatter all records for longevity. The unorthodox policies also, of course, left a lasting imprint on the relationship between the Fed and the Treasury.

15

The Aftermath and the Backlash

We saved the economy, but we kind of lost the public doing it.
—TIM GEITHNER, INTERVIEW WITH JOHN CASSIDY, 2010

Tim Geithner was in an excellent position to know. He started battling the financial fires of 2007–2008 from his post as president of the Federal Reserve Bank of New York and then moved over in January 2009 to fight the fiscal battles as President Barack Obama's first secretary of the treasury. It was no accident that Geithner chose the title *Stress Test* for his excellent book on the episode (Geithner 2014). His personal stress test lasted far longer than the banks' stress tests, starting during the 2008–2009 presidential transition and continuing right through Obama's first term.

The American economy deteriorated sharply during the presidential transition period between November 2008 and January 2009. It was hemorrhaging jobs at an alarming rate: 727,000 net jobs lost in November, 706,000 in December, and another 784,000 in January. The modest fiscal stimulus that Congress had passed in February 2008 helped a bit, as certainly did the Troubled Assets Relief Program (TARP). The Federal Reserve, for its part, was throwing everything at the recession, including the kitchen sink. It was clear, however, that their strenuous efforts were insufficient to the task. Monetary policy needed more help from fiscal policy—much more. But President George W. Bush had all but disappeared from sight, and Congress was ill-suited to take the lead. So, further fiscal stimulus during the transition was a pipe dream. It would have to await the new presidency.

The Obama administration came in raring to go and with starkly different attitudes from those of the outgoing Bush administration. As the campaign's chief economic adviser put it in a November 2008 interview, "We're out with the dithering; we're in with a bang" (Goolsbee 2008). True to that promise, one of the new administration's first initiatives was a massive fiscal stimulus program: the American Reinvestment and Recovery Act (ARRA). The ARRA was legislated quickly, in the first month of the Obama administration, although with great political difficulty. A newcomer to Washington,[1] President Obama displayed his inexperience by naively believing that Republicans would join him in trying to lift the nation out of the ditch. He soon learned otherwise.

The Acrimonious Debate over Fiscal Stimulus

During the transition months, the press had reported that the president-elect would ask for a fiscal stimulus package in the $700–800 billion range, or roughly 5 percent of GDP. Too much, said Republicans, who steadfastly opposed everything in the bill that was not a tax cut. Those were odd days for Keynesians. The need for fiscal stimulus was enormous, but so was the reluctance to act. House minority leader John Boehner (R-OH) even took to calling the spending portions of the stimulus bill "job-killing government spending." Here was a nation in dire need of stimulus—both monetary and fiscal—on a grand scale, yet many Republicans were speaking of the fiscal multiplier as negative!

---

1. Obama was a U.S. senator when elected president but had held that job for less than two years, much of which he had spent campaigning.

"Job-killing government spending." Try parsing those words. It is, of course, possible to object to any particular government spending program as wasteful, poorly targeted, an inappropriate use of public money, and so on. But a job killer? How was that supposed to happen? After all, more government spending means either buying items from private companies or cutting checks to people or businesses, who then buy things. Nonetheless, elements of the attack stuck. The illogic of the political backlash was captured perfectly during the heated debate over Obamacare in the summer of 2009, when a South Carolinian famously warned his congressman to "keep your government hands off my Medicare."[2] Try parsing those words!

But if the size of the stimulus was politically contentious, its composition was even more so. A substantial chunk of the administration's proposal took the form of tax cuts. Republicans like cutting taxes, but Obama's tax proposals were far more progressive than the tax cuts that the GOP favored. For example, the president wanted (and got) a "Make Work Pay" tax credit that was "refundable," meaning it would be paid even to workers who did not earn enough money to pay income taxes but who did pay payroll taxes. Republicans derided that idea as "welfare." Another part of the president's plan was to spend more money on infrastructure. Republicans didn't like that idea either; it was more government spending, not tax cuts. A third piece was aid to state and local governments so they would not have to slash their payrolls and raise taxes quite as much. Republicans opposed that too, claiming it would not stimulate the economy.

Fortunately for the new president, Democrats held majorities in both Houses of Congress at the time. Led by its clever new Speaker, Nancy Pelosi (D-CA), the House went along with the Obama proposals eagerly, passing a version of what would eventually become the stimulus bill by a comfortable margin on the eighth day of the new administration. Did someone say that fiscal policy moved too slowly to be an effective countercyclical tool? That old belief was dying. Notably, however, and even a bit chilling, not a single Republican voted "yes" on ARRA. Instead, a united Republican

---

2. This quote was reported in many places. One example is Rucker (2009).

Party decried any federal spending as suspect and wasteful, even in a deep recession.

The fight was harder in the Senate, where Republicans utilized the threat of a filibuster—and thus the need for sixty votes—to force huge concessions out of Obama and the Democrats. These concessions included a variety of business tax cuts that the president didn't want and probably would not stimulate much spending.[3] In return, the Republicans' "cooperation" turned out to consist of exactly three votes. It wasn't many, but all three proved essential as the bill barely squeezed through the Senate filibuster barrier by a vote of 60–38. The price tag originally placed on the ARRA was $787 billion, or roughly 5.5 percent of GDP, spread over several years. Subsequent reestimates by the Congressional Budget Office raised the cost to around $830 billion.

A debate ensued at the time and has continued to this day over whether the Obama stimulus program was too small, given the severity of the recession. Liberal economists such as Paul Krugman (publicly) and Council of Economic Advisers Chair Christina Romer (privately) applied conventional fiscal policy multipliers to the estimated GDP gap and argued that $787 billion was not enough to do the enormous job. Other more pragmatic advisers and commentators judged that it was the biggest package they could get through Congress. Both sides may have been right: the stimulus may have been too little economically even though it was nearly too much politically.

Early in Obama's first term, Treasury Secretary Geithner had insisted to his new boss that "your signature accomplishment is going to be preventing a Great Depression," to which Obama responded, "That's not enough for me" (Scheiber 2012, 15–16). But Obama had not consulted the Republican Party. Even before the ink was dry on the ARRA, Republicans attacked it as misguided, futile, laden with pork, ineffective, and even a step toward socialism. Almost immediately after its passage they even began a futile symbolic campaign

---

3. One particularly egregious example was extending the "carry back" period for net operating losses. How can reducing past taxes retroactively stimulate future investment?

Tim Geithner (1961–)

Indefatigable Firefighter

Timothy Geithner was born in New York City. But since his father worked for years for USAID and then the Ford Foundation, Geithner was raised mostly outside the United States in Zimbabwe, Zambia, India, and Thailand, where he completed high school. He then followed his father and paternal grandfather to Dartmouth College, from which he graduated in 1983. Two years later, Geithner earned a master's degree in international economics and East Asian studies at Johns Hopkins

All that seemed like perfect training for a career in international economic diplomacy. And indeed, when Geithner first joined the U.S. Treasury, it was as an attaché at the U.S. embassy in Tokyo. When Bill Clinton was elected president, Geithner jumped over to the political side and quickly rose through the hierarchy in a series of international economic positions of ever-increasing importance, culminating in 1998 as undersecretary of the treasury for international affairs. While in the Clinton Treasury, Geithner honed his skills as a financial firefighter, dealing with crises in Mexico, Brazil, and several East Asian countries.

When the Clinton administration ended, Geithner served a stint at the International Monetary Fund before being selected as president of the Federal Reserve Bank of New York in 2003. That post made him both the vice chair of the Federal Open Market Committee and, in essence, the Fed's chief operating officer. As president of the New York Fed, Geithner criticized sloppy practices in trading financial derivatives, but he also supported the Basel II accord that, critics argued, would leave banks with thin capital bases.

The presidency of the New York Fed made Geithner a central figure in the ad hoc responses to the emergencies at Bear Stearns, Lehman Brothers, the American International Group, and others in 2008 and also in the Fed's creation of a variety of novel lending facilities mentioned in the previous chapter. In both contexts, he often emphasized the need to "put foam on the runway" in case of a crash-landing.

In January 2009, Geithner made the proverbial jump from the frying pan into the fire when President Obama made him secretary of the treasury. There, Geithner's oft-repeated motto was "plan beats no plan." And there were plenty of plans. Still teaming up with Ben Bernanke (but no longer with Hank Paulson), Geithner oversaw the TARP, the 2009 fiscal stimulus program, a number of mortgage modification programs, the bank stress tests, the negotiations over the fiscal cliff in 2013 (discussed in the next chapter), and much else. When he left the Treasury in January 2013, he must have been exhausted. It was quite a stress test.

to repeal it, arguing that the stimulus had failed long before it could possibly have worked. While Republicans lacked the votes needed for repeal, their campaign succeeded in giving stimulus in general— and the ARRA in particular—a bad name. Perhaps that was their intent.

The ensuing antigovernment backlash helped found the far-right Tea Party movement, which transformed American politics. The day after Obama unveiled his relatively minimalist "Making Home Affordable" plan to limit foreclosures in February 2009, Rick Santelli, a high-strung reporter and commentator for CNBC, was on the floor of the Chicago Mercantile Exchange denouncing it. Here's an excerpt of what soon became famous as "the Rick Santelli rant":

> You know, the government is promoting bad behavior! . . .
>
> Why don't you put up a website to have people vote on the Internet as a referendum to see if we really want to subsidize the losers' mortgages?
>
> This is America! How many of you people want to pay for your neighbor's mortgage that has an extra bathroom and can't pay their bills? Raise their hand!
>
> [*boos from traders in the background*]
>
> President Obama, are you listening?
>
> [*A trader in the background*: "How about we all stop paying our mortgage? It's a moral hazard."]
>
> We're thinking of having a Chicago Tea Party in July. All you capitalists that want to show up to Lake Michigan, I'm going to start organizing. [*cheers*] (Blinder 2013, 339)[4]

Commodity traders are hardly a random sample of American society. They are gamblers at heart, have much higher incomes than average, and are unlikely to have been worried about losing their homes. Contrary to what soon become an urban myth, Santelli and his band of merry men were not giving voice to American public opinion that day. In fact, a Gallup poll just a few days later found that Americans favored "giving [federal] aid to homeowners who are in danger of losing their homes to foreclosures" by a whopping 64–33 percent margin (Newport 2009).

Nonetheless, the Santelli rant went viral, creating the false belief that Americans were not much happier about bailing out distressed homeowners than they were about bailing out distressed bankers.

---

4. Oddly, CNBC has no transcript of the rant even though it may be the most famous words ever uttered on that network. An internet search surfaces numerous alleged "transcripts," but they are inaccurate. I compiled this one myself from the video clip while writing my book *After the Music Stopped* (2013).

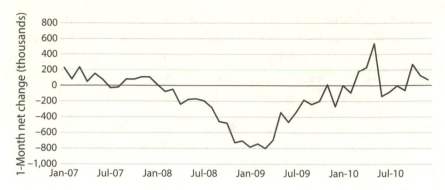

FIGURE 15.1. Change in payroll employment, monthly, 2007–2010.
Source: Bureau of Labor Statistics.

But it wasn't true. The aforementioned Gallup poll found respondents opposing federal aid to "U.S. banks and financial companies in danger of failing" by a decisive 59–39 percent margin. Santelli had a loud megaphone, however, and he was shouting what many conservatives wanted to hear: that homeowners facing foreclosure had been irresponsible and did not deserve help. Santelli didn't seem to blame the bankers who had signed off on these irresponsible loans.

Was the fiscal stimulus effective? Circumstantial evidence certainly says yes. The monthly job gains or losses from January 2007 through December 2010 first shown in figure 13.5 are repeated for convenience in figure 15.1. The graph depicts a U.S. economy in free fall from the time of the Lehman Brothers collapse through the first quarter of 2009, with truly terrifying rates of job loss. Then a big fiscal stimulus bill passed Congress in February 2009 and job losses started to abate immediately and dramatically, dropping from about 780,000 a month in January–March 2009 to under 40,000 a month in January–February 2010. The graph virtually conjures up an image of Barack Obama riding in on horseback to save the day. Several scholarly studies back up that view.[5]

The public didn't see it that way, however. As mentioned earlier, the economy hit bottom in June 2009, but the recovery was not exactly rip-roaring. Growth averaged just 3 percent over the remaining two

5. See, for example, Chodorow-Reich et al. (2012), Feyrer and Sacerdote (2011), and Wilson (2012).

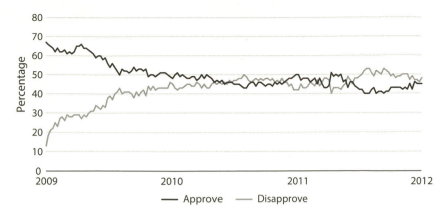

FIGURE 15.2. To approve or not to approve.
Source: The Gallup Organization.

quarters of 2009, 2.7 percent over the first six quarters of the recovery, and a mere 2.3 percent over its first ten quarters. Monthly payroll employment reports did not switch from showing net job losses to showing net job gains until March 2010, and even then there was a streak of four more job-losing months from June to September 2010. The national unemployment rate kept rising to a peak of 9.9 percent in April 2010 and was still sitting at a high 8.5 percent at the end of 2011.

So, what the American public saw was that a new president was elected in November 2008 promising change, and yet unemployment kept rising. The recession, although officially declared over by the National Bureau of Economic Research in June 2009, seemed to last forever, with the economy showing precious few signs of life. Times were tough, wages and incomes stagnated, jobs were excruciatingly hard to get, and many families lost their homes. That was not the sort of change Americans sought. Few were feeling good about the economy's performance. Even fewer realized that jobs normally recover more slowly than GDP.

Figure 15.2 depicts the devastating effect of this on President Obama's approval rating, which began to plunge almost immediately after he took office and continued to drop into 2010. While Obama was not on the ballot in 2010, the entire House of Representatives was, as were 37 senators. And the results were disastrous for the

Democrats. Going into the election, there were 256 Democrats in the House. Coming out, there were just 193. It was the sharpest seat swing by any party since 1938 and left the House with the most Republican members since 1946. Changes in the Senate were less dramatic, but Republicans still picked up six seats there. Many governorships and state legislatures also swung Republican.

The paradox was stunning. For their prodigious and largely successful efforts to right the economy, Obama and his party got a big Bronx cheer from the electorate, who saw instead a 9.4 percent unemployment rate on election day and believed that the U.S. economy was still in recession.[6] Former president Bill Clinton, as astute a political observer as we have, wrote that "one of the most interesting things to me [about the 2010 elections] is how easy it was to persuade so many Americans . . . to join in the government-bashing" (Clinton 2011, 7). History records that the Tea Party movement played a major role in that bashing.

The electoral debacle for the Democrats had numerous consequences. One of them became apparent when the weak economy needed further fiscal support in the years 2011–2013. No politician even dared utter the word "stimulus," which had become an eight-letter word. That was bad news for Keynesian economics. It was also bad news for Fed Chair Ben Bernanke, who was practically begging Congress to take action to boost aggregate demand. Instead, concern with the budget deficit, which had gone into hibernation during the Bush years, awoke with a vengeance.

The large fiscal stimulus plus the extraordinary outlays from TARP and other measures to combat the financial crisis plus the normal losses of tax revenue in a recession combined to raise the federal budget deficit to extraordinary heights, from a mere 1.2 percent of GDP in 2007 to a mind-boggling 10 percent of GDP in 2009. Ten percent of GDP? The number itself—over $1.4 trillion in dollar

6. Poll after poll in 2010 showed that. See, for example, *USA Today* (2010). That particular poll, conducted in August 27–30, 2010, showed 82 percent of respondents answering "yes" to the question "Do you think the economy is now in a recession, or not?" Only 16 percent answered "no."

terms—was shocking at the time. The U.S. government hadn't run budget deficits that large, relative to GDP, since World War II. The previous postwar high, under Ronald Reagan, was a mere 6 percent of GDP in 1983. In consequence, the debt-to-GDP ratio soared from about 30 percent at the end of 2007 to about 55 percent at the end of 2011, a stunning rise in just four years. Even some deficit doves started raising their eyebrows.

Republicans piled on. Some of the same congressmen and senators who had blithely ignored deficits while George W. Bush was president suddenly decided that deficits now posed a clear and present danger to American prosperity, if not to its morality. The notion that fiscal stimulus shrinks the economy is, of course, profoundly anti-Keynesian, not to mention nonsensical. But since opposing Obama required Republicans to turn sharply against Keynesian economics, they did so with gusto. As *The Economist* put it in April 2011, "If there is one ideology that unites today's Republicans, it is Keynesianism, whose nefarious influence they are determined to stamp out" (*The Economist* 2011). Indeed, some conservatives started arguing that the best way to grow the economy was to reduce federal spending.[7] To Keynesians, this sounded Orwellian: right is wrong, war is peace, up is down.

The political hysteria was partially echoed and partially justified by voices from the academy. Stanford's John Taylor and coauthors, for example, argued in a series of papers that the stimulus program had essentially no effect on aggregate demand despite costing over $800 billion (Taylor 2011a).[8] Taylor added that "I do not think this finding should come as a surprise" (Taylor 2011b). Not a surprise? Lord Keynes would have been shocked.

So were I and other modern Keynesians at the time. For example, Mark Zandi and I had estimated that real GDP in 2011 was $1.8 trillion higher than it would have been without all the rescue operations (fiscal, monetary, and financial) (Blinder and Zandi 2010). That much

---

7. See Hirsh (2009). Note the early date of this article (January 28), just eight days into the Obama administration.

8. This work is summarized in Taylor (2011a).

more output translated into 9.8 million more jobs and an unemployment rate 6.5 percentage points lower, according to our estimates. Those were huge effects that transformed what might have been an utter catastrophe into something that was merely awful. Even if you rejected the avowedly Keynesian model we used to make those estimates, there was still a question to confront: How in the world can you spend that much money, even if wastefully, without creating plenty of jobs?

President Obama responded to the Sturm und Drang over the budget deficit by creating the bipartisan National Commission on Fiscal Responsibility and Reform in February 2010. That eighteen-member commission, cochaired by Republican Alan Simpson and Democrat Erskine Bowles, included both politicians and nonpoliticians. When its recommendations were delivered in December 2010, they were praised lavishly by editorialists and other pundits around the country—and totally ignored by both Republican and Democratic politicians. At last, the two parties had reached bipartisan agreement on something!

Ironically, the partisan stalemate that paralyzed Washington in 2010 and 2011 may have been better than taking fiscal action.[9] After all, Democrats wanted to repeal the Bush income tax cuts for upper-income groups, and Republicans wanted to repeal Obama's payroll tax cuts for workers. Those were left-of-center and right-of-center versions of something the economy most emphatically did not need at the time: a tax hike. Unable to agree, the two parties compromised by doing neither. Instead, a series of last-minute budget deals reached in December 2010, December 2011, and February 2012 each kicked some proverbial cans down the proverbial road, thereby setting the nation up for what came to be called "the fiscal cliff" in January 2013 (see the next chapter).

On balance, fiscal policy was notably contractionary over the years 2011, 2012, and 2013, despite unemployment rates that averaged 8.9 percent, 8.1 percent, and 7.4 percent, respectively. Over those

9. In fairness to the Simpson-Bowles commission, their recommendations for deficit reduction were intended for the future, not for early 2011.

twelve quarters, the Congressional Budget Office's measure of the budget deficit, abstracting from automatic stabilizers, fell from a large 6.5 percent of GDP to a below-average 1.9 percent of GDP, a policy shift of about 1.5 percent of GDP per year for three years running.

At the Federal Reserve, Chair Bernanke was gnashing his teeth over this perverse shift in fiscal policy. As he later observed, "After enacting President Obama's stimulus package in February 2009, Congress had shifted into austerity mode. . . . This headwind was no soft breeze. . . . Tight fiscal policies were arguably offsetting much of the effect of our monetary efforts" (Bernanke 2015, 504). Not only had monetary policy become "the only game in town," it was also playing against a fiscal foe rather than working with it.

The Political Backlash against the Fed

The political backlash against the apparent success of the emergency stabilization policies was not limited to the Obama administration and Congress. Some of it was aimed at the Federal Reserve. The alphabet soup of lending facilities and especially the Fed's participation in a variety of "bailouts"—whether real or imagined—unleashed a considerable outcry against the central bank. Some of it came in real time, such as the chorus of objections to the second round of quantitative easing (QE2) mentioned in the previous chapter. Some of it came after the fact. Some of it came from the political Left: too many bankers bailed out. And some of it came from the political Right: the Fed was an unaccountable agency with too much power. But it came in torrents.

The paradox was tremendous. The financial crisis was the result of a series of grievous errors, misjudgments, and even frauds by private-sector companies and individuals, aided and abetted by leaders such as George W. Bush and Alan Greenspan, who were unduly enamored of laissez-faire and viscerally attached to the vaunted wisdom of the market. The American economy in 2005–2008 was plainly a victim of too little regulation, not too much, and some of the blame could justifiably be laid at the Fed's doorstep. Only after the blow-up in September 2008 did the formerly passive government turn interventionist—in desperation. And it worked. The worst was avoided. Financial markets returned to something approximating normalcy much sooner than seemed likely. There was no Great Depression 2.0.

You might have thought that such a bravura, if belated, performance would have restored faith in government and put the advocates of laissez-faire to rout. But no. In a cruel twist of fate, the coincidence in time of the horrible recession with multiple policy interventions gave the antigovernment crowd an opening to vilify and blame the government, which they took with gusto and with devastating effectiveness.

Perhaps the counterfactual notion that things would have been much worse but for the extensive policy interventions is too subtle for politics. As Congressman Barney Frank (D-MA) put it in a subsequent TV debate, "It is not a good political slogan to say things would have been worse without me. You don't win on that" (Ryan et al. 2011). In any case, it never caught on with the electorate. Instead, the critics fomented a severe backlash against the Federal Reserve, the Obama administration, and Congress. After all, policy levers were pulled all over Washington, and the economy tanked anyway. Right?

No, wrong. By that same reasoning, firefighters cause fires and people age faster in Florida. The real errors of bank regulators (including the Fed)—and there were many—was failing to step in earlier to stop the madness and restore some modicum of "safety and soundness." But logic rarely rules the political roost; ideology often does. And the ideologically driven backlash that powered Tea Party candidates to electoral victories in 2010 also produced a wave of criticisms of the Fed for overreaching, for enacting "quasi-fiscal" policies, and even for violating the Federal Reserve Act. (The latter was demonstrably false. The Fed has cautious lawyers.)

When Congress passed the Dodd-Frank financial reform act in July 2010, it limited the Fed's emergency lending powers by rewriting the now-famous Section 13(3) of the Federal Reserve Act. Thereafter, the Fed could not make an emergency loan to an individual institution; emergency loans could only be made to "a program or facility with broad-based eligibility." Even then, the Fed would need approval from the secretary of the treasury. A number of experts worried at the time that these provisions would tie the Fed's hands when the next crisis struck. But in 2020, Secretary of the Treasury Steven Mnuchin was only too happy to approve any lending the Fed would or could do and to provide it with backstop funding to do even more. Future uses of 13(3) are, of course, anybody's guess.

Monetarism's Last Gasp?

One final monetary policy issue merits discussion here. Milton Friedman famously declared that inflation is "always and everywhere" a monetary phenomenon. If that's more than a tautology, it must mean that large increases in the money supply (somehow defined) lead to large increases in prices, perhaps with lags but with little doubt.

The Fed's profusion of lending facilities, especially its various rounds of quantitative easing, led to a massive expansion of the asset side of the Fed's balance sheet during and after the financial crisis, an increase of about 140 percent from Lehman Day to November 2008 and an almost fivefold increase by the end of 2014. The liabilities side, of course, grew pari passu, with more than half of that showing up as a massive increase in bank reserves. Any reader of Friedman and Schwartz's *Monetary History* would naturally think that the money supply must have increased almost as rapidly, sowing the seeds of high inflation. Did it?

In a word, no. Figure 15.3 traces the behavior of three key monetary variables—Federal Reserve assets, bank reserves, and the M2 money supply—from 2008 through 2014. (Because it is on such a different scale, the graph actually plots one-sixth of M2; the other two series are in their natural units.) It is apparent that the Fed's assets and bank reserves both skyrocketed immediately after the Lehman failure. Specifically, assets more than doubled, and reserves rose an astonishing 27-fold. (Yes, you read that right.) The growth of the money supply was far more subdued, however. M2 moved up only negligibly from September to November 2008 and grew by less than 50 percent over the entire six-year period.

Figure 15.4 displays one obvious implication of this huge disparity: the money multiplier, defined here as the ratio of M2 to the monetary base, collapsed from 9.2 in August 2008 to just 5.4 three

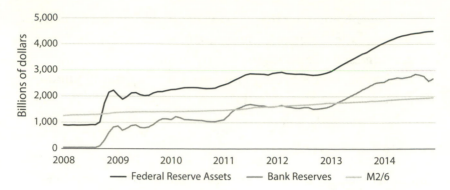

FIGURE 15.3. Federal Reserve assets, bank reserves, and M2, 2008–2014 (M2 scale adjusted).

Source: Board of Governors of the Federal Reserve System.

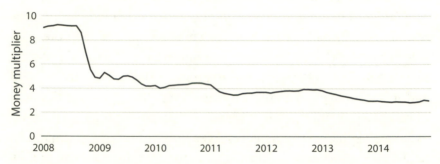

FIGURE 15.4. The money multiplier (M2/monetary base), 2008–2014.

Source: Author's computations from Board of Governors of the Federal Reserve System data.

months later and eventually to under 3.0. What happened here? Banks decided they were content to hold on their balance sheets the huge volumes of reserves the Fed was creating, thereby cutting the textbook money multiplier process short. What made banks content to hold so many reserves, whereas they held approximately zero prior to the Lehman bankruptcy?

There were several reasons. The biggest was probably a "minor" provision in the TARP legislation that allowed the Fed to pay interest on reserves. That "little" change transformed bank reserves into ersatz T-bills, only in a more convenient form for bankers, thus making them a far more attractive asset than previously. Perhaps more important, the provision annihilated the traditional link between bank reserves and money. Now paying interest on reserves, the Fed could expand its balance sheet massively without seeing the money supply expand pari passu.

In addition, with financial problems still surrounding the banks during the first few years covered by figure 15.4, they were fearful of further calamities and thus eager to stockpile liquidity rather than lend. In the later years covered by the figure, new regulatory requirements, which demanded higher liquidity buffers, added yet more to the demand for bank reserves. All that said, I still find it amazing that by, say, 2015 banks were still holding trillions of dollars in excess reserves.

What about inflation? Unlike in the case of the Great Contraction, the Fed did not allow the collapse of the money multiplier to drag down the money supply. The compound annual growth rate of M2 over this six-year period was about 7 percent. The Bernanke Fed thus redeemed the promise that the chair had made to Milton Friedman and Anna Schwartz years earlier. That said, if even a little bit of monetarist blood flowed through your veins, you might have expected 7 percent money growth to produce a lot higher inflation rate than the roughly 1.75 percent rate that was actually observed. Indeed, it seems that some members of the Federal Open Market Committee (FOMC) were worried about eventual inflation, even if they didn't voice their concerns in old-fashioned monetarist terms.

The most prominent such critic was Thomas Hoenig, president of the Federal Reserve Bank of Kansas City at the time, who dissented in the hawkish direction against every FOMC decision in 2010. Here's how the FOMC statement characterized his dissent from the committee's dovish forward guidance in April 2010: "Thomas M. Hoenig . . . believed that continuing to express the expectation of exceptionally low levels of the federal funds rate for an extended period was no longer warranted because it could lead to a build-up of future imbalances and increase risks to longer run macroeconomic and financial stability, while limiting the Committee's flexibility to begin raising rates modestly" (FOMC 2010b). Raise rates? In 2010?

Hoenig was not alone in worrying that the FOMC was keeping monetary policy too loose for too long, perhaps because of the strong growth of money and reserves. Over the twenty-four FOMC meetings held during the years 2011–2013, Chair Bernanke experienced twenty-five total dissenting votes, of which twenty-one were in the hawkish direction. Outside critics such as John Taylor of Stanford and Allan Meltzer of Carnegie-Mellon also criticized the Fed for keeping monetary policy too loose for too long even before Hoenig began dissenting.[10] But what was once a tight link between M2 growth and subsequent inflation had disappeared years before.

The Federal Reserve finally started raising rates, albeit cautiously, on December 16, 2015. By then, the near-zero federal funds rate had been in effect for seven years.

Chapter Summary

American fiscal policy makers turned sharply Keynesian—though more in deed than in word—in the early days of the Obama administration, passing a fiscal stimulus bill in excess of 5 percent of GDP. The ARRA was a partisan affair, however, with only three Republican senators and no Republican members of the House voting for it despite a collapsing economy and soaring unemployment. Some liberals argued that the stimulus was too small, though I believe history will judge that it tested the limits of what Congress would have accepted at the time. As a piece of evidence in support of that judgment, President Obama found it extremely difficult to get any further stimulus measures through Congress in the ensuing years.

The spending from the 2009 ARRA, the outlays from TARP,[11] and the adverse budget swing that always accompanies a recession conspired to balloon the federal budget deficit to almost 10 percent of GDP in fiscal 2009, an unheard-of number in peacetime America. That alarming figure quickly roused deficit hawks from their slumber. And it seemed to be no coincidence that many of those

10. Their criticisms started quite early. See, for example, Taylor (2009b) and Meltzer (2009d).

11. TARP outlays were loans, not expenditures, and those loans were mostly repaid with a profit to the Treasury. But U.S. budget conventions counted the loan amounts, when granted, as adding to the deficit.

hawks were the same Republicans who had shown no concern over large deficits whatsoever during the Bush presidency. Could deficits really be worrisome when run by Democratic administrations but not when run by Republican administrations? There is no economic explanation for why that might be so. But there is a straightforward political explanation.

Perhaps the biggest irony of this period was the powerful and multifaceted political backlash against President Obama, the Democrats in Congress, and the Fed (not to mention against Lord Keynes). While their antirecessionary actions were certainly not perfect, strong fiscal, monetary, and financial policy responses to the financial crisis and the Great Recession mitigated the decline of economic activity and almost certainly shortened the recession. Yet Obama and the Democrats were vilified for the large budget deficits that ensued, the Fed was accused of overstepping its authority, and both the Treasury and the Fed were excoriated for bailing out banks.

An interesting question for history is whether the political backlash would have been milder if (a) more financial miscreants had been charged, tried, and sent to jail and (b) more help had been provided to distressed homeowners rather than to distressed banks. My own guesses are yes on both counts. But neither happened, and the powerful backlash led, among other things, to the rise of the Tea Party in 2010. More speculatively, the lingering anger likely contributed to the implausible rise of Donald Trump, the grievance candidate, in 2015–2016.

Despite massive expansion of the Fed's balance sheet, a dizzying increase in bank reserves, and a large increase in the money supply, inflation remained quiescent after 2008. In fact, the Federal Reserve would spend much of the following decade trying to nudge inflation up, not down. On the intellectual front, these developments seemed to drive the last nails into the coffin of monetarism.

Well, maybe not quite the last. Similar concerns about money creation driving up inflation arose in some quarters in 2020 and 2021, when the Fed engaged in even more massive provision of liquidity, credit, and money in response to the far greater crisis brought on by the COVID-19 pandemic. But this time inflation did rise—sharply.

16

The Record Expansion of the 2010s

And the beat goes on.
—SONNY AND CHER, 1967

Economic events rarely align with the decadal calendar. The soaring "Sixties" really began with the Kennedy-Johnson tax cuts of 1964. The inflationary "Seventies" began in earnest with the first Organization of the Petroleum Exporting Countries shock in the fall of 1973. And so on. The record-shattering expansion of the 2010s is the exception that proves the rule. According to National Bureau of Economic Research dating, it began when the so-called Great Recession bottomed out in June 2009 and ended abruptly after February 2020 when the COVID-19 pandemic decimated economic activity all over the world. The expansion therefore encompassed the entire decade.

That said, the U.S. economy did not take off like a rocket in June 2009; the deep recession had caused far too much damage for that. As noted in the previous chapter, real GDP growth averaged just 3 percent over the last half of 2009 and a mere 2.6 percent over the four quarters of 2010. Net job gains did not appear until March 2010, and even then they were not sustained. What would eventually grow into a record-breaking run of consecutive job gains did not begin until October. All in all, the American people could be forgiven for thinking they were still living in a recession—as they did.

It turned out, however, that Americans of the day were experiencing the start of the longest business expansion in U.S. history, one that would likely have lasted even longer had the pandemic of 2020 not ended it abruptly. Over the forty-two quarters spanning 2009:3 through 2019:4, real GDP growth averaged 2.3 percent per annum; payroll employment rose for a record-setting 113 consecutive months, adding 21.3 million net new jobs in total; and the unemployment rate tracked down gradually but steadily from 9.9 percent to 3.5 percent, the lowest rate since 1969.

One important fact, however, seems to have been lost in most of the discussions since. The "secret" behind how the U.S. economy managed to bring the unemployment rate down so far while growing at just 2.3 percent per annum is no secret at all but rather a simple matter of arithmetic—and a profoundly negative piece of arithmetic at that: labor productivity performed miserably. After soaring in 2009 as frightened businesses reduced their labor hours more vigorously than they reduced output, productivity advanced at a sluggish 1 percent annual rate from the first quarter of 2010 through the last quarter of 2019, after which the pandemic turned the lights out.[1] For historical comparison, the previous worst productivity performance over a protracted period was the notorious—and still poorly understood—productivity slowdown of 1973–1995, when output per hour grew at a lackluster 1.5 percent annual rate. Thus, the U.S. economy experienced an employment boom without a GDP boom.

---

1. There was a hint in the data that nonfarm labor productivity growth might have been returning to normal in 2019, when it averaged 2.4 percent at an annual rate. In 2020 and 2021, productivity (like much other data) bounced around wildly from quarter to quarter but also averaged a strong 2.4 percent per annum.

The 2012 Election

With the economy still weak in 2012, any talk of fiscal consolidation in the federal budget was clearly premature on economic grounds. But that was a presidential election year—the silly season, I like to call it—and antideficit sentiment was at or near its zenith. So, the 2012 campaign featured considerable discussion of fiscal "exit" strategies from the huge budget deficits of the day, despite the fact that the unemployment rate in 2012 averaged 8.1 percent.

President Obama's opponent was Mitt Romney, the former governor of Massachusetts who had made a fortune in the private equity business. Republicans may have thought they could sell a successful businessman as just the person to fix an underperforming economy. After all, real GDP growth averaged barely over 1 percent during the politically sensitive second and third quarters of 2012, and the unemployment rate was still 7.7 percent on election day. Those are not the kinds of economic numbers an incumbent wishes to run on, and Romney argued that they should be blamed on Obama. Somewhat incongruously, by the way, he also ran against Obama's signature legislative achievement—which Republicans derisively called "Obamacare"—even though it had been closely patterned on "Romneycare" in Massachusetts.

History records that the Republican sales pitch failed to work. Obama defeated Romney by about 4 percentage points in the popular vote and by a comfortable 332–206 margin in the electoral college. But Obama's coattails were short, and the congressional win for the Democrats was modest. They added to their slim majority in the Senate but fell well short of the sixty votes needed to block Republican filibusters. In the House the Democrats picked up a few seats, but the Republicans hung onto their majority. President Obama therefore would still have to contend with stonewalling from Speaker John Boehner, egged on by the Tea Party faction in the House that was constantly pulling Boehner to the right. The configuration of the White House and Congress in January 2013 was thus tailor-made for partisan sniping and continued gridlock.

The Fiscal Cliff

Not long after the election, President Obama and Congress confronted what was ominously called "the fiscal cliff," a term popularized by Federal Reserve Chair Ben Bernanke, who worried about it and sought to draw attention to it. The cliff was remarkably steep. Had the American economy fallen off, a recession very likely would have followed.

The fiscal cliff of 2012–2013 was man-made, though presumably accidentally. By sheer coincidence, various budget agreements reached in prior years had left both the Obama payroll tax cuts and the Bush income tax cuts set to expire in January 2013. In addition, long-term unemployment benefits were slated to be curtailed severely just then, and drastic formulaic spending cuts enacted as part of the budget agreement of August 2011 (but never intended to take effect) were also set to be triggered. Adding it all up, the nation was headed for a massive fiscal contraction—in the neighborhood of 4 percent of GDP—unless actions were taken to avert it.

Bernanke warned repeatedly that the Federal Reserve "cannot offset the full impact of the fiscal cliff. It's just too big, given the tools that we have available and the limitations on our policy toolkit at this point" (Bernanke 2012b, 12). But partisan intransigence seemed poised to push the economy over the cliff nonetheless until a last-minute deal was reached on New Year's Day 2013, technically one day after the U.S. government went over the cliff. (Luckily, January 1 is a holiday, so nothing happened.) The deal delayed sequestration by two months, extended some of the Bush tax cuts, let the payroll tax cut lapse but added some tax credits for low-income families, extended federal unemployment benefits, and more.

Washington's fiscal battles were far from over, however. During the summer and fall of 2013, congressional Republicans sought to delay funding for President Obama's signature policy achievement: the Affordable Care Act. Obama and congressional Democrats refused to accept the delay. The standoff produced another politically charged government shutdown when congressional spending authority expired on the last day of fiscal year 2013 (September 30, 2013). Raising the national debt ceiling—a hardy perennial—also became a political hot potato once again. Concerns actually arose that the U.S. government might default on its debt, not because the nation couldn't afford to pay its bills but because Congress was mired in gridlock.

After sixteen arduous days, an agreement to end the shutdown was finally cobbled together in the Senate, passed by the House, and quickly signed by President Obama. The 2013 government shutdown was both long (as shutdowns go) and consequential. Some eight hundred thousand federal employees were furloughed, the national parks were closed, and a number of government services were severely disrupted. Much like the shutdowns of 1995 and 1996, shuttering substantial portions of the federal government did not redound to the political benefit of the Republican Party. Popular sentiment swung more toward Obama and the Democrats.

Theatrics aside—and there were plenty of them—fiscal policy was notably contractionary over the years 2011, 2012, and 2013, despite unemployment rates that averaged 8.9 percent, 8.1 percent, and 7.4 percent, respectively. As mentioned in the previous chapter, the Congressional Budget Office's measure of the budget deficit, abstracting from automatic stabilizers, fell from a large 6.5 percent of GDP to just 1.9 percent of GDP over those twelve quarters, a policy shift of about 1.5 percent of GDP per year in an economy in which aggregate demand was still weak. Keynes was presumably rolling in his grave. Ben Bernanke, very much alive, was grimacing.

It was in 2013–2014 that Lawrence Summers (2014) began to revive an old theory originally due to Alvin Hansen (1939): secular stagnation, the notion that the U.S. economy faced a chronic (not just cyclical) shortage of aggregate demand. Curiously, Summers did not offer the recent years of contractionary fiscal policy as one of the possible (but easily reversible!) causes of that stagnation. Rather, he focused on the decline in the equilibrium rate of interest.

The Only Game in Town

Fiscal policy may have forsaken its role as a macroeconomic stabilizer. But true to its new designation as "the only game in town," monetary policy did not. The Fed's alphabet soup of special lending facilities was mostly wound down by 2011 for a simple reason: they were no longer needed. And having ruled out negative interest rates, the Fed could not push either the federal funds rate or the interest rate paid on reserves down any further. Ever since the end of 2008, the Fed had been relying on two main monetary policy instruments, each with many variants: quantitative easing (QE) and forward guidance. The Fed continued using those two tools through the end of Bernanke's term and into Janet Yellen's. (Those same tools, by the way, came roaring back in 2020.)

QE was discussed earlier. The twin ideas behind it were to shrink risk premiums in interest rates (e.g., by buying mortgage-backed securities instead of treasuries) and to shrink term premiums in interest rates (e.g., by buying long-term treasury securities instead of short-term treasuries). Three waves of "large-scale asset purchases," as the Fed preferred to call them, were announced in November 2008 (QE1), November 2010 (QE2), and September 2012 (QE3). There was also Operation Twist, which came between QE2 and QE3. As mentioned in the previous chapter, the first episode of QE achieved the most dramatic results: the Fed succeeded in resurrecting the deceased market for mortgage-based securities (MBS). But the second round of QE was the most controversial politically, even though the Fed bought only treasuries.

The third QE episode marked a major departure for the Fed in that it did not prespecify a maximum value of treasuries to be purchased but instead left QE3 open-ended. In total, the Fed increased its balance sheet by $1,725 billion, most of which was agency MBS in QE1 and another $600 billion (all in treasuries) in QE2. In designing QE3, however, the Federal Open Market Committee (FOMC) decided to buy $40 billion per month in agency MBS and another $45 billion per month in longer-dated treasuries. No terminal date—and thus no cumulative amount—was announced.

Chair Bernanke gave the first hint of QE3 purchases coming to an end in congressional testimony on May 22, 2013. In answering a question, he observed that "if we see continued improvement and we have confidence that that's going to be sustained then we could in the next few meetings . . . take a step down in our pace of purchases" (Reuters 2019). A mild statement, you might think. The Fed thought of it as indicating an intent to ease its foot off the gas pedal. Besides, "in the next few meetings" could mean months away, as it eventually did. Nonetheless, markets reacted strongly. Bond yields leaped; a month later, ten-year Treasury yields were about 50 basis points higher than they were before Bernanke's statement. The stock market also reacted badly. The episode was quickly labeled the "taper tantrum." Markets clearly did not relish the thought of their support being taken away—or even "tapered"—and let the Fed know. The central bank seemed surprised by the strength of the market reaction. It remembered this episode well when it started considering tapering again in 2021. It gave markets repeated advance notice, and this second taper went smoothly—no tantrum.

As it turned out, it was not until December 2013 that the Fed actually began to taper its QE3 asset purchases, ending them entirely in October 2014. By that time, the Fed had acquired just over $1.6 trillion in net new assets under QE3, making the grand total over the three QE episodes almost $4 trillion. Net of redemptions and maturing assets, the Fed balance sheet, which had started the crisis under $1 trillion, reached a peak of around $4.5 trillion in 2014.

Did these various QE programs achieve their goals? A naive look at Treasury rates would certainly suggest that they did; interest rates mostly fell during the QE period (figure 16.1). But, of course, interest rates had been falling for almost three decades prior to QE, and the downward trend during the QE period does not look especially sharp by eyeball. Econometric studies are far more sophisticated, and the consensus among them is that QE did work: interest rate spreads on MBS narrowed, and the Treasury yield curve flattened.[2]

2. Many studies could be cited. See, for example, Krishnamurthy and Vissing-Jorgensen (2011) and Hamilton and Wu (2012).

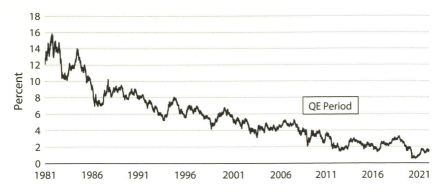

FIGURE 16.1. Ten-year Treasury interest rates, 1981–2021.
Source: Board of Governors of the Federal Reserve System.

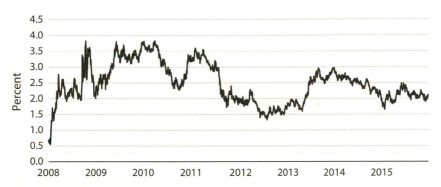

FIGURE 16.2. Spread between ten-year and three-month Treasury interest rates, 2008–2015.
Source: Board of Governors of the Federal Reserve System.

What is less frequently mentioned, however, is that the largest effects on interest rates appear to have come from QE1, the one QE episode that looks more like emergency relief from a financial crisis than "normal" monetary policy applied to bolster aggregate demand by shrinking risk or term premia (Krishnamurthy and Vissing-Jorgensen 2011). Figure 16.2 displays the spread between ten-year Treasury rates and three-month bill rates over the period 2008–2015. The sharp drop at the time of QE1 (November 2008) is evident. But there are no similarly dramatic drops at the time of QE2 (November 2010) or QE3 (September 2012).[3]

3. It is possible, however, that some of the sharp drop in the spread in August 2012 came in anticipation of QE3.

The FOMC's other big "new" weapon was forward guidance, which the committee began to rely on more strongly, albeit in an ad hoc way, at its momentous December 2008 meeting. Its words at the time were "the Committee anticipates that weak economic conditions are likely to warrant exceptionally low levels of the federal funds rate for some time." "Exceptionally low" was easy enough to parse; it meant the just-established range of 0–25 basis points for the funds rate, the closest thing to zero that the Fed was willing to consider. The phrase "for some time" was more cryptic. Was that months? Years?[4] In its March 2009 statement, the FOMC amended those words to "for an extended period," which markets read (correctly) as "longer than we said in December 2008." And that still-vague commitment to a near-zero funds rate remained intact until the August 2011 FOMC meeting.

At that point the FOMC, seeking to put more teeth into its forward guidance, began a series of experiments that it ultimately judged to be unsatisfactory. The first few attempts involved naming specific dates. The August 2011 FOMC statement observed that "the Committee currently anticipates that economic conditions . . . are likely to warrant exceptionally low levels for the federal funds rate at least through mid-2013" (FOMC 2011). Despite the clear escape clause provided by the words "at least," that time frame was shockingly specific by the Fed's historically tight-lipped standards. But as the calendar rolled into 2012, the "mid-2013" date started to look too close for comfort. Remember, the main idea behind forward guidance is to keep intermediate to long rates low. So, the FOMC changed its "zero" interest rate pledge again in January 2012, this time extending it to "at least through late 2014" (FOMC 2012a).

Several other major changes in Fed transparency were also made at the January 2012 FOMC meeting, including official adoption of numerical targets for inflation (2%) and the nonaccelerating inflation rate of unemployment (between 5.2% and 6% at the time) and the publication of the FOMCs first-ever "dot plot," showing where members believed (or was it hoped?) the funds rate would go over

---

4. It turned out to be seven years, but I'm pretty sure no member of the FOMC thought so at the time.

the next several years. If there was any remaining doubt, this was now Ben Bernanke's transparent Fed, not Alan Greenspan's opaque Fed.[5]

Meanwhile, Charles Evans, president of the Federal Reserve Bank of Chicago, was arguing that forward guidance on interest rates should be tied to economic conditions, not to any particular date. His arguments made sense, and in December 2012 the FOMC adopted them with these words: "the Committee . . . currently anticipates that this exceptionally low range for the federal funds rate will be appropriate at least as long as the unemployment rate remains above 6-1/2 percent, inflation between one and two years ahead is projected to be no more than a half percentage point above the Committee's 2 percent longer-run goal, and longer-term inflation expectations continue to be well anchored" (FOMC 2012b). It was a complex message. So, perhaps naturally, market participants focused on the numerical unemployment-rate target. The number 6.5 percent soon became a Holy Grail.

During 2013 the unemployment rate kept tracking downward, from 8 percent in January to 6.7 percent in December. With the FOMC still far from ready to raise rates and Ben Bernanke's eight years at the helm drawing to a close, something had to give. But the December 2013 statement merely added that "the Committee now anticipates . . . that it likely will be appropriate to maintain the current target range for the federal funds rate well past the time that the unemployment rate declines below 6-1/2 percent" (FOMC 2013). The phrase "well past the time" left traders wondering. Wasn't $U = 6.5$ percent the magic number that would trigger rate hikes?

Passing the Baton: Monetary Policy under Janet Yellen

For markets craving continuity and also feeling a bit perplexed by the Fed's clumsy messaging late in 2013, it would have been hard to imagine a better replacement for Ben Bernanke than Janet Yellen.

---

5. Bernanke also began to hold live press conferences after the April 2011 FOMC meeting. Having been a colleague of Greenspan's on the Federal Reserve Board, I can testify that this degree of openness was inconceivable under Greenspan. Not even a transparency superhawk like me dared to suggest it.

President Obama's choice shouted continuity, not change. For openers, no one could see much intellectual daylight between Bernanke and Yellen because there wasn't much. Both were accomplished academic macroeconomists from elite universities (Princeton and the University of California, Berkeley, respectively.) Both were Keynesians, even though Bernanke was then a Republican and Yellen was a Democrat. More than that, when Yellen was named to replace Bernanke, she was serving under him as the Fed's vice chair.

No Federal Reserve chair in history had ever served as many apprenticeships for the top spot as Janet Yellen. Her unprecedented Federal Reserve résumé began in August 1994,[6] when President Bill Clinton appointed her to the Federal Reserve Board. About two and a half years later Clinton asked her to move to the White House to chair his Council of Economic Advisers, which she did for roughly another two and a half years before returning to her professorship at Berkeley. The Fed would soon beckon her again, however. In June 2004 Yellen was installed as president of the Federal Reserve Bank of San Francisco, and in October 2010 President Barack Obama elevated her to become vice chair of the Federal Reserve Board. Many Fed watchers speculated at the time that there must have been some understanding, though certainly no guarantee, that she would become the next chair when Bernanke's term ended in January 2014.[7] Otherwise, why would she leave the San Francisco bank?

By the time her turn came, Yellen had basically run the table. She had been a Fed governor, a Federal Reserve bank president, and vice chair of the Federal Reserve Board. She had worked shoulder-to-shoulder with Ben Bernanke for years. On top of all that, President Obama would surely relish the opportunity to appoint the first female head in the Fed's history. Right? Well, yes. But not before a firestorm broke out.

It seems that Lawrence "Larry" Summers, the ex-secretary of the treasury, ex-president of Harvard, and ex-director of Obama's

6. I do not count here a stint as a Fed staff economist early in her career.

7. There are no term limits on Fed chairs. Bernanke could have requested a third term but did not.

National Economic Council, had thrown his large hat into the ring, where it landed loudly. Or maybe Obama threw it in for him.[8] Summers wanted the Fed chairmanship for himself and, having served in the Obama administration for its first two years, looked well positioned to claim it. Virtually all of the top-ranking economic officials in the Obama administration in 2013 were either declared or covert Summers supporters. That group probably included Obama himself.

As soon as Summers's name became public, however, a media firestorm broke out. Ghosts from his past came from everywhere to oppose him. Women's groups remembered his unfortunate remarks about women being unable to compete with men at the top echelons of science and math. Labor unions and Democratic senators remembered his rather conservative views on financial issues. For example, lots of people remembered—and not fondly—his laissez-faire (or worse) attitudes toward regulating derivatives in 2000 and his lack of enthusiasm for using Troubled Assets Relief Program money to mitigate foreclosures in 2009–2010. Summers was looked upon as more of a friend to Wall Street than to Main Street.

All that said, Obama was nonetheless attracted by Summers's obvious intelligence and deep experience. However, the president was also warned of a potentially nasty confirmation battle that could end in a rejection of the nomination by the Senate Banking Committee, where several members, led by Senator Jeff Merkley (D-OR), were hostile to Summers. So, Obama returned to the safety of nominating Yellen, who was confirmed easily by a 56–26 Senate vote on January 6, 2014, and took office on February 1, right on schedule.

It fell to Yellen to complete the monetary policy exit plan that Bernanke had often discussed but barely acted upon: reducing asset purchases under QE3 and modifying the Fed's forward guidance. Forward guidance presented itself as the more immediate problem because of the muddle over 6.5 percent unemployment at the end of

8. In his memoir *A Promised Land*, Obama acknowledged what had long been rumored: Summers had been all but promised the Fed chairmanship years earlier as part of the deal that induced him to take the National Economic Council job in January 2009 (Obama 2020, 506–7).

Bernanke's term. The communication task looked difficult because the Fed was widely assumed to be poised to start raising rates once the unemployment rate reached that magic number, which was just slightly below where unemployment stood on March 2014 (6.7%). In fact, however, the FOMC was by no means ready.

Yellen quickly proved herself to be a master of the fine art of Fed-speak. The March 2014 FOMC statement, her first as chair, repeated verbatim Bernanke's warning "that it likely will be appropriate to maintain the current target range for the federal funds rate for a considerable time after the asset purchase program ends" (FOMC 2014), an ending that was still at some indeterminate time in the future. But then the statement noted that "with the unemployment rate nearing 6-1/2 percent, the Committee has updated its forward guidance. The change in the Committee's guidance does not indicate any change in the Committee's policy intentions as set forth in its recent statements." Try figuring that one out. Updated guidance but no change in policy intentions? In fact, the financial markets accepted the Fed's newest tortured prose with barely a hiccup. Chair Yellen had passed her first test with flying colors.

By the next FOMC meeting (April 2014) all traces of the 6.5 percent unemployment rate had vanished from the statement, never to appear again. QE3 asset purchases were also nearing their end. Yet the statement stuck with the previous forward guidance: "it likely will be appropriate to maintain the current target range for the federal funds rate for a considerable time after the asset purchase program ends." When would that be? The end of QE3 finally arrived in October, with the unemployment rate down to 5.7 percent. But the committee stuck to its view that rate hikes were not yet imminent. The dovish consensus on the FOMC was fraying, however. At the December 2104 meeting Yellen suffered three dissents, which is akin to a mass mutiny on the consensus-driven FOMC.

The central issue under debate at the time was familiar, especially to Yellen who had been a Fed governor in 1996–1997 when Greenspan debated—mostly with himself—how low the unemployment rate could go without causing inflation to erupt. Well after Yellen had left the Fed for the Clinton administration in 1997, the Greenspan Fed had allowed the unemployment rate to drift all the way down

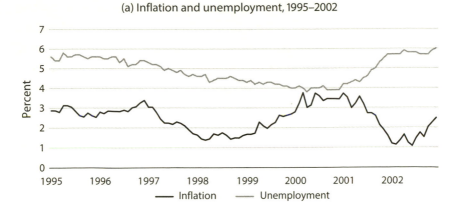

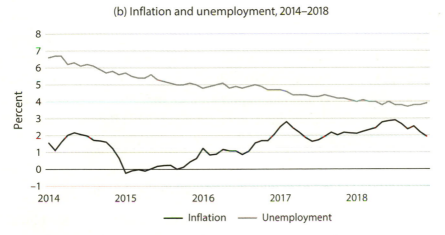

FIGURE 16.3. Inflation and unemployment, 1995–2002 and 2014–2018.
Source: Bureau of Labor Statistics.

to 3.9 percent in the closing months of 2000, yet there never was an inflationary price to pay. Notice in panel (a) of figure 16.3 that it wasn't just a matter of a long delay, as Milton Friedman might have suggested. The inflationary consequences of superlow unemployment never came. Would the 2010s look the same?

The time to raise rates finally arrived at the December 16, 2015, meeting, when the FOMC decided unanimously to increase the target range by 25 basis points. It was no wonder they chose such a small increment. As the Fed's first rate hike in seven years, it would be widely noticed and commented upon. By then the unemployment rate was down to 5.1 percent, a number low enough to frighten the FOMC's inflation hawks and worry even some of its doves, a group that certainly included Chair Yellen. But despite widespread expectations that the Fed's rate hike would be the first in a series, the 25 basis points in December 2015 proved to be a one-shot affair. The funds rate was bumped up that one time and then stayed put for a full year. No one could accuse the Yellen Fed of embarking on a crusade to vanquish some invisible inflationary dragon. Yellen and her colleagues wanted to see a live, fire-breathing enemy, which they did not.

In total, the Yellen Fed engineered just five rate hikes, each of 25 basis points, over her four years in the chair. Not much. It also began to shrink the huge balance sheet it had acquired, though again not by much. During that time, the FOMC watched the unemployment rate drift down from 6.6 percent to 4.1 percent and watched the core Consumer Price Index (CPI) inflation rate rise from 1.6 percent to 2.3 percent (see figure 16.3b).[9] These were the "initial conditions" when President Donald Trump refused to reappoint Yellen (a Democrat) and handed the reins over to Jerome ("Jay") Powell (a Republican) in February 2018.

The Yellen-to-Powell Handoff: Continuity Continues

Because Powell's heroic actions in the 2020 pandemic made him a historic figure, it is easy to forget now that his chairmanship began as a smooth continuation of what markets had grown accustomed to seeing over the twelve Bernanke-Yellen years. At first, a few Fed watchers wondered about the fact that the patrician Powell was the first Fed chief since G. William Miller who did not have a PhD in economics. Greenspan, Bernanke, and Yellen had created a model. Going back through Volcker and Burns, an economist had led the Fed since Martin's retirement except for Miller's brief reign.

---

9. To remind the reader, the Fed's 2 percent inflation target was for core personal consumption expenditure inflation, not core CPI inflation. The former ran consistently below the latter throughout this period.

Janet Yellen (1946–)
_____

Serial Glass Ceiling Breaker

Janet Yellen is a distinguished economist who at this writing is serving as U.S. secretary of the treasury.[10] Her remarkable career changed abruptly from successful academic to important policy maker one fateful day in 1994 during an airport stop en route from Berkeley to Yale. She was interrupted while changing planes by a call from the White House: Please reroute to Washington, DC, the caller said; the president wants to announce your nomination to the Federal Reserve Board today.

Yellen's head was spinning when she arrived at the White House later that day. (I know; I met her there.) But no one could have predicted the amazing success story that would unfold over the coming years. Janet Yellen is the only person ever to lead all three key economic agencies: the Council of Economic Advisers, the Federal Reserve, and the U.S. Treasury. More remarkably, she was the first woman to chair the Federal Reserve Board (2014–2018) and is currently the first woman secretary of the treasury. For Yellen, there are no more glass ceilings left to break.

Janet Yellen was born and raised in Brooklyn, New York. She graduated as valedictorian of her high school class and went on to academic success at Brown University before enrolling in Yale's PhD program. When she completed her Yale PhD in 1971, she was the only female to do so that year. She was already a pioneer.

After a few years of teaching at Harvard, Yellen joined the staff of the Federal Reserve Board in Washington, where one day in the cafeteria she met George Akerlof, a brilliant economic theorist who would later win a Nobel Prize. The two married in 1978, and in 1980 they both joined the faculty of the University of California, Berkeley. She was a Berkeley professor on that fateful day in 1994.

Yellen served for about two and a half years as a Fed governor. While there, she developed a reputation as a monetary policy dove, a skilled debater, and a person who always came assiduously prepared. In February 1997, President Clinton persuaded her to become his chair of the Council of Economic Advisers. After another two and a half years in the White House, she returned to Berkeley in 1999.

But Janet Yellen was hooked—on policy making in general, and on the Federal Reserve in particular. So, when the directors of the Federal Reserve Bank of San Francisco offered her the bank's presidency (the first woman to hold that position, of course), she accepted with alacrity.

Yellen was so successful at the San Francisco Fed that President Obama nominated her to become vice chair of the Federal Reserve Board in 2010. In that post, she cemented her reputations for dovishness, competence, and hard work. She also helped Chair Ben Bernanke persuade the FOMC to adopt inflation targeting in 2012. After a fierce though mostly behind-the-scenes battle over Bernanke's successor, she emerged as the Fed's next leader.

Yellen tuned in another fine performance at the Fed's helm, including extremely rapid job growth with no rise in inflation and a start on "normalizing" interest rates from their financial crisis lows. President Trump, who had criticized Yellen for being too political,

_____

10. Truth-in-writing demands that I reveal that Janet Yellen has been a dear friend for more than twenty-five years.

reportedly considered reappointing her in 2018 but opted instead for Governor Jerome Powell, a Republican.

But Yellen's illustrious career in public service was not yet over. President Joe Biden surprised many people—probably including Yellen—by tapping her to be his first secretary of the treasury in 2021. Among Yellen's first jobs was helping to pass the huge pandemic relief bill known as the American Rescue Plan. Much more action followed, including a remarkable international tax agreement intended to reduce corporate tax shelters and sanctions on Russia when it invaded Ukraine.

Few people, if any, have played such a large role in the *Monetary and Fiscal History of the United States, 1961–2021* as Janet Yellen.

They need not have been worried, however, and soon they were not. First of all, Powell proved to be a great Fed chair, but that's a story for chapter 18. Second, he was reassuring and did indeed follow the Bernanke-Yellen script in his early years. Specifically, the Yellen Fed had raised interest rates three times in 2017, in each case by 25 basis points. The Powell Fed nearly replicated that performance in 2018, with four rate hikes of 25 basis points each. Markets thought that was about right. After all, as 2019 opened, inflation remained quiescent, the unemployment rate was 4 percent, and the federal funds rate range was only 2.25–2.5 percent. This did not look like tight money—except at 1600 Pennsylvania Avenue.

President Donald Trump raged against every rate hike, insulted the Fed, attacked Powell personally, and even threatened to remove him from office until some lawyer in the White House, I suppose, convinced him that he lacked the legal authority to do so.[11] (Readers of chapter 1 may recall that Lyndon Johnson received that same advice.) Long before the COVID-19 pandemic made Powell's job substantively difficult, Trump made it politically difficult. But Powell soldiered on bravely, pointing out on many occasions that the Fed is an independent agency that does not take orders from the president; that the Fed chief can be removed from office only "for cause," not because his policy decisions displease the president; and that he had every intention of serving out his four-year term. Support for Powell came from everywhere except the Oval Office.

---

11. At one point, Trump threatened to demote Powell to an ordinary Fed governor. Such an action, never anticipated by the Fed's framers in 1913, would have precipitated a legal case. But it never happened.

Chapter Summary

Despite urgings from Fed Chair Ben Bernanke and many other economists, most of the fiscal policy changes over the years 2011, 2012, and 2013 reduced the budget deficit, leaving monetary policy as the only game in town when it came to supporting aggregate demand. In fact, the nation barely escaped falling off a 4 percent-of-GDP "fiscal cliff" on New Year's Day 2013. The short-lived devotion to stimulative fiscal policy in 2008–2009 was clearly wobbling, to put it mildly.

Having lowered the federal funds rate to (its version of) zero in December 2008, the FOMC pursued easy money during the decade of the 2010s mainly by relying on several variants of QE and on dovish forward guidance about future rates. Federal Reserve talk thus changed in character. Communication had long been thought of as a supplementary tool that helped to explain the Fed's interest rate policy and therefore reduce uncertainty and manage expectations. After 2009, it became an important monetary policy tool in its own right, possibly the Fed's most important tool.

With fiscal and monetary policy pulling in opposite directions for much of the 2010s, the economy limped along. GDP grew slowly, but it grew. More salient politically, however, job growth did much better than GDP growth because productivity performance was so poor. The unemployment rate trailed downward year after year with only minor breaks.

In February 2014 President Obama passed the Fed's reins from Ben Bernanke to Janet Yellen, who brought QE to a gradual halt and led the FOMC to promulgate its first rate hike in December 2015. Both were delicate transitions, deftly handled. But Yellen never raised rates very high before her term expired, nor did she put much of a dent in the Fed's large balance sheet.

The Bernanke-to-Yellen handoff was about as smooth as a handoff could be, and so in its early years was the Yellen-to-Powell handoff. The federal funds rate kept edging up during Powell's early years, and the Fed's balance sheet was reduced a bit more. Just as Yellen could be said to be following the Bernanke playbook, Powell could be said to be following the Yellen playbook.

Until the roof caved in.

17

Trumponomics before the Pandemic

Not only will this tax plan pay for itself, but it will pay down debt.

—STEPHEN MNUCHIN, SECRETARY OF THE TREASURY, 2017

Hardly any political expert—one of my favorite oxymorons—saw Donald Trump coming. When the flamboyant real estate developer kicked off his campaign for the presidency by riding down a golden elevator at Trump Tower in Manhattan on June 16, 2015, few people took his candidacy seriously. The crowd that greeted him that day was small and, we later learned, some of them had been paid to show up. The main headline Trump made that day was accusing Mexico of sending the United States a bunch of rapists. MAGA hats would come later.

Trump had never held any public office or even ran for one, though he had flirted ostentatiously with running for president several times before. His 2015 effort, however, was for real. The Republican field was wide open; unlike the usual situation in which, according to the political aphorism, "Republicans fall in line," there was no heir apparent. Trump had a masterful flair for publicity, had hosted a popular TV show for years, and had thrust himself into political notoriety by claiming (with no factual basis) that Barack Obama was not a U.S. citizen, the so-called birther claim. With his wealth, huge name recognition, finely honed ability to garner publicity, and keen understanding of how to manipulate the media, Trump propelled himself to the top of the pack in a fractious Republican field and remained there throughout the primaries.

Then in the 2016 general election, he shocked the world by defeating Democrat Hillary Clinton in the electoral college despite losing the popular vote by about three million votes (roughly 2 percentage points). Trump's narrow upset victory—cobbled together by about seventy thousand votes in the states of Pennsylvania, Michigan, and Wisconsin—surprised just about everybody, probably including Trump himself.[1]

"Make America Great Again" was a pretty vague slogan, though it carried the clear implication that America was no longer great. Candidate Trump fleshed it out by railing against immigration (promising to build a wall that Mexico would pay for), trade agreements (such as the North American Free Trade Agreement and the recently negotiated Trans-Pacific Partnership), climate change (which he branded a Chinese hoax), and Obamacare (which Republicans had been trying to repeal ever since it was enacted). And he clearly wanted to cut taxes.

During the presidential campaign, Trump frequently insisted that recent GDP growth rates were far too low. The U.S. economy could grow much faster, he claimed, intimating that he knew how to make that happen. For example, in the televised presidential debate on October 19, 2016, he repeated his oft-made claim that "we're bringing [the GDP growth rate] from 1 percent up to 4 percent. And I actually think we can go higher than 4 percent. I think you can go to 5 percent or 6 percent" (Politico 2016).

Mainstream economists wondered how Trump proposed to do that. Consider some obvious arithmetic: population was growing at less than 1 percent per annum, productivity was barely making 1 percent per annum, and resource utilization was presumably

1. See, for example, Jacobs and House (2016).

close to full employment, leaving little if any slack to take up. Those stark facts made many macroeconomists wonder whether even the recent 2.5 percent growth rate could be sustained. In fact, the Federal Reserve's last published estimate of the growth rate of potential GDP prior to the election was only 1.8 percent, as was the Congressional Budget Office's (CBO) January 2017 estimate for 2018. By the way, those modest assessments of potential GDP growth helped explain why the unemployment rate had fallen for years during the Obama presidency despite GDP growth in the 2.5 percent range. That meager speed was apparently faster than the growth rate of potential GDP.

None of these numbers bothered Trump and the Republicans, however. They lined up solidly behind what had become the standard Republican Party fiscal attitude since Ronald Reagan: No matter what the circumstances and no matter what the condition of the budget, always advocate tax cuts. Then hope for a supply-side miracle. Even if you don't get it, taxes will be lower than previously.

The Trump Tax Cut of 2017

To observers old enough to remember U.S. fiscal policy in the 1960s, the Trump tax cut proposal conjured up images of 1965, when President Lyndon Johnson piled a lot more federal spending on top of an economy that was already at full employment. The predictable result—which was in fact predicted at the time—was rising inflation from too much aggregate demand. Nonetheless, in 2017 President Trump was determined to pass what he insisted on calling the largest tax cut in history. (It wasn't, though it was large.)

In addition to the incipient inflation problem (which did not materialize), the medium- to long-term prospects for the federal budget deficit looked terrible at the time, even though no one imagined what was to come in 2020. The CBO's ten-year budget projection published in June 2017 saw the deficit ballooning from about $700 billion in fiscal year 2017 (3.6% of GDP) to almost $1,500 billion (5.2% of GDP) by 2027. And that was without the Trump tax cuts. The big reasons were escalating expenditures on Social Security,

Medicare, and Medicaid, all items that had figured prominently in the fiscal debate for decades. Over that same period, the national debt held by the public was projected to soar from 76.7 percent of GDP to 91.2 percent (CBO 2017b). Deficit hawks were alarmed.[2] Republican members of Congress, eyeing big tax cuts, were not.

The Tax Cut and Jobs Act of 2017 was a complicated piece of legislation that turned out to be the lone major legislative achievement of the Trump administration. (President Trump did accomplish many other things but mainly through executive orders and refusal to enforce regulations.) Supporters of the act touted it as an important tax "reform" that would improve incentives, reduce distortions, and simplify the tax code, thereby giving the economy a big boost from the supply side. There were in fact a few elements of simplification and (arguably) some loophole closings in the act. But this alleged tax reform also opened up some gigantic new loopholes (especially for pass-through entities) and added new complexities to the code. A fair assessment would probably be that it was much more of a tax cut than a tax reform, just as the law's title says.

Major changes embedded in the Tax Cut and Jobs Act included reducing tax rates for both businesses and individuals, eliminating personal exemptions but increasing the standard deduction (which did constitute simplification), limiting deductions for state and local income taxes and property taxes (a tax hike clearly aimed at residents of blue states), and reducing the estate tax. The corporate tax cut was particularly large: the basic tax rate was reduced from 35 percent to 21 percent and expensing was substantially liberalized, all without closing loopholes to recoup some of the lost revenue.

Kevin Hassett, who chaired Trump's first Council of Economic Advisers, frequently repeated the claim that the large corporate tax cut would (eventually) raise household incomes by about $4,000 a year, a large increment, and that some of this benefit would start accruing right away (CEA 2017). The presumed mechanism was that the tax cut would lead to a surge in business investment, which would raise productivity and hence real wages. Note the familiar ring

---

2. See, for example, CRFB (2017).

of this line of logic. Would-be deficit reducers had argued for years, even before Bill Clinton's election, that lower budget deficits would crowd out less business investment, thereby boosting productivity and real wages. Could both a fiscal contraction and a fiscal expansion have the same salutary effect? That seemed implausible. But Hassett's argument was different. It came from the supply side and was all about tax incentives, not about interest rates.

As it turned out, the share of real nonresidential fixed investment in real GDP rose from an average of 14 percent in 2016 and 2017 (the tax cut passed in December 2017) to an average of 14.7 percent in 2018 and 2019 (before the coronavirus hit). The direction was right, though the increment of 0.7 percentage point could hardly be called a surge. The whole episode brought to mind Charles Schultze's old quip that there was nothing wrong with supply-side economics that dividing by ten couldn't cure.

Notably, the corporate tax cuts were legislated to be permanent, while the rate cuts for individuals and pass-through entities were scheduled to fade out over time. That last feature was redolent of the budgetary gimmickry used to reduce the cost of the Bush tax cuts in 2001 and later President Joe Biden's Build Back Better proposals in 2021. It enabled the Senate to pass the bill under budget reconciliation, thereby obviating the need to defeat a filibuster.[3] With all that, the bill barely squeaked through the Senate with just fifty-one votes. It was quickly signed into law by President Trump on December 22, 2017.

Regarding the size of the tax cut, the CBO estimated that individuals and pass-through entities (partnerships and S corporations) would receive about $1,125 billion in net benefits over ten years, while corporations would receive around $320 billion. All told and including debt service, the CBO estimated that implementing the Tax Cut and Jobs Act would add about $2.3 trillion to the national debt over ten years, or about $1.9 trillion under dynamic scoring that took account of macroeconomic feedback effects.

---

3. The special reconciliation procedure allows budget-related measures to pass the Senate by a simple majority vote rather than the usual sixty votes needed to terminate debate.

Those numbers made it a large tax cut for sure, roughly 1 percent of GDP, but a far smaller share of GDP than, say, the Reagan tax cuts of the early 1980s, which were closer to 3 percent of GDP (though phased in over three years). The Trump administration disputed these (and other) estimates of revenue losses, however. In fact, both the president and his secretary of the treasury, Stephen Mnuchin, actually claimed that the tax cuts would stimulate so much economic activity that they would more than pay for themselves (see this chapter's epigraph).[4] It was Laffer redux.[5]

As noted, the debt-to-GDP ratio was already projected to rise sharply before the Trump tax cuts were enacted. With the tax cuts, it would rise even faster. Treasury yields did rise a bit at first; the ten-year rate went from about 2.5 percent when the tax bill passed in December 2017 to about 3.1 percent in May 2018. But then rates stabilized for months before beginning a notable decline in November (figure 17.1). As a general matter, the larger Trump deficits did not seem to spook the bond market. Perhaps traders were delirious with joy over their own reduced tax liabilities.

Amazingly for a tax cut, however, the Trump tax cuts never proved popular with the broad American public. Just before the law passed, only 34 percent of Americans polled by Gallup thought the tax cuts would help their family's finances; 57 percent said it would not. Only a few percentage points more thought it would help the national economy (Gallup Organization 2017). Two years later the bill remained unpopular, and Americans remained confused about its provisions. Tellingly, only 14 percent thought their taxes had been reduced (Brenan 2019). One obvious reason, emphasized by the law's critics, is that the tax cuts, taken as a whole, were remarkably regressive, showering benefits on corporations, pass-through businesses, and large estates while many households of modest means received little if anything.

4. See, for example, Davidson (2017).
5. The icing on the cake: Most economists winced in June 2019 when President Trump awarded Arthur Laffer a presidential medal of freedom. See, for example, Weissmann (2019).

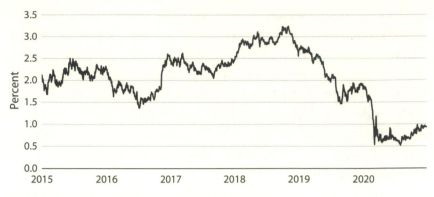

FIGURE 17.1. Ten-year Treasury yield, 2015–2020.
Source: Board of Governors of the Federal Reserve System.

On the spending side of the budget, the partisan wars of the Obama years morphed into a series of less dramatic skirmishes, leading to stopgap spending bills ("continuing resolutions") in May 2017, September 2017, December 2017, January 2018, and February 2018 until a genuine agreement was reached in March 2018. The most notable of these agreements was the September 2017 budget-busting deal reached mainly by Trump, House minority leader Nancy Pelosi, and Senate minority leader Chuck Schumer, with relatively little input from congressional Republicans despite their majorities in both chambers at the time. That deal, which averted a debt ceiling crisis, raised the caps on discretionary spending by about $300 billion over two years. Later those same spending caps were essentially inscribed in the March 2018 budget agreement, which narrowly averted a government shutdown.

Trump, though bellicose by nature and perhaps the most partisan president the country has ever known, showed little appetite for either a government shutdown or brinkmanship over the national debt ceiling, both of which had become standard Republican fare since the Clinton administration. Instead, the bipartisan budget deal of 2017–2018 added more stimulus on the spending side to the large stimulus already coming on the tax side. Hardly any congressional Republicans expressed concern about the widening budget deficit. They were, however, disappointed by Trump's propensity to deal mostly with Democrats on spending and also by his failure to mount a serious attack on the welfare state, a long-held Republican wish.

There was one big exception, however: health care. The president enthusiastically joined congressional Republicans in their efforts to "repeal and replace" President Obama's signal achievement: the Affordable Care Act. Amazingly, they were attempting to repeal Obamacare without replacing it, for the Republicans never came up with an alternative plan. Several attempts at repeal passed the House but failed narrowly in the Senate. The last of these went down in particularly dramatic fashion in the wee hours of July 28, 2017, when an ailing Senator John McCain (R-AZ), the party's standard-bearer in 2008, turned a "thumbs down" (literally) in the well of the Senate. McCain died about a month later. But the effort to repeal Obamacare legislatively died that night in the Senate.[6]

Trump and the Fed

As early as 2015, while still a candidate for the Republican nomination, Trump began attacking the Federal Reserve in general and its chair, Janet Yellen, in particular. His charge at the time was that she was keeping interest rates too low for political purposes, specifically to support the Obama economy and thereby assist the Democratic nominee, who was widely expected to be Hillary Clinton. In October 2015, Trump told Bloomberg that "Janet Yellen for political reasons is keeping interest rates so low that the next guy or person who takes over as president could have a real problem" (McMahon 2015). In September 2016, speaking then as the Republican nominee, Trump said that Yellen should be "ashamed of herself" for keeping interest rates so low and creating a "false stock market" to help Clinton win the election (La Monica 2016). These are just two of many examples. Trump's anti-Fed, anti-Yellen drumbeat was incessant.

---

6. But not judicially. A court case that threatened to repeal Obamacare judicially was filed in February 2018. It went all the way to the U.S. Supreme Court, where in June 2021 the justices rejected the suit on lack of standing.

The relationship improved a bit when candidate Trump became president in January 2017. But in early November 2017 he decided against retaining Yellen as Fed chair for another four years, opting to replace her by promoting Jerome "Jay" Powell, who was then a Fed governor. Powell was a Republican—something very important to Trump—though far from a Trump Republican. At the Rose Garden announcement at which Trump introduced Powell, the president was complimentary: "He's strong, he's committed, he's smart. I am confident that Jay [will be] a wise steward of the Federal Reserve" (Swanson and Applebaum 2017). Years later, most observers judged those words to be accurate. But Trump himself basically ate them.

The new president's other early appointments to the Federal Reserve Board were also mainstream; they gave no impression that the White House was at war with the Fed or trying to pack it with acolytes or quacks.[7] On the contrary, Randal Quarles, who joined the board in October 2017 as vice chair for supervision (a post Obama had left vacant), and Richard Clarida, who became the Fed's vice chair in September 2018, were both experienced and well-qualified Bush Republicans. Indeed, both had served in George W. Bush's Treasury Department. They were confirmed easily by Senate votes of 66–33 and 69–26, respectively.

Trump's honeymoon with the Fed was short-lived, however. Powell took over the helm from Yellen on February 5, 2018. As noted earlier, Yellen had led the Federal Open Market Committee (FOMC) to raise interest rates three times during 2017, each by just 25 basis points. The Powell Fed followed almost the same script, pushing rates up four times during 2018, again by 25 basis points each time. Even after those seven rate hikes, however, the federal funds rate was barely positive in real terms: just 2.25 to 2.5 percent against an inflation rate around 1.75 percent. Arguably, monetary policy was

---

7. That was unlike most of Trump's subsequent selections. He sought to put Herman Cain, Stephen Moore, and Judy Shelton on the Federal Reserve Board. None of these controversial choices made it through the Senate. Trump's one late-term mainstream candidate, Christopher Waller, did, however.

close to neutral. But the president of the United States didn't see it that way.

In an unusual display of restraint for him, Trump somehow held his tongue after the Powell Fed's first rate hike in March 2018. Trump's personal dam broke, however, when the FOMC raised rates again that June. "I'm not thrilled," he told CNBC. "I'm not happy about it." Yet, he allowed as to how Powell—his own appointee—was "a very good man" (Cox 2018). By Trumpian standards, it was a mild rebuke, certainly not accompanied by any sort of threat.

Things went downhill from there, however. After the FOMC raised rates again in late September 2018, Trump told a campaign rally that "they're so tight. I think the Fed has gone crazy," adding a few days later that the central bank was "going loco." He later called the Fed the "biggest threat" to the growth of the U.S. economy even though he recognized that the central bank is "independent so I don't speak to them." Trump also said that he was not going to fire Powell, as if he had the authority to do so. Shortly after the FOMC took the funds rate up another 25 basis points on December 19, 2018, Trump tweeted that "the only problem our economy has is the Fed" (Condon 2019).

The FOMC held the funds rate steady, in the 2.25 to 2.5 percent range it had established in December 2018, through July 2019. But the central bank's long pause did not induce a corresponding pause in Trump's criticism of monetary policy. In June 2019, for example, the president told CNBC that the Fed had "made a big mistake. They raised interest rates far too fast" (Oprysko 2019).

In 2019 real economic growth was mediocre and inflation continued to run below target, but words such as the president's made it hard for the FOMC to reduce rates without appearing to cave to White House pressure. The FOMC did so anyway, starting with a rate cut of 25 basis points on July 31. The FOMC statement said the rate cut was done "in light of the implications of global developments for the economic outlook as well as muted inflation pressures." Two district bank presidents (Esther George of Kansas City and Eric Rosengren of Boston) dissented against the cut, preferring to hold the funds rate constant. Many outside observers attributed the Fed's move—as well as the two rate cuts that followed—to the deleterious macroeconomic effects of the White House's trade war with China.

But Trump was far from placated. In August, he tweeted that "the only problem we have is Jay Powell and the Fed. He's like a golfer who can't putt, has no touch" (Elliott 2019). On September 11, the president lambasted Federal Reserve decision makers as "bone-heads" and said that interest rates should be zero or negative. One week later the FOMC cut the funds rate by another 25 basis points, with George and Rosengren again dissenting. Then on October 30, 2019, the FOMC made one final cut of 25 basis points, with the same two dissents, setting the federal funds rate range at 1.5–1.75 percent. Since that was about the same as the inflation rate at the time, the real funds rate was approximately zero.

Good enough? Well, not quite. About two weeks later, Trump blasted the Fed again in a speech to the Economic Club of New York. It was a strange venue to choose for an attack on the central bank; the Wall Street–dominated club is about as Fed-friendly an audience as you can find outside the Fed's own buildings. A few days later, Powell met with the president at the White House in a meeting described as "cordial." But Trump continued to call for lower rates. The Fed, as it turned out, was finished cutting rates. But the president was not finished complaining that rates were too high. For whatever reasons, however, the verbal war between the White House and the Fed went comparatively quiet after that. Soon the pandemic started consuming everyone's attention.

The Trump Economy before the Crash

Donald Trump, you will recall, promised a sharp acceleration in economic growth, presumably sparked by the tax cut. But he did not deliver on that pledge. From 2017:1 through 2019:4 (before the pandemic struck), real GDP growth averaged the same boring 2.5 percent per annum that had prevailed for years before. Perhaps more important politically, however, weak productivity performance continued to translate that mediocre GDP growth into

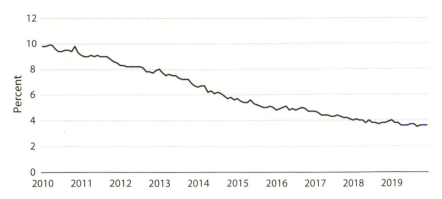

FIGURE 17.2. Unemployment rate, 2010–2019.
Source: Bureau of Labor Statistics.

strong job growth, just as it had for Obama. Net job creation averaged slightly less in the first three Trump years than it had during the preceding six Obama years: 2.19 million net new jobs per year versus 2.44 million. But it was still notable.

The unemployment rate, which had tracked down from a peak of 9.9 percent (in March and April 2010) to just 4.7 percent in Obama's last month in office (January 2017), continued to decline, reaching a fifty-year low of 3.5 percent in September 2019. There is no observable acceleration of that downward trend after January 2017 (figure 17.2). In fact, a regression test detects a tiny flattening of the curve after that date, which is the "wrong sign" for the Trump claim. But basically, the preexisting downward trend just continued until the pandemic interrupted the ongoing experiment to see how low the unemployment rate could go.

In short, if you ignored the name on the White House door and looked only at the economic numbers, you could not tell when the "Obama economy" ended and the "Trump economy" began. That said, the state of the economy on the eve of the pandemic was excellent: record-low unemployment, especially for minorities; reasonable rates of net job creation; moderate GDP growth; and very low inflation. As Trump was making plans for his 2020 reelection campaign, the economy looked like his strong suit.

Fiscal policy had boosted the budget deficit from 3.4 percent of GDP in fiscal year 2017 to 4.6 percent in fiscal year 2019, but no one except a few policy wonks cared about that. In fact, even within that small community, a new view had begun to take hold: that with interest rates so low and the world's demand for safe assets such as U.S. treasuries so high, there was room to push the national debt considerably higher.[8] Regarding monetary policy, the federal funds rate target range was 100 basis points higher in December 2019 than it had been in January 2017. So, monetary and fiscal policy were, in the literal sense, clashing as they had in Reagan's first term. But the clash was not sharp. In general, the situation was sunny, as was the outlook.

Chapter Summary

Donald Trump inherited a strong economy in January 2017. GDP growth was mediocre. But with productivity growth so weak, jobs were being created at a healthy enough pace to keep the unemployment rate tracking downward. (It finally hit a fifty-year low of 3.5 percent in September 2019.) Trump was not content to leave well enough alone, however. (Was he ever?) He had run on a campaign promise to cut taxes, and the Republican-dominated Congress did exactly that in December 2017. He had also run against both the Federal Reserve's leadership (Janet Yellen at the time) and its policy of low interest rates. His attitude regarding the latter changed dramatically on election day 2016, however, from sharp criticism that interest rates were too low to railing against keeping interest rates too high. In early 2018, Trump replaced Yellen with Jay Powell as chair of the Fed.

The highly partisan Trump tax cut of December 2017, coupled with a bipartisan relaxation of spending caps in 2018, provided significant fiscal stimulus to an economy that most economists thought was already near full employment. Yet inflation did not rise, just as it had not in the late 1990s. In fact, the Fed's inability to push inflation up to its 2 percent target, coupled with concerns over what the trade war with China would do to the economy, induced the Fed to

8. See, for example, Blanchard (2019).

switch from raising rates (slowly) in 2017 and 2018 to cutting rates (slowly) in 2019.

The effects of the fiscal stimulus on real growth appear to have been minor. The growth rate of real GDP, which had averaged 2.3 percent over the years 2015, 2016, and 2017, rose to 2.5 percent and 2.4 percent in 2018 and 2019.[9] Small beer, you might say, almost certainly smaller than measurement error. The Fed's switch to more expansionary monetary policy in 2019 was also minor, just 75 basis points in total. But the pandemic of 2020 turned the lights out before anyone could draw a judgment on its effects or on how low unemployment could go. Soon, both fiscal policy and monetary policy faced a far darker situation.

---

9. I divide the years this way rather than by political administration because the Trump fiscal stimulus began in the closing days of 2017.

18

Responding to the Great Pandemic

The scope of the crisis required an all-in government response.
—JEROME POWELL, *WALL STREET JOURNAL*, MARCH 19, 2021

The COVID-19 pandemic, which began in China late in 2019, reached the United States in January 2020, with the first U.S. case confirmed on January 20 and the first death attributed to COVID recorded on February 29 in Washington state.[1] The spread was frighteningly rapid. By May 1, 2020, the cumulative number of confirmed cases in the United States was about 1.12 million, and over 68,000 people had died. By the end of 2020, those numbers were roughly 20 million cases and 352,000 deaths. By the end of 2021, they were a staggering 56 million cases and over 800,000 deaths—and rising. Worldwide numbers were, of course, multiples of U.S. numbers.

The pandemic was, in the first instance, a public health catastrophe of the first rank, the worst since the badly misnamed Spanish flu pandemic of 1918–1920. But it also brought on an economic

---

1. It was later learned that several COVID deaths had occurred earlier in California.

catastrophe with blinding speed. The recession of 2020 was the deepest contraction the United States had witnessed since the 1930s, dwarfing the Great Recession of 2007–2009, and by far the sharpest recession ever. For comparison, the peak-to-trough decline in real GDP over the six quarters from 2007:4 to 2009:2 was 4 percent, while the decline in 2020 was 10.1 percent, almost all which occurred in a single frightening quarter: 2020:2. Real GDP in that dreadful palindromic quarter declined at a mind-numbing 31.2 percent annual rate, cutting this comprehensive measure of economic activity all the way back to its 2015:1 level.[2] The unemployment rate soared to almost 15 percent.

At first, most of that horrific decline was laid at the doorstep of government-ordered lockdowns. But subsequent examinations of high-frequency data from a variety of unconventional sources soon showed that people stopped shopping, traveling, going out to restaurants and movies, and so on well before any shutdowns were ordered.[3] What happened in the United States and in other countries was pretty simple and pretty devastating: fear ran rampant, and absent any proven medical interventions, people just pulled away from one another as they had during the plagues of centuries gone by.

Even in this electronic age, human contact is an essential part of economic activity, and human contact suddenly looked dangerous. People and businesses quickly learned which economic activities could be conducted online and which could not. On the employment side that division was, sadly but obviously, highly skewed toward upper-income and better-educated segments of the population, many of whom normally worked at computers anyway. They suffered relatively small losses of earnings, if any. Less educated workers, whose jobs were in restaurants, hotels, retail shops, and the like, lost far more. Once recovery began, it was labeled K-shaped

2. Quarterly data follow the calendar, but the worst three months were actually March, April, and May.

3. See, for example, Goolsbee and Syverson (2021) and Gupta, Simon, and Wing (2020).

to connote that upper-income groups fared well while lower-income groups remained mired in recession longer.

In addition to the astonishing speed of the decline, another highly unusual aspect of the recession of 2020 was its concentration in consumer expenditures and especially in spending on consumer services, which not only collapsed but came back agonizingly slowly. In previous business cycle downturns, consumer spending normally held up well compared to, say, business investment and housing, and spending on services barely registered any declines at all. In 2020, however, many service jobs that we thought of as noncyclical suddenly disappeared in droves.

By March, there was little doubt that both fiscal policy and monetary policy had to respond quickly and massively. Both faced challenges. But there was little doubt that fiscal policy had to do the heavier lifting this time around because monetary policy had little conventional ammunition left. The Fed's target range for the federal funds was 1.5–1.75 percent on March 1, 2020. By March 15 it was down to 0–0.25 percent, which was the Fed's effective lower bound.[4] This meant that asset purchases on a grand scale, in the style of quantitative easing (QE), would be required. So would deficit-financed public spending by the federal government. The budget-deficit ogre would have to be put back in its cage again.

First Responders: Fiscal Policy

Federal spending is the province of Congress, of course, and the U.S. Congress responded to the clear and present danger posed by the coronavirus extremely aggressively. A series of emergency response bills started small with an $8.3 billion supplemental appropriation to the fiscal year 2020 budget, enacted on March 6. At the time, the economic impact of the virus was barely registering; the earliest shutdowns and stay-at-home orders were still a week or two away.

---

4. Just as it had in 2008–2009, the Fed steadfastly refused to lower the funds rate below the 0–0.25 percent range even though many other central banks had moved their overnight rates into negative territory.

Understandably, that first dollop of money was appropriated mainly for public health purposes, including vaccine development. The bill contained nothing controversial and garnered near-unanimous support in both houses of Congress. No one knew at the time that the $8.3 billion would turn out to be the tiniest tip of a gigantic iceberg.

Within two weeks the World Health Organization declared the novel coronavirus to be a global pandemic, and Congress passed the much larger ($104 billion) Families First Coronavirus Response Act, again with huge majorities in both the House (363–40) and the Senate (90–8). That law provided for paid sick leave at an employee's full salary (up to $511 per day), legislated paid family leave at two-thirds of a parent's usual salary, required Medicare and private health insurance plans to cover COVID-19 testing, and expanded unemployment insurance (though ever so slightly). The usual resistance to public spending was largely dissipated by widespread recognition that the United States was facing a national emergency, though no one knew how dire that emergency would turn out to be.

But in perhaps an omen of things to come, all 48 "no" votes in Congress were cast by Republicans. Still, the fact that 140 House Republicans voted "yes" showed that few people in Washington were seeing things through partisan lenses in mid-March, except perhaps for Donald Trump, who seemed to see everything that way. In his eyes, the Democrats, the press and the Chinese were ganging up on him to make a big deal over a disease that would soon disappear on its own. On March 10, he advised Americans that "it will go away. Just stay calm" (Colvin 2020). On March 22, referring to state-ordered lockdowns, he declared that "we cannot let the cure be worse than the problem itself" (Haberman and Sanger 2020), and two days later he said that "I would love to have the country opened up and just raring to go by Easter" (Watson 2020), which was just two and a half weeks away.

As they say, hope is not a plan. And COVID-19 was spreading like wildfire. The daily count of confirmed cases in the United States (based on the seven-day moving average) rose from just 13 on March 1 to 436 on March 15 and to almost 21,000 by April 1. President Trump may have been assuring everyone that it would be all but over by Easter, but the American population and Congress were frightened. Late in March, after a bit of partisan wrangling, Congress passed the enormous Coronavirus Aid, Relief, and Economic Security (CARES) Act, with a price tag of around $2.2 trillion. It still stands as the largest spending bill in history; President Joe Biden's American Rescue Plan (ARP) in March 2021 clocked in at $1.9 trillion. Partisanship was set aside in passing CARES by a voice vote in the House and by 96–0 in the Senate, with 4 Republicans not voting. President Trump signed the bill into law on March 27. On that day, 417 Americans died of COVID-19. By April 15, that number would be 2,289.

To put the size of the CARES Act into perspective, $2.2 trillion amounted to more than 10 percent of GDP and was almost exactly half of total federal spending during the previous fiscal year. The scope of CARES was equally impressive. Its long list of major provisions included, among other things, the following:

- Checks in the amount of $1,200 for "every" adult ($2,400 for a married couple and $500 per child). In fact, however, millions of low-income Americans received nothing because the checks were paid out as rebates on 2019 tax liabilities, and they were too poor to have filed income tax returns.
- The Paycheck Protection Program (PPP), originally budgeted at $366 billion but quickly oversubscribed, which provided forgivable loans (thus, really grants) to "small" businesses that maintained their payrolls. (Some weren't all that small.) About four weeks later, Congress infused a great deal more money into the popular program via the PPP and Health Care Enhancement Act ($484 billion in total), another noncontroversial bill that passed with bipartisan support.
- A huge increase ($600 per week) in unemployment insurance benefits plus extension of coverage to many previously uncovered workers. To economists, the $600 flat amount was an odd structure; it meant that about two-thirds of American workers would receive more income by being unemployed than employed (Ganong, Noel, and Vavra 2020).

- About $150 billion in aid to struggling state and local governments. Aid to states and localities would later become a major partisan sticking point, with Democrats wanting more and Republicans steadfastly opposed. Some people, it seemed, had noticed that COVID-19 in its early stages was mostly a blue states phenomenon.
- A large bailout for the airline industry and grants to other transportation industries, all of which had been decimated by the pandemic. Airlines, of course, had gone through bankruptcies before, but this time they did not have to.
- Over $180 billion in health and health-related spending.
- A variety of business tax cuts amounting to about $280 billion. These were not among Democrats' favorite provisions.
- Moratoria on foreclosures and evictions though without enforcement mechanisms.

Taken together, this was powerful fiscal relief. The transfer payments to individuals—mainly the "rebate" checks and the extra unemployment benefits—created an unprecedented situation in which disposable income actually went up in 2020, even though earnings crumbled. That stunning development helped support consumer spending even though most of the transfers were saved. The personal saving rate reached heights never seen in America (figure 18.1). Well over $2 trillion in "excess" saving was accumulated in 2020 and 2021; much of it wound up in bank accounts.

By summer, several of the major provisions of the CARES Act were drawing to a close, and many more were set to expire by December. Democrats, who then held the majority in the House but were in the minority in the Senate, began agitating for another emergency relief bill, but Republicans were not convinced of the need. Among other reasons, the economy started to revive in June. In the third quarter (July–September), real GDP growth soared at a 33.8 percent annual rate, thereby making up most of its sharp second-quarter decline. Real GDP in 2020:3 stood just 3.3 percent below its 2019:4 level. In addition, the budget deficit had soared

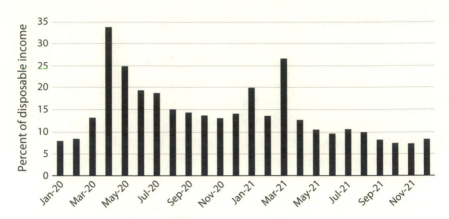

FIGURE 18.1. Personal saving rate, monthly, 2020–2021.
Source: Bureau of Economic Analysis.

to levels previously thought unimaginable, and some Republicans "remembered" that a large deficit could be a problem.

The two parties deadlocked for months over two issues in particular. Democrats wanted to send much more federal aid to state and local governments. Republicans, seeing that much of the money would flow to the more heavily impacted blue states, opposed that. Instead, they wanted to provide legal protections for employers whose workers might become ill from workplace exposure, an idea Democrats opposed. With a modicum of bipartisan comity, those two issues could have been compromised away. But bipartisanship had disappeared by then, giving way to months of rancorous partisan sniping with little movement on either side.

Finally, with end-of-year expiration dates of several key COVID relief programs concentrating the minds of legislators, the four congressional leaders—House Speaker Nancy Pelosi (D-CA), Senate majority leader Mitch McConnell (R-KY), Senate minority leader Chuck Schumer (D-NY), and House minority leader Kevin McCarthy (R-CA)—hammered out a deal with roughly $900 billion in new COVID relief. The package included $600 checks to most Americans (including children), $300 per week in enhanced federal unemployment benefits (until March 14, 2021), and another large dollop of funding (over $280 billion) for the immensely popular (though poorly designed) PPP.

At the eleventh hour President Trump, never a piker, threw a monkey wrench into the negotiations by proclaiming that the checks should be for $2,000, not $600. Many Democrats—including President-elect Joe Biden—warmly embraced the $2,000 figure, but Republicans did not, and Congress stuck with the agreed-upon $600. Despite calling that paltry sum a "disgrace," President Trump signed the bill into law just after Christmas. Biden insisted that more aid would come once he became president. Meanwhile, Trump stubbornly refused to concede that he had lost the 2020 election. In fact, he never did concede, hewing to what came to be called the Big Lie: that the election had been stolen from him by a wide variety of illegal acts, none of which proved to be true.

Ironically, two runoff elections for Georgia senators were scheduled for January 5, and the Democratic challengers (the two incumbents were Republicans) ran in part on supporting Trump's $2,000 checks. In a huge surprise, they both won, thereby making the Senate an even 50–50 split, which effectively made the Democrats the majority party because Vice President–elect Kamala Harris could cast the deciding vote if the chamber deadlocked 50–50. That 50–50 Senate "majority" would quickly prove to be incredibly important.

On the very next day, January 6, 2021, Americans suddenly had a lot more than relief checks to worry about as a crowd of over two thousand Trump supporters stormed and vandalized the U.S. Capitol, demanding that the Senate—with Vice President Mike Pence still presiding—not certify the electoral college count. Pence and the Senate refused their demands, though many Republican members of both houses of Congress continued to spout the Big Lie.

First Responders: Monetary Policy

While fiscal policy acted fast, monetary policy acted even faster. The Federal Reserve's initial policy response to the threat posed by the pandemic—a drop of 50 basis points in the already-low federal funds rate—came at a hurriedly arranged Federal Open Market Committee (FOMC) meeting on March 3. The committee's statement that day observed that "the coronavirus poses evolving risks to economic activity" (FOMC 2020a), which subsequently proved to be quite an understatement. (But the Fed never wants to frighten people.) Two painfully obvious problems faced the Fed, however.

One was that when a central bank starts an easing cycle with an overnight rate in the 1.5–1.75 percent range, there is a sharp limit to how much rate cutting it can do. In past recessions, which were far less severe than that of 2020, the Fed had often cut rates by 500 basis points or more to boost aggregate demand and end the downturn. But in the pandemic recession, the FOMC limited itself to 150 basis points of rate cutting, which it finished doing on March 15, just twelve days after it started.

The second big problem for monetary policy was speed, but not speed in decision making; as just noted, the FOMC moved with alacrity. Rather, the speed issue stemmed from the well-known lags between interest rate changes and their effects on spending. Econometric estimates of these lags in normal times showed small effects in the first few quarters after a Federal Reserve action, building into larger effects after, say, six to eight quarters. In the crisis atmosphere of 2020, that would plainly be far too slow. Would the effects of expansionary monetary policy arrive faster in such desperate times? Or, as seemed more likely, would the interest sensitivity of spending on new automobiles and new homes be attenuated because people were afraid to go shopping?

But that wasn't the end of the Fed's problems. There is, of course, two-way contagion between financial markets and the real economy. Ructions in the financial world can disrupt the normal credit-granting mechanisms and, by dint of that, imperil real economic activity—as happened dramatically in 2007–2009. But damage to the real economy can also cause severe problems, even panic, in financial markets, as it did in February and March 2020. So, the Fed's attention quickly turned to stabilizing the financial markets. The central bank was powerless to stem the spread of the virus or even to reduce the fear of shopping, but it could nip financial panics in the bud.

As traders started processing the economic hazards that lay ahead and the huge uncertainties they posed, stock prices cratered. The

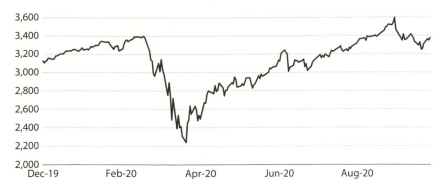

FIGURE 18.2. S&P 500 stock index, December 2019–September 2020.
Source: S&P Dow Jones Indices.

S&P 500 began dropping on February 19, gradually at first but then dramatically in March (figure 18.2). Between March 11 and March 23 (which turned out to be the market's bottom), the S&P lost a stunning 22.4 percent in just nine trading days. The total peak-to-trough decline from February 19 to March 23 was a confidence-shattering 33.8 percent in little more than a month. As figure 18.2 shows, the stock market recovered remarkably quickly, however, regaining all those losses by mid-August and then going much higher.[5] But no one knew that in March, and few dared dream it. The Fed is normally content to pay little heed to stock market gyrations, but a drop that large and that fast grabbed its attention.

Disruptions in fixed-income markets were also happening at the time, and they got even more of the Fed's attention. Figure 18.3, which displays an index of the interest rates on junk bonds, shows one extreme example.[6] That index soared from under 4 percent to almost 11 percent over the same period in which the stock market cratered. Figure 18.4 exhibits a less extreme example: the spread

5. By comparison, it took more than five years for the S&P to gain back its fall 2008 losses from the financial crisis.

6. The index is compiled by the Bank of America, which says it "tracks the performance of US dollar denominated below investment grade rated corporate debt publicly issued in the US domestic market." It is available on the St. Louis Fed's FRED database (Ice Data Indices 2022).

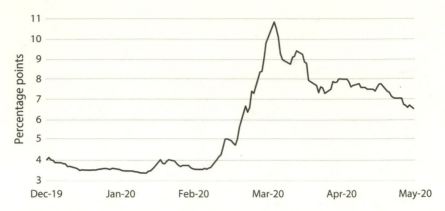

FIGURE 18.3. Interest rate on junk bonds, index, December 2019–May 2020. (ICE BofA U.S. high yield index option-adjusted spread.)
Source: ICE Data Indices, LLC.

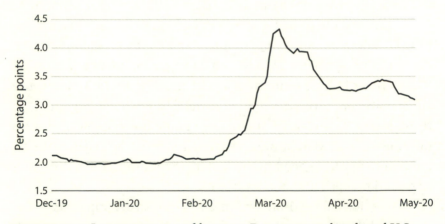

FIGURE 18.4. Interest rate spread between Baa corporate bonds and U.S. treasuries, December 2019–May 2020.
(Moody's seasoned Baa corporate bond yield relative to yield on ten-year Treasury constant maturity.)
Source: Federal Reserve Bank of St. Louis.

between Baa-rated corporate bonds and ten-year treasuries, which rose by about 425 basis points over that same period.

There was even, amazingly and disconcertingly, a severe hiccup in the Treasury markets in March. Yields on T-bills actually dipped below zero for a frightening few days as traders scrambled for liquidity that securities dealers could not provide. And it wasn't just T-bills; rates on longer-maturity treasuries also gyrated wildly for a short time. The Fed was now witnessing disruptions right in its own backyard and jumped in to soothe the markets. That meant providing liquidity to meet the "dash for cash" and eventually creating a standing loan facility to ensure that the repo market wouldn't crash again.

First Responders: Lending Facilities

Close inspection of these last three graphs reveals that all three markets hit bottom on March 23, 2020, and then started to improve rapidly. That was no coincidence. At 8 A.M. that day, following yet another unscheduled meeting (FOMC 2020b), the FOMC announced that "the Federal Reserve is committed to use its full range of tools to support the U.S. economy in this challenging time." More specifically, "The Federal Open Market Committee is taking further actions to support the flow of credit to households and businesses by addressing strains in the markets for Treasury securities and agency mortgage-backed securities," continuing "to purchase Treasury securities and agency mortgage-backed securities in the amounts needed to support smooth market functioning," and continuing "to offer large-scale overnight and term repurchase agreement operations." It also pledged to take "additional measures to support the flow of credit to households and businesses" (FOMC 2020b). In short, the Fed was all in.

The central bank's virtually open-ended commitment to backstop most forms of credit served as a powerful tonic to the financial markets, which were teetering at the time and looking for a lifeline. The markets' quick reactions were redolent of what had happened in European sovereign debt markets in July 2012 when European Central Bank president Mario Draghi made his famous "whatever it takes" pledge (Draghi 2012). The words—Draghi's then, the Fed's now—were galvanizing and stopped the incipient financial panic in its tracks. In Draghi's case, the European Central Bank never had to back up his words with a single euro. In the case of the Fed's announcement on March 23 the market reactions came swiftly, long before the central bank committed a dime, and the eventual volume of Federal Reserve lending, though sizable, turned out to be minimal relative to the enormity of the problem. Words matter, especially if they are credible and backed by mountains of cash.[7]

Although the whole process unfolded quickly, it is useful to think of the Fed's emergency lending facilities as coming in two tranches. First, the central bank reinstated several of the facilities it had created during the financial crisis of 2008–2009 but had let lapse when they were no longer needed. These arrangements, justified by Section 13(3) of the Federal Reserve Act (as amended by Dodd-Frank in 2010), concentrated on stabilizing the money markets, including the commercial paper market,[8] but they also reprised the Term Asset-Backed Securities Loan Facility to support the issuance of asset-backed securities backed by student loans, auto loans, credit card loans, Small Business Administration loans, and the like.

The Fed didn't stop there, however. Its legal and accounting staffs must have worked overtime to create two new facilities to support the corporate bond market,[9] one to support the municipal bond market,[10] and two more to assist banks in lending to Main Street businesses (as opposed to Wall Street firms).[11] All of these new lending facilities, especially the last two, meant that the Federal Reserve was venturing into places it had never gone before and about which it had little or no relevant experience. Yet the central bank stood up all these facilities in about three weeks. That was not exactly typical central bank speed.

Speed was one thing; scope was another. Supporting the corporate bond market, whether doing so when bonds are originally issued or later in the secondary market, was something the Fed had

---

7. The Fed did, however, start buying enormous quantities of treasuries and mortgage-based securities as QE.

8. For example, the Commercial Paper Funding Facility, the Primary Dealer Credit Facility, and the Money Market Mutual Fund Liquidity Facility.

9. The Primary Market Corporate Credit Facility and the Secondary Market Corporate Credit Facility.

10. The Municipal Liquidity Facility.

11. The PPPLF and the MSLP.

never attempted during the 2008–2009 financial crisis. But it was at least on relatively familiar turf there, dealing in large-denomination bonds carrying high credit ratings.[12]

The Municipal Liquidity Facility (MLF) was a bird of a different feather. While the Federal Reserve Act explicitly allows the FOMC to conduct open-market operations in municipal debt, it restricts the scope to instruments with maturities "not exceeding six months, issued in anticipation of the collection of taxes or in anticipation of the receipt of assured revenues" (Federal Reserve Act 1913, sect. 14). The MLF was designed to be much broader and longer-term than that, so it was structured as an emergency lending facility under Section 13(3) rather than as open-market operations. (The Fed had used this legal fig leaf extensively in 2008 and 2009.) The special purpose vehicle created for that purpose was capitalized by $35 billion from the U.S. Treasury and authorized to purchase up to $500 billion in municipal obligations (broadly defined). It was barely used, however. The cash-strapped state of Illinois was first in line, eventually taking out several loans, but the line proved to be short. At their peak in early 2021, the MLF's total outstanding loans were a mere $6.4 billion. Apparently, the availability of the Fed as a backstop, starting with the dramatic March 23, 2020, pronouncement, was enough to calm the municipal bond markets, making actual MLF lending almost superfluous. Shades of Draghi.

The Main Street Lending Program (MSLP) was an even bigger departure from Fed norms. The idea behind it was (in the Fed's words) "to support lending to small and medium-sized for-profit businesses and nonprofit organizations that were in sound financial condition before the onset of the COVID-19 pandemic" (Federal Reserve 2022). More specifically, MSLP loans under Section 13(3) were targeted at businesses too small to issue corporate bonds but too large for the PPP. To put it mildly, such businesses were not even on the Fed's radar screen before the crisis. Like most central

12. Well, not all the ratings were high. At one point the Fed decided to support "fallen angels" in the secondary market, that is, formerly investment-grade issues that had been downgraded to high yield status by the rating agencies.

banks, the Fed had plenty of experience with large-dollar loans to financial businesses but basically none with small-dollar loans to nonfinancial businesses.

Lacking the experience and resources relevant to that sort of lending but mandated by the CARES Act (March 2020) to do so, the Fed had to scramble. Naturally, it turned to commercial banks to originate the loans, insisting that the banks retain 5 percent of each loan. The Fed would then buy the other 95 percent. The MSLP's lending volume was budgeted as high as $600 billion, with the Treasury providing $75 billion in equity to capitalize the special purpose vehicle the Fed created for this purpose.

To put it bluntly, the MSLP was a failure, just as many observers predicted when it was first announced. The Fed's initial term sheet (April 2020) invited banks to sell loan participations ranging from $500,000 to $25 million from loans made to companies employing up to ten thousand workers or with revenues of less than $2.5 billion. Those are "Main Street" businesses? The lower loan limit of $500,000 was subsequently reduced to $100,000. Yet take-up was still modest. Many banks were less than delighted by the requirement that they retain 5 percent of each loan, many businesses found the Fed's terms less than attractive, and not many Main Street businesses wanted to borrow $500,000. The MSLP was terminated by the Treasury in the closing days of the Trump administration. At the time, outstanding MSLP loans were a mere $16.5 billion. Could MSLP lending have been made to work better? Almost certainly, yes. But the Fed was the wrong agency to do it.

The Paycheck Protection Program Liquidity Facility (PPPLF), another strange venture for the Fed, grew much larger and lasted much longer (until July 2021). The PPP itself was an important component of the mammoth CARES Act that Congress passed in late March 2020. Its animating idea was to offer small businesses forgivable loans—implicitly, grants—so they could continue paying their workers through what Congress then thought would be a short interruption. As it turned out, the interruption wasn't short at all. So, Congress boosted the size of the program and extended its expiration date several times.

The Fed's involvement in PPP came because the law authorized the twelve Federal Reserve Banks to provide nonrecourse loans to financial institutions (mainly banks) that made PPP loans to eligible businesses. Notice the two important adjectives: *nonrecourse* loans to banks backed by *forgivable* loans to bank customers. That sounds like a sure-fire recipe for large losses. Everyone realized that, of course, and rather than make a hash of Bagehot's dictum (explained in chapter 13), PPP loans were fully guaranteed by the Small Business Administration, making them perfect collateral for the Fed. If the place where loan losses were booked mattered to you—and it certainly mattered to the Fed—the Small Business Administration guarantee took them off the Fed's books.

Unlike the Main Street and municipal facilities, the take-up of the PPP program, and thus of the PPPLF, was enthusiastic and swift. The PPPLF was launched on April 16, 2020, and within three weeks it had lent out almost $30 billion. The sums kept climbing from there, requiring several replenishments by Congress. By November 2021, the PPP had made over 11 million loans totaling nearly $800 billion, of which over $600 billion had already been forgiven (figure 18.5). The Fed's backup commitments, of course, were far smaller. When it closed out its program in July 2021, the PPPLF held about $61 billion. Even so, that was almost triple the sum of all Federal Reserve lending under the municipal and Main Street facilities.

Lest anyone miss the point, Federal Reserve Chair Jerome Powell repeatedly stated that in all these unorthodox operations, the Fed was "lending, not spending." It became his mantra. And, of course, all this lending activity was dwarfed by the Fed's pandemic-induced QE asset purchases, which eventually topped $4 trillion.

The lending facilities were all temporary, of course, designed to cope with an emergency. But Powell did not stop there. In August 2020, he led the FOMC in adopting the biggest changes in its monetary policy procedures in decades. Four aspects of those changes stand out.

First and foremost under the harrowing circumstances, the Fed changed the operational weights on the two parts of its dual mandate, making clear that it would prioritize reducing unemployment

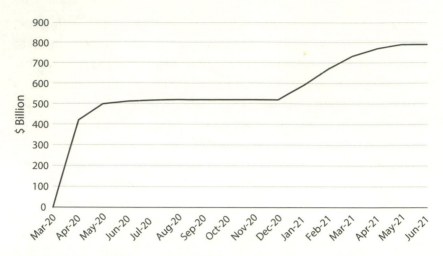

FIGURE 18.5. Cumulative lending by the Paycheck Protection Program, monthly, March 2020–June 2021.
Source: Small Business Administration. Calculations courtesy of Robert Jackman (Faulkender, Jackman, and Miran 2022).

and that the mandate for a strong labor market would be interpreted broadly—not limited to the official unemployment rate.

Second, the Fed made the employment objective explicitly asymmetric; the FOMC cared much more about employment that was too low than about employment that was too high.

Third, in recognition of the disappearance of a reliable Phillips curve, the FOMC stated that it would not take preemptive action (based on a forecast) against inflation but would wait until it saw inflation rising.

Fourth, the Fed replaced its 2 percent inflation target by something it dubbed "Flexible Average Inflation Targeting," an intellectual cousin of price-level targeting. The message was that the Fed would no longer strive for 2 percent inflation every year but would instead seek to make inflation average 2 percent "over time," a deliberately vague phrase that did not specify the length of the averaging period or its starting and ending points. Amazingly, even as inflation skyrocketed in 2021, few Fed watchers paid much attention to the inflation averaging period, which was never specified. Flexible indeed!

"Some have greatness thrust upon them."[13]

When Jerome "Jay" Powell took over the reins of the Federal Reserve from Janet Yellen in 2018, things looked peaceful on the monetary policy front. Yellen had begun to normalize interest rates from their financial crisis lows, and there seemed to be no good reason to deviate from her script. Then COVID-19 struck and changed everything, including monetary policy. The Yellen script became useless, with nothing obvious to replace it. The way Jay Powell rose to the occasion assures his place in history.

Powell was born in Washington, D.C., one of six children. His father, also Jerome Powell, was a lawyer, which is how his son began his career. The younger Powell graduated from Princeton University and then from the Georgetown University law school. While there, he was editor in chief of the *Georgetown Law Journal*. Obviously he was a promising young lawyer, but not for long.

In 1984 Powell switched from law to investment banking, where he remained more or less for twenty-six years. That period included time out for a brief stint at the U.S. Treasury under George H. W. Bush in 1992–1993. Between 2010 and 2012, Powell was a visiting scholar at the Bipartisan Policy Center, a Washington think tank, where he worked on predicting and minimizing the damage from hitting the national debt ceiling.

In December 2011, President Barack Obama paired Powell with Jeremy Stein, a Harvard professor and a Democrat, in order to get two nominees to the Federal Reserve Board through a recalcitrant Senate. Obama's strategy worked but, in the view of some, set a terrible precedent; it was as if the board had "Democratic" and "Republican" seats.

On the job, Powell proved himself to be political only in the good senses of that term. He spoke regularly with members of Congress of both parties, he understood that the Federal Reserve and Congress operate in separate "lanes" (a favorite metaphor of his), and he staunchly defended the Fed's independence. In 2018, when President Trump decided that he would not reappoint Democrat Janet Yellen as Fed chair, he turned to Powell, a registered Republican though certainly not a Trump Republican. The Trump-Powell relationship soon soured, as recounted in chapter 17. Powell stood his ground as the FOMC nudged interest rates slowly upward.

Then COVID-19 hit, requiring unprecedented actions from the Fed beginning in March 2020. Soon Powell was looking and behaving like the most dovish Fed chair in history, leading the central bank, among other things, to the major changes in its operating procedures discussed in this chapter. As events unfolded, the Fed emphasized the need to improve weak labor markets. Until December 2021, it regularly branded the sharp increases in inflation as "transitory." All in all, this did not look like Volcker redux.

In the fall of 2021, President Biden faced a difficult decision. Should he renominate Chair Powell for a second term, in recognition of his superb performance on monetary policy? Or should he replace Powell with a Democrat (Governor Lael Brainard was the most frequently mentioned name) who was more sympathetic to Democrats' regulatory agenda? In November 2021 Biden chose Powell, calling the decision "a testament to decisive action by Chair Powell and the Federal Reserve to cushion the impact of the pandemic and get America's economy back on track" (White House 2021). And cushion they did.

---

13. The quote is from Shakespeare, *Twelfth Night*, Act 2, Scene 5. The bard presumably knew nothing about monetary policy.

President Biden Ups the Ante

The atmosphere was tense as Joseph R. Biden was sworn in as the forty-sixth president of the United States on January 20, 2021. The defeated Donald Trump was still wailing that the election had been stolen from him, and his acolytes had stormed the Capitol only two weeks before. As president-elect, Biden had stated emphatically that the $900 billion relief package passed in the closing days of the Trump administration was not nearly enough, and in the early days of his administration a combination of events enabled him to do much more. The most important of these events were the Senate runoff victories in Georgia mentioned earlier. They installed Raphael Warnock and Jon Ossoff as two new Democratic senators, thereby producing a 50–50 tie in the Senate. If needed, the tie-breaking vote could now come from Vice President Kamala Harris, acting in her capacity as president of the Senate.

The second important ingredient propelling Biden's early success was the Senate's arcane budget "reconciliation" procedure, which was familiar to the cognoscenti but almost unknown outside the beltway. Reconciliation is governed by a special set of rules that allow the annual budget to pass the Senate with just fifty-one votes rather than the sixty votes needed to overcome a filibuster. In plain if oversimplified English, the minority party may not filibuster the budget, which in this case opened the door to a COVID relief bill voted in only by Democrats.

Thus armed for battle, President-elect Biden surprised many observers, including many of his supporters, when he proposed his mammoth $1.9 trillion American Rescue Plan six days before his inauguration. The ARPs gigantic price tag, including its huge dollop of money for state and local governments ($350 billion), was probably enough to ensure that no Republicans would support the bill. But Biden, apparently thinking about passing the bill with only fifty votes anyway, threw in several more items that were anathema to Republicans, such as an increase in the federal minimum wage to $15 an hour (which was later dropped) and a huge increase in the child tax credit, including making it refundable. He also included $1,400 tax "rebate" checks, thereby bringing the $600 bipartisan number enacted in December 2020 up to the $2,000 figure that Trump had favored (but congressional Republicans had not).

At the end of a relatively short debate, the ARP passed the Senate 51–50, with every Republican voting no, and then passed the House by 220–211, with every Republican again voting no. Bipartisan support for COVID relief packages was plainly a thing of the past. The attitude of House minority leader Kevin McCarthy (R-CA) captured the Republican Party's hostility: "This isn't a rescue bill. It isn't a relief bill. It's a laundry list of left-wing priorities that predate the pandemic and do not meet the needs of American families" (Cochrane 2021).

The bill's critics did not come exclusively from the political Right, however. Former treasury secretary (under Bill Clinton) Lawrence Summers caused a stir with a February 4, 2021, op-ed in the *Washington Post* warning that adding $1.9 trillion of further stimulus to the $0.9 trillion that had just been enacted was probably too much. It would, Summers said, likely lead to an overshoot of potential GDP and possibly to "inflation pressures of a kind we have not seen in a generation" (Summers 2021). That criticism, which subsequently looked prophetic, raised eyebrows and provided fodder for Republicans, basically all of whom were opposing the bill. It did not, however, persuade any Democratic legislators. Still, Summers's central point was worth noting: $2.8 trillion in additional spending was more than a quarter larger than the landmark CARES Act. Even though many ARP programs had "low multipliers," a lot of stimulus would be put in the hopper.

Was There an Inflationary Danger?

In March 2021, the month the ARP passed, some nervousness developed in the bond market. It was hardly surprising. After all, the Federal Reserve's near-zero interest rate policy and its rapid balance sheet expansion policy were proceeding apace even as massive fiscal stimulus was coming on line. The ten-year Treasury bond rate, which had fallen to barely above 50 basis points during the worst of the pandemic's financial panic, began climbing in August 2020.

And that climb accelerated in the early months of 2021, from about 1 percent in late January 2021 to about 1.7 percent by late March (after which it leveled off and even declined a bit). Even at 1.7 percent, however, the level of the long rate could not be called high in any meaningful sense; after all, the Fed had loudly and frequently proclaimed its desire to return inflation to 2 percent, which would make a 1.7 percent nominal bond rate negative in real terms. But the speed of the climb attracted attention and, in some quarters, worries.

It was not hard to think of reasons why bond rates might have risen. After all, the economy was plainly on the mend, with strong growth anticipated for 2021. (That strong growth subsequently materialized.) As just mentioned, large amounts of fiscal stimulus were coming online, where they would join what looked to be sizable pent-up demand from consumers who had been more or less forced to save an inordinate share of their incomes. On top of all this, the Fed was continuing its supereasy monetary policies. Conventional macroeconomic thinking could certainly lead to the conclusion that inflation from excess demand was on the way, as Summers and others fretted.

On the other hand, however, many economists remembered that the once-reliable Phillips curve had apparently died a mysterious death two decades earlier, as mentioned at the end of chapter 3. Just before the pandemic struck, the U.S. economy had enjoyed an unemployment rate near 3.5 percent for six months and at or below 4 percent for nearly two years, all without the slightest sign that inflation was perking up. It would be a long time before the United States got back to 3.5 percent unemployment. Even when the bond market was getting agitated about inflation in late March 2021, the break-even inflation rate implied by the Treasury Inflation-Protected Securities (TIPS) market stood at only around 2.25 percent, which was almost exactly the Fed's long-run inflation target.[14] If inflationary alarm bells were sounding, they certainly were not loud.

14. The Fed posts a target for the PCE deflator, not for the Consumer Price Index. Inflation measured by the PCE deflator tends to run about 20–40 basis points below inflation measured by the Consumer Price Index.

Then the inflation picture began to change. The early months of the pandemic had beaten the monthly inflation numbers for February–May 2020 down into negative territory. But in February–May 2021 as these aberrant months were replaced by 2021 figures in the twelve-month average, measured inflation was destined to rise—which it did, though quite a bit more than expected. The Consumer Price Index inflation rate, for example, soared at an annualized 7.4 percent pace over the January–May 2021 period, compared to –3.1 percent over January–May 2020. That alone boosted the headline-making twelve-month inflation rate to 5 percent, which got some alarmists talking about a return to the inflation of the 1970s and early 1980s. As spring gave way to summer, fall, and then finally winter, inflation crept even higher. Apparently, however, few of those inflation alarmists were bond traders. Both ten-year Treasury rates and ten-year breakeven rates on TIPS rose only modestly.

The big controversy of the day was over whether these high inflation rates were transitory—a joint product of the data rotation just mentioned and various shortages and bottlenecks from reopening—or something more lasting. The bond market and most of the FOMC, prominently including Chair Powell, were firmly in the transitory camp. For example, the FOMC "Summary of Economic Projections" issued in June 2021 projected a personal consumption expenditure (PCE) inflation rate of only 2.1 percent in 2022. And so, certainly, was the White House. But a few FOMC members were getting nervous about prospective inflation, and Summers and others continued to sound the alarm. As high inflation numbers accumulated over the summer and fall of 2021, inflation worries grew. Was all this really transitory?

On November 3, 2021, the FOMC announced its intention to begin tapering its asset purchases over the coming months (FOMC 2021). (Remember, as long as it was engaging in QE purchases, the Fed was tapping on the accelerator, not the brake.) But this time, unlike in 2013, the markets reacted calmly; there was no taper tantrum. After all, the Fed had all but announced its decision prior to issuing the official word, and everyone could see that the economy was growing strongly and that inflation was too high. By the end of November, Chair Powell made it clear in congressional testimony that the FOMC would accelerate the taper. He also jettisoned the word "transitory" when referring to the rise in inflation, saying "it's probably a good time to retire that word and explain more clearly what we mean" (Timiraos and Omeokwe 2021). As 2021 drew to a close, markets expected an end to tapering by March 2022, with interest rate liftoff following shortly thereafter. (Both of those did indeed happen.) That said, the specter of yet another COVID variant—this one labeled "omicron"—was casting a shadow of uncertainty over the recovery. Infections soared to record heights, but the economy soldiered on.

Building Back Better

Meanwhile, the two makers of fiscal policy—the White House and the Congress—were engaged in pitched battle yet again. In addition to the ARP, President Biden had proposed an American Jobs Plan and an American Families Plan, each in the $2 trillion range over ten years and each financed mainly by higher taxes, especially on the rich and on corporations. Republicans in Congress were appalled by the gigantic expansion of government, basically unsympathetic to Biden's list of public "needs" (except for physical infrastructure), and adamant about not raising taxes.

Since Democrats held only a slender majority in the House and the Senate was evenly split, Biden could push legislation through Congress only if he held on to every Democratic senator and used reconciliation to avoid filibusters. On top of all that, Senator Joe Manchin (D-WV), after providing one of the fifty votes for the ARP, insisted on bipartisanship thereafter. That attitude essentially handed a veto pen to Senate minority leader Mitch McConnell, who was only too happy to wield it.

Part of the Republican strategy was to separate the physical infrastructure provisions from the rest of the Biden package. And indeed, in July 2021 a fragile bipartisan agreement emerged on physical infrastructure and passed the Senate. The House, however, delayed passage until November, wanting to pair the infrastructure bill with the much larger package of social, educational, and climate measures that combined elements of Biden's American Jobs Plan and American Families Plan. The House passed that second bill, now dubbed "Build Back Better," on a strictly partisan vote on November 19. But the Senate proved a tougher nut to crack, and as 2021 drew to a close, Build Back Better looked dead (which it was).

Chapter Summary

COVID-19 hit the U.S. economy and indeed all the world's economies hard, leading to a terrifying recession in 2020 that, while short, was far from sweet. Large monetary and fiscal responses were clearly imperative. But they had very different targets.

Fiscal policies delivered cash relief, largely through tax cuts and transfer payments, to those who lost their jobs, those who lost their incomes, businesses threatened with oblivion, and so on. The combined fiscal effort under the Trump and Biden administrations added up to about $6 trillion, an enormous sum even for the gigantic U.S. economy.

In the Washington budget argot, almost none of this was "paid for." So, the already-large federal budget deficit soared to levels not seen since World War II. But nobody in Washington seemed to care. Neither did the bond market; interest rates remained low. In its early stages, the fiscal expansion was strongly bipartisan; in its later stages, it turned bitterly partisan.

Monetary policy was hampered a bit by starting the crisis period with a very low federal funds rate, which it quickly dropped to near zero. So, the Fed concentrated on holding the shaky financial system together via both reassuring talk and the rapid creation of a large number of liquidity facilities. Bagehot on steroids, one journalist called it (Timiraos 2022, chap. 10).

Central bank independence was both maintained and forgotten during the crisis. On the one hand, President Trump stopped berating the Fed when the central bank turned to cutting rates instead of raising them. And President Biden reverted to the status quo ante, enabling the Fed to decide matters independently. On the other hand, however, central bank independence melted away as it had in 2008, as the Treasury and the Fed worked together to stand up several liquidity facilities, often with the Treasury offering backstop funding in case the facility suffered losses. As Fed Chair Powell was fond of saying, the central bank was "lending, not spending."

Initially, the steep recession and the accompanying fears that things would get worse drove inflation down from about 2.5 percent in the twelve months ending January 2020 to a low barely above zero in the twelve months ending May 2020. But the recovery was V-shaped, and high and rising inflation became the big macroeconomic story of 2021 and 2022. The twelve-month inflation rate soared from 1.7 percent in February 2021 to 6.9 percent in November 2021, the highest since the early 1980s. Then, in early 2022, it went even higher.

At the Fed, Powell and Company took their feet off the proverbial accelerator by tapering QE purchases quickly and penciling in several rate hikes for 2022. But neither monetary nor fiscal policy could do much to alleviate the unconventional problems with supply chains, which were unable to keep up with burgeoning demand for things that come in boxes. That unusual problem, unfixable by either fiscal or monetary means, grew even worse when Russia invaded Ukraine in March 2022.

•

19

Sixty Years of Monetary and Fiscal Policy: What's Changed?

Like a circle in a spiral. Like a wheel within a wheel. Never ending or beginning, on an ever spinning reel.
—FROM THE SONG "WINDMILLS OF YOUR MIND"

While writing this book, I was asked many times "What's your punch line, your 'elevator pitch,' the ninety-second capsule summary of sixty years of monetary and fiscal history?" As the work progressed, the answer became more and more obvious: there is no punch line. You can't summarize sixty years of fascinating history in an elevator pitch. What is clear is that the complex interplay among ideas, events, politics, and policy that is at the core of this book did not proceed in a linear fashion. Rather, it looked more like a bunch of wheels within wheels, spinning endlessly in time and space. That said, certain themes do emerge from the historical narrative, and this concluding chapter pulls some of those themes together. I have selected four that carry lessons for today.

Monetary versus fiscal policy. The book's title, of course, evokes Milton Friedman and Anna Schwartz's (1963) classic work

A Monetary History of the United States, 1857–1960. But the addition of two vitally important words—*and Fiscal*—to my title broadens the focus considerably. Readers who have come this far know that the waxing and waning of monetary versus fiscal policy over time, both in the intellectual realm and in the world of practical policy making, is an important thread that runs through the historical narrative. Economists in 2021 thought about the two types of stabilization policy quite differently than they had in 1961, and policy makers in 2021 acted quite differently than policy makers in 1961. How and why that changed so many times over sixty years is perhaps the principal focus of this book. The addition of fiscal policy to the narrative also forced me to delve much more deeply into the politics of policy than Friedman and Schwartz did.

Keynesian economics. Friedman and Schwartz were, of course, monetarists who rejected Keynesianism both as theory and as policy, and they were not alone. So, a second major theme of this book is the repeated ascendance and descendance of Keynesianism, a process that accompanied and in some ways underpinned the evolving attitudes toward monetary and fiscal policy.

Budget deficits. Discussions of fiscal policy over sixty years have often revolved around implications for the federal budget deficit. Here, changes have been both revolutionary and momentous. At the beginning, large budget deficits were viewed as dangerous if not immoral. By the end, they were viewed as mother's milk. The administrations of George W. Bush, Barack Obama, Donald Trump, and Joe Biden each boosted the federal deficit by amounts that would have been unthinkable to Dwight Eisenhower or even to John F. Kennedy. Notice that the post-2000 list of budget busters is nonpartisan; it includes two Democrats and two Republicans. The true break with prior history came with Ronald Reagan in 1981. But just as with views on monetary versus fiscal policy, the evolution of thought on budget deficits was far from linear.

Central bank independence. One final theme of this book has received far less public attention: attitudes toward central bank independence. These days, the independence of the central bank is taken for granted as one of the main—and most obvious—pillars of best monetary policy practice. Hardly anyone questions its wisdom. But that was far from the case in 1961. Attitudes since then have changed drastically.

Who Sits in First Chair, Fiscal Policy or Monetary Policy?

Who should take the lead in formulating and executing stabilization policy, the central bank or the fiscal authorities? The choice matters for any number of reasons. Some involve effects on major macroeconomic variables such as interest rates, exchange rates, and asset prices. For example, while looser fiscal policy generally raises interest rates, looser monetary policy generally lowers them. Other considerations are allocative. For example, easier money favors the homebuilding and automobile industries, while income tax cuts promote general consumer spending. The distributional effects of the two varieties of stabilization policy also differ. Monetary policy generally has its biggest effects, for good or ill, on asset holders. Fiscal policies can be tailored to favor the rich or the poor, as the politicians please. U.S. history holds examples of each.

So, whether a nation relies more on fiscal policy or more on monetary policy is consequential. Prior to 1961, the answer to this question was clear, at least in the United States: neither one.[1] Yes, there had been fiscal changes before 1961, sometimes large ones with profound effects on aggregate demand (e.g., wartime spending and subsequent demobilizations). But those policies were not deliberately aimed at speeding up or slowing down the growth of the economy.

It is also worth remembering that the U.S. government's official commitment to achieving "conditions under which there will be afforded useful employment for those able, willing, and seeking to

1. Sweden, for example, already had a long history of fiscal stabilization policy. See, for example, Lundberg (1985).

work" dates only to the Employment Act of 1946, and that landmark act concentrated on fiscal, not monetary, policy. It created, for example, a new Council of Economic Advisers in the White House, and it required an annual *Economic Report of the President*. But the act did not alter the Federal Reserve in any way or require it to report on the economy. Times have certainly changed. Economy watchers now dote on the Fed and don't read the *Economic Report of the President*.

Kennedy's 1962 speech, his subsequent advocacy of a tax cut, and the tax cut's eventual passage in 1964 constituted a major break with prior history. It was the first time America deliberately used discretionary fiscal policy to move aggregate demand, and Kennedy advocated it despite a budget deficit. The widely trumpeted success of the Kennedy-Johnson tax cuts helped secure Lyndon Johnson's landslide victory in 1964, elevated the stature of fiscal policy, and turned Council of Economic Advisers Chair Walter Heller into a national celebrity. Monetary policy was relegated to second fiddle.

The accolades thrown at the Kennedy-Johnson tax cuts also enhanced the prestige of Keynesian economics, though only fleetingly as it turned out. Keynesian theory was basically symmetric, and consistent with that, the Heller and Okun Council of Economic Advisers urged Johnson to raise taxes (or cut spending) to fight an overheating economy. Johnson, a master politician, naturally resisted, and Congress resisted even longer. So, the 1968 tax surcharge came far too late to stop inflation. That failure had two important consequences. In the realm of ideas, monetarism made deep inroads by falsely claiming that Keynesianism was inherently inflationary. In the realm of policy, the 1968 surtax marked basically the first and last time discretionary fiscal policy would be used to cool the U.S. economy.[2] Keynesianism turned out to be symmetric in theory but asymmetric in practice.

The long-delayed tax cut also dragged the Federal Reserve into the center of the battle against inflation. And that brought its chair, William McChesney Martin, into direct conflict with President

2. There were subsequent fiscal contractions, but they were rationalized by reducing the budget deficit, not by slowing growth.

Johnson, who toyed with the idea of firing Martin (but could not). As fiscal policy turned sharply expansionary to prosecute the Vietnam War, Martin felt it was the Fed's duty to lean against the inflationary wind. This episode marked the first major clash between tight monetary policy and loose fiscal policy but not the last.

Any such conflict disappeared when President Richard Nixon installed his old chum, Arthur Burns, at the helm of the Fed in 1970. No one had to ask which branch of stabilization policy was dominant because the two acted in concert, starting with highly expansionary fiscal and monetary policies designed to get Nixon reelected in 1972 and followed by major fiscal and monetary tightenings once the desired political result had been achieved. It is tempting to say that fiscal policy dominated monetary policy in those years, but it is probably more accurate to say that Nixon dominated both.

Shortly thereafter, stagflation hit the United States and other nations, first with food and energy shocks in 1972–1974 and later with energy shocks in 1979–1980. Both fiscal and monetary policy thus faced a strange new dilemma. Should policy makers tighten to fight soaring inflation or ease to combat rising unemployment? Since no one knew the right answer, the question of who was in charge went moot.

In fact, policy became schizophrenic. President Gerald Ford first called for a tax increase to combat inflation in 1974 but then reversed himself and persuaded Congress to cut taxes in 1975 to fight the deep recession. The Fed vacillated between turning expansionary to give the economy a boost or contractionary to slow inflation down. However, as public revulsion with inflation grew in the 1970s, the focus of monetary policy clearly shifted away from mitigating recessions and toward reducing inflation. Especially once Paul Volcker became the Fed's chair, monetary policy took the lead. Fiscal policy was not just relegated to the back seat; it was not even invited along for the ride.

Fiscal policy made a strong comeback, however, under President Ronald Reagan. Although the outrageous supply-side claims of the Reaganites were proven false, the standard demand-side effects of the Reagan tax cuts were both evident and large. By 1984, the American people were enjoying the convivial combination of rapid growth and lower inflation. The idea that fiscal policy could be ignored fared about as well as Reagan's opponent in the lanslide 1984 election.

The dominant fiscal concern did, however, change dramatically within Reagan's eight years, from stimulating the economy to reducing the budget deficit. If aggregate demand was to be managed, the job would be left to the Federal Reserve, not to Congress, which according to the Washington wisdom of the day needed to concentrate on reducing the deficit. Happily, Volcker started the job and Alan Greenspan finished it. In fact, the Fed might have achieved a perfect soft landing in 1990 were it not for Saddam Hussein and the sharp oil price shock. One striking fact of the period was that no one in authority even mentioned fiscal stimulus as a possible remedy for the minirecession of 1990–1991.

Fiscal policy made another big comeback, however, under President Bill Clinton, albeit with a major twist. Worried about the deficit, Clinton staked his administration on what economists normally think of as contractionary fiscal policy: raising taxes and cutting spending. Naturally, Clinton did not advertise his economic program as a way to slow down the economy. Rather, he trumpeted the virtues of deficit reduction that, he claimed, would somehow create jobs. How, exactly, this was supposed to happen was never clear. But in a political environment in which budget deficits had become an obsession, good things were supposed to flow from reducing the deficit.

Clinton understood very well that whether his deficit reduction gamble would succeed or fail hung on the behavior of the Federal Reserve under its very Republican chair, Alan Greenspan. Perhaps even more frightening, it hung on the reactions of a bunch of bond traders in New York, London, and Tokyo.

Both delivered, sort of. The Federal Open Market Committee (FOMC) held the federal funds rate at just 3 percent—about zero in real terms—for about a year. Greenspan turned out to be the consummate fine-tuner. The Fed's first rate hike in years had to come on February 4, 1994, and it had to be 25 basis points, not the 50 basis points that the majority of the FOMC preferred. Such exquisite fine-tuning continued throughout Greenspan's long tenure as Fed chief. Walter Heller may have been unable to fine-tune the economy, and Charles Schultze may have been disinclined to try. But Alan Greenspan did both.

The U.S. economy performed splendidly under the Clinton-Greenspan policy mix of easy money and tight budgets.[3] Business investment rose as a share of GDP, inflation remained low, and tens of millions of new jobs were created. What most surprised mainstream economists was that the sizable fiscal contraction (without any monetary easing) seemed not to slow the economy at all. Rather, it precipitated a strong bond market rally that overwhelmed the fiscal contraction. Now, that was something new.

The Clinton boom was lengthened and strengthened by Greenspan's subsequent gamble with monetary policy. As the economy soared and the unemployment rate fell to levels not seen in decades, Greenspan saw that inflation was not rising. Why not? He hypothesized that rapid productivity growth from New Economy innovations was pushing potential GDP up faster than people realized. It was a hunch at first, but the data subsequently vindicated his iconoclastic view. Due largely to this "great call," the Fed let the good times roll into the late 1990s, and inflation stayed put at around 3 percent.

Taken together, the perfect soft landing in 1994–1995, the expert fine-tuning, and the great call of 1996–1999 elevated Greenspan to near godlike status. He was riding high. So was the Federal Reserve and monetary policy. Who needed fiscal policy?

A fair question. But fiscal policy came back anyway with the election of George W. Bush in 2000. Bush campaigned on a large Reaganesque tax cut, which Congress subsequently passed. During the congressional debate in 2001, Greenspan tarnished his gold-plated reputation by seeming to endorse the Bush tax cuts. His thinly disguised advocacy not only crossed the line between monetary and fiscal policy but also struck many people as way too political for the Federal Reserve. Democrats were naturally displeased. But

---

3. Soaring productivity after 1995 no doubt played a major role as well.

Greenspan's endorsement of the Bush tax cuts probably didn't hurt his chances for reappointment by Bush in 2004.

When Ben Bernanke replaced Alan Greenspan in February 2006, the U.S. economy was performing well. But this didn't last. As what became the worldwide financial crisis surfaced and then worsened in 2007, the FOMC began cutting interest rates in September 2007, slowly at first but later aggressively. Finally, in December 2008 the Bernanke Fed hit rock bottom at a federal funds rate range of zero to 25 basis points, its version of the effective lower bound. All told, the drop in the funds rate from September 2007 to December 2008 was almost 525 basis points. In a word, monetary policy took the lead in fighting the recession (and the financial panic) in both timing and magnitude.[4] Fiscal policy once again played second fiddle. But this time it did play: the Bush administration managed to get a modest tax cut through Congress, roughly 1 percent of GDP.

The relative roles of fiscal and monetary policy changed once again and dramatically when Barack Obama arrived at the White House. Within a month, the new president (barely) pushed a large fiscal stimulus package—about 5 percent of GDP—through a recalcitrant Congress. But fiscal policy was not back in the driver's seat for long. Most of the Obama administration's subsequent efforts to combat the recession were stymied by Congress, especially after Democrats lost control of the House in the 2010 midterm elections. Monetary policy once again became the only game in town, despite Fed Chair Bernanke practically begging Congress for help. Pulling the economy out of the Great Recession was a big job, and Bernanke was worried that the Fed could not do it alone.

That last thought was a relatively new one for the Fed and for many macroeconomists at the time. In most previous recessions, several of which were caused by tight monetary policy, the central bank thought it could perform the entire job by itself, basically by cutting interest rates. Fiscal policy was thought to be too tied up in political knots to be of much help. But in the deep recession of

---

4. Interest rate cuts were hardly the whole story for the Fed. Details are in chapters 13 and 14.

2007–2009, the Fed found itself confronting what it had previously thought of as a Japanese problem: the "zero" lower bound on nominal interest rates. Even a wide array of unconventional monetary policies seemed insufficient to pull the economy out of the ditch. Rather than ask whether it was better to rely on monetary or fiscal policy to boost demand, Bernanke concluded that the right answer was both. It was a thought that Alan Greenspan and Paul Volcker may never have entertained.

However, fiscal stabilization policy effectively shut down after the 2009 stimulus. In fact, it turned contractionary for most of the years 2011, 2012, and 2013. Partly because the inability to push interest rates down further reduced the potency of monetary policy and partly because fiscal policy turned procyclical, the recovery from the June 2009 trough was agonizingly slow. Payroll employment did not return to its January 2008 peak until May 2014.

Both the macroeconomy and monetary policy went pretty quiet from then until the pandemic hit in early 2020. But fiscal policy did not. President Trump pushed through large cuts in personal and corporate taxes in December 2017 even though the economy was humming along, showing no signs of needing stimulus. The Trump tax cuts reminded many economists of Lyndon Johnson's Vietnam episode, dropping more fiscal kindling into an already hot economy. But just as in 1965, fiscal policy in 2017 was dictated by politics, not economics.

Many economists feared higher inflation from excess demand, as had happened after 1965. But it didn't happen this time. Inflation remained roughly flat at slightly below the Fed's 2 percent target even as the unemployment rate tracked down to a fifty-year low in September 2019. A few months later, the COVID-19 pandemic turned the lights off on the economic data—and almost turned off the economy.

As economic activity cratered in March, April, and May 2020, what Ben Bernanke had argued a decade earlier became patently obvious: ending the vicious recession would require maximum effort from both monetary and fiscal policy. Fortunately, both Congress and the Fed delivered.

The FOMC moved first, dropping interest rates to the floor, stating that they would remain there "until it is confident that the economy has weathered recent events" (FOMC 2020c), and announcing a wide variety of emergency lending and liquidity facilities, many backed by the Treasury. Those actions and words quickly calmed the turbulent financial waters.

Congress passed the massive Coronavirus Aid, Relief, and Economic Security (CARES) Act on March 27, followed it with another large relief package in December 2020, and then capped off roughly $5 trillion in total fiscal support with President Biden's huge American Relief Plan in March 2021. Amazingly, personal disposable income actually rose despite the economic devastation.

It was, of course, the pressure of events, not any new developments in the world of ideas, that elevated both monetary and fiscal policy to DEFCON 1 in 2020–2021. No one worried then about whether monetary or fiscal policy should sit in first chair. Nor did many people worry—at least at first—about the possible ill-effects of hyperloose monetary policy or mammoth budget deficits.

Looking back over the sixty years covered in this book, the proverbial arc of history bent slightly toward monetary policy. Both economists and policy makers looked more toward the Fed than toward Congress in 2021 than in 1961. But that trend was minor compared to the notable cycles, the spinning wheels. Fiscal policy was on top in the 1960s, Richard Nixon dominated both in the early 1970s, and Paul Volcker didn't seek fiscal help in conquering inflation in the 1980s. The Reagan and Clinton administrations thrust fiscal policy into the spotlight again, albeit in starkly different ways. Reagan slashed taxes and ballooned the deficit; Clinton seemed to grow the economy by shrinking the deficit. Through most of the 1984–2008 period, fiscal policy was preoccupied by the budget deficit and left the stabilization job to the Fed. But this monopoly position became untenable when the financial crisis and then the pandemic recession exceeded the central bank's ability to stimulate the economy. Major assists from fiscal policy were needed.

The Rise and Fall and Rise and . . .
of Keynesian Economics

Most of the ups and downs of fiscal versus monetary policy in the real world over these sixty years reflected the press of events. But some reflected the ups and downs of Keynesian ideas, at least where fiscal policy was concerned. Monetary policy, in contrast, was always Keynesian in the practical sense of turning expansionary when the economy slumped and contractionary when inflation rose.[5] The Fed's monetarist experiment of 1979–1982 was in some sense the exception that proved the rule: it ended because the economy needed "Keynesian" stimulus.

Keynesianism first came to dominate Washington thinking in the Kennedy administration and quickly scored a major policy victory with the Kennedy-Johnson tax cuts. However, the sands soon shifted away in both the intellectual and policy arenas.

In the intellectual arena, the shoots of what would subsequently blossom into monetarism started to sprout with Friedman and Schwartz's (1963) monumental work. Monetarism continued to ascend during the 1960s on Friedman's persuasiveness and on a wave of rising inflation, which monetarists successfully blamed on Keynesian policies. Inflation gave monetarism another boost when a series of supply shocks struck the United States and other countries in the 1970s and early 1980s. It was ironic: inflation actually soared for reasons unrelated to the money supply, but monetarists and other foes of Keynesianism successfully blamed Keynesianism again.

In the policy arena, the long delay in passing the 1968 tax surcharge and its apparent failure to curb inflation had two major effects. First, it tarnished the soft glow of Keynesianism. Second, it suggested that fiscal policy might be usable only to boost demand, not to rein it in. Contractionary policy to fight inflation fighting would have to be left to the Fed.

The stagflation of the 1970s also opened the door to another intellectual challenge to Keynesian theory: new classical economics.

5. Stagflation posed an obvious dilemma.

That academic approach was and still is often termed the "rational expectations revolution," but that's a misnomer. What gave new classical models their startlingly anti-Keynesian implications was not the assumption of rational expectations but rather the obviously false assumption that all markets clear quickly. In this imaginary world, monetary policy could affect output or employment only if it surprised economic agents, a tall order under rational expectations.

New classical economics, with this "policy ineffectiveness" result, conquered vast swaths of academia in the 1970s and 1980s, but it never developed much of a following among central bankers or among the many PhD economists who worked for them.[6] After all, the doctrine said they were all wasting their time. Neither Arthur Burns nor Paul Volcker, the two Fed chairs for most of that period, ever believed in monetary policy ineffectiveness. More important, central bankers all over the world saw that both inflation and real economies were crushed by Margaret Thatcher's excruciatingly tight money in the United Kingdom and by Volcker's excruciatingly tight money in the United States. No real effects?

As Keynesianism declined in intellectual circles, monetarism rose in policy circles, culminating in the Federal Reserve's alleged conversion to monetarism in 1979. Monetarists felt vindicated. But Keynesians winced, having absorbed William Poole's (1970) lesson: wild fluctuations in money demand would likely lead to wild gyrations in both money growth (displeasing monetarists) and interest rates (displeasing everyone). Both happened, dealing a body blow to monetarism.

Nonetheless, Keynesian ideas were still under siege in the academy when Ronald Reagan demonstrated both the power and appeal of Keynesian tax cuts in the real world, though he called them "supply-side" tax cuts instead. Ironically, this episode marked the last gasp for fiscal policy as a macro stabilizer for quite a while. Rather, the large chronic deficits left behind by Reaganomics made reducing

---

6. In those days, it was rare to find a monetary policy maker with a PhD in economics. (Arthur Burns was the rare exception.) Governments wanted "prudent men" (yes, men) running their central banks.

the yawning budget deficit the new focus of fiscal policy. What might be called the anti-Keynesian era began with repealing most of the Reagan business tax cuts in 1982, went through several false starts (e.g., Gramm–Rudman–Hollings) in the mid-1980s, and became the focus of President George H. W. Bush's fiscal policy, culminating in the landmark 1990 budget agreement.

All that was prologue to the Clinton presidency, which focused like a laser beam (a favorite Clintonism) on reducing the federal budget deficit. The success of Clintonomics fostered some thoroughly anti-Keynesian thoughts, such as negative fiscal multipliers. You can create jobs by reducing the budget deficit? This anti-Keynesian view of the world would come back to haunt policy makers in the Obama years.

But did U.S. prosperity under Clinton really prove Keynes wrong? No. Clinton's deficit reduction program was heavily back-loaded; there was little budget cutting in the near term. So, perhaps the correct lesson was that fiscal policy can stimulate the economy today by credibly promising deficit reduction in the future. The likely mechanism works through the term structure of interest rates: the promise of lower short rates in the future, if believed, should reduce long rates today. High credibility, not a negative fiscal multiplier, is the key to making this trick work.

When George W. Bush and Al Gore battled for the presidency in 2000, the major economic policy debate was over what to do with the federal government's mounting surpluses. Bush wanted a supply-side tax cut. Gore wanted to pay down the national debt. Neither camp's rhetoric sounded Keynesian. Thus, during the entire period from 1982 to 2001, most economists who thought about stabilization policy thought first, second, and third about monetary policy.

While that was happening in the policy world, Keynesians in the academy were busy fighting off monetarism, supply-side econom-ics, new classical economics, and even so-called real business cycle theory, a curious doctrine that viewed recessions as instances of negative productivity growth. But academic fashions began to turn back toward Keynesianism in the late 1990s as proponents of new classical economics began to admit that macro markets do not clear instantly. Rather, prices and wages are "sticky," as Keynesians had always insisted, and such stickiness leads to Keynesian policy implications even under rational expectations.[7]

Just as there are no atheists in foxholes, even policy makers who profess hostility to Keynesianism in principle tend to turn Keynesian in practice when a recession strikes. This is exactly what happened in 2001. George W. Bush found a new rationale for his supply-side tax cuts: the economy needed fiscal stimulus. The Federal Reserve, for its part, slashed the federal funds rate even though Alan Greenspan never (to my knowledge) called himself a Keynesian. The outcomes would not have been much different if monetary and fiscal policy had been run by James Tobin and Walter Heller.

But this was just a small preview of what was to come. As the global financial crisis brought on the Great Recession of 2007–2009, policy makers all over the world turned very Keynesian very quickly. In a series of hastily arranged summit meetings in 2008 and 2009, leaders of the world's major countries pledged to pursue Keynesian policies though without invoking Lord Keynes's name.

Though hailed at the time as marvelous examples of international cooperation, those summits were actually foxhole behavior writ large. Since virtually every nation faced the same problem—a shortage of aggregate demand—virtually every nation pursued its own national interest by boosting aggregate demand. The world went Keynesian by necessity. Oddly enough, "communist" China led the way with a massive fiscal stimulus in the neighborhood of 10 percent of GDP. The United States followed with about 5 percent of GDP at the start of the Obama presidency.

Once again, however, the romance did not last. In the United States, the Republican-dominated Congress quickly reverted to fretting about the budget deficit, and fiscal policy turned contractionary during the years 2011–2013 over the objections of both President Obama and Fed Chair Bernanke. In fact, Congress nearly drove the economy over a steep fiscal cliff in 2013.

When Donald Trump assumed the presidency in January 2017, it was déjà vu all over again. His income tax cuts resembled George W.

7. See, for example, Christiano, Eichenbaum, and Evans (1999).

Bush's in magnitude and structure, but there were a few noteworthy differences. Trump's tax cuts came at a time of low unemployment, whereas in 2001 the economy needed stimulus. Bush's tax cuts originated amid growing budget surpluses, while Trump's were piled atop an already-large budget deficit. Finally, Trump's supply-side rhetoric far surpassed anything the Bush team ever dared claim. If you took Trump at his word, the tax cuts would propel annual GDP growth into the 5–6 percent range, reduce the budget deficit, and then produce surpluses large enough to pay down the national debt. Of course, no serious economist believed those claims. I wonder if the Trump White House did.

Regardless, the 2017 tax cuts left the federal budget far out of balance when the pandemic struck early in 2020. At that point, just as in 2008–2009, it was all Keynesian hands on deck all over the world, with nobody caring much about labels. The Fed cut interest rates to the bone in March 2020. By the end of that month, Congress had passed the monumental CARES Act, and more fiscal relief would come in December 2020 and then again in March 2021. Overall, the massive fiscal response to COVID reminded some people of the mobilization to fight World War II. So did the rising national debt.

Looking back over sixty years of fiscal policy, attitudes in 2021 were certainly more Keynesian than they had been in 1961. But the road was both bumpy and political. Defining Keynesian policy as belief in using fiscal policy to influence aggregate demand, I would classify American presidents into three baskets. Kennedy, Johnson, Nixon, Ford, Carter, Obama, and Biden were all basically Keynesians, both in principle and in practice. Reagan, Bush II, and Trump shunned the Keynesian label but acted Keynesian in practice. The only fiscal episodes that can be characterized as truly anti-Keynesian occurred under Bush I and Clinton, when the policy focus was squarely on reducing the deficit no matter what.

Monetary policy leaders from Martin through Jerome Powell are easier to classify. With the possible exceptions of Bernanke and Janet Yellen, none of them wanted to be called Keynesians. But they all sought to manage aggregate demand along Keynesian lines. What's in a name?

Do Budget Deficits Matter?

Attitudes toward the federal budget deficit and the national debt changed dramatically over the sixty years covered in this volume. Indeed, they changed several times.

President Dwight D. Eisenhower would have thought the question "Do deficits matter?" silly. To him and many others in the 1950s (and since), deficits were fiscally imprudent, morally repugnant, a burden on our children and grandchildren and, if you listened to any of his economic advisers, also raised interest rates and crowded out private investment. Deficits were thought to be inflationary even if they were not monetized by the Fed, although it was not clear exactly how.[8] Keynesianism, not incidentally, got a black eye because it seemed to countenance, perhaps even to advocate, budget deficits.

The Kennedy and Johnson administration marked the first big break from this tradition, as taxes were cut despite a preexisting deficit. As the 1960s progressed, the accusation that budget deficits were inflationary even without money creation faded away, perhaps under the intellectual pressure of monetarism. (*Inflation is always and everywhere a monetary phenomenon.*) A different accusation replaced it: deficits burdened future generations by crowding out investment.[9] That burden, however, did not deter Richard Nixon from running large deficits to assist his reelection efforts in 1972. No ideologue he.

Jimmy Carter, whose presidency followed the Nixon-Ford years, took deficits more seriously, perhaps even as a moral outrage. (Carter was a stern moralist.) The federal deficit nevertheless hung around 2.5 percent of GDP throughout his term. Ironically, that "large" deficit was one of the points on which candidate Reagan pummeled Carter in the 1980 campaign.

8. What modern economists call "the fiscal theory of the price level" played no role in this debate.

9. A few academics argued that "burdening" future generations that way was fine, even preferable, because future generations would be richer. This view never caught on with the general public, however. Indeed, it was barely ever heard there.

Ironically indeed. Early in the Reagan presidency, the budget deficit exploded from 2.5 percent of GDP in fiscal 1981 to nearly 6 percent of GDP in fiscal 1983, at the time the largest relative to GDP since World War II.[10] Yet the balanced budget ideology remained alive even as fiscal policy was pushing actual budget deficits to new heights. You want consistency? Supply-siders squared the circle by claiming that the Reagan program would balance the budget within four years (White House 1981).

That didn't happen, of course, and reducing the budget deficit became the preoccupation of fiscal policy for the next fifteen years or so. The pay-as-you-go (PAYGO) system that had been agreed to by President George H. W. Bush and the Democrats in 1990 can be thought of as requiring budget balance at the margin, because any deficit-increasing policy had to be accompanied by equal and opposite deficit-reducing policies. Indeed, the rhetorical attraction of a balanced budget was so strong in the 1990s that both Bill Clinton and Al Gore routinely referred to budget surpluses as "balanced budgets." Arithmetic be damned.

That background makes it all the more astonishing that President George W. Bush returned the nation to large budget deficits so quickly and so easily. Congress terminated pay-as-you-go. The tax cuts of 2001 and 2003 were not paid for. The wars in Afghanistan and Iraq were not paid for. Even a big new entitlement program, the Medicare prescription drug benefit, was not paid for. All this quickly transformed the federal budget position from a surplus of 1.2 percent of GDP in fiscal 2001 into a deficit of 3.3 percent in fiscal 2003. No more Eisenhower Republicans.

By this time, a clear political pattern had emerged: Republicans railed against budget deficits when a Democrat was in the White House but accepted them willingly, even eagerly, when a Republican was in the White House, especially if the deficits stemmed from tax cuts for the wealthy. In retrospect, the Reagan episode was not a deviation from the norms of the party that once stood for fiscal

---

10. It is true that 1983 was a recession year, and recessions depress revenue. But the budget deficit was still 5 percent of GDP two years later.

discipline. Rather, it marked the start of a new normal, interrupted by Bush I and Clinton.

Barack Obama took office in January 2009 at approximately the bottom of the Great Recession. His new administration managed to push through a large deficit-increasing stimulus bill with negligible Republican help. But after that, the fiscal stimulus door slammed shut again. Increasing the deficit further was out of the question politically. That frugal attitude condemned the United States to contractionary fiscal policy for most of the remainder of the Obama administration. But it did not survive the election of the next Republican president.

The large tax cuts that Trump pushed through Congress in 2017 were, once again, not paid for. And I wonder how many members of Congress actually believed the outlandish claims by the president and his secretary of the treasury that yet another supply-side miracle would rescue the budget from revenue losses. After all, the promised supply-side miracles of 1981 and 2001 had not happened.

When the pandemic struck in early 2020, no one in either party fretted much about the budget deficit, which was already 4.6 percent of GDP in fiscal 2019. The nation mobilized fiscal policy for war on the coronavirus, only the federal government had sufficient borrowing capacity, and the Treasury paid extremely low interest rates to borrow. Furthermore and important, the Federal Reserve purchased a large share of the newly issued Treasury debt,[11] dropped interest rates to the floor, and vowed to keep them there. It was all hands on deck to minimize the damage that COVID-19 was wreaking on the economy, even if that meant epic deficits, substantially monetized.

The relaxed and seemingly bipartisan attitude toward deficits didn't last, however. As funds from the CARES Act (March 2020) started to peter out, a fiercely partisan debate emerged over the advisability and size of any follow-up relief package. With tax cuts no longer commanding center stage, congressional Republicans bridled at the large budget deficit, which hit a mind-blowing 15 percent of

11. Not exactly. The Fed actually purchased treasuries in the secondary market, not at original issue.

GDP in fiscal 2020. Nonetheless, Congress eventually agreed on a new relief bill, which passed with large bipartisan majorities in December 2020. President Trump even groused that the relief checks were too small.

Enter President Joe Biden. With majorities in both Houses of Congress, albeit razor-thin ones, Biden was able to pass another huge budget-busting COVID relief bill in March 2021, including another round of relief checks. Tellingly, the votes in both chambers were entirely partisan, forcing Vice President Harris to break a 50–50 tie in the Senate. Republicans objected on many grounds, one of which was the explosion of the national debt, which hit 96 percent of GDP by the end of fiscal 2021. The nation had come full circle, from a balanced budget in fiscal 1960 to a deficit of over 12 percent of GDP in 2021.

Against this backdrop, Biden and the Democrats had trouble pushing through more spending. A bipartisan infrastructure bill amounting to over $1 trillion did pass in 2021, but it at least carried a fig leaf of being paid for. The rest of the Biden plan encountered a brick wall of Republicans—plus Senator Joe Manchin (D-WV)—in the Senate.

The Rise (without a Fall) of Central Bank Independence

One of the starkest and yet least remarked-upon changes in the monetary-fiscal realm since 1961 has been the prevailing attitude toward central bank independence (CBI). The value of CBI has been axiomatic to economists for decades. More important, most of the world's democratic governments apparently agree; they have granted their central banks a remarkable degree of independence, either de jure or de facto. But many economists I've talked to are surprised to learn that the doctrine of CBI was not widely accepted in the 1960s and 1970s, not even in the United States, where the Federal Reserve's independence stood out as unusual by world standards.

Even some prominent economists questioned the wisdom of CBI. As noted in chapter 11, two economic giants of the Left and the

Right, James Tobin and Milton Friedman, respectively, disagreed on almost everything. But they nonetheless agreed that the Fed should not be independent. Even Fed Chair Martin thought of the Federal Reserve as part of the economic team.

Attitudes toward CBI were starkly different by 2021. But that evolution of ideas did not happen overnight. The low point for CBI in the United States probably came under Nixon and Burns, when the president thought he could and should heavily influence monetary policy and the Fed chair seemed to acquiesce.

A few years later, with Paul Volcker leading the Fed, the situation changed dramatically. Jimmy Carter knew that Volcker would be staunchly independent, but he gave his new Fed chief free rein to fight inflation anyway. Volcker grabbed the reins like a man on a mission, asserted the Fed's independence, and relentlessly pursued an aggressive anti-inflation policy that caused a deep recession. The virtues of CBI have rarely been questioned since then, at least not in the United States.

Yet in the 1980s, if you looked around the world, independent central banks were still the exception, not the rule. The Federal Reserve, the Deutsche Bundesbank, and the Swiss National Bank stood nearly alone. The inflationary experience of the 1970s and 1980s helped change all that. Yes, Margaret Thatcher had conquered Britain's high inflation from 10 Downing Street without an independent central bank. But most other nations, led (intellectually) by New Zealand, saw more promise in the Volcker/Bundesbank examples: make your central bank independent and give it a mandate to reduce inflation. The United Kingdom subsequently adopted that norm too.

When the Treaty of Maastricht was drafted and approved by European governments in 1992, it seemed only natural to make CBI a condition for membership in the currency union. And when the European Central Bank opened for business in 1999, it was the most independent central bank in the world, having essentially no government to which to report. Since then, despite occasional grumblings about the "democracy deficit" posed by the ECB's extreme independence, there have been no serious threats to that independence, which after all is inscribed in a multinational treaty.

The final two chapters of the story of Fed independence were strikingly different from the earlier ones. They also pose questions for the future.

In fighting the megacrises of 2007–2009 and 2020–2021, the Fed, like other central banks, found itself cooperating with the Treasury in unusual ways. Some critics saw such close cooperation as tantamount to subordinating the central bank to the Treasury. For example, Allan Meltzer (2009c, 13) opined that "Chairman Ben Bernanke seemed willing to sacrifice much of the independence that Paul Volcker restored in the 1980s. He worked closely with the Treasury and yielded to pressures from the chairs of the House and Senate Banking Committee and others in Congress." Other than the phrase "worked closely with the Treasury," Bernanke disagreed completely. Was the Treasury or the Fed in first chair?

It is worth noting that the Fed's enormous display of power in 2008–2009 led Congress to consider several ways to clip its wings in the Dodd-Frank Act of 2010. But the Bernanke Fed successfully fended off almost every proposal to curtail its powers and emerged from the debate with more authority than when it went in.[12] So, who was subordinated to whom?

The more recent episode was mostly wound down when this book went to press. When Congress, the Treasury, and the Federal Reserve geared up to fight the COVID-19 crisis in 2020, the Fed was pushed into a wide variety of unusual measures. Some of the central bank's assignments were traditional: turn monetary policy highly expansionary and safeguard financial stability. But Congress and the Treasury also called upon the Fed to promulgate some lending facilities that were far from normal.[13] One example was the ill-fated Main Street Lending Program, which the Fed was ill-equipped to execute. Another was backstopping loans that banks made to small businesses under the Paycheck Protection Program, most of which were not expected to be repaid.

12. The major exception was that Dodd-Frank placed some restrictions on emergency lending under Section 13(3).

13. Incidentally, some of these policies involved liberal use of Section 13(3) lending powers, which the Treasury gleefully granted.

As Chair Jerome Powell never tired of pointing out at the time, the Federal Reserve is in the business of "lending, not spending"; it doesn't expect to take losses on its loans. So, Congress squared the circle by having the Small Business Administration absorb any losses from Paycheck Protection Program loans. Nonetheless, the program's never-to-be-repaid loans were a pretty unusual entry on the Fed's balance sheet. That said, the Fed did not push back hard against assuming these new responsibilities under the unusual and exigent circumstances of 2020. So, as long as the post–COVID-19 world does not deviate importantly from what came before, central bank independence seems likely to survive the pandemic.

Last Word

Ideas, events, and policy decisions interact, with causation running in every direction. Certainly in the case of fiscal policy and sometimes in the case of monetary policy, politics also plays an important role.

In the fiscal policy realm, economists have been advising politicians and suggesting policies for a long time. A few have been highly influential. Discretionary fiscal policy, though new in 1961, is familiar now, although the 2020–2021 episode was unprecedented in scope and magnitude. Looking back over sixty years of fiscal history, some of America's major decisions look wise, others not so much. But regardless, the big decisions have always been made by politicians. That has not changed and probably never will. We call it democracy.

When it comes to monetary policy, both the locus of decision-making power and the style of thinking are radically different now than they were in 1961. Apart from Donald Trump, U.S. presidents since Bill Clinton (though not before him) have taken a hands-off attitude toward the Federal Reserve. America's central bank is an economists' organization, not a politicians' organization. Metaphorically, it thinks, speaks, and acts like a bunch of economists. To some observers, that creates a democracy deficit. But a large number of observers over the last sixty years have seen Federal Reserve independence as a valuable contributor to superior macroeconomic performance.

Monetary and fiscal policies will continue to evolve over the next sixty years just as they did over the past sixty, with many unpredictable twists and turns. I nonetheless finish this book with one fearless prediction: fiscal policy decisions will continue to be made largely on political grounds while monetary policy decisions will continue to turn on technocratic, economic considerations. The twain will not soon meet.

REFERENCES

Abrams, Burton A. 2006. "How Richard Nixon Pressured Arthur Burns: Evidence from the Nixon Tapes." *Journal of Economic Perspectives* 20 (4): 177–88.

Abrams, Burton A., and James L. Butkiewicz. 2017. "The Political Economy of Wage and Price Controls: Evidence from the Nixon Tapes." *Public Choice* 170 (1): 63–78.

Agarwal, Sumit, and Wenlan Qian. 2014. "Consumption and Debt Response to Unanticipated Income Shocks: Evidence from a Natural Experiment in Singapore." *American Economic Review* 104 (12): 4205–30.

Alesina, Alberto, and Lawrence Summers. 1993. "Central Bank Independence and Macroeconomic Performance: Some Comparative Evidence." *Journal of Money, Credit and Banking* 25 (2): 151–62.

American Banker. 1982. "Volcker Speech Announcing Temporary Deemphasis of M1." October 13.

Andersen, Leonall C., and Jerry L. Jordan. 1968. "Monetary and Fiscal Actions: A Test of Their Importance in Economic Stabilization." *Federal Reserve Bank of St. Louis Review* 50 (11): 11–23.

Anderson, Martin. 1991. "Promises the Supply-Siders Made—and Didn't." *Wall Street Journal,* August 13.

Ando, Albert, and Franco Modigliani. 1965. "The Relative Stability of Monetary Velocity and the Investment Multiplier." *American Economic Review* 55 (4): 693–728.

Andrews, Edmund L. 2008. "Greenspan Concedes Error on Regulation." *New York Times,* October 23.

Bade, Robin, and Michael Parkin. 1988. "Central Bank Laws and Monetary Policy." Working Paper, University of Western Ontario, London, Ontario, October 1988. https://economics.uwo.ca/people/parkin_docs/CentralBankLaws.pdf

Ball, Deborah. 2018. "Mnuchin Brushes Off Concern about Dollar, Trade." *Wall Street Journal,* January 24.

Barr, Nicholas. 2004. "Phillips, Alban William Housego (1914–1975)." Oxford Dictionary of National Biography, September 23. https://www.oxforddnb.com/.

Barro, Robert J. 1977. "Unanticipated Money Growth and Unemployment in the United States." *American Economic Review* 67 (2): 101–15.

Barro, Robert J. 1979. "On the Determination of the Public Debt." *Journal of Political Economy* 87 (5): 940–71.

Barro, Robert J. 1986. "The Behavior of United States Deficits." In *The American Business Cycle: Continuity and Change*, ed. Robert J. Gordon, 361–94. Chicago: University of Chicago Press for NBER.

Beckner, Steven K. 1996. *Back from the Brink: The Greenspan Years.* New York: Wiley.

Benati, Luca, and Paolo Surico. 2009. "VAR Analysis and the Great Moderation." *American Economic Review* 99 (4): 1636–52.

Berke, Richard L. 1990. "The Budget Agreement: The Opposition; Rebellion Flares among Republicans over Accord." *New York Times*, October 2.

Bernanke, Ben S. 1983. "Nonmonetary Effects of the Financial Crisis in Propagation of the Great Depression." *American Economic Review* 73 (3): 257–76.

Bernanke, Ben S. 2002. "On Milton Friedman's Ninetieth Birthday." Remarks by Governor Ben S. Bernanke before the Conference to Honor Milton Friedman, University of Chicago, Chicago, November 8, 2002.

Bernanke, Ben S. 2004. "The Great Moderation." Remarks by Governor Ben S. Bernanke at the meetings of the Eastern Economic Association, Washington, DC, February 20, 2004.

Bernanke, Ben S. 2006. "Monetary Aggregates and Monetary Policy at the Federal Reserve: A Historical Perspective." Speech by Chairman Ben S. Bernanke at the Fourth ECB Central Banking Conference, Frankfurt, Germany, November 10, 2006.

Bernanke, Ben S. 2012a. "The Economic Club of New York, 426th Meeting, 105th Year, November 20, 2012: The Honorable Ben S. Bernanke, Chairman, Federal Reserve System." https://www.econclubny.org/documents/10184/109144/2012BernankeTranscript.pdf.

Bernanke, Ben S. 2012b. "Transcript of Chairman Bernanke's Press Conference, December 12, 2012." Board of Governors of the Federal Reserve System. https://www.federalreserve.gov/mediacenter/files/FOMCpresconf20121212.pdf.

Bernanke, Ben S. 2015. *The Courage to Act: A Memoir of a Crisis and Its Aftermath.* New York: Norton.

Berry, John M. 2001. "Greenspan Supports a Tax Cut." *Washington Post*, January 26, 2001.

Birnbaum, Jeffrey H., and Alan S. Murray. 1987. *Showdown at Gucci Gulch: Lawmakers, Lobbyists, and the Unlikely Triumph of Tax Reform.* New York: Random House.

Blanchard, Olivier J. 1984. "Current and Anticipated Deficits, Interest Rates and Economic Activity." *European Economic Review* 25 (1): 7–27.

Blanchard, Olivier J. 2019. "Public Debt and Low Interest Rates." *American Economic Review* 109 (4): 1197–229.

Blinder, Alan S. 1979. *Economic Policy and the Great Stagflation.* New York: Academic Press.

Blinder, Alan S. 1980. "The Consumer Price Index and the Measurement of Recent Inflation." *Brookings Papers on Economic Activity* 2: 539–65.

Blinder, Alan S. 1981a. "It's a Peter Pan Style of Economics." *Boston Globe*, April 10.

Blinder, Alan S. 1981b. "Temporary Income Taxes and Consumer Spending." *Journal of Political Economy* 89 (1): 26–53.

Blinder, Alan S. 1982. "The Anatomy of Double Digit Inflation in the 1970s." In *Inflation: Causes and Effect*, ed. Robert E. Hall, 261–82. Chicago: University of Chicago Press for NBER.

Blinder, Alan S. 1984. "Reaganomics and Growth: The Message in the Models." In *The Legacy of Reaganomics: Prospects for Long-Term Growth*, ed. Charles R. Hulten and Isabel V. Sawhill, 199–227. Washington, DC: Urban Institute Press.

Blinder, Alan S. 1987a. *Hard Heads, Soft Hearts: Tough-Minded Economics for a Just Society*. Reading, MA: Addison-Wesley.

Blinder, Alan S. 1987b. "Keynes, Lucas, and Scientific Progress." *American Economic Review* 77 (2): 130–36.

Blinder, Alan S. 1987c. "Paul Volcker was the Babe Ruth of Central Banking." *Business Week*, June 29.

Blinder, Alan S. 1988. "The Fall and Rise of Keynesian Economics." *Economic Record* 64 (4): 278–94.

Blinder, Alan S. 1990. "Can Congress Make the Budget Stick? Don't Bet on It." *Business Week*, December 31.

Blinder, Alan S. 1991. "Set the Record Straight on Violation of Trust." *Wall Street Journal*, August 21.

Blinder, Alan S. 2010. "In Defense of Ben Bernanke." *Wall Street Journal*, November 15.

Blinder, Alan S. 2013. *After the Music Stopped: The Financial Crisis, the Response, and the Work Ahead*. New York: Penguin Books.

Blinder, Alan S. 2018. *Advice and Dissent: Why America Suffers When Economics and Politics Collide*. New York: Basic Books.

Blinder, Alan S. 2021. "BPEA and Monetary Policy over 50 Years." *Brookings Papers on Economic Activity*, spring, 231–50.

Blinder, Alan S., and Stanley Fischer. 1981. "Inventories, Rational Expectations, and the Business Cycle." *Journal of Monetary Economics* 8 (3): 277–304.

Blinder, Alan S., and Douglas Holtz-Eakin. 1984. "Public Opinion and the Balanced Budget." *American Economic Review* 74 (2): 144–49.

Blinder, Alan S., and William J. Newton. 1981. "The 1971–1974 Controls Program and the Price Level: An Econometric Post-Mortem." *Journal of Monetary Economics* 8 (1): 1–23.

Blinder, Alan S., and Ricardo Reis. 2005. "Understanding the Greenspan Standard." In *Proceedings of the Federal Reserve Bank of Kansas City Symposium: The Greenspan Era; Lessons for the Future*, 11–96. Jackson Hole, WY, August 25–27, 2005. Kansas City, MO: Federal Reserve Bank of Kansas City.

Blinder, Alan S., and Jeremy B. Rudd. 2013. "The Supply-Shock Explanation of the Great Stagflation Revisited." In *The Great Inflation: The Rebirth of Modern Central Banking*, ed. Michael D. Bordo and Athanasios Orphanides, 119–75. Chicago: University of Chicago Press for NBER.

Blinder, Alan S., and Robert M. Solow. 1974. "Analytical Foundations of Fiscal Policy." In *The Economics of Public Finance: Essays*, ed. Alan S. Blinder, 3–115. Washington, DC: Brookings Institution Press.

Blinder, Alan S., and Janet L. Yellen. 2001. *The Fabulous Decade: Macroeconomic Lessons from the 1990s.* New York: Century Foundation Press.

Blinder, Alan S., and Mark Zandi. 2010. "How the Great Recession Was Brought to an End." *Moody's Analytics*, July 27, 2010.

Bordo, Michael D., and Barry Eichengreen. 2013. "Bretton Woods and the Great Inflation." In *The Great Inflation: The Rebirth of Modern Central Banking*, ed. Michael D. Bordo and Athanasios Orphanides, 449–89. Chicago: University of Chicago Press for NBER.

Bordo, Michael D., Christopher Erceg, Andrew Levin, and Ryan Michaels. 2017. "Policy Credibility and Alternative Approaches to Disinflation." *Research in Economics* 71 (3): 422–40.

Bordo, Michael D., and Athanasios Orphanides, eds. 2013. *The Great Inflation: The Rebirth of Modern Central Banking.* Chicago: University of Chicago Press for NBER.

Boston Herald. 2007. "McCain Says Greenspan's His Choice, Dead or Alive." October 6. https://www.bostonherald.com/2007/10/06/mccain-says-greenspans-his-choice-dead-or-alive/.

Bouey, Gerald K. 1982. "Monetary Policy–Finding a Place to Stand." Per Jacobsson Lecture, University of Toronto, September 5, 1982. Washington, DC: Per Jacobsson Foundation, International Monetary Fund. http://www.perjacobsson.org/lectures/1982.pdf.

Brenan, Megan. 2019. "Tax Day Update: Americans Still Not Seeing Tax Cut Benefit." Gallup News, April 12, 2019. https://news.gallup.com/poll/248681/tax-day-update-americans-not-seeing-tax-cut-benefit.aspx.

Broda, Christian, and Jonathan A. Parker. 2014. "The Economic Stimulus Payments of 2008 and the Aggregate Demand for Consumption." *Journal of Monetary Economics* 68 (December): S20–36.

Brown, E. Cary. 1956. "Fiscal Policy in the 'Thirties: A Reappraisal." *American Economic Review* 46 (5): 857–79.

Brunner, Karl. 1968. "The Role of Money and Monetary Policy." *Federal Reserve Bank of St. Louis Review* 50 (7): 9–24.

Bruno, Michael, and Jeffrey D. Sachs, 1985. *Economics of Worldwide Stagflation.* Cambridge, MA: Harvard University Press.

Burns, Arthur F. 1979. "The Anguish of Central Banking." Per Jacobssen Lecture, Belgrade, Yugoslavia, September 30, 1979. Washington, DC: Per Jacobssen Foundation, International Monetary Fund. http://www.perjacobsson.org/lectures/1979.pdf.

Bush, George W. 2000. "Address Accepting the Presidential Nomination at the Republican National Convention, Philadelphia, August 3, 2000." The American Presidency Project. https://www.presidency.ucsb.edu/node/211699.

Bush, George W. 2006. "Remarks to the Business and Industry Association of New Hampshire, Manchester, NH, February 8, 2006." The American Presidency Project. https://www.presidency.ucsb.edu/node/214730.

Campbell, John Y., and Robert J. Shiller. 1991. "Yield Spreads and Interest Rate Movements: A Bird's Eye View." *Review of Economic Studies* 58 (3): 495–514.

Carter, James Earl, Jr. 1979. Transcript of "Crisis of Confidence" Speech, July 15, 1979. The Miller Center of Public Affairs, University of Virginia. https://web.archive.org/web/20090721024329/http://millercenter.org/scripps/archive/speeches/detail/3402.

Case, Karl E., and Robert J. Shiller. 2003. "Is There a Bubble in the Housing Market?" *Brookings Papers on Economic Activity* 2: 299–362.

Cassidy, John. 2010. "On Tim Geithner." *The New Yorker*, March 9.

CBO (Congressional Budget Office). 1990. *The 1990 Budget Agreement: An Interim Assessment.* CBO Papers 217, December 1990. Washington, DC: CBO. https://www.cbo.gov/sites/default/files/101st-congress-1989-1990/reports/90doc217.pdf.

CBO (Congressional Budget Office). 1997. *The Economic and Budget Outlook: Fiscal Years 1998–2007.* CBO Report 10330, January 1997. Washington, DC: CBO. https://www.cbo.gov/publication/10330.

CBO (Congressional Budget Office). 1998a. *The Economic and Budget Outlook: Fiscal Years 1999–2008.* CBO Report 10607, January 1998. Washington, DC: CBO. https://www.cbo.gov/publication/10607.

CBO (Congressional Budget Office). 1998b. *Projecting Federal Tax Revenues and the Effect of Changes in Tax Law.* CBO Paper, December 1998. Washington, DC: CBO.

CBO (Congressional Budget Office). 2000. *The Budget and Economic Outlook: An Update.* CBO Report 12477, July 2000. Washington, DC: CBO. https://www.cbo.gov/publication/12477.

CBO (Congressional Budget Office). 2001. *The Budget and Economic Outlook: Fiscal Years 2002–2011.* CBO Testimony before the Committee on the Budget, U.S. Senate, January 31, 2001. Washington, DC: CBO. https://www.cbo.gov/sites/default/files/107th-congress-2001-2002/reports/entire-testimony.pdf.

CBO (Congressional Budget Office). 2004a. *The Budget and Economic Outlook: Fiscal Years 2005–2014.* CBO Report 15179, January 2004. Washington, DC: CBO. https://www.cbo.gov/publication/15179.

CBO (Congressional Budget Office). 2004b. *A Detailed Description of CBO's Cost Estimate for the Medicare Prescription Drug Benefit.* CBO Paper, July 2004. Washington, DC: CBO. https://www.cbo.gov/sites/default/files/108th-congress-2003-2004/reports/07-21-medicare.pdf.

CBO (Congressional Budget Office). 2014. *Competition and the Cost of Medicare's Prescription Drug Program.* CBO Report to the Chairman of the Subcommittee on Health Care of the Senate Finance Committee, 45552, July 2014. Washington, DC: CBO. https://www.cbo.gov/publication/45552 and https://www.cbo.gov/sites/default/files/113th-congress-2013-2014/reports/45552-PartD.pdf.

CBO (Congressional Budget Office). 2017a. *CBO's Economic Forecasting Record: 2017 Update.* CBO Report 53090, October 2017. Washington, DC: CBO. https://www.cbo.gov/system/files/115th-congress-2017-2018/reports/53090-economicforecastaccuracy.pdf.

CBO (Congressional Budget Office). 2017b. *An Update to the Budget and Economic Outlook: 2017 to 2027.* CBO Report 52801, June 29, 2017. Washington, DC: CBO. https://www.cbo.gov/publication/52801.

CBO (Congressional Budget Office). 2019. *The Budget and Economic Outlook: 2019 to 2029.* CBO Report 54918, January 2019. Washington, DC: CBO. www.cbo.gov/publication/54918.

CBO (Congressional Budget Office). 2021. Budget and Economic Data: Potential GDP and Underlying Inputs. Washington, DC: CBO. https://www.cbo.gov/data/budget-economic-data#6.

CBO (Congressional Budget Office). 2022. Noncyclical Rate of Unemployment [NROU Dataset]. Retrieved from FRED, Federal Reserve Bank of St. Louis. https://fred.stlouisfed.org/series/NROU.

CEA (Council of Economic Advisers). 1964. *Economic Report of the President,* January 1964. Washington, DC: U.S. Government Printing Office.

CEA (Council of Economic Advisers). 1965. *Economic Report of the President.* Washington, DC: U.S. Government Printing Office.

CEA (Council of Economic Advisers). 1968. *Economic Report of the President.* Washington, DC: U.S. Government Printing Office.

CEA (Council of Economic Advisers). 1969. *Economic Report of the President: Hearings before the Joint Economic Committee, Congress of the United States.* Washington, DC: U.S. Government Printing Office.

CEA (Council of Economic Advisers). 2017. *Corporate Tax Reform and Wages: Theory and Evidence.* October 2017. Washington, DC: U.S. Government Printing Office. https://trumpwhitehouse.archives.gov/sites/whitehouse.gov/files/documents/Tax%20Reform%20and%20Wages.pdf.

Chandler, Adam. 2017. "Why Would Trump Want a Weaker Dollar? *The Atlantic,* January 18, 2017.

Chodorow-Reich, Gabriel, Laura Feiveson, Zachary Liscow, and William Gui Woolston. 2012. "Does State Fiscal Relief during Recessions Increase Employment? Evidence from the American Recovery and Reinvestment Act." *American Economic Journal: Economic Policy* 4 (3): 118–45.

Christiano, Lawrence J., Martin Eichenbaum, and Charles L. Evans. 1999. "Monetary Policy Shocks: What Have We Learned and to What End?" In *The Handbook of Macroeconomics,* Vol. 1A, ed. John B. Taylor and Michael Woodford, 65–148. Amsterdam: North-Holland.

Clinton, William J. 1992. *Putting People First: How We Can All Change America.* New York: Three Rivers.

Clinton, William J. 1998. State of the Union Address, January 27, 1998. William J. Clinton Presidential Library. The Miller Center of the University of Virginia. https://millercenter.org/the-presidency/presidential-speeches/january-27-1998-state-union-address.

Clinton, William J. 2011. *Back to Work.* New York: Knopf.

CNN (Cable News Network)/Knight Ridder. 1992. Gallup/CNN/Knight Ridder Poll: Town Meeting Study 31088130, Version 3. Gallup Organization. Cornell

University, Ithaca, NY: Roper Center for Public Opinion Research. https://ropercenter.cornell.edu/ipoll/study/31088130.

Cochrane, Emily. 2021. "Congress Clears $1.9 Trillion Aid Bill, Sending It to Biden." *New York Times*, March 10.

Colvin, Jill. 2020. "As Americans Take Virus Precautions, Trump Flouts Advice." *Associated Press News*, March 10. https://apnews.com/article/michael-pence-public-health-donald-trump-ap-top-news-virus-outbreak-55466402fcfd1234f4120623f364772a.

Condon, Christopher. 2019. "Key Trump Quotes on Powell as Fed Remains in the Firing Line." Bloomberg News, August 22.

Cox, Jeff. 2018. "Trump Lays into the Federal Reserve, Says He's 'Not Thrilled' about Interest Rate Hikes." CNBC News, July 19. https://www.cnbc.com/2018/07/19/trump-lays-into-the-fed-says-hes-not-thrilled-about-interest-rate-.html.

CRFB (Committee for a Responsible Federal Budget). 2017. "Today's CBO Report Makes Clear Just How Far the President's Budget Is from Balance." CRFB Press Release, July 13. https://www.crfb.org/press-releases/todays-cbo-report-makes-clear-just-how-far-presidents-budget-balance.

Davidson, Kate. 2017. "Treasury Secretary Steven Mnuchin: GOP Tax Plan Would More Than Offset Its Cost." *Wall Street Journal*, September 28.

Dionne, E. J., Jr. 1988. "Political Memo; Yes, Late Voter Swings Do Happen, but Underdogs Can't Count on Them." *New York Times*, November 5.

Draghi, Mario. 2012. Speech by the European Central Bank President at the Global Investment Conference, London, July 26, 2012. https://www.ecb.europa.eu/press/key/date/2012/html/sp120726.en.html.

Eckstein, Otto. 1981. *Core Inflation*. New York: Prentice Hall.

The Economist. 2011. "The Rise of the Anti-Keynesians: Paul Ryan's Intellectual Hinterland." April 14, 2011.

Eisner, Robert. 1969. "What Went Wrong?" *Journal of Political Economy* 79 (3): 629–41.

Eizenstat, Stuart E. 2018. *President Carter: The White House Years*. New York: St. Martin's.

Elliott, Larry. 2019. "Trump Raises Pressure on Federal Reserve to Cut Interest Rates." *The Guardian*, August 21, 2019.

Evans, Paul. 1987. "Do Budget Deficits Raise Nominal Interest Rates? Evidence from Six Countries." *Journal of Monetary Economics* 20 (2): 281–300.

Fair, Ray C. 1978. "The Effect of Economic Events on Votes for President." *Review of Economics and Statistics* 60 (2): 159–73.

Fair, Ray C. 1993. "Testing the Rational Expectations Hypothesis." *Oxford Economic Papers* 45 (2): 169–90.

Faulkender, Michael, Robert Jackman, and Stephen I. Miran. 2022. "The Job-Preservation Effects of Paycheck Protection Program Loans." Office of Economic Policy Working Paper, U.S. Department of the Treasury.

FCIC (Financial Crisis Inquiry Commission). 2011. *The Financial Crisis Inquiry Report: Final Report to the National Commission on the Causes of the Financial and Economic Crisis in the United States.* Washington, DC: U.S. Government Printing Office.

Federal Reserve Act. 1913. Section 14, Open-Market Operations, December 1913. https://www.federalreserve.gov/aboutthefed/section14.htm.

Federal Reserve Bank of St. Louis. 2022. FRED (Federal Reserve Economic Data), FRASER (Federal Reserve Archival System for Economic Research). https://fred.stlouisfed.org/ and https://www.loc.gov/item/lcwaN0003909.

Federal Reserve System. 2006. "G. William Miller, 1925–2006." *Federal Reserve History.* Federal Reserve Bank of St. Louis. https://www.federalreservehistory.org/people/g_william_miller.

Federal Reserve System, Board of Governors. 2008. "Board Announces Creation of the Commercial Paper Funding Facility (CPFF) to Help Provide Liquidity to Term Funding Markets." Board of Governors of the Federal Reserve System Press Release, October 7, 2008. https://www.federalreserve.gov/newsevents/pressreleases/monetary20081007c.htm.

Federal Reserve System, Board of Governors. 2022. Main Street Lending Program. https://www.federalreserve.gov/monetarypolicy/mainstreetlending.htm.

Feldstein, Martin. 1994. *American Economic Policy in the 1980s.* Chicago: University of Chicago Press.

Feyrer, James, and Bruce Sacerdote. 2011. "Did the Stimulus Stimulate? Real Time Estimates of the Effects of the American Recovery and Reinvestment Act." NBER Working Paper 16759. Cambridge, MA: National Bureau of Economic Research.

Fischer, Stanley. 1977. "Long-Term Contracts, Rational Expectations, and the Optimal Money Supply Rule." *Journal of Political Economy* 85 (1): 191–206.

FOMC (Federal Open Market Committee). n.d. Washington, DC: Board of Governors of the Federal Reserve System. https://www.federalreserve.gov/monetarypolicy/fomc.htm.

FOMC (Federal Open Market Committee). 1975. "Meeting, February 19, 1975: Memorandum of Discussion." Washington, DC: Board of Governors of the Federal Reserve System.

FOMC (Federal Open Market Committee). 1982. "Meeting, October 5, 1982: Transcript." Washington, DC: Board of Governors of the Federal Reserve System.

FOMC (Federal Open Market Committee). 1994a. "Federal Reserve Press Release." Board of Governors of the Federal Reserve System Press Release, February 4, 1994.

FOMC (Federal Open Market Committee). 1994b. "Meeting, February 3–4, 1994: Transcript." Washington, DC: Board of Governors of the Federal Reserve System.

FOMC (Federal Open Market Committee). 2004. "Meeting, January 27–28, 2004: Transcript." Washington, DC: Board of Governors of the Federal Reserve System.

FOMC (Federal Open Market Committee). 2010a. "Meeting, January 26–27, 2010: Transcript." Washington, DC: Board of Governors of the Federal Reserve System.

FOMC (Federal Open Market Committee). 2010b. "Meeting, April 27–28, 2010: Transcript." Washington, DC: Board of Governors of the Federal Reserve System.

FOMC (Federal Open Market Committee). 2011. "Meeting, August 9, 2011: Transcript." Washington, DC: Board of Governors of the Federal Reserve System.

FOMC (Federal Open Market Committee). 2012a. "Federal Reserve Issues FOMC Statement." Board of Governors of the Federal Reserve System Press Release, January 25, 2012.

FOMC (Federal Open Market Committee). 2012b. "Federal Reserve Issues FOMC Statement." Board of Governors of the Federal Reserve System Press Release, December 12, 2012.

FOMC (Federal Open Market Committee). 2013. "Federal Reserve Issues FOMC Statement." Board of Governors of the Federal Reserve System Press Release, December 18, 2013.

FOMC (Federal Open Market Committee). 2014. "Federal Reserve Issues FOMC Statement." Board of Governors of the Federal Reserve System Press Release, March 19, 2014.

FOMC (Federal Open Market Committee). 2020a. "Federal Reserve Issues FOMC Statement." Board of Governors of the Federal Reserve System Press Release, March 3, 2020.

FOMC (Federal Open Market Committee). 2020b. "Federal Reserve Press Release." Board of Governors of the Federal Reserve System, March 23, 2020.

FOMC (Federal Open Market Committee). 2020c. "Federal Reserve Press Release." Board of Governors of the Federal Reserve System, July 29, 2020.

FOMC (Federal Open Market Committee). 2021. "Federal Reserve Issues FOMC Statement." Board of Governors of the Federal Reserve System, November 3, 2021.

Friedman, Milton. 1948. "A Monetary and Fiscal Framework for Economic Stability." *American Economic Review* 38 (3): 245–64.

Friedman, Milton. 1956. "The Quantity Theory of Money–A Restatement." In *Studies in the Quantity Theory of Money*, ed. Milton Friedman, 1–21. Chicago: University of Chicago Press.

Friedman, Milton. 1957. *A Theory of the Consumption Function*. Princeton, NJ: Princeton University Press.

Friedman, Milton. 1959. "The Demand for Money: Some Theoretical and Empirical Results. *Journal of Political Economy* 67 (4): 327–51.

Friedman, Milton. 1960. *A Program for Monetary Stability*. New York: Fordham University Press.

Friedman, Milton. 1968. "The Role of Monetary Policy." *American Economic Review* 58 (1): 1–17.

Friedman, Milton. 1969. *The Optimum Quantity of Money and Other Essays.* Chicago: Aldine.

Friedman, Milton. 1974a. "Is Money Too Tight?" *Newsweek*, September 23.

Friedman, Milton. 1974b. "Perspective on Inflation." *Newsweek*, June 24.

Friedman, Milton. 1975a. "Congress and the Federal Reserve." *Newsweek*, June 2.

Friedman, Milton. 1975b. "Perspectives on Inflation." *Newsweek*, June 24.

Friedman, Milton. 1979. *Free to Choose: A Personal Statement*. New York: Harcourt Brace Jovanovich.

Friedman, Milton. 1980. "Monetary Overkill." *Newsweek*, July 14.

Friedman, Milton. 2017. *Milton Friedman on Freedom: Selections from the Collected Works of Milton Friedman*. Edited by Robert Leeson and Charles G. Palm. Stanford, CA: Hoover Institution Press.

Friedman, Milton, and Rose D. Friedman. 1962. *Capitalism and Freedom*. Chicago: University of Chicago Press.

Friedman, Milton, and Walter W. Heller. 1969. *Monetary vs. Fiscal Policy*. New York: Norton.

Friedman, Milton, and David Meiselman. 1963. "The Relative Stability of Monetary Velocity and the Investment Multiplier in the United States, 1897–1958." In *Stabilization Policies*, 165–268. Commission on Money and Credit. Englewood Cliffs, NJ: Prentice Hall.

Friedman, Milton, and David Meiselman. 1965. "Reply to Ando and Modigliani and to DePrano and Mayer." *American Economic Review* 55 (4): 753–85.

Friedman, Milton, and Anna Jacobson Schwartz. 1963. *A Monetary History of the United States, 1867–1960*. Princeton, NJ: Princeton University Press.

Fullerton, Don, and Yolanda Kodrzycki Henderson. 1984. "Incentive Effects of Taxes on Income from Capital: Alternative Policies in the 1980s." In *The Legacy of Reaganomics: Prospects for Long-Term Growth*, ed. Charles R. Hulten and Isabel V. Sawhill, 45–90. Washington, DC: Urban Institute Press.

Fuster, Andreas, Greg Kaplan, and Basit Zafar. 2021. "What Would You Do with $500? Spending Responses to Gains, Losses, News, and Loans." *Review of Economic Studies* 88 (4): 1760–95.

Gali, Jordi, and Luca Gambetti. 2009. "On the Sources of the Great Moderation." *American Economic Journal: Macroeconomics* 1 (1): 26–57.

Gallup Organization. 2001. "Presidential Approval Ratings—Bill Clinton." Gallup News, November 9, 2021. https://news.gallup.com/poll/116584/presidential-approval-ratings-bill-clinton.aspx.

Gallup Organization. 2017. Gallup Poll: December 2017, Question 1, USGALLUP. 120617A.R03 [Dataset]. Cornell University, Ithaca, NY: Roper Center for Public Opinion Research. https://news.gallup.com/poll/1714/taxes.aspx.

Ganong, Peter, Pascal J. Noel, and Joseph S. Vavra. 2020. "US Unemployment Insurance Replacement Rates During the Pandemic." *Journal of Public Economics* 191 (104273): 1–12.

GAO (General Accounting Office [now Government Accountability Office]). 1996. *Financial Audit: Resolution Trust Corporation's 1995 and 1994 Financial Statements*, GAO/AIMD-96-123. Washington, DC: Accounting and Information Management Division.

Garten, Jeffrey E. 2021. *Three Days at Camp David: How a Secret Meeting in 1971 Transformed the Global Economy*. New York: HarperCollins.

Geithner, Timothy F. 2014. *Stress Test: Reflections on Financial Crises*. New York: Broadway Books.

Goldfeld, Stephen M. 1976. "The Case of the Missing Money." *Brookings Papers on Economic Activity* 3: 683–739.

Goldfeld, Stephen M., and Alan S. Blinder. 1972. "Some Implications of Endogenous Stabilization Policy." *Brookings Papers on Economic Activity* 3: 585–644.

Goodman, Peter S. 2008. "Taking Hard New Look at a Greenspan Legacy." *New York Times*, October 9.

Goodwin, Doris Kearns. 1976. *Lyndon Johnson and the American Dream*. New York: Harper & Row.

Goolsbee, Austan. 2008. "Looking for Lasting Solutions." *Face the Nation*, CBS News. Transcript of interview with Bob Schieffer, November 23. http://www.cbsnews.com/htdocs/pdf/FTN_112308.pdf.

Goolsbee, Austan, and Chad Syverson. 2021. "Fear, Lockdown, and Diversion: Comparing Drivers of Pandemic Economic Decline 2020." *Journal of Public Economics* 193 (January): 104311. SI: The Public Economics of COVID-19.

Gordon, Robert J. 1970. "The Recent Acceleration of Inflation and Its Lessons for the Future." *Brookings Papers on Economic Activity* 1: 8–47.

Gordon, Robert J. 1972. "Wage-Price Controls and the Shifting Phillips Curve." *Brookings Papers on Economic Activity* 2: 385–421.

Gordon, Robert J. 1975. "The Impact of Aggregate Demand on Prices." *Brookings Papers on Economic Activity* 3: 613–70.

Gordon, Robert J. 1977. "Can the Inflation of the 1970s Be Explained?" *Brookings Papers on Economic Activity* 1: 253–79.

Gordon, Robert J. 1982. "Price Inertia and Policy Ineffectiveness in the United States, 1890–1980." *Journal of Political Economy* 90 (6): 1087–117.

Gordon, Robert J., ed. 1986. *The American Business Cycle: Continuity and Change*. Chicago: University of Chicago Press for NBER.

Gordon, Robert J. 2011. "The History of the Phillips Curve: Consensus and Bifurcation." *Economica* 78 (309): 10–50. SI: A. W. H. Phillips 50th Anniversary Symposium.

Gorton, Gary B. 2010. *Slapped by the Invisible Hand: The Panic of 2007*. New York: Oxford University Press.

Granville, Kevin. 2017. "A President at War with His Fed Chief, 5 Decades before Trump." *New York Times*, June 13.

Greenhouse, Steven. 1993. "Fed Abandons Policy Tied to Money Supply." *New York Times*, July 23.

Greenspan, Alan. 1993. "Semiannual Monetary Policy Report to the Congress." Testimony of Alan Greenspan before the Committee on Banking, Finance, and Urban Affairs, U.S. Senate, February 19. Washington, DC: Board of Governors of the Federal Reserve System.

Greenspan, Alan. 2007. *The Age of Turbulence: Adventures in a New World*. New York: Penguin Books.

Grilli, Vittorio, Donato Masciandaro, Guido Tabellini, Edmond Malinvaud, and Marco Pagano. 1991. "Political and Monetary Institutions and Public Financial Policies in the Industrial Countries." *Economic Policy* 6 (13): 342–92.

Gupta, Sumedha, Kosali I. Simon, and Coady Wing. 2020. "Mandated and Voluntary Social Distancing during the COVID-19 Epidemic: A Review." *Brookings Papers on Economic Activity*, Summer, 269–326.

Haberman, Maggie, and David E. Sanger. 2020. "Trump Says Coronavirus Cure Cannot 'Be Worse Than the Problem Itself.'" *New York Times*, March 23.

Hamilton, James D., and Jing Cynthia Wu. 2012. "The Effectiveness of Alternative Monetary Policy Tools in a Zero Lower Bound Environment." *Journal of Money, Credit, and Banking* 44 (1): 3–46.

Hansell, Saul. 1999. "Business Travel; Priceline.com Stock Zooms in Offering." *New York Times*, March 31.

Hansen, Alvin. 1939. "Economic Progress and Declining Population Growth." *American Economic Review* 29 (1): 1–15.

Hegel, Georg Wilhelm Friedrich. 1899. *The Philosophy of History*, Vol. 10. Translated by J. Sibree. New York: Colonial Press. https://www.bartleby.com/73/570.html.

Heller, Walter W. 1966. *New Dimensions of Political Economy*. Godkin Lectures on the Essentials of Free Government and the Duties of the Citizen. Cambridge, MA: Harvard University Press.

Hirsh, Michael. 2009. "The Party of Goldwater?" *Newsweek,* January 28.

Holston, Kathryn, Thomas Laubach, and John C. Williams. 2016. "Measuring the Natural Rate of Interest: International Trends and Determinants." Federal Reserve Bank of San Francisco Working Paper 2016-11, December. https://doi.org/10.24148/wp2016-11.

Hulse, Carl, and David M. Herszenhorn. 2008. "Behind Closed Doors, Warnings of Calamity." *New York Times*, September 19.

Ice Data Indices, LLC. 2022. ICE Bank of America US High Yield Index Effective Yield [BAMLH0A0HYM2EY]. Retrieved from FRED, Federal Reserve Bank of St. Louis. https://fred.stlouisfed.org/series/BAMLH0A0HYM2EY.

Iša, Ján. 2006. "Profiles of World Economists: Nicholas Kaldor–One of the First Critics of Monetarism." *Biatec* 14 (12): 26–30. National Bank of Slovakia, Bratislava. https://www.nbs.sk/_img/Documents/BIATEC/BIA12_06/26_30.pdf.

Jacobs, Jennifer, and Billy House. 2016. "Trump Says He Expected to Lose Election Because of Poll Results." Bloomberg News, December 13.

Jordan, Jerry L. 1986. "The Andersen-Jordan Approach after Nearly 20 Years." *Federal Reserve Bank of St. Louis Review* 68 (8): 5–8.

Kennedy, John F. 1962. Commencement Address at Yale University, New Haven, CT, June 11, 1962. https://www.jfklibrary.org/archives/other-resources/john-f-kennedy-speeches/yale-university-19620611.

Kilborn, Peter T. 1987a. "The Business Cycle Rolls Over and Plays Dead." *New York Times*, January 11.

Kilborn, Peter T. 1987b. "Walter Heller, 71, Economic Adviser in 60s, Dead." *New York Times*, June 17.

Kilian, Lutz. 2008. "The Economic Effects of Energy Price Shocks." *Journal of Economic Literature* 46 (4): 871–909.

Kindleberger, Charles P. 1978. *Manias, Panics, and Crashes: A History of Financial Crises*. New York: Basic Books.

King, Robert G., and Charles I. Plosser. 1984. "Money, Credit, and Prices in a Real Business Cycle." *American Economic Review* 74 (3): 363–80.

Klamer, Arjo. 1984. *The New Classical Macroeconomics: Conversations with New Classical Economists and Their Opponents*. Brighton, UK: Wheatsheaf Books.

Kliesen, Kevin L. 2002. "Die Another Day? Budget Deficits and Interest Rates." Federal Reserve Bank of St. Louis, National Economic Trends, December 2002. https://files.stlouisfed.org/files/htdocs/datatrends/pdfs/net/20021201/cover .pdf.

Krishnamurthy, Arvind, and Annette Vissing-Jorgensen. 2011. "The Effects of Quantitative Easing on Interest Rates: Channels and Implications for Policy." *Brookings Papers on Economic Activity*, Fall, 215–87.

Krugman, Paul R. 2001. *Fuzzy Math: The Essential Guide to the Bush Tax Plan*. New York: Norton.

Kudlow, Larry. 2010. "Kudlow's Money Politics: My Interview with George W. Bush." *National Review,* November 2, 2010. https://www.nationalreview.com /kudlows-money-politics/my-interview-george-w-bush-larry-kudlow/.

Kydland, Finn E., and Edward C. Prescott. 1977. "Rules Rather Than Discretion: The Inconsistency of Optimal Plans." *Journal of Political Economy* 85 (3): 473–91.

Kydland, Finn E., and Edward C. Prescott. 1982. "Time to Build and Aggregate Fluctuations." *Econometrica* 50 (6): 1345–70.

La Monica, Paul R. 2016. "Trump: Janet Yellen Should Be 'Ashamed of Herself.'" *CNN Money*, September 13, 2016. https://money.cnn.com/2016/09/13 /investing/stocks-donald-trump-janet-yellen-federal-reserve/index.html.

Leeper, Eric M. 1991. "Equilibria under 'Active' and 'Passive' Monetary and Fiscal Policies." *Journal of Monetary Economics* 27 (1): 129–47.

Leonhardt, David. 2001. "Back in Business; Supply-Side Economists Regain Influence under Bush." *New York Times*, April 10.

Lipsey, Richard G. 1960. "The Relation between Unemployment and the Rate of Change of Money Wage Rates in the United Kingdom, 1862–1957: A Further Analysis." *Economica* 27 (105): 1–31.

Louis Harris & Associates. 1977. Louis Harris Poll: September 1977, Question 71, [USHARRIS.103177.R1]. Cornell University, Ithaca, NY: Roper Center for Public Opinion Research. https://ropercenter.cornell.edu/ipoll/study/31103250.

Lovell, Michael C. 1986. "Tests of the Rational Expectations Hypothesis." *American Economic Review* 76 (1): 110–24.

Lucas, Robert E., Jr. 1972a. "Econometric Testing of the Natural Rate Hypothesis." In *The Econometrics of Price Determination: Conference, October 30–31, 1970*, ed. Otto Eckstein, 50–59. Washington, DC: Board of Governors of the Federal Reserve System.

Lucas, Robert E., Jr. 1972b. "Expectations and the Neutrality of Money." *Journal of Economic Theory* 4 (2): 103–24.

Lucas, Robert E., Jr. 1973. "Some International Evidence on Output-Inflation Trade-offs." *American Economic Review* 63 (3): 326–34.

Lucas, Robert E., Jr. 1976. "Econometric Policy Evaluation: A Critique." *Carnegie-Rochester Conference Series on Public Policy* 1 (1): 19–46.

Lucas, Robert E., Jr. 1995. "Robert E. Lucas Jr., Biographical." NobelPrize.org. Nobel Prize Outreach. https://www.nobelprize.org/prizes/economic-sciences /1995/lucas/biographical/.

Lucas, Robert E., Jr., and Leonard A. Rapping. 1969. "Price Expectations and the Phillips Curve." *American Economic Review* 59 (3): 342–50.

Lucas, Robert E., Jr., and Thomas J. Sargent. 1978. "After Keynesian Macroeconomics." In *After the Phillips Curve: Persistence of High Inflation and High Unemployment*, 49–83. Federal Reserve Bank of Boston Conference Series 19. Federal Reserve Bank of Boston.

Lundberg, Erik. 1985. "The Rise and Fall of the Swedish Model." *Journal of Economic Literature* 23 (1): 1–36.

Macleod, Iain. 1965. "Economic Affairs." Hansard Transcript of House of Commons Debate, U.K. Parliament, Vol. 720, Cols. 1155–284, November 17, 1965. https://hansard.parliament.uk/Commons/1965-11-17/debates/06338c6d-ebdd -4876-a782-59cbd531a28a/EconomicAffairs?highlight=stagflation.

Martin, William McChesney, Jr. 1955. Address before the New York Group of the Investment Bankers Association of America, New York, October 19, 1955. Board of Governors of the Federal Reserve System. https://fraser.stlouisfed .org/title/448/item/7800.

Mayer, Martin. 1990. *The Greatest-Ever Bank Robbery: The Collapse of the Savings and Loan Industry.* New York: Scribner.

McMahon, Madeline. 2015. "Trump: Janet Yellen Keeping Interest Rates Low as Political Favor to Obama." Bloomberg News, October 16.

Meltzer, Allan H. 1995. "Monetary, Credit and (Other) Transmission Processes: A Monetarist Perspective." *Journal of Economic Perspectives* 9 (4): 49–72.

Meltzer, Allan H. 2009a. *A History of the Federal Reserve*, Vol. 2, Bk. 1, *1951–1969.* Chicago: University of Chicago Press.

Meltzer, Allan H. 2009b. *A History of the Federal Reserve*, Vol. 2, Bk. 2, *1970–1986.* Chicago: University of Chicago Press.

Meltzer, Allan H. 2009c. "Policy Principles." In *The Road Ahead for the Fed*, ed. John D. Ciorciari and John B. Taylor, 13–52. Stanford, CA: Hoover Institute Press.

Meltzer, Allan H. 2009d. "Preventing the Next Financial Crisis." *Wall Street Journal,* October 22.

Meyer, Laurence H. 2004. *A Term at the Fed: An Insider's View.* New York: HarperCollins.

Mishkin, Frederic S. 1982. "Does Anticipated Monetary Policy Matter? An Econometric Investigation." *Journal of Political Economy* 90 (1): 22–51.

Mishkin, Frederic S. 1995. "Symposium of the Monetary Transmission Mechanism." *Journal of Economic Perspectives* 9 (4): 3–10.

Mitchell, Daniel. 1992. "Bad Numbers, the Price for Bad Tax Policy." *Wall Street Journal,* July 28.

Mohr, Charles. 1976. "Vance Is Selected by Carter to Run State Department." *New York Times*, December 4.

Moore, Stephen. 1992. "Crime of the Century: The 1990 Budget Deal after Two Years." Cato Institute Policy Analysis 182, October 12. https://www.cato.org /sites/cato.org/files/pubs/pdf/pa182.pdf.

Moynihan, Daniel Patrick. 1986. "The Diary of a Senator." *Newsweek*, August 25.

Muller, Christopher. 2015. "Delivering Food to the Front Door: A New, or Very Old, Convenience?" Boston Hospitality Review, Boston University School of Hospitality Administration. https://www.bu.edu/bhr/2015/02/01/780/.

Mundell, Robert A. 1960. "The Monetary Dynamics of International Adjustment under Fixed and Flexible Exchange Rates." *Quarterly Journal of Economics* 84: 227–57.

Mundell, Robert A. 1971. "The Dollar and the Policy Mix: 1971." *Essays in International Finance* 85:1–40. International Finance Section, Department of Economics, Princeton University. Princeton, NJ: Princeton University Press.

Muth, John F. 1961. "Rational Expectations and the Theory of Price Movements." *Econometrica* 29 (3): 315–35.

Nelson, Edward. 2007. "Milton Friedman on Inflation." Federal Reserve Bank of St. Louis Economic Synopses 1. https://doi.org/10.20955/es.2007.1.

Nelson, Edward. 2013. "Milton Friedman and the Federal Reserve Chairs, 1951–1979." Working Paper presented at Economics History Seminar, University of California, Berkeley, October 23. http://citeseerx.ist.psu.edu/viewdoc/download ?doi=10.1.1.404.5347&rep=rep1&type=pdf.

Nelson, Edward. 2020. *Milton Friedman and Economic Debate in the United States, 1932–1972,* Vol. 2. Chicago: University of Chicago Press.

Newport, Frank. 2009. "Views on Government Aid Depend on the Program." Gallup News, February 24. https://news.gallup.com/poll/116083/views-government -aid-depend-program.aspx.

New York Times. 1987. "Arthur F. Burns Is Dead at 83; A Shaper of Economic Policy." June 27. https://timesmachine.nytimes.com/timesmachine/1987/06/27 /754287.html?pageNumber=1.

Nixon, Richard M. 1962. *Six Crises*. Garden City, NY: Doubleday.

Nixon, Richard M. 1972. Transcript of a Recording of a Meeting between the President and H. R. Haldeman in the Oval Office, The White House, Washington, DC, June 23. Richard Nixon Presidential Library & Museum, Yorba Linda, CA. https://www.nixonlibrary.gov/sites/default/files/forresearchers/find/tapes /watergate/wspf/741-002.pdf.

Noble, Holcomb B. 2002. "James Tobin, Nobel Laureate in Economics and an Adviser to Kennedy, Is Dead at 84." *New York Times*, March 13.

Nordhaus, William D. 2007. "Who's Afraid of a Big Bad Oil Shock?" *Brookings Papers on Economic Activity* 2: 219–38.

Obama, Barack. 2020. *A Promised Land*. New York: Crown.

O'Brien, Patrick Joseph. 1935. *Will Rogers: Ambassador of Good Will, Prince of Wit and Wisdom*. Philadelphia: John C. Winston.

Okun, Arthur M. 1970. *The Political Economy of Prosperity*. Washington, DC: Brookings Institution Press.

Okun, Arthur M. 1971. "The Personal Tax Surcharge and Consumer Demand, 1968–70." *Brookings Papers on Economic Activity* 1: 167–211.

Oliner, Stephen D., and Daniel E. Sichel. 2002. "The Resurgence of Growth in the Late 1990s: Is Information Technology the Story?" *Journal of Economic Perspectives* 14 (4): 3–22.

O'Neill, Michael. 1999. Issue cover. *TIME*, February 15. http://content.time.com /time/magazine/0,9263,7601990215,00.html.

Oprysko, Caitlin. 2019. "Trump Accuses the Fed of Making a 'Big Mistake' with Its Interest Rate Hikes." POLITICO, June 10, 2019. https://www.politico.com /story/2019/06/10/trump-federal-reserve-interest-rate-hikes-1358816.

Orphanides, Athanasios. 2003. "The Quest for Prosperity without Inflation." *Journal of Monetary Economics* 50 (3): 633–63.

Palin, Sarah. 2010. "'Refudiation' of $600 Billion Printed Out of Thin Air." Letter to the Editor. *Wall Street Journal,* November 18. https://www.wsj.com/articles /SB10001424052748703326204575616901259121246.

Parker, Jonathan A., Nicholas S. Souleles, David S. Johnson, and Robert McClelland. 2013. "Consumer Spending and the Economic Stimulus Payments of 2008." *American Economic Review* 103 (6): 2530–53.

Passell, Peter. 1991. "Spurning Fine-Tuning; Any Fixes Washington Might Do to Help Could Just as Well Harm, Economists Say." *New York Times*, December 11.

Paulson, Henry M., Jr. 2009. "Statement on Comprehensive Approach to Market Developments." U.S. Department of the Treasury Press Release, September 19. http://www.treasury.gov/press-center/press-releases/Pages/hp1149.aspx.

Paulson, Henry M., Jr. 2010. *On the Brink: Inside the Race to Stop the Collapse of the Global Financial System*. New York: Business Plus.

Perloff, Jeffrey, and Michael L. Wachter. 1979. "The New Jobs Tax Credit: An Evaluation of the 1977–78 Wage Subsidy Program." *American Economic Review* 69 (2): 173–79.

Perry, George L. 1975. "Policy Alternatives for 1974." *Brookings Papers on Economic Activity* 1: 222–37.

Pew Research Center. 2012. "Auto Bailout Now Backed, Stimulus Divisive." Pew Research Center Survey Report, February 23. https://www.pewresearch.org /politics/2012/02/23/auto-bailout-now-backed-stimulus-divisive/.

Phelps, Edmund S. 1967. "Phillips Curves, Expectations of Inflation and Optimal Unemployment over Time." *Economica* 34 (135): 254–81.

Phelps, Edmund S. 1968. "Money-Wage Dynamics and Labor-Market Equilibrium." *Journal of Political Economy* 76 (4): 678–711.

Phelps, Edmund S. 1978. "Commodity-Supply Shock and Full-Employment Monetary Policy." *Journal of Money, Credit and Banking* 10 (2): 206–21.

Phillips, Alban William. 1958. "The Relation between Unemployment and the Rate of Change of Money Wage Rates in the United Kingdom, 1861–1957." *Economica* 25 (100): 283–99.

Pierce, James L., and Jared J. Enzler. 1974. "The Effects of External Inflationary Shocks." *Brookings Papers on Economic Activity* 1: 13–61.

POLITICO. 2016. "Full Transcript: Third 2016 Presidential Debate, October 19, 2016." POLITICO, October 20, 2016. https://www.politico.com/story/2016/10/full-transcript-third-2016-presidential-debate-230063.

Poole, William. 1970. "Optimal Choice of Monetary Policy Instruments in a Simple Stochastic Macro Model." *Quarterly Journal of Economics* 84 (2): 197–216.

Powell, Jerome. 2021. "Jerome Powell on the Pandemic Year: Tools to Avoid a Meltdown and Save Livelihoods" *Wall Street Journal*, March 19.

Presidential Task Force on Market Mechanisms. 1988. *Report of the Presidential Task Force on Market Mechanisms: Submitted to the President of the United States, the Secretary of the Treasury and the Chairman of the Federal Reserve Board*. Washington, DC: U.S. Government Printing Office. https://catalog.hathitrust.org/Record/005316860.

Reagan, Ronald. 1984. *Address before a Joint Session of the Congress on the State of the Union*, January 25, 1984. Online by Ronald Reagan Presidential Library. https://www.reaganlibrary.gov/archives/speech/address-joint-session-congress-state-union-january-1984.

Reeves, Richard. 1993. *President Kennedy: Profile of Power*. New York: Simon & Schuster.

Reinhart, Carmen M., and Kenneth S. Rogoff. 2009. *This Time Is Different: Eight Centuries of Financial Folly*. Princeton, NJ: Princeton University Press.

Reuters. 1971. "Nixon Reportedly Says He Is Now a Keynesian." *New York Times*, January 7. https://www.reuters.com/article/us-usa-fed-2013-timeline-idUSKCN1P52A8.

Reuters. 2019. "Key Events for the Fed in 2013: The Year of the 'Taper Tantrum.'" January 11. https://www.reuters.com/article/us-usa-fed-2013-timeline-idUSKCN1P52A8.

Romano, Lois. 1986. "Warren Rudman and His New Cause." *Washington Post*, January 22.

Rucker, Philip. 2009. "Sen. DeMint of S.C. Is Voice of Opposition to Health-Care Reform." *Washington Post*, July 28.

Ryan, Paul, George F. Will, Barney Frank, and Robert B. Reich. 2011. "Transcript: The Great American Debate, Part 1: There's Too Much Government in My Life." ABC News and the Miller Center of the University of Virginia, moderated by Christiane Amanpour, Washington, DC, December 18. https://abcnews.go.com/Politics/transcript-great-american-debates/story?id=15182473.

Safire, William. 1984. "On Language; Free World, So-Called." *New York Times*. December 16.

Samuelson, Paul Anthony. 1947. *Foundations of Economic Analysis*. Cambridge, MA: Harvard University Press.

Samuelson, Paul Anthony. 1948. *Economics: An Introductory Analysis*. New York: McGraw-Hill.

Samuelson, Paul Anthony. 1985. "Reagan's Tax Plan: A Help, but Not as Good as Treasury Proposal." *Boston Globe,* May 31.

Samuelson, Paul Anthony, and Robert M. Solow. 1960. "Analytical Aspects of Anti-inflation Policy." *American Economic Review* 50 (2): 177–94.

Samwick, Andrew. 1996. "Tax Shelters and Passive Losses after the Tax Reform Act of 1986." In *Empirical Foundations of Household Taxation*, ed. Martin Feldstein and James Poterba, 193–233. Chicago: University of Chicago Press for NBER.

Sargent, Thomas J. 1971. "A Note on the 'Accelerationist' Controversy." *Journal of Money, Credit and Banking* 3 (3): 721–25.

Sargent, Thomas J., and Neil Wallace. 1975. "'Rational' Expectations, the Optimal Monetary Instrument, and the Optimal Money Supply Rule." *Journal of Political Economy* 83 (2): 241–54.

Scheiber, Noam. 2012. *The Escape Artists: How Obama's Team Fumbled the Recovery.* New York: Simon & Schuster.

Schultze, Charles. 2011. "Slaying the Dragon of Debt: Fiscal Politics and Policy from the 1970s to the Present: A Project of the Walter Shorenstein Program in Politics, Policy and Values." Conducted by Martin Meeker in 2010, Regional Oral History Office, The Bancroft Library, University of California, Berkeley. https://digitalassets.lib.berkeley.edu/roho/ucb/text/schultze_charles.pdf.

Seru, Ami, and Luigi Zingales. 2020. "Save Capitalism from the Cares Act." *Wall Street Journal*, March 30.

Shiller, Robert J. 1989. "Investor Behavior in the October 1987 Stock Market Crash: Survey Evidence." *Market Volatility*, 379–402. Cambridge, MA: MIT Press.

Shultz, George P., and Kenneth W. Dam. 1977. "Reflections on Wage and Price Controls." *Industrial and Labor Relations Review* 30 (2): 139–51.

Solomon, Robert. 1982. *The International Monetary System: 1945–1981.* New York: Harper & Row.

Solow, Robert. 2018. "A Theory Is a Sometime Thing." *Review of Keynesian Economics* 6 (4): 421–24.

Sorkin, Andrew Ross. 2010. *Too Big to Fail: The Inside Story of How Wall Street and Washington Fought to Save the Financial System—and Themselves.* New York: Penguin.

Sperling, Gene B. 2001. "Greenspan Should Have Thought Twice." Brookings, February 5. The Brookings Institution, Washington, DC. https://www.brookings.edu/opinions/greenspan-should-have-thought-twice/.

Statista. 2021. Foreclosure Rate in the United States from 2005 to 2019. ATTOM Data Solutions. Statista Research Department, April 15, 2021. https://www.statista.com/statistics/798766/foreclosure-rate-usa/.

Stein, Herbert. 1969. *The Fiscal Revolution in America.* Chicago: University of Chicago Press.

Stock, James H., and Mark W. Watson. 2002. "Macroeconomic Forecasting Using Diffusion Indexes." *Journal of Business and Economic Statistics* 20 (2): 147–62.

Stock, James H., and Mark W. Watson. 2003. "Has the Business Cycle Changed? Evidence and Explanations." In *Proceedings of the Federal Reserve Bank of Kansas City Symposium on Monetary Policy and Uncertainty: Adapting to a Changing*

Economy, 11–96. Jackson Hole, WY, August 28–30, 2003. Federal Reserve Bank of Kansas City.

Stockman, David A. 1986. *The Triumph of Politics: Why the Reagan Revolution Failed*. New York: Harper & Row.

Summers, Lawrence H. 2014. "U.S. Economic Prospects: Secular Stagnation, Hysteresis, and the Zero Lower Bound." *Business Economics* 49 (2): 65–73.

Summers, Lawrence H. 2021. "Opinion: The Biden Stimulus Is Admirably Ambitious. But It Brings Some Big Risks, Too." *Washington Post,* February 4, 2021.

Suskind, Ron. 2004. *The Price of Loyalty: George W. Bush, the White House, and the Education of Paul O'Neill*. New York: Simon & Schuster.

Swagel, Phillip. 2009. "The Financial Crisis: An Inside View." *Brookings Papers on Economic Activity*, Spring, 1–78.

Swanson, Ana, and Binyamin Applebaum. 2017. "Trump Announces Jerome Powell as New Fed Chairman." *New York Times*, November 2.

Tax Foundation. n.d. "Federal Individual Income Tax Rates History: Nominal Dollars, Income Years 1913–2013." https://files.taxfoundation.org/legacy/docs/fed_individual_rate_history_nominal.pdf.

Tax Policy Center. 2017. Historical Capital Gains and Taxes [Dataset]. Urban Institute, Brookings Institution. https://www.taxpolicycenter.org/statistics/historical-capital-gains-and-taxes.

Taylor, John B. 1980. "Aggregate Dynamics and Staggered Contracts." *Journal of Political Economy* 88 (1): 1–23.

Taylor, John B. 1981. "On the Relation between the Variability of Inflation and the Average Inflation Rate." *Carnegie-Rochester Conference Series on Public Policy* 15 (1): 57–85.

Taylor, John B. 2009a. *Getting Off Track: How Government Actions and Interventions Caused, Prolonged, and Worsened the Financial Crisis*. Stanford, CA: Hoover Institution Press.

Taylor, John B. 2009b. "How Government Created the Financial Crisis." *Wall Street Journal,* February 9.

Taylor, John B. 2011a. "An Empirical Analysis of the Revival of Fiscal Activism in the 2000s." *Journal of Economic Literature* 49 (3): 686–702.

Taylor, John B. 2011b. "The 2009 Stimulus Package: Two Years Later." Testimony before the Committee on Oversight and Government Reform, Subcommittee on Regulatory Affairs, Stimulus Oversight and Government Spending, U.S. House of Representatives, February 16. http://citeseerx.ist.psu.edu/viewdoc/download?doi=10.1.1.362.5150&rep=rep1&type=pdf.

Tempalski, Jerry. 2006. "Revenue Effects of Major Tax Bills." OTA Working Paper 81, revised September 2006. Office of Tax Analysis, U.S. Department of the Treasury. https://www.treasury.gov/resource-center/tax-policy/tax-analysis/Documents/WP-81.pdf.

Thomas, Kenneth H. 2000. "Doubling Deposit Insurance Would Compound S&L Error." *American Banker*, September 1. https://www.americanbanker.com/search?q=%22Doubling+deposit+insurance+would+compound+%2C%22#nt=navsearch.

TIME. 1961. "The Economy: The Pragmatic Professor." March 3.

TIME. 1965. "The Economy: We Are All Keynesians Now." December 31.

Timiraos, Nick. 2022. *Trillion Dollar Triage: How Jay Powell and the Fed Battled a President and a Pandemic—and Prevented Economic Disaster*. New York: Little, Brown.

Timiraos, Nick, and Amara Omeokwe. 2021. "Powell Lays Groundwork for Faster End to Stimulus as Inflation Outlook Worsens." *Wall Street Journal*, November 30.

Tobin, James. 1974. *The New Economics One Decade Older*. Princeton, NJ: Princeton University Press.

Tufte, Edward. 1978. *Political Control of the Economy*. Princeton, NJ: Princeton University Press.

Türegün, Adnan. 2017. "Revisiting Sweden's Response to the Great Depression of the 1930s: Economic Policy in a Regional Context." *Scandinavian Economic History Review* 65 (2): 127–48.

Turner, Adair. 2016. *Between Debt and the Devil: Money, Credit, and Fixing Global Finance*. Princeton, NJ: Princeton University Press.

Turnovsky, Stephen J., and Marcus H. Miller. 1984. "The Effects of Government Expenditure on the Term Structure of Interest Rates." *Journal of Money, Credit and Banking* 16 (1): 16–33.

USA Today. 2010. *USA Today*/Gallup Poll: August Wave 1, Question 43, USGALLUP.10AGT027.R17 [Dataset]. Gallup Organization. Cornell University, Ithaca, NY: Roper Center for Public Opinion Research.

U.S. Congress. 1993. *Congressional Record: Proceedings and Debates of the U.S. Congress*. 103rd Congress, 1st Session, Vol. 139, Part 2, February 2, 1993. Washington, DC: U.S. Government Printing Office. https://www.congress.gov/bound -congressional-record/1993/02/02/house-section.

U.S. Department of the Treasury. 2009. "Secretary Geithner Introduces Financial Stability Plan." U.S. Department of the Treasury Press Release, February 10. https://www.treasury.gov/press-center/press-releases/pages/tg18.aspx.

U.S. Department of the Treasury. 2021. Troubled Assets Relief Program. TARP Investment Program Transaction Reports. https://home.treasury.gov /data/troubled-assets-relief-program/reports/tarp-investment-program -transaction-reports.

U.S. Department of the Treasury, Office of the Secretary. 1984. *Tax Reform for Fairness, Simplicity, and Economic Growth, Report to the President*, Vol. 1, *Overview*. November 1984. https://www.treasury.gov/resource-center/tax-policy /Documents/Report-Tax-Reform-v1-1984.pdf.

U.S. Department of the Treasury, Office of the Secretary. 1985. *The President's Tax Proposals to the Congress for Fairness, Growth, and Simplicity*. May 29. https:// home.treasury.gov/system/files/131/Report-Reform-Proposal-1985.pdf.

U.S. House Committee on Financial Services. 2010. *Monetary Policy and the State of the Economy*. Hearing, Committee on Financial Services, U.S. House of Representatives, Serial No. 111-64, July 21, 2009. Washington, DC: U.S. Government

Printing Office. https://www.gpo.gov/fdsys/pkg/CHRG-111hhrg53244/pdf/CHRG-111hhrg53244.pdf.

U.S. Joint Economic Committee. 1979. *The Economic Report of the President: Hearings before the Joint Economic Committee, U.S. Congress.* 96th Congress, 1st Session, Part 1, January 29, 1979. Washington, DC: U.S. Government Printing Office. https://fraser.stlouisfed.org/title/5332/item/536835.

U.S. Senate Committee on Banking, Housing, and Urban Affairs. 1971. *Hearings, Committee on Banking, Housing, and Urban Affairs, U.S. Senate*, March 1971. Washington, DC: U.S. Government Printing Office. https://www.banking.senate.gov/.

Volcker, Paul A. 1979. "Transcript of Press Conference Held in Board Room, Federal Reserve Building, Washington, DC, October 6, 1979." https://fraser.stlouisfed.org/title/statements-speeches-paul-a-volcker-451/transcript-press-conference-held-board-room-federal-reserve-building-washington-dc-8201.

Volcker, Paul A. 1990. "The Triumph of Central Banking." Per Jacobssen Lecture, International Monetary Fund, September 23, 1990. Washington, DC: Per Jacobsson Foundation, International Monetary Fund. http://www.perjacobsson.org/lectures/1990.pdf.

Volcker, Paul A. 2018. *Keeping at It: The Quest for Sound Money and Good Government.* New York: PublicAffairs.

Wall Street Journal. 1998. "Bush Pins 1992 Election Loss on Fed Chair Alan Greenspan." August 25. https://www.wsj.com/articles/SB904002475770183000.

Wanniski, Jude. 1978. *The Way the World Works: How Economies Fail and Succeed.* New York: Basic Books.

Watson, Kathryn. 2020. "Trump Says He Wants the Country 'Raring to Go by Easter,' Later Says It Will Be Based on 'Hard Data.'" *CBS News*, March 24. https://www.cbsnews.com/news/trump-says-he-wants-the-country-raring-to-go-by-easter-despite-warnings-from-many-health-experts-2020-03-24/.

Weissmann, Jordan. 2019. "Trump Gives World's Worst Economist the Presidential Medal of Freedom." Slate, May 31. https://slate.com/business/2019/05/trump-gives-art-laffer-the-worlds-worst-economist-the-presidential-medal-of-freedom.html.

Wessel, David. 2009. *In Fed We Trust: Ben Bernanke's War on the Great Panic.* New York: Random House.

Wessel, David, and Thomas T. Vogel Jr. 1993. "Arcane World of Bonds Is Guide and Beacon to a Populist President." *Wall Street Journal*, February 25.

White, Lawrence J. 1991. *The S&L Debacle: Public Policy Lessons for Bank and Thrift Regulation.* New York: Oxford University Press.

White House. 1981. *America's New Beginning: A Program for Economic Recovery.* Office of the President Report to the U.S. Congress, February 18. Washington, DC: U.S. Government Printing Office. https://fraser.stlouisfed.org/title/america-s-new-beginning-1221.

White House. 2021. "President Biden Nominates Jerome Powell to Serve as Chair of the Federal Reserve, Dr. Lael Brainard to Serve as Vice Chair." White

House Release, November 22. https://www.whitehouse.gov/briefing-room /statements-releases/2021/11/22/president-biden-nominates-jerome-powell-to -serve-as-chair-of-the-federal-reserve-dr-lael-brainard-to-serve-as-vice-chair/.

Wicker, Tom. 1985a. "In the Nation: Congress, Good and Bad." *New York Times*, November 29.

Wicker, Tom. 1985b. "In the Nation: Keeping It Simple." *New York Times*, January 18.

Wilentz, Sean. 2008. *The Age of Reagan: A History, 1974–2008*. New York: Harper Collins.

Wilson, Daniel. 2012. "Fiscal Spending Jobs Multipliers: Evidence from the 2009 American Recovery and Reinvestment Act." *American Economic Journal: Economic Policy* 4 (3): 251–82.

Woodward, Bob. 1994. *The Agenda: Inside the Clinton White House*. New York: Simon & Schuster.

Woodward, Bob. 2000. *Maestro: Greenspan's Fed and the American Boom*. New York: Simon & Schuster.

Wray, Randall. 1993. "Money, Interest Rates, and Monetarist Policy: Some More Unpleasant Monetary Arithmetic?" *Journal of Post Keynesian Economics* 15 (4): 541–69.

Yang, John E. 1990. "Budget Negotiators Meet at Andrews in Cheery, Summer Camp-Like Mood." *Washington Post*, September 8.

INDEX

NOTE: Page numbers in *italics* refer to figures and tables and associated captions. Note information is indicated by n following the page reference.